PATRONAGE AND THE BRITISH NAVY, 1775–1815

PATRONAGE AND THE BRITISH NAVY, 1775–1815

Catherine S. Beck

THE BOYDELL PRESS

© Catherine S. Beck 2025

All Rights Reserved. Except as permitted under current legislation
no part of this work may be photocopied, stored in a retrieval system,
published, performed in public, adapted, broadcast,
transmitted, recorded or reproduced in any form or by any means,
without the prior permission of the copyright owner

The right of Catherine S. Beck to be identified as the author of this work has
been asserted in accordance with sections 77 and 78 of the Copyright, Designs
and Patents Act 1988

First published 2025
The Boydell Press, Woodbridge

ISBN 978 1 83765 227 3

The Boydell Press is an imprint of Boydell & Brewer Ltd
PO Box 9, Woodbridge, Suffolk IP12 3DF, UK
and of Boydell & Brewer Inc.
668 Mt Hope Avenue, Rochester, NY 14620-2731, USA
website: www.boydellandbrewer.com

A CIP catalogue record for this book is available
from the British Library

The publisher has no responsibility for the continued existence or accuracy
of URLs for external or third-party internet websites referred to in this book,
and does not guarantee that any content on such websites is,
or will remain, accurate or appropriate

CONTENTS

List of Illustrations	vi
Acknowledgements	viii
List of Abbreviations	ix
Introduction	1
1. Time and Place: The Geography of Naval Patronage	18
2. Friends and Family: Markham's Network	50
3. Followers and Strangers: Markham's Admiralty Correspondents	88
4. Constituents and Corporations: The Expectations of Political Connection	144
5. Gender and Parenthood: The Power of Brokers	181
6. Fees and Resistance: Lower-Level Patronage	216
Conclusion	264
Appendix I	274
Appendix II	277
Appendix III	286
Appendix IV	289
Bibliography	293
Index	305

ILLUSTRATIONS

Figures

1.1   Map of average sailing times. Jonathan Scott, *When the Waves Ruled Britannia: Geography and Political Identities, 1500–1800* (Cambridge, 2011), 74; Ian Steele, *The English Atlantic 1675–1740: An Exploration of Communication and Community* (Oxford, 1986), 31 and 91; Julian Gwyn, *Frigates and Foremasts: The North American Squadron in Nova Scotia Waters 1745–1815* (Vancouver, 2003), 88; Peter Ward, *British Naval Power in the East 1794–1805: The Command of Admiral Peter Rainier* (Woodbridge, 2013), 93; James Davey, *In Nelson's Wake: The Navy and the Napoleonic Wars* (London, 2015), 105.   26

2.1   Markham's family network. NMM, MRK/107–108; Markham, *Naval Career* (1883); Scone, NRAS776; *Oxford Dictionary of National Biography*, vols. 17–59 (Oxford, 2004).   59

2.2   Correspondents by frequency in Markham Papers 1801–1807. NMM, MP, MRK/101–104.   79

3.1   Markham's correspondents grouped by their rating, social rank and position. Markham's Correspondents Database.   93

3.2   Broker-recipient relationships. Markham's Correspondents Database.   96

3.3   Broker-recipient relationships grouped by rating, social rank and position of the broker. Markham's Correspondents Database.   97

6.1.1   Plymouth gratuities: overview of the payment of fees for appointment and promotion in Plymouth yard. *The Sixth Report of the Commissioners of Naval Inquiry. Appendix 126. Plymouth yard, Woolwich yard* (London 1804), 419–421.   230

6.1.2   Plymouth gratuities: detail of broker Robert Duins.   231

ILLUSTRATIONS

6.1.3	Plymouth gratuities: detail of broker Luke Hammet.	231
6.1.4	Plymouth gratuities: detail of broker Mrs Rippon.	232
6.1.5	Plymouth gratuities: others accepting fees.	233
6.2	James Jagoe's network. The timber yard 1801–1803. LMA, P97/MRY/008–009, P97/MRY/050, P97/MRY/024, St Mary Magdalene Woolwich; TNA, ADM 106/2984, Woolwich 1799, ADM 106/2985, Woolwich 1802, ADM 106/2979, Plymouth 1779, IR 1/31–36 Board of Stamps: Apprenticeship Books, PROB 11/1099/245, PROB 11/1381/24, PROB 11/1400/29, PROB 11/1483/88, PROB 11/1532/63, PROB 11/1549/528, PROB 11/1784/51, PROB 11/1858/188, PROB 11/2123/368, RG 4/1770.	240

Table

6.1	Movement of shipwrights from the yard of their apprenticeship. TNA, ADM 106/2975, Chatham 1779; ADM 106/2979, Plymouth 1779; ADM 106/2980, Portsmouth 1779; ADM 106/2982, Sheerness 1779; ADM 106/2984, Woolwich 1779; ADM 106/2986, Deptford 1784.	252

The author and publisher are grateful to all the institutions and individuals listed for permission to reproduce the materials in which they hold copyright. Every effort has been made to trace the copyright holders; apologies are offered for any omission, and the publisher will be pleased to add any necessary acknowledgement in subsequent editions.

ACKNOWLEDGEMENTS

My special thanks to Stephen Conway and James Davey, for their gentle and diligent guidance in the early stages of this work. Also to Roger Knight for all his kind support, not only for his insight and advice but also for sharing his research with me. I am truly grateful to all my friends and colleagues for their constant support, especially Evan Wilson for all his advice and Misha Ewen, Eilish Gregory and Alys Beverton for their tireless proofreading, and Elaine Murphy for her endless support. Particular thanks go to Ann Coats and the Navy Dockyards Society for advice on the very early stages of the work in Chapter 6. Also to Christina Petterson for her editorial suggestions in the final stages of writing after many hurdles and interruptions (including a global pandemic). My thanks also, most especially, to Tine Ravnsted-Larsen Reeh for her optimism and tireless encouragement to keep going.

My thanks also go to the staff at the various libraries and archives I have visited over the course of my research. I would like to especially thank Martin Salmon at the Caird Library, National Maritime Museum, for his constant, cheerful support, and Jane Knight for her work as a volunteer cataloguing the Markham collection. I would also like to thank Scone Palace for allowing me to view the private papers of the Murray family.

Most of all, my heartfelt thanks go to Susan Beck for her willingness to read every draft I sent her, even at the eleventh hour.

ABBREVIATIONS

BL	British Library
CRL	Cadbury Research Library and Special Collections, University of Birmingham
LMA	London Metropolitan Archive
HL	Huntingdon Library, California
HRO	Hampshire Record Office
NMM	Caird Library, National Maritime Museum, Greenwich
NLS	National Library of Scotland
NRS	Publications of the Navy Records Society
ODNB	*Oxford Dictionary of National Biography*
Scone	Scone Palace Archives
UoA	University of Aberdeen Special Collections
UoN	University of Nottingham Special Collections

INTRODUCTION

> … if any thing should happen to you I have No other frind to assist me or famely wich is the Reason of my trubling you so offten wich I hop you will forgive …
>
> Russel White, Carpenter of *Salvador del Mundo*, 30 June 1802[1]

In 1802, after twenty-six years as a carpenter in the British Royal Navy, Russel White wrote to his old messmate John Markham, to ask for his patronage. Captain Markham was now a lord commissioner on the board of Admiralty under the First Lord John Jervis, Earl St Vincent, and was inundated with requests from friends and strangers across the navy and wider British society. White was the carpenter in ordinary of a first rate ship of the line, in fear of being paid off and laid up during the pause in hostilities with France following the Peace of Amiens that had been signed several months earlier. To our eyes the distance between the two seems stark and perhaps it is hard to imagine what White meant when he called Markham his friend. Their connection, however, began at a time when they had been on much more intimate terms despite the differences in their background and status.

In March 1776, Markham, as a boy of fifteen with just a year of naval service under his belt, followed his captain to a new ship, *Perseus,* ready to serve in the North American station.[2] White, who was approaching forty years of age, had joined the ship only a few months earlier as a newly warranted naval carpenter.[3] Sharing their meals and free time on board in the same mess brought White and Markham into close quarters with one another. As

---

[1] NMM, Markham Papers, MRK/104/3/49.

[2] Clements Markham, *A Naval Career during the Old War: Being a narrative of the Life of Admiral John Markham, M.P. for Portsmouth for Twenty-Three Years (Lord of the Admiralty, 1801–4 and 1806–7)* (London, 1883), 27.

[3] TNA, ADM 29/1/254 Navy Pay Office: Entry Books of Certificates of Service (Warrant Officers); ADM 6/346/125 ff.630–634. Elizabeth White, widow of Russel White, carpenter Royal Navy who died 27 July 1809; Medway Archives, P153/1/49 f.141: Russel White, b. 1738, died 1809, age 71, buried 30 July 1809, Gillingham, St Mary Magdalene.

2   PATRONAGE AND THE BRITISH NAVY, 1775–1815

was common on naval ships, White assumed an almost paternal role, guiding Markham's early shipboard life.[4] They parted ways when Markham left the ship in 1777, in command of a merchant prize that would later lead to his shipwreck, rescue and return to Britain, while White remained as carpenter of *Perseus* until 1780.[5] However, their connection continued. Markham repaid White's kindness by recommending him to his father's patronage in 1779 and 1780.[6] When Markham was appointed to the board of Admiralty in 1801, White wrote several letters soliciting him for his newly acquired patronage.[7] White was respectful of Markham's status in the way he wrote to him and Markham was diligent in his replies but rarely offered more than he could easily obtain through vacancies already available. Their letters reflect their intimate yet inherently unequal relationship first forged on *Perseus*, one that was both paternalistic and loaded with the weight of differences in status, connection and access to power. But they are also revealing of the varied and complex origins of late eighteenth-century patronage relationships and the tangled threads of obligation, trust, expectation and anxiety that bound them together.

This book is about patronage, or rather the multifaceted, highly personal and sometimes contradictory system of personal connection and guarantee that underpinned naval employment, promotion and support at the end of the eighteenth and beginning of the nineteenth centuries. Patronage was the water in which all eighteenth-century people swam. Indeed, dip into almost any eighteenth-century archive and you are likely to stumble across some facet of patronage; whether it be as explicit as a direct application to an elite patron for their favour and support, more indirect as in the exchange of news about a child sent away for work to a friend of the family, or even as subtle as a casual request for assistance tagged onto the end of a letter between close friends.

The final decades of the eighteenth century in Britain were marked by great administrative and social change born of the galvanising forces of war, population growth, the explosion of the popular press, changes of labour force and global colonial and economic expansion, all of which threatened to upset the established hierarchy of British society. In the world of 'how to' literature, the explicit and strategic patronage advice of the mid-century gave way to letter-writing manuals that encouraged the use of sensible ideals of friendship when asking for support from elite patrons, as well as of distress and gratitude in petitions and poor relief letters.[8] One letter from Thomas

---

4   Markham, *A Naval Career*, 45; Evan Wilson, *A Social History of British Naval Officers 1775–1815* (Woodbridge, 2017), 27.

5   Markham, *A Naval Career*, 47–48.

6   NMM, MRK/107/1/5–6, Markham to William Markham, 30 October 1799 and 13 May 1780.

7   NMM, MRK/104/3/48–50, White to Markham, 29 April 1801–30 June 1802.

8   Philip Carter, *Men and the Emergence of Polite Society, Britain 1660–1800*

INTRODUCTION

Cooke's *Universal Letter-Writer*, reprinted in 1801, entitled 'From a Gentleman of decayed Circumstances in the Country, to another lately returned from the East-Indies, recommending his Son to his Protection', reveals this shift neatly. It included the line: 'I rather think that my present distressed circumstances will plead more powerfully in favour of the youth, than if he was supported even by the recommendation of the whole body of directors.'[9] The deep cultural anxiety about the sincerity of friendship and the morality of patronage provoked by earlier texts like *Letters written by Lord Chesterfield to His Son* (1774) may have caused the language of patronage to change, but the system itself did not disappear.[10]

The Royal Navy was deeply enmeshed in the tensions that coursed through British society, both driving and resisting the transition from the old to the new. Throughout the eighteenth century, the navy varied considerably in size because, unlike its counterparts in other European countries, it operated on a system of peacetime demobilisation. But the extended period of war between 1775 and 1815, with only roughly a decade of peace separating the American War of Independence and the beginning of the French Revolutionary Wars, created a unique set of pressures on employment. During this period, the navy experienced times when there was a shortage of sailors, resistance from dockyard workers to government control, and a surfeit of junior commissioned officers for the limited number of vacancies available.[11] The navy also saw rapid growth in its unwieldy bureaucracy and the increasingly centralised control of appointments motivated by both ideological and practical concerns about the most effective way to manage the entry and promotion of trustworthy and able personnel throughout the navy, especially officers.[12] The bureaucratic pressures and practical demands of this shift in the navy's size and

---

(London, 2001), 79; Thomas Sokoll, 'Writing for Relief: Rhetoric in English Pauper Letters 1800–1834', in Andreas Gestrich, Steven King and Lutz Raphael (eds.), *Being Poor in Modern Europe: Historical Perspectives 1800–1940* (Oxford, 2006), 100; Eve Tavor Bannet, *Empire of Letters: Letter Manuals and Transatlantic Correspondence, 1688–1820* (Cambridge, 2005).

[9] Thomas Cooke, *The Universal Letter-Writer; or, New Art of Polite Correspondence* (Gainsborough, 1801), 123.

[10] Carter, *Emergence of Polite Society*, 79.

[11] Jeremiah Dancy, *The Myth of the Press Gang: Volunteers, Impressment and the Naval Manpower Problem in the Late Eighteenth Century* (Woodbridge, 2015), 28–29; Roger Morriss, 'Government and Community: The Changing Context of Labour Relations, 1770–1830', in Kenneth Lunn and Ann Day (eds.), *History of Work and Labour Relations in the Royal Dockyards* (London, 1999), 26–30, 116; N. A. M. Rodger, *The Command of the Ocean: A Naval History of Britain, 1649–1815* (London, 2004), 518–519.

[12] Wilson, *British Naval Officers*, 129; S. A. Cavell, *Midshipmen and the Quarterdeck Boys in the British Navy 1771–1831* (Woodbridge, 2012), 116.

administration collided with a patronage system that traditionally relied on personal connection and favour to guarantee that good people filled the right positions while also allowing patrons to pay into wider networks of reciprocity and connection maintenance that extended far beyond the navy.

It is perhaps tempting to frame patronage as the opposing force to the modernising effects of growing bureaucracy and centralisation rather than a broader social mechanism that adapted to changing social and economic landscapes.[13] At its bare essentials, patronage is the use of personal connection to act as a guarantee within the distribution of appointments and social support. In some ways then, it can refer to corruption, or the circumvention by well-placed friends and the social elite of what many contemporary writers, as well as historians, may perceive as superior or fairer meritocratic systems of preferment.[14] However, patronage can just as equally refer to the role that reputation, knowledge and reciprocity played in employment and support structures throughout all levels of society, similar to the term *social capital*, especially in social network analysis.[15]

As a social mechanism with personal connection at its heart, patronage varied hugely in style, especially in the language people used to describe it. So how do we define it? When we look beyond individual interactions between the applicant, often referred to as the *client* or the person who needed a favour, and the *patron*, the one with the power to bestow it, key structural aspects appear again and again. From a sociological perspective, studies usually define patronage relationships by the reciprocal exchange of physical and social resources which created strong or long-lasting bonds of obligation between connections.[16] Within this frame, these interactions, or *exchanges*, were both intimate and inherently unequal, usually operating

---

[13] J. M. Bourne, *Patronage and Society in Nineteenth Century England* (London, 1986), 5–6; Philip Harling, *The Waning of 'Old Corruption': The Politics of Economical Reform in Britain, 1779–1846* (Oxford, 1996), 18–21; C. I. Hamilton, 'John Wilson Croker: Patronage and Clientage at the Admiralty, 1809–1857', *Historical Journal* 43:1 (2000), 55–56; Linda Colley, 'Whose Nation? Class and National Consciousness in Britain, 1750–1830', *Past and Present* 113 (1986), 113; Rodger, *The Command of the Ocean*, 513; Ellen Gill, *Naval Families, War and Duty in Britain 1740–1820* (Woodbridge, 2016), 104.

[14] Michael Lewis, *A Social History of the Navy 1793–1815* (London, 1960), 232.

[15] S. N. Eisenstadt and Luis Roniger, *Patrons, Clients and Friends: Interpersonal Relations and the Structure of Trust in Society* (Cambridge, 1984), 48–49; Nan Lin, *Social Capital: A Theory of Social Structures and Action* (Cambridge, 2001); David Sunderland, *Social Capital, Trust and the Industrial Revolution, 1780–1880* (London, 2007); Charles Kadushin, *Understanding Social Networks: Theories, Concepts and Findings* (Oxford, 2012), 4 and 170–172.

[16] Eisenstadt and Roniger, *Patrons, Clients and Friends*, 48–49; John Levi Martin, *Social Structures* (Princeton, 2009), 189–231.

INTRODUCTION 5

vertically within a social hierarchy. Many sociological studies that have dealt with patronage in this way were based on anthropological research into small-scale, pre-industrial or feudal communities and structural approaches consequently defined the inequality of the exchange almost exclusively in the context of socio-economic status.[17] In contrast, sociologists who approached the same structures of reciprocity and obligation from the perspective of social network analysis recognised how patronage also worked as a mechanism within lateral relationships between friends, neighbours and family members.[18] Within both of these frames, patronage is principally a mechanism of trust, reciprocity and obligation.

When we view patronage as a system of networks grounded in trust and obligation, which relied on personal relationships within social networks, it is possible to see how it extended beyond the social elite throughout all levels of society. Certainly patronage can be used by historians to refer simply to the *gift* that a lofty patron bestowed on a favoured connection lower down the social scale, such as an artist or protégé.[19] But in other ways, historians have used patronage as a way to understand more complex interactions in the eighteenth century. In political connection, where the reciprocity between connections on a similar social standing is often easier to identify, patronage helps to make sense of the soft power wielded peer-to-peer by politicians, or, more recently, how this informal power structure allowed greater access for women as active agents in political recommendation networks.[20] Even at

---

[17] J. C. Scott, 'Patron-Client Politics and Political Change in South-East Asia', *American Political Science Review* 66:1 (1972), 92. There is a great deal of discussion in sociology about how best to define patronage in regard to class. For discussion of the reliance on anthropological studies see Sydel F. Silverman, 'Patronage and Community-Nation Relationships in Central Italy', in S. W. Schmidt, L. Guasti, C. H. Landé and J. C. Scott (eds.), *Friends, Followers, and Factions: A Reader in Political Clientelism* (London, 1977), 293–295; Eric Wolf, 'Kinship, Friendship, and Patron-Client Relations in Complex Societies', in Michael Banton (ed.), *The Social Anthropology of Complex Societies* (London, 1966), 1–20. For discussion of the importance of class see Y. Michal Bodemann, 'Relations of Production and Class Rule: The Hidden Basis of Patron-Clientage', in Barry Wellman and S. D. Berkowitz, *Social Structures: A Network Approach* (Cambridge, 1988), 198–216; and complexity of class: S. N. Eisenstadt and Luis Roniger, 'Patron-Client Relations as a Model of Structuring Social Exchange', *Comparative Studies in Society and History* 22:1 (1980), 42–77.

[18] Martin, *Social Structures*, 189–231; Eisenstadt and Roniger, *Patrons, Clients and Friends*, 48–49; Bourne, *Patronage and Society*, 5–6; Kadushin, *Understanding Social Networks*, 4 and 170–172.

[19] See for example Mark Ledbury, 'Patronage', in *The Oxford Handbook of the Ancien Régime* (Oxford, 2012), 388–408.

[20] Lewis Namier, *The Structure of Politics at the Accession of George III* (2nd

lower-level political culture, patronage was intimately linked with the eighteenth-century concept of friendship and can be understood as one of a series of ties which operated both vertically and horizontally within a community.[21] As one historian dubbed it, the ties of obligation that came from patronage acted as a 'glue' that bound society together, especially as the direct reciprocity of traditional 'gift-giving' practices became stretched as more and more intermediaries, or *brokers*, entered the chain between applicant and patron.[22] Within epistolary networks we can see that these same ties of obligation among the middling sort were well-suited to surviving the great pressure that the distance of trans-Atlantic migration placed on families and friendships.[23]

Other historians have noted how patronage operated as a form of social maintenance within a broader culture of gift-giving or as a method of distributing charity, creating the ties of obligation which provided support outside the family unit in the lower levels of society.[24] The arrangement of apprenticeships lower down the social scale mirrored the patronage of the elite because they also relied on personal connection and were just as vulnerable to personal offence and manipulation.[25] As with the blurred distinction between patronage and social capital in social network analysis, comparing trends in language and network structure allows us to consider patronage in such a way that includes parts of society whose direct participation in the exchange is less visible in the written record, particularly women and the non-elite.

So how do we define *naval* patronage? In many ways, the inequality of Russel White and John Markham's relationship that we began with epitomises the traditional view of eighteenth-century patronage, as an inherently unequal social system involving a supplicant or *client*, and a magnanimous albeit perhaps slightly uncaring *patron*.[26] It is a useful place to start, but it is not the whole picture. The highly personal nature of patronage meant that the way it operated was often extremely varied and dependent on the unique contexts of the connection between applicant and patron, as well as the time

---

edn 1957; reprint London, 1961), 24; Elaine Chalus, *Elite Women in English Political Life c.1754–1790* (Oxford, 2005), 106–156.

21 Naomi Tadmor, *Family and Friends in Eighteenth-Century England: Household, Kinship, and Patronage* (Cambridge, 2001), 10–11 and 29.

22 Linda Levy Peck, *Court Patronage and Corruption in Early Stuart England* (Boston, 1990), 2–3, 18 and 40.

23 Sarah Pearsall, *Atlantic Families: Lives and Letters in the Later Eighteenth Century* (Oxford, 2008); Lindsay O'Neill, *The Opened Letter: Networking in the Early Modern British World* (Philadelphia, 2014).

24 Ilana Krausman Ben-Amos, *The Culture of Giving: Informal Support and Gift-Exchange in Early Modern England* (Cambridge, 2008), 197–199.

25 Ibid., 288.

26 For discussion of validity of patronage as inherently unequal see Bourne, *Patronage and Society*, 5–6.

INTRODUCTION 7

and place in which the application was made. Take, for example, another patronage request that John Markham received while he was a lord of the Admiralty. Edward Pellew wrote in 1806 asking for Markham's assistance in promoting his son: 'Do me all the kindness for my son you can; I may live to return it to one of your's, for you see the wheel goes round and round.'[27] Unlike White, Pellew was on a similar professional, and by extension social, standing to Markham. Pellew avoided using patronage as a term, although his frank sketch of the system suggests he saw no need to hide his use or expectations for it. Nor did he minimise his sense of Markham's obligation to him as a serving naval officer or the direct reciprocity he offered in return for his help. His style and approach are radically different from White's, to the extent that some may argue that White's letter falls more easily into a definition of *charity* than *patronage*.

Indeed, Pellew's quote is often used by naval historians to illustrate how naval patronage worked, particularly beyond the paternalistic relationship between a captain and the young boys who entered the service aboard his ship.[28] However, few of those who wrote to Markham were as explicit as he was. Most framed their patronage in terms of friendship but very few laid out either their direct sense of obligation or expectations of reciprocity. The opening of a letter from Captain John Perkins to Markham at the Admiralty in 1803 is a typical example: 'I take the liberty in troubling you once more for your Interest and Friendship, to get me kept out on this station'.[29] Others referred to Markham's patronage directly but did so in terms of charity and duty, such as Lieutenant John Lake who wrote in 1806: 'I must again apologise for this letter having no claim to your patronage but your candour and justice'.[30] Markham himself rarely referred to promotion in the navy as patronage, except when he referred to what was in the gift of the Admiralty, as he did in reply to a request from Captain John Whitby in 1802: 'The Board will not attend to captain's recommendations of Lieuts which will take away their patronage.'[31] At the furthest extent of this attitude, deep within the blurred edges of what we may consider to be patronage, Markham's wife Maria was never explicit about her role in any of her diaries or correspondence despite being vital in maintaining his patronage networks whilst he served at sea.

Pellew's letter gives the impression that the bestowal of appointments and promotions in the navy relied on strong friendships between fellow

---

[27] NMM, MRK/101/13/100, Pellew to Markham, 15 August 1806.
[28] Rodger, *Command of the Ocean*, 513; Stephen Taylor, *Commander: The Life and Exploits of Britain's Greatest Frigate Captain* (London, 2012), 201; Gill, *Naval Families*, 105; Wilson, *British Naval Officers*, 116.
[29] NMM, MRK/102/5/13, Perkins to Markham, 8 May 1803.
[30] NMM, MRK/102/4/4, Lake to Markham, 1 November 1806.
[31] NMM, MRK/102/6/28, Whitby to Markham, 30 April 1802.

8   PATRONAGE AND THE BRITISH NAVY, 1775–1815

officers who were above all else blunt in their application of patronage. However, the way men like Markham framed patronage was not all that different from their civilian counterparts. Consequently, *naval* patronage is difficult to define in terms of style. The friendships which Pellew's 'wheel' relied upon also extended beyond the navy and between social levels, so naval patronage networks rarely contained just officers. The bestowal of appointments within the navy is one way to identify *naval* patronage, but the manner in which applicants secured favours was variable and dependent on the character and social contexts of the patron and applicant. In many respects, other than the subject matter, it seems that only subtle preferences for brevity, duty and service delineated naval patronage requests from those made in other social spheres.

The Royal Navy provides a useful case study to explore the values and great personal variation of patronage. The mobility of officers coupled with a fashion for honour and plain-speaking provides a detailed record of the priorities and expectations of the patronage exchange in the letters sent to family members and to patrons in Britain and overseas. The power of appointment was technically in the hands of the Admiralty but standards of honour, politeness and convention meant that admirals, captains and even lieutenants still had a lot to offer their followings, and even felt in certain cases that they had the right to demand their allotment of patronage from the Admiralty. Captain John Oaks Hardy wrote to Markham to complain that the lieutenant of the ship to which he had been newly appointed had filled all the vacancies. Hardy was aggrieved to have 'utter strangers *imposed upon me* contrary to the general practice of the service'.[32] However, the behavioural standards which governed naval patronage were unclear even to contemporaries and often shifted depending on the amount of vacancies available during war and peace.[33]

Captains were expected to look out for the young men whom they entered aboard their ships, often as favours to connections in their extended network. Despite promises that were made to families and friends upon the boy's initial entry to the ship, some captains did not uphold their end of the bargain. Major Thomas Thorpe Fowke of the Royal Marines wrote to advise his son George Fowke, midshipman aboard *Brune*, who faced the apparent neglect of his captain: 'as to your looking out for a ship commanded by his acquaintance, [it] is ridiculous if that's all he intends doing for you, its no more than fifty of my acquaintance wou'd do that never saw you'.[34] He then advised George to write politely to his captain and re-emphasise that when George entered the ship Fowke considered him to be under the captain's protection, and

[32] NMM, MRK/102/3/13, Hardy to Markham, 13 June 1802. Emphasis in original.

[33] Wilson, *British Naval Officers*, 128; Thomas Wareham, *Frigate Commander* (Barnsley, 2004), 77, 79.

[34] NMM, FOW/2/1, Fowke to George Fowke, 25 April 1783.

INTRODUCTION 9

that he had turned down the patronage of 'Adml Drake, Cap^tns Sutherland, Knatchbul, and others that you [George] might follow him'.[35] The system was not as simple as finding a captain to assist a young man's entry into the navy and then finding further support to make him lieutenant. The semi-informal aspect of naval patronage meant that much of it was done on trust and captains could back out of an arrangement in order to assist boys with better connections who were worth their limited attention in a period of peace when fewer vacancies were available.

Fowke solicited the support of his naval connections in the marines and maintained correspondence with his son's various captains throughout the 1780s, to safeguard his son's position and to push for his promotion to lieutenant at every opportunity. Even after George passed for lieutenant in 1786, Fowke continued to solicit on his behalf, although pressing connections for their favour continued to be a delicate issue. In November 1790, Fowke wrote to George that there was no use cultivating a connection with Admiral Howe or Admiral Gower and that 'it's against any one's promotion to be a follower' of them because 'Sr Roger has more interest than either'.[36] Fowke then wrote that he had not applied to his political friend in Tavistock for fear of damaging their chances with Sir Roger Curtis and alienating their already staunch patron Captain Marshall: '[I] refrained applying to my Borough friend fearing to offend the great man or Cap M who says he hopes there's no such thing as bribery.'[37] The Fowkes had many connections, but in the peacetime navy, they had to be doubly cautious in using every connection they had, particularly political connections, because of the damage that could be done to those acquaintances they had cultivated.

Whether it was a 'wheel' of reciprocity between equals or a 'spring' for promotion that operated alongside, or even *undermined*, the navy's meritocracy, patronage is a facet of naval life that few historians have been able to avoid writing about.[38] In his foundational social study, Michael Lewis framed his discussion of patronage firmly around the idea of haves and have-nots, calling 'interest' a bell which struck a 'merry carillon' for those who had it and a 'mournful toll' for those who did not.[39] Although he recognised the role that personal recommendations played in promoting meritorious young officers, his discussion veered at many points into an assumption of corruption.

The navy was not immune to accusations of patronage corruption, even from contemporaries. John Montagu, earl of Sandwich, frequently faced

[35] Ibid.

[36] He most likely referred to Admiral Sir Roger Curtis.

[37] NMM, FOW/2/1, Fowke to George Fowke, 18 November 1790.

[38] N. A. M. Rodger, *The Wooden World: An Anatomy of the Georgian Navy* (Glasgow, 1986), 301.

[39] Lewis, *A Social History of the Navy*, 202.

10 PATRONAGE AND THE BRITISH NAVY, 1775–1815

accusations of corruption when he served as First Lord of the Admiralty from both political allies and sea officers he did not oblige.[40] Some officers were particularly vocal about the various patronage failings of the Admiralty or commanders-in-chief. Cuthbert Collingwood was dismissive of the distribution of patronage in the Mediterranean until he took up the command and faced the difficulties of making appointments under the pressure from the Admiralty, the fleet and his networks at home. Even so, he promoted the interests of his friends, on the express condition that they were worthy of his favour.[41] John Jervis, earl of St Vincent, was also quick to criticise other officers in command and at the Admiralty, but saw his own distribution of patronage as inherently moral despite often obliging connections to secure his political position.[42] Patronage relied on trust, not just in the fulfilment of the exchange, but that the right men were promoted. In a system where vacancies were relatively scarce and applicants were passed over in favour of those who offered merit or security, one man's moral patronage inevitably seemed corrupt to another.

Naval historians since Lewis have taken a more structural view of patronage, stepping away from a focus on it as inherently corrupt to look at it instead as a facet of the way that talent and merit were recognised in an increasingly large body of officers.[43] Recent cultural and statistical studies have also challenged the idea that the navy was flooded with the sons of the nobility and well-connected, an attitude which at least partly originated in the condemnations of the time from vocal critics such as St Vincent.[44] These studies have touched on both the existence of subtler forms of engagement in patronage, including the active participation of women, and also how important networks and connections within the navy were for officers' careers, with more sons of officers entering and rising through the navy during wartime, as opposed to peacetime.[45] Others have shown that during wartime an officer's skill and conduct took priority in his promotion, but these factors were underpinned by the support of his connections which were naturally associated with his social

[40] N. A. M. Rodger, *The Insatiable Earl: The Life of John Montagu, Fourth Earl of Sandwich 1718–1792* (London, 1993), 166–167 and 174–192.

[41] Edward Hughes (ed.), *The Private Correspondence of Admiral Lord Collingwood* (NRS, 1957).

[42] St Vincent's attitude to patronage when he was First Lord of the Admiralty will be looked at in greater detail in Chapter 4.

[43] Rodger, *Wooden World*, 273 and 301.

[44] Rodger, *Command of the Ocean*, 513; Cavell, *Midshipmen and the Quarterdeck Boys*, 118–119.

[45] Chalus, *Elite Women in English Political Life*; Margarette Lincoln, *Naval Wives and Mistresses* (London: National Maritime Museum, 2007), 56–65; Cavell, *Midshipmen and the Quarterdeck Boys*, 124; Rodger, *Command of the Ocean*, 380–381; building on his work in 'Commissioned Officers' Careers in the Royal Navy, 1690–1815', *Journal for Maritime Research* 3:1 (2001).

INTRODUCTION   11

background.[46] Patronage in the navy, with all its added pressures and priorities, was not necessarily a question of merit versus connection, but ultimately an interwoven fabric of both.

'Interest' extended far beyond the individual patronage exchange of applying and recommending for promotion. An individual's values and social circle affected how a patron viewed their application. In peacetime years some naval patrons were more inclined to listen to the politically influential connections of officers because there was less urgency to select for talent.[47] But equally, when vacancies were limited, patrons used any excuse to politely refuse applications from unprofitable connections, and an unwillingness to make decisions on political grounds was favoured by many naval officers, from captains to the First Lord of the Admiralty. To understand patronage, we must expand our definition of it beyond the simple exchange between a high-status patron and a low-status client, to include these other aspects of social interaction which supported the system. Patronage was more than just favours, it was the maintenance of intricate networks of support which were vulnerable to the offence of the patron and influenced by their fashion.

The story of eighteenth-century naval patronage is often told from the perspective of individual officers and the role of connection, or lack thereof, in their careers.[48] In one sense, this book is no different. It uses John Markham, and most importantly his collection of papers and correspondence from his time at the Admiralty, as its spine.[49] Although a small proportion of the letters were published in 1904 by the Navy Records Society, the rest of the collection was uncatalogued when it was acquired by the National Maritime Museum, Greenwich, in 2013 and has never been thoroughly researched.[50]

Born in 1761, John Markham had a fortunate naval career marked by lucky timing, his useful family connections and his ability to foster the goodwill of his superiors. He was the second son of William Markham, who was Archbishop of York from 1776 and who had previously held positions as headmaster of Westminster school, Dean of Christ Church, Oxford, and also private tutor to the Prince of Wales. John entered the navy in March 1775, just before the commencement of the American Revolutionary War, through the connection of his father's Scottish friends to his first captain George Keith Elphinstone, who remained a solid connection and friend for the rest of his life. A few weeks after his fourteenth birthday, they set sail for Newfoundland

[46] Wilson, *British Naval Officers*, 109–112.
[47] Cavell, *Midshipmen and the Quarterdeck Boys*, 124–125, 216; Wilson, *British Naval Officers*, 128.
[48] Lewis, *A Social History of the Navy*, 202.
[49] NMM, MRK/100–109.
[50] Clements Markham (ed.), *Selections from the Correspondence of Admiral John Markham during the Years 1801–4 and 1806–7* (NRS, 1904).

and John would spend the majority of the next seven formative years serving in the North American and West Indian stations.[51]

The first few years of his early career were a rapid success. He made acting-lieutenant on board *Roebuck* in 1779 and was confirmed in May 1781 in *Royal Oak*, making the step to commander less than a year later in March 1782 at the hands of Sir Peter Parker, commander-in-chief of the Jamaica station. In May that year, he suffered a nearly disastrous setback to his career when he was court-martialled for having fired on a French ship that turned out to have been sailing under a flag of truce. He was officially dismissed from his command and the service. However, this court martial did not greatly damage his career, most likely thanks to his family connections and the good impression he had made on his superior officers. Admiral George Rodney reinstated him to his rank the following December and he was quickly made acting-captain of *Carysfort*. He was promoted to post-captain officially on 3 January 1783 at the age of twenty-one.

Markham's fortune continued when, unlike many of his peers, he remained employed after the end of the war and served in the Mediterranean in command of *Sphinx* for three years, until he was finally paid off and put on half-pay in 1786. He returned to active service in 1793 with the outbreak of the French Revolutionary War, where he commanded *Blonde* and *Hannibal* in the Channel and West Indies where he came to the attention of John Jervis, who would later become Earl St Vincent after the battle of Cape St Vincent in 1797. Markham was not at this battle; the high rates of sickness in the West Indies hit his ships hard and in 1795 he left *Hannibal* as an invalid himself and returned to Britain. He did not return to sea again until 1797, just after marrying Maria Rice, the daughter of a family friend and twelve years his junior. In command of *Centaur* he served variously under St Vincent and Elphinstone's command in Ireland, the Channel and the Mediterranean until February 1801 when he followed St Vincent to the Admiralty.

John Markham had a reputation for being even-handed in his distribution of patronage and in his commands, albeit with a strong propensity for prayer.[52] One of his midshipmen from the 1790s, who later wrote a richly embellished memoir, described him through the anonymous mouth of a fellow midshipman as 'a tight one' with a tendency to pray well and 'heartily' in hurricanes.[53] In the first of his two times at the Admiralty, from February 1801 to May 1804, he was instrumental to St Vincent's management as First Lord, especially in pushing reforms through parliament and in being delegated control of most officer appointments, therefore shouldering much of the administrative burden

---

[51] See Appendix I for a chronology of Markham's career.

[52] Frederick Hoffman, *A Sailor of King George: The Journals of Captain Frederick Hoffman RN 1793–1814* (London, 1901; reprint 1999), 22.

[53] Ibid., 3.

INTRODUCTION 13

of Admiralty patronage. He was promoted to Rear-Admiral of the Blue in April 1804, shortly before leaving the Admiralty for the first time. St Vincent had also used his influence with the political corporation in Portsmouth to have Markham elected MP in November 1802, which proved especially useful for defending St Vincent's reforms in the House of Commons once they were out of the Admiralty.[54]

When the government of 'All the Talents' formed in January 1806, Markham re-joined the Admiralty under Charles Grey, Lord Howick. When the ministry was reshuffled again in September 1806, the new First Lord, Thomas Grenville, in deciding whether to retain Markham, wrote: 'I am still quite at a loss for a sheet anchor, and wish Markham had not made so many enemies, for in zeal and quickness of resource he seems to me to have great merit'.[55] Grenville ultimately decided to keep Markham on his board and he served for another seven months until March 1807 when he finally retired to the country.

He lived out the rest of his life in the family home with Maria in Ades near Lewes, where they had moved in 1802 at St Vincent's recommendation.[56] He occasionally championed the causes of his most precious remaining followers, such as Thomas John Williamson who had served as midshipman and clerk on board *Centaur* and was the (possibly illegitimate) son of one of Markham's brother's friends from his time in Bengal with the East India Company.[57] Otherwise, Markham remained mainly occupied by his duties as MP for Portsmouth until he was unseated in 1818. He never served at sea again.

The influence of connection on Markham's career is obvious even from this brief sketch. The role of his family and friends in particular will be explored in more detail in Chapter 2. In many ways, however, the most useful part of the Markham collection for our purposes is from his time as a commissioner of the board of Admiralty from 1801 to 1804 and 1806 to 1807. During

[54] R. G. Thorne (ed.), *The History of Parliament: The House of Commons 1790–1820* (Woodbridge, 1986), iv.546–548.

[55] Quoted in Markham (ed.), *Selections from the Correspondence of Admiral John Markham*, xii.

[56] Markham, *A Naval Career*, 246.

[57] NMM, MRK/105/3/95, Markham to Lord Mulgrave, First Lord of the Admiralty, 15 June 1809; TNA, ADM 36/14167 and 14168, Muster Books: HMS *Centaur*, 1 December 1800–30 April 1801. Thomas John Williamson joined *Centaur* in January 1800 and is recorded in the following muster as being aged twenty at the time of entry and coming from Bengal. I suspect he was the natural born son of one of William Markham's connections in Bengal, perhaps Captain Thomas George Williamson of the army in Bengal. He also seems to have been connected to the Griffiths family and by extension the Parkers through the marriage of Anne Parker to Captain Anselm Griffiths. See: NMM, MRK/107/4/8, William Markham to John Markham, 9 August 1803; TNA, PROB 11/1771/432 Will of Thomas John Williamson, Purser in the Royal Navy of Hampton Court, 3 May 1830.

this time Markham received applications for promotion, appointments, leave, assistance in court martial proceedings, information and advice, and for his influence with the First Lord. The collection also includes correspondence with his wife, family and wider circle of intimate friends throughout his career. Our period of focus begins with the American Revolutionary War and ends with the Napoleonic Wars, roughly framing Markham's sea-going and later political career, from when he entered the service in 1775 to when he lost his seat as MP for Portsmouth in 1818.[58]

Of course by focusing on Markham's papers at the core of this book, there will be parts of the picture that are not illuminated in as much detail as we may wish. The richest part of the collection is the correspondence Markham received while he was at the Admiralty. Many of the examples which we will explore in the following chapters will expose the kind of merit- and duty-focused patronage that teetered on the edge of bureaucracy, more so than if we focused on the patronage of someone like Edward Pellew as commander-in-chief of the East India station.[59] The great benefit of the Markham collection, however, is its survival and focus. The mobility of officers and others serving within or attached to the navy coupled with a fashion for honour and plain-speaking makes the navy particularly useful for understanding eighteenth-century patronage. Markham's papers provide a wealth of evidence for the language used in patronage solicitation, the sorts of connections and relation-ships that facilitated it and the priorities of patrons and applicants. They reveal how patronage operated both explicitly and implicitly underneath individual presentations of sensibility, friendship, duty and honour.

There is also a strength in focusing on Markham as a lord of the Admiralty rather than the First Lord himself. He was delegated a lot of control, especially in the appointment and promotion of commissioned and warrant officers. Many applicants also seem to have preferred to make more difficult requests to him, rather than risk directing them through public channels via the Admiralty's secretary, or troubling the First Lord. This also meant that Markham received requests from less fortunate or less elite applicants who are typically excluded from our discussion of patronage, those who perhaps had less claim on the First Lord personally, who did not feel the nature of their connection or status would give them licence to interrupt his business or even warrant his attention. Looking at Markham as a lord commissioner of the navy gives us an insight into how patronage operated for the type of applicant who made up the bulk of the navy, rather than the few who might survive in a First Lord's correspondence collection.

However, the patronage exchange leaves an incomplete historical record in many ways. We can surmise that many applications happened informally in

---

[58] Thorne, *House of Commons 1790–1820*, iv.546–548.

[59] John Morrow, *British Flag Officers in the French War, 1793–1815: Admiral's Lives* (London, 2018), 128–129.

INTRODUCTION 15

person, over dinner, in the drawing room, at the club, on ship, in inns, or in government offices like the Admiralty. The letters in the Markham collection show an expectation for face-to-face meetings. Captain George Lumsdaine apologised to Markham at the beginning of his request because 'a rheumatic complaint prevents me from paying my personal respect to you'.[60] Civilian applicants, soliciting on behalf of their sons in the navy, often waited at the Admiralty to be personally seen by a commissioner. One letter from William Baker, on behalf of William Eldridge, the son of a friend, shows that he intended to see Markham in person and had already spoken to St Vincent: 'I was unwilling to stop you in your way through Mr Parker's room, this morning when I perceived you was in a hurry to proceed to Lord St Vincent's apartments'.[61] Elizabeth Collier similarly mentioned wanting a face-to-face meeting with Markham as she opened her letter with 'The other morning when at the Admiralty, I regretted not being so fortunate to obtain a few minutes conversation with you.'[62] An interview was vital for some applicants to achieve their patronage goals, especially those lower down the social scale approaching elite patrons with whom they would have had fewer mutual connections and consequently had to work harder to establish the necessary trust. One way they could gain an audience with a patron was with a brokered letter from a mutual acquaintance. White was sent by Markham as the bearer of a letter to his father, the Archbishop of York.[63] Mary Higg, a female connection of Markham's from Plymouth, also sent a friend as the bearer of a letter recommending him to Markham's favour.[64]

This side of patronage is generally lost in the record, where only the letter to the patron survives. Focusing solely on solicitation letters and direct applications for patronage can distort our understanding of patronage and it is why this study expands the definition to include all forms of assistance in friendships and communities, including those instances where even the broker themselves did not conceive of their actions as patronage. To address the gaps in the record, the book also draws on network methodologies to reconstruct the potential avenues of patronage access and support, both for men like Markham and those lower down the social scale.[65] In doing so it includes some players not traditionally considered in the story of naval patronage. In this case, the networks of mutual trust and support that underpinned employment, support

---

[60] NMM, MRK/102/4/57, Lumsdaine to Markham, 3 May 1802.

[61] NMM, MRK/104/5/20, Baker to Markham, 25 June 1803.

[62] NMM, MRK/104/4/54, Collier to Markham, 6 January 1807.

[63] NMM, MRK/107/1/6, Markham to William Markham, 15 May 1780.

[64] NMM, MRK/104/4/44, Higg to Markham, 24 August 1803.

[65] Mark Granovetter, 'The Strength of Weak Ties', *American Journal of Sociology* 78:6 (May, 1973), 1360–1380; Lin, *Social Capital*, 29–54; Kadushin, *Understanding Social Networks*, 1–45; Sheryllyne Haggerty and John Haggerty, 'Visual Analytics of an Eighteenth-Century Business Network', *Enterprise and Society* 11:1 (March, 2010), 1–25.

16 PATRONAGE AND THE BRITISH NAVY, 1775–1815

and promotion in the Royal Dockyards. Although often overlooked, these networks and relationships were strong enough to resist the extending reach of Admiralty control to such an extent it excited the pique of St Vincent and his reforming zeal to stamp out corruption, instigating a large-scale government commission to investigate the corruption in the dockyards.[66]

To encompass the wide spectrum of connections and relationships that facilitated patronage across social levels, this book is therefore structured thematically rather than by dividing the navy by rank. The following chapters tackle in turn the three core aspects that determined the character of an individual's patronage: time, place and connection. The first chapter introduces us to our first two factors together within the framework of *geography*, and how the nature of the patronage a person had access to varied greatly depending on the station and time in which they served, and the location of the core of their network. The second chapter introduces the power of connection and with it John Markham's particular network context, surrounded by his family and friends. Chapter 3 expands the concept of connection even further, looking beyond Markham's intimate connections to consider in detail how patronage operated among Markham's wide and varied correspondents. Chapters 4 and 5 build on this to consider in turn the specific factors of politics and gender in the style of applicants' letters to Markham and his distribution of patronage in response. Chapter 6, our final chapter, expands the discussion beyond the close analysis of the Markham Papers, to consider how our three factors of time, place and connection moulded patronage at lower levels of society using the Royal Dockyards as a case study.

Establishing patronage as a broad social mechanism undermines the assumption that elite patronage was an inherently corrupt expression of control as opposed to lower-level 'community' often framed instead as driven by altruistic filial bonds.[67] Corruption and altruism happened at every level of society. Equally, in viewing patronage in this way this study avoids representing both female and lower-level applications to elite patrons, via petitions or direct solicitations, as condescendingly exceptional. Russel White was careful and solicitous when he approached Markham because of the disparity in their social statuses. His disadvantage came from the reduced likelihood of his and Markham's social circles being integrated, a factor which strengthened the claims made by Markham's social peers. It did not come from his lack of patronage skills produced by his lower social position. He was not ignorant of the way patronage worked, it was a system which operated throughout

---

[66] Morriss, 'Government and Community', 28; Roger Morriss, *The Royal Dockyards during the Revolutionary and Napoleonic Wars* (Leicester, 1983), 113.

[67] See Gill, *Naval Families*, 197–199; David Garrioch, *Neighbourhood and Community in Paris, 1740–1790* (Cambridge, 1986); Susan Whyman, *Sociability and Power in Late Stuart England* (Oxford, 1999).

INTRODUCTION 17

society at every level. Uncovering lower-level patronage networks proves the value of considering the focal points of patronage throughout society rather than merely judging degrees of access to elite control.

This book changes our understanding of the operation of patronage in the eighteenth century and provides a new model for female and lower-level agency. It combines the discussions of historical infrastructures of trust and informal support, and applies these frameworks to both elite and non-elite society.[68] Obligations connected individuals vertically and horizontally within social hierarchies. Networks of indebtedness shaped social circles and a person's identity, as well as their access to financial support and appointments. But relationships also shifted and changed with each interaction, causing a subtle interplay of societal pressures and priorities which affected how individuals approached patrons or distributed their patronage. Patronage was pervasive and lay between formal and informal social structures, relying on rules of honour and politeness which were not immune to personal offence or quirks. But most crucially, it was a system dictated by trust founded on an individual's ability, character and connections. In this way, we can see how the need for patronage shaped eighteenth-century society.

[68] See Sunderland, *Social Capital*; Ben-Amos, *Culture of Giving*.

1

Time and Place: The Geography of Naval Patronage

> I respectfully leave it to your command to discharge him from the *Zealand* to *any* destination where you judge that the letter with which you intend to honor him will be most effective and will best suit your own convenience; whether on the East or West Indies Stations, Mediterranean or Channel or in what Quarter you think proper.
>
> David P. Watts, 26 November 1806[1]

When Captain John Perkins wrote to Markham from Jamaica in 1806 to thank him for soliciting the First Lord, he wrote: 'I shall have the Happyness to convince a few out here that I have so good a friend at home as you'.[2] In his letter, Perkins presented Britain as the 'home' and centre of the perceived geography of the Royal Navy. Perkins was born in Jamaica, the son of an enslaved woman, and served his entire career in the West Indies. He first went to sea as the enslaved servant of a carpenter but after the Seven Years War he escaped this service and become a pilot; a skilled and vital role in the difficult waters of the West Indies.[3] His expertise secured his entry as a freeman to the navy in 1771 and he rose first to lieutenant in 1781 and then post-captain in 1800. Perkins is remarkable as one of the only known black commissioned officers in the navy in the late eighteenth century and his career is testament to the influence of talent, connection and timing on an officer's life.[4] Aside from catching the attention of influential admirals George Rodney and Peter Parker, Perkins also made friends with officers like Markham while serving in the West Indies. In 1802, this friendship paid off when Markham appointed Perkins to the fifth rate *Tartar*, the largest command of his career.[5]

---

[1]   NMM, MRK/104/3/41.

[2]   NMM, MRK/102/5/15, Perkins to Markham, 6 June 1806.

[3]   Douglas Hamilton, '"A Most Active, Enterprising Officer": Captain John Perkins, the Royal Navy and the Boundaries of Slavery and Liberty in the Caribbean', *Slavery and Abolition*, online (2017), DOI: 10.1080/0144039X.2017.1330862, 5–6. My thanks to Douglas Hamilton for sharing his work with me pre-publication.

[4]   Wilson, *British Naval Officers*, 123–124.

[5]   Hamilton, '"A Most Active, Enterprising Officer"', 9; NMM, MRK/102/5/14,

TIME AND PLACE: THE GEOGRAPHY OF NAVAL PATRONAGE   19

Perkins only visited Britain twice, once in 1784 and again in 1786.[6] This is perhaps not surprising given that his reputation was founded on his specialised knowledge of West Indian waters and his active avoidance of colder stations which aggravated his asthma. However, despite being so firmly rooted in the West Indies, when writing to Markham he almost always referred to Britain explicitly as 'home'.[7] In doing so, Perkins may have sought to emphasise his connection to Markham through their shared British identity, similar to the way many other writers maintained trans-Atlantic networks in their correspondence through their use of sentimental language evoking family and friendship.[8] But Perkins's letter also illustrates how Britain was the perceived centre of administration, culture and friendship in naval patronage, which ultimately placed stations like the West Indies at the periphery.

Location drastically shaped patronage, especially in the Royal Navy. Naval patronage operated on a global scale. Appointments relied on administrative, professional and social networks which extended from the Mediterranean to the Atlantic and Indian Ocean. Environmental factors in each station dictated patronage limitations and opportunities. While service closer to home allowed easy access to home-networks and the Admiralty, it also meant greater Admiralty control and limited the patronage autonomy of senior officers. For those without strong connections to the Admiralty or home politics, serving in distant stations offered more opportunity. However, this greater autonomy also meant that an applicant needed strong ties with the civilian and naval communities of overseas stations to ensure their patronage success. Furthermore, although the rate of disease in certain stations presented great risks, it increased the number of vacancies and an applicant needed less patronage to gain promotion.

Applicants solicited Markham at the Admiralty from across the wide spread of the navy drawing on the opportunities offered them by their stations. Others sought to be sent out to stations where they could prove themselves or gain quick promotion. There were also those who requested his influence in keeping them out of stations which were considered too risky to their health. Many applicants who mentioned the West or East Indies used their health as an excuse to be stationed elsewhere. Lieutenant Thomas Hand mentioned his ill health in hot climates but also his willingness to serve: 'I was obliged to quit the East, and West Indies for the liver-complaint. I must however (tho' I should not volunteer those stations on *that* account) take my chance like

---

Perkins to Markham, 18 May 1806 [catalogued as 12 May 1806]; NMM, MRK/104/5/52, Perkins to Markham, 31 March 1802.

6   NMM, MRK/102/5/13, Perkins to Markham, 8 May 1803.

7   See particularly NMM, MRK/102/5/12 and 13, Perkins to Markham, 7 September 1801 and 8 May 1803.

8   Pearsall, *Atlantic Families*, 55 and 64.

20 PATRONAGE AND THE BRITISH NAVY, 1775–1815

others and am ready to serve my country wherever it calls me.'[9] Lady Rebecca Peshall's application on behalf of her son reflected her fear of foreign stations far more explicitly: 'I have not the least objection to his going to any port in Europe, that you may think proper to direct, but the Climates of the East and West Indies have proved so fatal to my family, few advantages would tempt me to risque my son there.'[10]

Many officers were prepared to take the risk in the pursuit of the vacancies that inevitably arose from high rates of death and disease. Thomas John Peshall overruled his mother's request and managed to secure service in the West Indies anyway in the hopes of promotion.[11] Many other officers simply could not afford to damage their patronage relationships by making overbearing requests. David Watts, a wine merchant and the civilian applicant quoted at the beginning of this chapter, was keen to stress that his nephew would go to any station which suited Markham.[12] Some officers warned their families against requesting the Admiralty to spare them from certain stations because such inflexible demands could damage their reputation.[13] Flexibility was crucial in naval patronage, especially for lieutenants and commanders in a period where there were more officers than appointments. As St Vincent wrote in response to Admiral Archibald Dickson: 'Your son in law is plac'd on a very long list of Candidates, several of whom made application for service in any Clime, several months ago, and I am sure you will admit are entitled to preference.'[14]

The geography of patronage is a useful way to frame an introduction to the central roles of time and place on naval promotion structure, as well as its variation and complexity. But it is also important to note that the navy was not static. Officers and seamen moved readily between stations and some

---

9 The 'liver-complaint' was a general term for ill health in hot climates, sometimes referred to as hepatitis in the period, but could also refer to ill health in the aftermath of recovering from intermittent fever (malaria) or yellow fever. See Thomas Girdlestone, *Essays on the Hepatitis and Spasmodic Affections in India; Founded on Observations made while on Service with His Majesty's Troops in Different Parts of that Country* (London, 1787); for detailed discussion of association of ill health and climate in India during the Seven Years War see Erica Charters, *Disease, War and the Imperial State: The Welfare of the British Armed Forces during the Seven Years' War* (London, 2014); NMM, MRK/102/3/6, Hand to Markham, 28 May 1803.

10 NMM, MRK/104/4/42, Peshall to Markham, 10 June 1803.

11 Peshall avoided the disease of the West Indies which his mother feared, but he did not escape death in the service, and died a prisoner of war after wrecking his ship in South America. *The Naval Chronicle for 1812: Containing a general and biographical history of the Royal Navy of the United Kingdom; with a variety of original papers on nautical subjects*, 27, January–June (London, 1812), 273.

12 NMM, MRK/104/3/41, Watts to Markham, 26 November 1806.

13 Gill, *Naval Families*, 105 and 107–108.

14 BL, Add MS 31167, St Vincent to Dickson, 2 April 1803.

TIME AND PLACE: THE GEOGRAPHY OF NAVAL PATRONAGE 21

types of service, such as convoy duty, were especially mobile. The type of action seen in various fleets also differed greatly in times of war and peace. This chapter uses home-waters, the Mediterranean, Newfoundland and the West and East Indies as case studies in understanding the effect of location on patronage. The first section considers the role of distance and the second considers the opportunities and limitations each station offered.

Naval Administration

Control of appointments was distributed across the offices, the fleets and the dockyards. The offices of the navy were its administrative heart. The Admiralty was led by the First Lord, who was a member of cabinet, often a politician and in some cases also a naval officer. Beneath the First Lord were six commissioners, four of whom were usually politicians and two were sea officers. Commissioners dealt with the administration of the navy. They also dealt with the high volume of patronage requests made by officers at sea and in the dockyards, as well as solicitations from broader British society. The amount of control the commissioners had depended on the temperament of the First Lord. Markham was one of the sea officers on St Vincent's board between 1801 and 1804. St Vincent was a micro-manager of appointments but was also inclined to dismiss applications out of hand. Early in his time as First Lord he delegated control of appointments to his sea officers, Markham and Thomas Troubridge, although he also often intervened. Thomas Grenville, on the other hand, kept diligent records of those who applied to him.[15] When under Grenville's direction in 1806 and 1807, Markham still had the power of appointment, but Grenville was more consistently involved in his distribution of Admiralty patronage.

The Admiralty controlled all appointments in the navy and fielded the recommendations of the other boards, as well as those from commanders-in-chief and officers in the fleets. The Admiralty also technically presided over sub-departments and Markham received applications for his assistance from officers in the dockyards, who usually were under the control of the Navy Board, as well as ships' surgeons and physicians, who likewise answered to the Sick and Hurt Board.[16] In many cases, however, the response of a commissioner like Markham was to either pass the solicitation on or to ask

[15] HL, Stowe Papers, ST102, Thomas Grenville: Promotion Books. My thanks to Roger Knight for sharing his research with me.

[16] Roger Morriss, *Naval Power and British Culture, 1760–1850: Public Trust and Government Ideology* (Aldershot, 2004), 132–134; for letters from officers in the dockyard see for example William Browne, previously master of *Centaur* appointed master attendant at Portsmouth yard: NMM, MRK/104/1/34–39, William Browne to Markham, 18 May 1802–17 December 1807.

the applicant to ask elsewhere.[17] Similarly, the commander-in-chief had the power of appointment in his fleet. However, he was increasingly restricted in the appointments he could make. He was limited by the 'Admiralty list' of candidates drawn up by the First Lord and commissioners from those who had solicited them. Just as at the Admiralty, the patronage of a commander-in-chief was a balancing act between satisfying the needs of their intimate friends, their political and naval allies, and the needs of the service. Commanders-in-chief bought their patronage control through their cooperation with seeing to the wishes of the Admiralty in appointments.

Similarly, although the commander-in-chief had technical control of the appointments in the fleet under his command, each captain was entitled to his say in the appointment of officers to his ship. The captain also had complete control over the entry to the service of volunteer class boys or captain's servants who were often the young sons of his friends and connections.[18] St Vincent, suspicious as he was of all patronage that was not his own, saw the practice as damaging to the navy.[19] It certainly contributed to the crisis in the promotion of sea officers in the early nineteenth century, where there were too many lieutenants for the number of ships and positions available.[20] However, the appointment of the 'young gentlemen' remained the captain's primary patronage throughout the Napoleonic Wars. The most important thing to a captain outfitting a ship was to fill it with men he could trust, both officers and seamen. Patronage played a key role in this because the network of obligations and officers' reputations acted as some guarantee of the client's competence. However, the shift towards a more centralised system of appointment controlled by the Admiralty at the end of the century curtailed officers' powers of appointment, especially those of admirals and commanders-in-chief. Consequently, many captains' applications to the Admiralty commissioners were requests to exchange officers between ships simply because the captain had been landed with an officer he disliked or considered incompetent.

Of course, because patronage relied on influence and connection, the well-connected often circumvented the technical control of appointments. Lieutenants sometimes had more influence than their captain, which allowed

---

[17] See Markham's note to his secretary on how to respond to a request by Henrietta Moriarty to be appointed to matron of the Royal Naval Asylum. The asylum was a charitable institution which did not come under the jurisdiction of the Admiralty until its amalgamation with Greenwich Hospital and Hospital School in 1821; NMM, MRK/104/4/22, Moriarty to Markham, 9 January 1807.

[18] Cavell, *Midshipmen and the Quarterdeck Boys*, 10.

[19] David Bonner Smith (ed.), *Letters of Admiral of the Fleet the Earl of St Vincent while First Lord of the Admiralty 1801–1804* (NRS, 1927), vol. 2, 254–255. St Vincent to Elizabeth Fane, 29 June 1802.

[20] Cavell, *Midshipmen and the Quarterdeck Boys*, 116.

TIME AND PLACE: THE GEOGRAPHY OF NAVAL PATRONAGE   23

them to recommend their own friends to profitable positions. Captain John Oakes Hardy wrote to Markham to complain that a newly appointed lieutenant had filled all the vacancies with his own friends before Hardy arrived.[21] Captains and admirals also had the power to promote men on their ship to acting appointments. The power of local networks in distant stations and difficulties in communication with the Admiralty meant that in some stations gaining an acting appointment was as good as an official promotion. They provided greater opportunities for glory and prize money, and were often eventually approved.

The dockyards were another focal point of naval patronage. Appointments were ostensibly controlled by the Navy Board. The Admiralty could intervene in the appointment of the commissioner of the dockyard and the most senior officers such as the master attendant and master shipwright. The appointment of commissioners to important home yards and overseas yards was also open to the influence of prominent admirals and politicians. Isaac Coffin was appointed commissioner at Halifax dockyard in Nova Scotia through the influence of St Vincent in 1800. While there, he carried out St Vincent's reforming agenda with apparent zeal and disregard for the expertise of officers long-established in the yard. However, the commissioner relied on the support of the dockyard officers who in turn had the support of civilian connections in the local community. Coffin soon angered everyone of influence in Halifax and alienated his command, prompting his recall to Britain only six months after his initial appointment.[22]

Patronage in the dockyards was not simply a question of whether appointments were controlled by the Navy Board or the Admiralty. The dockyards were largely semi-autonomous. Difficulties in communication and the sheer magnitude of the paperwork involved in organising the navy meant that the Navy Board did not have direct control of appointments even in the home yards. Equally, the Admiralty was filled with sea officers and politicians who had little practical experience of the needs of the dockyards.[23] Both boards relied on the recommendations of the principal yard officers who in turn, due to the nature of shipwright promotion, listened to their extended networks both within the yard and in the local parish community.

The largest or the most strategically significant yards were commanded by a commissioner who was often a retired sea officer. Beneath the commissioner, the running of the dockyard fell to the principal officers, usually five in the large British yards and three in smaller overseas yards. In overseas yards they were the master shipwright, the master attendant and the naval storekeeper or

[21] NMM, MRK/102/3/13, Hardy to Markham, 13 June 1802.

[22] Julian Gwyn, *Ashore and Afloat: The British Navy and the Halifax Naval Yard before 1820* (Ottawa, 2004), 73–74.

[23] Morriss, *Royal Dockyards*, 167.

clerk of the cheque. Each officer oversaw part of the yard and the appointment of men therein. The master shipwright oversaw all shipwrights, labourers and other artificers including the carpenters, sawyers and caulkers. The master attendant was responsible for the piloting of ships in the harbour and had control of the appointments of artificers who worked afloat such as the riggers and sailmakers. The clerk of the cheque and the naval storekeeper saw to the pay and victualling of the yard and largely controlled the appointments of the clerks in the offices and cabin-keepers who were the storekeepers for particular sections of the yard. Appointments were also made by the commissioner, who recommended men for positions by writing to the Admiralty or Navy Board, often depending on where he had the firmest connections.[24] Each yard had its own recommendation network defined by friendship and religious ties in the community. Unlike the sea service, officers and men often served their whole careers together in the same parish. Patronage was not restricted to operating within the yard's hierarchy. This was particularly true for the home yards because the size and stability of the workforce allowed for greater integration with parish churches and merchant yards.

The six main home yards were Plymouth, Portsmouth, Chatham, Sheerness, Deptford and Woolwich. There were also smaller bases and depots such as Leith in Scotland or Kinsale in Ireland. There were naval bases and depots spread across the world, although the largest were found in strategic locations to supply and refit the fleets. Gibraltar and the naval base at Port Mahon, Minorca supplied the Mediterranean fleet, Halifax the North American fleet when in northern waters, Kingston and Port Royal in Jamaica serviced the Jamaica fleet and the North American fleet depending on its service, and English Harbour at Antigua saw to the Leeward Islands fleet. The navy did not, however, have any yards in the East Indies, and instead relied on the East India Company bases at Bombay and Madras. Commanders-in-chief had influence in overseas yards in the absence of a commissioner or adequate communication with the Navy Board. Although the Navy Board was not in complete control of dockyard appointments, it fiercely protected the autonomy of yard officers in disputes with senior sea officers, port admirals and commanders-in-chiefs of overseas yards. Position in the dockyards, therefore, could be secured in several ways, but a link to the dockyard commissioner or one of the principal officers was perhaps the most effective, rather than connection to the Navy Board or Admiralty in Britain. Dockyard patronage was essentially local, and this meant that shipwrights and artificers in overseas yards faced different opportunities and limitations than officers and seamen in the fleet.

---

[24] See Appendix IV for a more detailed description of these roles. Gwyn, *Ashore and Afloat*, 76–77; Morriss, *Royal Dockyards*, 168–170.

Distance and Admiralty Control

Distance from Britain, the conceptual and administrative centre of the scattered stations, fleets and yards of the navy, greatly contributed to the variation of patronage. The Admiralty at Whitehall and the Navy Board at Somerset House had technical, administrative control of all naval appointments but the physical distance between these stations, compounded by difficulties in communications caused by packet routes, conflict and seasonal differences in sailing times to the East Indies and Newfoundland, meant that patronage control across the navy varied by distance from the Admiralty. N. A. M. Rodger called the Admiralty and commanders-in-chief in overseas stations the 'twin poles' of naval patronage because these communication problems meant admirals overseas had to make appointments immediately rather than wait for Admiralty approval.[25] Michael Lewis also incorporated distance into his framework for naval advancement, separating naval patronage into captains, the Admiralty and 'the admiral-on-the-spot'.[26] Social distance also greatly affected the control of patronage, as revealed by the strength of lateral ties within the communities surrounding the Royal Dockyards explored in Chapter 6. Fundamentally, alienation from home-networks by social or physical distance changed the way that clients sought and patrons distributed patronage.

Figure 1.1 shows the relative sailing times to the stations discussed in this chapter. Stations in home-waters could be reached within a couple of days and the Mediterranean within a week. The West Indies could take up to nine weeks sailing from Britain and up to fourteen weeks returning from Jamaica, the furthest west of the islands.[27] Newfoundland was physically closer to Britain but harsh winters meant that for five months of the year the station could become extremely isolated.[28] The East Indies, the furthest by sea with an average sailing of five to six months, was also isolated by the monsoon season in the spring which made sailing so dangerous that many merchantmen forwent sailing in winter from Britain entirely.[29]

Letters were key to conducting patronage at a distance.[30] Patrons and brokers based in British home-networks sent out letters on behalf of their clients to captains and admirals, soliciting their interest and directly asking for appointments or promotion. These letters in many ways acted as proxies for

[25] Rodger, *Wooden World*, 282.

[26] Lewis, *A Social History of the Navy*, 202–205.

[27] Ian Steele, *The English Atlantic 1675–1740: An Exploration of Communication and Community* (Oxford, 1986), 31.

[28] Ibid., 91; Julian Gwyn, *Frigates and Foremasts: The North American Squadron in Nova Scotia Waters 1745–1815* (Vancouver, 2003), 88.

[29] Peter Ward, *British Naval Power in the East 1794–1805: The Command of Admiral Peter Rainier* (Woodbridge, 2013), 93.

[30] Pearsall, *Atlantic Families*, 124.

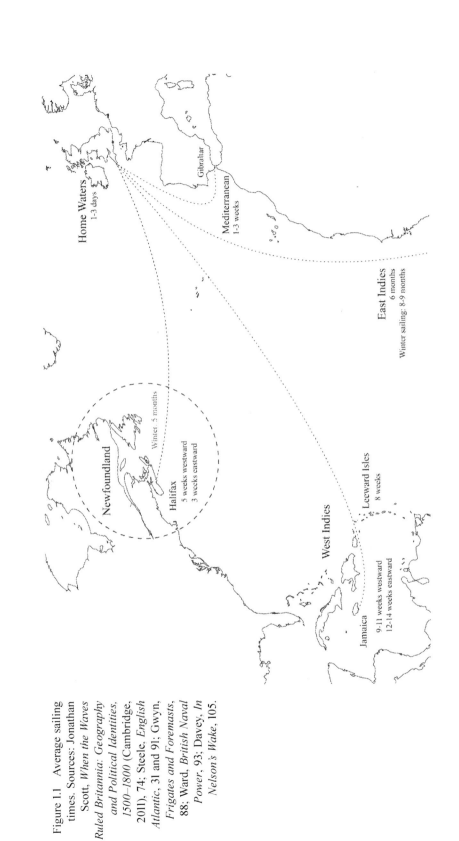

Figure 1.1 Average sailing times. Sources: Jonathan Scott, *When the Waves Ruled Britannia: Geography and Political Identities, 1500–1800* (Cambridge, 2011), 74; Steele, *English Atlantic*, 31 and 91; Gwyn, *Frigates and Foremasts*, 88; Ward, *British Naval Power*, 93; Davey, *In Nelson's Wake*, 105.

the patron, in lieu of a face-to-face meeting that would be desirable in Britain. Markham's father enclosed a duplicate letter from his friend David Murray, Viscount Stormont, to Admiral George Rodney, soliciting his interest in young Markham while he served in the Caribbean. He wrote: 'I was advised to look principally towards [Rodney] as having the means of serving you in much greater abundance than any other Ad^{ml} and accordingly got Ld Stormont to write an earnest letter to him in your favour, mentioning your repeated disappointments.' The duplicate letter was to be delivered by Markham to Rodney in case Stormont's original went astray: 'In case that letter should miscarry I desired him to write a duplicate, which I enclose to you, that if you have the opportunity, you may deliver it yourself.'[31] The duplicate letter acted as a proxy for the face-to-face solicitation of the patron at home.

Of course, distance made correspondence unreliable and patronage organised in this way was difficult to maintain. Major Thomas Thorpe Fowke had significant difficulty acting on his son's behalf when George Fowke served as a midshipman in the West Indies. In January 1789, he wrote to tell George that he had only just received a letter dated September of the previous year and had consequently not heard from George for twelve months. Fowke reasoned that the letter must have been 'left somewhere on the road' because otherwise they would have got it long before 'Easterly winds set in', increasing sailing times from the West Indies.[32] The delivery of letters to and from overseas stations was never sure. George fortunately had made 'friends' in Barbados who he assured his father would 'look after' him.[33] Certainly, enclosing a letter of introduction to local networks was one way an individual's home-network could conduct patronage at a distance.[34]

The transfer of private letters was disrupted to a greater degree than official Admiralty correspondence. Monthly packet ships sailed to Ireland, the Mediterranean, West Indies and North America, but there was no guarantee that the mail would make it in times of war. Some merchant ships also carried letters free of charge and had arrangements with post-masters in British ports to send the letters inland for the appropriate fee.[35] Very active service also gave officers little time to write to their friends and family, and some types of service such as blockading required a captain to keep a steady position, meaning he had little opportunity to pass his letters on to a captain going ashore. Markham had little time for letter-writing and little opportunity to send them when he served in the Mediterranean in 1798, which prompted his wife Maria to write, 'you will be convinced how great an object it is to me

---

[31] NMM, MP, uncatalogued, William Markham to Markham, 8 February 1782.
[32] NMM, FOW/2/1, Fowke to George Fowke, 29 January 1789.
[33] Ibid.
[34] C. Brant, *Eighteenth-Century Letters and British Culture* (London, 2006), 24.
[35] Lincoln, *Naval Wives*, 32–33.

28 PATRONAGE AND THE BRITISH NAVY, 1775–1815

to hear from you at every opportunity; and I should think even without being acquainted, no officer could think it trouble to a put a letter in the post for your poor Wiffy'.[36] She must have also rebuked him when he served in the Channel fleet for not corresponding with her frequently enough, as he wrote in a letter to her:

> I have only now got your letters and papers from the Africaine and Royal George. I am blamed I find for neglect, gracious God, why? I wish you could yourself be witness. Captain S[utton] is near the Ad[mrl] and has frequent opportunities of sending a boat, I am far, very far, from him, my station is more miles say thrice to leeward of him.[37]

The speed of correspondence to individual captains in certain stations, therefore, was not guaranteed and this meant that it was more difficult to reach their connections in Britain who could solicit the Admiralty on their behalf or arrange further patronage with officers and civilians in overseas stations.

Admiralty orders and dispatches, on the other hand, could take direct routes to reach their destinations. News of Nelson's victory at Trafalgar reached the Admiralty in ten days once Admiral Cuthbert Collingwood sent the dispatches on 26 October, including eight days at sea and two days overland from Falmouth to London.[38] The Admiralty also had use of the shutter telegraph system, established in 1796, which connected ports such as Portsmouth to Whitehall and cut communication time down to fifteen minutes for urgent news and a day for less sensitive orders such as appointments.[39] Consequently, in home-waters, including the Channel and North Sea fleets, as well as the Mediterranean, the Admiralty had greater control of appointments.

St Vincent's response to a patronage request from Captain William Aylmer illustrates the position that commanders-in-chief found themselves in in the Channel fleet, so close to Admiralty control. He wrote: 'Had a ship suitable to your Rank and ambition been selected for you in this Fleet you would have received every possible mark of attention from me.'[40] Aylmer could solicit St Vincent's assistance, but his support was of little material use to him until he had secured a ship from the Admiralty. The central feature of Admiralty control in home-waters was that there was less opportunity for acting commissions.

---

[36] NMM, MRK/107/3/22, Maria to John, 24 July [1798].

[37] NMM, MRK/107/2/27, John to Maria, 17 March 1800.

[38] James Davey, *In Nelson's Wake: The Navy and the Napoleonic Wars* (London, 2015), 105.

[39] Roger Knight, *Britain Against Napoleon: The Organization of Victory, 1793–1815* (London, 2013), 137–140; Markham also occasionally mentioned the telegraph in his memos or drafted replies to requests, in which it is clear he expected lower-priority messages to take a day to be transmitted.

[40] BL, Add MS31167, St Vincent to Aylmer, 8 January 1801.

When a vacancy arose in the small craft stationed around the coast, the Admiralty filled it from the long-list of candidates or those lieutenants on the half-pay list.

To gain the Admiralty's favour, officers or their brokers had to write either to the First Lord directly, a commissioner or the Admiralty secretary. Markham was solicited by captains both known and unknown to him in home-waters looking to exchange officers on their ship or to recommend their connections to other vacancies. They also asked for undesirable lieutenants to be discharged in favour of their own candidates who were sometimes known to the captain, but sometimes the captain knew of them by reputation alone. These sorts of applications blur the line between what we understand as patronage and what historians consider to be naval administration. Admiralty control in home-waters meant that officers had to solicit the board for any adjustments to appointments. However, a commissioner, like Markham, could approve an application as a mark of favour and this act opened a patronage relationship where officers approached Markham first or enhanced their application by writing to him alongside their letters to the Admiralty secretary.

Patronage in home-waters was characterised, then, by this careful exchange of letters between officers and Admiralty commissioners. The Admiralty's ability quickly to convey their orders for appointments gave them technical control over all vacancies in home-waters but officers' patronage also did not disappear entirely. Rather, an officer's patronage in home-waters was brokerage through their power of recommendation. As such, an officer's home-network truly characterised his patronage position. Proximity granted Admiralty control, but it also allowed an officer to communicate more effectively with influential friends who could then pressure the Admiralty to see him promoted or given a better appointment.

In the fleets stationed closer to Britain, such as the Channel or the Mediterranean fleet, it is difficult to distinguish Admiralty control because the ease in communication meant that commanders-in-chief could ask permission before making the appointment and so their autonomy is lost within the subtle system of patronage recommendation. However, some admirals were not afraid of showing their displeasure at Admiralty involvement, which highlights the burden that proximity to Britain placed on patronage in the fleets. St Vincent, in line with his tendency to view all decisions made by anyone but himself as incompetent or corrupt, was hugely critical of Admiralty appointments that were made to the Channel fleet when he was in command. He wrote a scathing letter to Evan Nepean, the Admiralty secretary, about the appointment of a captain to a ship that he considered to be extremely difficult to sail and consequently needed a competent officer in command, preferably one chosen by himself: 'You could not have selected a more unfit Man, to command the Courageux, than Tom Bowen, who beside being very near an idiot, is the

30   PATRONAGE AND THE BRITISH NAVY, 1775–1815

most Cow hearted fellow, on the whole list.'[41] Cuthbert Collingwood, when an admiral in the Mediterranean fleet, similarly complained to his sister about the appointments being made and his own limited authority to fill vacancies. He wrote: 'such numbers of unqualified, ignorant people are introduced into [the Navy] that my astonishment is that more accidents do not happen. I was never so sensible of this truth as since I came into this ship.'[42] Like St Vincent, Collingwood was similarly burdened when he became commander-in-chief of the Mediterranean in 1805. In 1808, he wrote to Rear-Admiral John Purvis:

> I need not assure you my sincere desire to do everything for your son that is in my power whenever I can give him an appointment I will most gladly, but I have never had one, those that have hitherto been made here were by the Admiralty.[43]

The Admiralty took control of most vacancies in the Mediterranean fleet, which left limited vacancies for the commander-in-chief to satisfy his own patronage network. The admirals of the fleet, such as Collingwood, were consequently restricted mainly to recommendations.

St Vincent was responsible for much of the Admiralty's seizing control of Mediterranean appointments. When he came to the Admiralty in 1801, he faced a crisis in the number of captains and lieutenants left unemployed and on half-pay, which only worsened when he secured peace in 1802. There were simply not enough vacancies to meet demand. Yet the Admiralty had to see to the requests of those powerful members of British society who supported the Addington ministry. St Vincent, although capricious, managed to deflect a great deal of political requests during his time as First Lord, as we will see in Chapter 4. However, to see to the Admiralty's political allies and to reduce the list of what he termed 'meritorious lieutenants on half-pay', St Vincent encroached on Mediterranean vacancies.[44] In 1801, he apologised to George Keith Elphinstone, the commander-in-chief, for having to 'trespass upon [his] patronage' because he had resolved not to promote at home until 'all the meritorious post-captains and commanders are provided for'.[45] Midshipman William Croft, one of Markham's protégés, also wrote in 1801 to say that he could not get a position from Keith because St Vincent had given the

---

[41] BL, Add MS 31173, St Vincent to Nepean, 21 January 1801.

[42] Edward Hughes (ed.), *The Private Correspondence of Admiral Lord Collingwood* (NRS, 1957), 101–102. Collingwood to his sister, 21 September 1799.

[43] Hughes, *Private Correspondence*, 234–235. Collingwood to Purvis, 1 February 1808.

[44] BL, Add MS 31168, St Vincent to William Dickson, 1 March 1801.

[45] Bonner Smith, *Letters of Admiral of the Fleet*, i.333. St Vincent to George Keith Elphinstone, 21 February 1801.

TIME AND PLACE: THE GEOGRAPHY OF NAVAL PATRONAGE 31

commander-in-chief a 'wrap *over the knuckles*' for granting acting commissions.[46] St Vincent spent much of his time at the Admiralty diverting the attentions of powerful applicants with hollow promises of future interest and acting commissions put him in an awkward position when a well-connected lieutenant could press to have his commission made full.

The Mediterranean was an extremely desirable station. The onset of the war with France in 1793 and the increased need to support Portugal against French and Spanish pressure in 1797 made the Mediterranean a focal point for naval activity in the late 1790s and early 1800s.[47] The fleet offered the opportunity for active service in large ships which in turn could take large prizes, and the chance for young officers to prove their talent in action. It was also considered a particularly healthy station; far from the risk of disease inevitable in most sea service, a cruise in the Mediterranean was seen to improve an officer's health.[48] Being in easy reach of communication from Britain also meant an officer was not isolated from his home-network and could manage his connections to continue to apply pressure to the Admiralty. Easy communication also made the Mediterranean a popular command for ambitious admirals with strong followings. Keith had a very strong regional base in his constituency in south-west Scotland and his family seat in north-east Scotland, which he managed by letter from the Mediterranean.[49] Much of Keith's correspondence with his sister Mary Elphinstone was taken up with discussion of favours and appointments.[50] His command of the fleet gave him access to desirable appointments as well as the proximity easily to correspond with his political, regional and familial connections.

However, the station's proximity and desirability also meant that the Admiralty was overwhelmed with requests from influential patrons that the First Lord needed to satisfy. A letter from St Vincent to Markham reveals the Admiralty's difficulty when he wrote requesting that Markham find an appointment in the Mediterranean for a client of the Queen's 'without naming the object to anyone'.[51] Proximity to Britain gave the Admiralty greater control of appointments which it then, in turn, had to use to satisfy influential patrons in a period of extreme competition for vacancies across the entire navy. Commanders-in-chief such as Keith or Collingwood, therefore, had very few vacancies which they could fill themselves, and admirals and captains

[46] NMM, MRK/105/3/39, Croft to Markham, 18 April 1801.

[47] Rodger, *Command of the Ocean*, 426–428, 454–472.

[48] See letter from Lieutenant Charles Wintour who sought passage to the Mediterranean for his health. NMM, MRK/103/2/42, 7 May 1801.

[49] Kevin McCranie, *Admiral Lord Keith and the Naval War Against Napoleon* (Gainesville, 2006), 4 and 30.

[50] BL, Add MS 86495–6, Keith to Mary Elphinstone, 1797–1800.

[51] NMM, MRK/101/1/7, St Vincent to Markham, 9 April 1802.

32 PATRONAGE AND THE BRITISH NAVY, 1775–1815

even fewer. For many, it was a choice between obliging their network back in Britain or avowing to promote only by merit, which is what St Vincent proclaimed on his entry to the Admiralty and was why he wanted Markham to keep the Queen's appointment quiet even if he had to oblige her by necessity.

Commanders-in-chief with strong regional affiliations, such as Keith, found placing the useless sons of connections in his limited vacancies particularly troublesome. In 1800, he wrote to his sister that 'this life does not suit me business and pleasure go ill together'. He was referring to his attempts to push forward the 'silly, idle and drunkern' William Leith.[52] In 1799, he had written proclaiming he would no longer 'be of use to boys' because of the disappointments he suffered at the poor service and character of Leith.[53] The fact that he had acted as patron for the boy at all illustrates the restriction his regional network placed on him. He did not stop promoting from his network but, increasingly, the pressure of Admiralty vacancies meant that he chose those connections who both satisfied his network obligations and had the skill to maintain his reputation. As Rodger framed it in his discussion on naval patronage, the failure of a protégé 'was as much the failure of the patron'.[54] Consequently, Keith promoted Charles Adam, a capable young officer and son of one of his largest network obligations, William Adam, a prominent Whig politician and his brother-in-law.[55] In the particularly competitive environment of the Mediterranean an officer needed both talent and connection to gain an appointment.[56]

The tension between Admiralty control and the autonomy of officers in the fleet is easier to see in stations where distance prevented reliable communication and, therefore, limited Admiralty control of immediate appointments. The time taken for the exchange of news and orders, as well as the transfer of officers, meant that commanders-in-chief 'on the spot' had much more control over acting appointments.[57]

The sailing time to the North American squadron and Halifax dockyard could be as short as three weeks but significant problems of communication in winter often made the station in effect more distant.[58] Sea ice and freezing temperatures played havoc with the reliability of mail coming via packet ships to New York. Commanders and dockyard commissioners in Newfoundland could wait up to five months for communications during winter. Rear-Admiral Sir Thomas Hughes attempted to set up a more reliable relay system between

---

52 BL, Add MS 86496, Keith to Elphinstone, 1 July 1800.
53 BL, Add MS 86496, Keith to Elphinstone 10 September 1799.
54 Rodger, *Wooden World*, 277.
55 McCranie, *Admiral Lord Keith*, 26.
56 Wilson, *British Naval Officers*, 127–129.
57 Lewis, *A Social History of the Navy*, 202–205.
58 Steele, *English Atlantic*, 90–91.

TIME AND PLACE: THE GEOGRAPHY OF NAVAL PATRONAGE 33

New York and Halifax in 1790 using two schooners hired at Dartmouth, Nova Scotia. One, unfortunately, met with a fierce storm and was driven off course to the West Indies while the second became trapped in ice in Nantucket for eight weeks.[59] Once the relay system became established in 1793, the ships took between four and six weeks to reach Halifax, meaning that correspondence carried via the packet to New York could take up to ten weeks to reach Newfoundland.[60] In several instances, commissioners of Halifax dockyard, when tired of their relatively isolated post, took it upon themselves to sail back to Britain rather than to request a change in appointment and await orders. Andrew Snape Hammond left his appointment as commissioner of Halifax dockyard without orders in 1784 and John Inglefield left the same position in 1807. Hammond eventually became the Comptroller of the Navy (after Charles Middleton) while Inglefield was commanded to return to his post, humiliated. Julian Gwyn suggests that Inglefield thought, perhaps misguidedly, that he had been invited by the First Lord to resign his post.[61] Inglefield's willingness to leave rather than await confirmation, however, reflects the perceived isolation of Halifax even if sailing times were relatively short.

The Admiralty's control in the West Indies, although present, was largely in name only. With reliable packet routes and average sailing times of eight weeks, the West Indies was better connected than more difficult to reach stations like Newfoundland or the East Indies. However, it could still take as much as fourteen weeks for news to come back to Britain from Jamaica and usually up to eight or nine weeks for replacement officers to arrive to fill a vacancy.[62] The patronage of commanders-in-chief in Jamaica and the Leeward Islands was consequently dependent on their making acting appointments which the Admiralty then approved or denied, although they were usually approved. Unfortunately, the Admiralty did not allow commanders-in-chief to fill vacancies which were created by death, sickness or court martial, even though it was these vacancies which most needed filling. The commander-in-chief therefore had to fill these vacancies with acting commissions while he awaited Admiralty orders. One exchange between Admiral John Thomas Duckworth and Evan Nepean reveals the nature of this relationship. On his initial appointment to commander-in-chief, Duckworth wrote to the Admiralty to fill several death and court martial vacancies. In his first letter of reply, Nepean approved Duckworth's appointments, complimenting him on his good choices.[63] In the second, however, he rebuked Duckworth and reminded him

---

[59] Gwyn, *Frigates and Foremasts*, 88.
[60] Ibid., 88.
[61] Gwyn, *Ashore and Afloat*, 72.
[62] Steele, *English Atlantic*, 31.
[63] NMM, DUC/8, Nepean to Duckworth, 29 January 1802 (1).

34 PATRONAGE AND THE BRITISH NAVY, 1775–1815

that he had no power to fill death and court martial vacancies, and that that power rested with the Admiralty alone.[64]

An Admiralty vacancy in the West Indies could take between sixteen and twenty weeks to be filled once the report of the vacancy arrived at Whitehall and the Admiralty's candidate made the voyage out, assuming they had been in Britain. Although commanders-in-chief like Duckworth obeyed the Admiralty's appointments, the role of acting-lieutenant and acting-captain became currency in patronage just like recommendations in home-waters. Those given acting appointments at the behest of Duckworth would either have the good fortune to have their appointment meet the approbation of the Admiralty or, if that position had been marked as an Admiralty vacancy, then they would be moved into another vacant position.[65] Eventually, if an officer served in enough acting positions he gained the experience needed to secure promotion. Therefore, appointment and promotion through connection to the commander-in-chief, admiral or flag-captain was in many ways more likely in the West Indies than in the Mediterranean or home-waters.

The same system technically existed in the East Indies but the commander-in-chief by necessity had to act with greater autonomy. Sailing time ranged from four to six months but the monsoon system and associated changes to wind and currents meant that a ship sailing from Britain to India in winter could expect to take up to nine months.[66] Dispatches could be sent overland at great expense. The communication time was shorter at three months but the available routes were often disrupted by conflict with France as well as the politics of the intervening countries.[67] Personal letters carrying familiar news or introductions for patronage connections most often followed the merchantmen or naval ships on the all sea route rather than face the expense of the overland route. Despite the expense to ensure speedy communication, Admiralty letters often went astray in the Indian Ocean itself, especially those to the commander-in-chief who moved around the extremely large station. Admiral Peter Rainier missed many communications from the Admiralty during his time in command of the station; one letter from the Navy Board sent in 1803 took eleven months to reach him.[68] The commander-in-chief of the East Indies had to be self-reliant and, as a consequence, East Indian patronage networks were largely self-contained.

The Admiralty's control of East Indian appointments was restricted to sending letters of recommendation with officers on their way to the station rather than sending lieutenants to fill specific vacancies. One of Markham's

---

64 NMM, DUC/8, Nepean to Duckworth, 29 January 1802 (2).
65 Cavell, *Midshipmen and the Quarterdeck Boys*, 22.
66 Ward, *British Naval Power in the East*, 93.
67 Ibid., 85–86.
68 Ibid., 92.

TIME AND PLACE: THE GEOGRAPHY OF NAVAL PATRONAGE   35

followers whom he managed to send out to the East Indies in search of promotion highlighted the reality of the Admiralty–East Indies relationship. Lieutenant Henry Hart wrote to Markham from *Culloden* in Madras to request Markham's 'Admiralty recommendation' to Admiral Edward Pellew to get him a profitable position.[69] East Indian appointments, promotions and discharges still needed Admiralty approbation but, whereas the West Indies worked on a system of recommendations, even the semblance of Admiralty power was not possible in the East Indies. With or without Admiralty approbation, appointments could be made and served in for up to a year before a replacement arrived or the Admiralty could voice its disapproval.

Pellew was commander-in-chief of the East Indies between 1804 and 1809 and his patronage demonstrates the autonomy an individual could wield when the turnaround of correspondence was ten to twelve months.[70] Upon his appointment, Pellew made great use of his position to promote his following, beyond their experience and seniority. He manipulated the system to get his fifteen-year-old son confirmed lieutenant in 1804 and then promoted him to post-captain a year later.[71] Pellew's position of autonomy was so powerful he was able to resist the First Lord, Lord Melville's attempts to undermine his control. Thomas Troubridge, Markham's fellow naval lord commissioner, was sent out to share the command in 1804, arriving in 1805.[72] Pellew used the long turnaround of correspondence to at first stall the division of his position and then to limit Troubridge's influence. Troubridge was eventually removed when Lord Howick became First Lord and Pellew's triumph of will shows how a self-serving commander-in-chief could protect his autonomy by exploiting difficulties in communication.[73]

Distance from Britain not only limited Admiralty control in overseas stations but also increased the influence of the local station communities and networks in the distribution of patronage. Letters of introduction to the commander-in-chief or local admirals were consequently essential for young officers leaving their home-networks. William Croft, one of Markham's protégés from *Centaur*, solicited Markham for a letter of introduction and recommendation to Duckworth when he discovered he was appointed to the storeship *Camel* for transferral to the West Indies. In reminding Markham of his request for a letter he stated that the prospect of 'a jaunt to the West Inds and back without any advantage ... will be consider'd a sufficient excuse for troubling you with this'.[74] Markham's recommendation to Duckworth

69 NMM, MRK/103/1/60, Hart to Markham, 8 August 1806.
70 Taylor, *Commander*, 189.
71 Ibid., 184 and 201.
72 Ibid., 187.
73 Ibid., 201–202.
74 NMM, MRK/103/1/44, Croft to Markham, 27 September 1803.

secured Croft an acting position on the flagship of the fleet on his arrival in Jamaica, as shown in Duckworth's reply to Markham: 'My dear Markham! From the Interest you take in the success of Lieut' Croft, I directly on His arrival put him into the Hercule.'[75] The journal of Maria Nugent, wife of the governor of Jamaica, shows the extent to which certain commanders-in-chief socialised with the white planter elite of the West Indies. Duckworth often invited members of the local government and prominent families to dine with him aboard his ship *Hercule* and held functions at the admiral's residence on shore in Jamaica.[76]

Siân Williams established in her work on the navy in the West Indies that the local elite were eager to incorporate the station commander and his officers into their circles, to ensure the navy protected West Indian trade, as well as to give them access to British social and political networks.[77] Vice-Admiral Hugh Seymour was 'deluged' with invitations to social events when he arrived at the island of St Vincent to take up his command in 1800.[78] The white elite of the West Indies ensured they were connected to influential station commanders, and naval officers strove to be connected to these influential planters. Forging connections with local land networks could give captains, lieutenants and non-commissioned officers the opportunity to be personally introduced to the station commander and his acquaintances. Letters of introduction to the networks on shore in the West Indies were, therefore, as important to naval officers serving in this station as letters of recommendation to other naval officers or letters directly soliciting the Admiralty at Whitehall. Indeed, Williams argues that letters of introduction, and the consequent expectation of future patronage, were a central feature of the social life of the West Indies, positioning itself firmly as an extension of mainland British culture.[79]

Newfoundland also had strong local networks which offered patronage support in the absence of strong British ties, and in some cases even resisted control from the metropole. In Halifax dockyard, those who had the weakest ties with the local Newfoundland community had the briefest careers in the area. As we have already seen, Isaac Coffin only served six months as commissioner of the dockyard at Halifax. Despite his strong connections in Britain, Coffin alienated himself from the communities in Halifax and Dartmouth by

---

75 NMM, MRK/103/1/46, Duckworth to Markham, 11 March 1804.

76 Maria Nugent, *Lady Nugent's Journal of Her Residence in Jamaica from 1801 to 1805* (Kingston, 1966), 200; Siân Williams, 'The Royal Navy and Caribbean Colonial Society during the Eighteenth Century', in John McAleer and Christer Petley (eds.), *The Royal Navy and the British Atlantic World, c.1750–1820* (London, 2016), 35–36.

77 Siân Williams, 'The Royal Navy in the Caribbean 1756–1815' (unpublished PhD thesis, University of Southampton, 2015), 85–86.

78 Williams, 'The Royal Navy and Caribbean Colonial Society', 33.

79 Williams, 'The Royal Navy in the Caribbean 1756–1815', 55 and 88.

TIME AND PLACE: THE GEOGRAPHY OF NAVAL PATRONAGE   37

his harsh punishment of key dockyard officers, as well as enforcing a strict disengagement with local mercantile networks which had previously been offered support through the yard.[80] Commissioner Philip Wodehouse, on the other hand, was so deeply entrenched in local networks that when he retired in 1819, with the yard's closure, he received expressions of regret and heartfelt thanks from clerks and artificers throughout the yard, as well as from the local government.[81] Wodehouse had served as commissioner between 1812 and 1819, which was, as Gwyn has argued, the Newfoundland station's most active period with over 120 ships serving in North American waters. This is partly why Wodehouse was so loved by the yard and surrounding community. Unlike Coffin who had forced his way into the yard using British patronage and exerted his administrative control by dismissing men he deemed troublesome, Wodehouse had acted as patron to shipwrights in the yard and a point of connection with British networks for the local mercantile community.[82]

However, the local networks at Halifax did not carry the same social cachet as the networks in the West Indies, nor did the naval squadron feature so prominently in the social life of Halifax and Dartmouth. Although isolation from British networks also meant that more distant stations like Halifax could offer opportunities for officers who had strong British connections because they had little competition. George Thomas, the naval storekeeper at Halifax in 1784, was the illegitimate son of Sir Hugh Palliser. When his authority in the yard was interrupted by the ministrations of Admiral Charles Douglas in command of the North American squadron, it was Thomas who gained Navy Board and Admiralty approval.[83]

Access to local networks at Halifax was more important for those in the dockyard than for officers serving in the squadron because it offered support in resisting the whims of commissioners or squadron commanders who tried to take too much control when isolated from Navy Board or Admiralty commands. The dockyard community itself was not static, and many officers served their time and then returned to yards in Britain, using Halifax yard as a 'step' in their career.[84] Many artificers stayed, however, and the importance of local communities in artificer patronage meant that the senior officers in the dockyard, such as the naval storekeeper or master shipwright, had strong connections in the community and with the resident commissioners. Master Shipwright William Hughes was dismissed by Coffin in 1799. He was reinstated, however, when Coffin was recalled, and remained in the post for the next eight years.[85]

[80] Gwyn, *Ashore and Afloat*, 73–75.
[81] Ibid., 76.
[82] Ibid., 75–76.
[83] Ibid., 84–85.
[84] Ibid., 78.
[85] Ibid., 78.

The isolation of Halifax had given a commissioner like Coffin an enormous amount of control and power. To be reinstated, Hughes could not rely on his connections in the community and had to return to England to gather the support of patrons such as Admiral Arbuthnot and Andrew Snape Hammond, the Comptroller of the Navy. Hammond had been the resident commissioner in the yard between 1781 and 1783 and he was perhaps already acquainted with Hughes. If he was not, Hughes may have drawn on mutual connections in the communities at Halifax and Dartmouth to be introduced. Halifax offered good access to local networks, but these networks lacked strength compared to home-networks.

There were, however, limitations in those stations which had stronger local networks. The East Indies was a difficult station to operate in without strong East India Company ties. Equally, other factors affected an officer's integration into these networks. In the West Indies, race could exclude an officer from the circles of white planter society which had such influence with commanders-in-chief. Douglas Hamilton has argued that John Perkins was probably limited in his later career because he was never truly welcomed into Jamaican planter society despite his naval credentials serving to include him in many social functions, and his having his own enslaved workers on a small plantation.[86] Williams has also argued that the importance of West Indian planter networks in the station's naval patronage pressured officers into supporting slavery, as those who objected or were marked as abolitionists were seen as ungrateful and excluded from important patronage network opportunities.[87]

The use of enslaved labourers in Jamaica also affected the opportunities available for artificers in the dockyards. The largest home yards of Plymouth, Portsmouth, Chatham, Sheerness, Deptford and Woolwich all relied heavily on lateral friendships and integration in the local community. In overseas yards, artificers could rise more quickly than in home yards where the importance of these community ties meant that shipwrights new to the parish had to spend years carefully forging connections. Vacancies also occurred more frequently within the yard hierarchy in overseas yards. Many artificers volunteered to serve in overseas yards as young men and returned to Britain after a few years' service to start or re-join their families, creating a quick turnaround in high-level positions. British artificers and clerks, through virtue of having apprenticed in a British yard, also entered overseas yards at a higher level than artificers or labourers from the local area. This was particularly the case for West Indian yards, where the main workforce was made up of enslaved artificers and labourers.[88] Dockyard patronage power was not restricted to

---

[86] Hamilton, "'A Most Active, Enterprising Officer'", 14–15.

[87] Williams, 'The Royal Navy in the Caribbean 1756–1815', 88.

[88] Charles Foy, 'The Royal Navy's Employment of Black Mariners and Maritime Workers 1754–1783', *International Journal of Maritime History* 28:1 (2016), 25.

TIME AND PLACE: THE GEOGRAPHY OF NAVAL PATRONAGE 39

the vertical hierarchy of the dockyard. Indeed, Chapter 6 establishes that there were labourers in Plymouth yard in the 1790s who wielded considerable patronage control through brokering entry to the yard because of their community connection to the master attendant. In the small yards of the West Indies, a white artificer travelling from Britain would miss out on experience building ships but would be placed into positions of more responsibility which would boost their promotion prospects when they returned to Britain. White British artificers would also be more likely to wield the most patronage control in overseas yards because enslaved labourers are unlikely to have held the same level of community power as labourers in Britain.[89]

Distance from the Admiralty determined the autonomy of sea officers but only if those officers had strong connections in the networks local to their station, who could offer different channels of influence. The distance which limited Admiralty control also limited the ability for an officer's influential connections to work on his behalf. In certain stations, this prompted officers to uproot their networks. Pellew brought his protégés and sons to India with him so that he could continue to support them. When Markham was first married to Maria in 1797, it was uncertain where he would be posted and it looked for a time that he would be sent to Newfoundland. Maria wrote that if he was sent to a faraway station, 'it would be the wish of my heart if consistent with your heart, to go with you, or at least follow you, and then establish myself in a House near the port you put in at'.[90] If an officer, however, was isolated from these local networks it was more difficult to reach out to the Admiralty, where an officer lacking connection could secure the interest of a commissioner even in competition with candidates with influential connections. The overseas fleets were at the mercy of the character of the commander-in-chief, although environmental factors such as the rate of vacancies created through death and disease, or the type of service available, meant that a badly connected officer could succeed through the necessity of placing an officer in command of a vacancy immediately.

---

[89] Some of the muster books for yards in the West Indies list black and white artificers separately and in others the employment of enslaved workers is stark in the lists of artificers described only by a single name. See ADM 36/16057 Jamaica Yard 1 April 1799–30 June 1800, or ADM 36/17235 Martinique Yard 1 January 1799–30 September 1802. The level of influence that enslaved dockyard workers had in comparison to artificers and labourers coming from Britain or other naval yards would be an interesting topic for future research, especially in comparison to the network research of Chapter 6. See also Ann Coats, 'Bermuda Naval Base: Management, Artisans and Enslaved Workers in the 1790s: The 1950s Bermudian Apprentices' Heritage', *Mariner's Mirror* 95:2 (March, 2013), 149–178.

[90] NMM, MRK/107/3/9, Maria to John, 7 November 1797.

Opportunity and Limitation

The perceived and real variations in opportunity across the navy affected the way applicants approached certain appointments and, in turn, underpins our understanding of the value of favours when writers asked for them or when patrons bestowed them. Some stations offered more in terms of desirable gift-goods, which could then be used to strengthen patronage ties across an extended network. Those stations with strong local networks gave officers or artificers with weak patronage ties in Britain access to patrons who had more autonomy. The frequency and type of vacancies available in each station also depended on local factors as well as the station's position in relation to French interests when at war. The West Indies was predominantly served by smaller vessels, whereas the Mediterranean fleet had a much larger complement of large ships better suited to engaging with French fleets. The rate of discharges through death and disease also varied by station and greatly impacted the availability of profitable positions. This section illustrates the variation in naval patronage with examples of access to gifts, local networks and the frequency of vacancies caused by type of service and disease.

Gift-giving was a crucial part of eighteenth-century connection maintenance and was particularly important in situations where connections were separated by distance and could not perform other maintenance acts such as face-to-face visits.[91] As the fashion for letter-writing became more familiar, so too did the giving of gifts. Items of particular interest to the intended recipient were favoured above all else.[92] Both seamen and officers had access to exotic objects such as shells, coral, furs and feathers, which they then distributed among their network, consolidating ties. Elin Jones, in her thesis on the spatial and material aspects of naval masculinity, emphasised the importance of 'curiosity' in the items young officers sent back home to their families. The objects sent home with accompanying letters, or via a friend, acted as a link with the place in which the young officer served.[93] Voyages of exploration, of course, provided the best opportunity for the collection of rare, interesting gifts, but the practice was by no means restricted to them. Midshipman George Perceval fixated on the collection of 'curiosities', and their subsequent delivery and distribution among his familial connections, while he served in the Mediterranean between 1807 and 1811.[94] Perceval intended his gifts for family and Jones has suggested

[91] Ben-Amos, *Culture of Giving*, 8–9; O'Neill, *Opened Letter*, 122–124.

[92] O'Neill, *Opened Letter*, 124–125.

[93] Elin Frances Jones, 'Masculinity, Materiality and Space on Board the Royal Naval Ship, 1756–1815' (unpublished PhD thesis, Queen Mary University London, 2016), 321–323 and 324.

[94] See: NMM, PER/1/23, PER/1/32, Perceval to his mother, 21 May 1807 and 1 November 1808; NMM, PER/1/40, Perceval to his father, 1 January 1811. Quoted in Jones, 'Masculinity, Materiality and Space', 325.

TIME AND PLACE: THE GEOGRAPHY OF NAVAL PATRONAGE   41

it was a part of his practising gentlemanly masculinity associated with the grand tour as well as demonstrating his purchasing power.[95] The sending of gifts home was also not restricted to officers. Jones highlighted how John Martindale Powell, an ordinary seaman, wrote a letter to his mother promising he would send her rock from Gibraltar. The rock was to add to a grotto made of rocks from his travels around the world, but it also shows the wide range of gifts and their meanings to the sender and recipient.[96]

Not all gifts were sent home as curiosities for the family. Some were sent to strengthen friendship or patronage ties in Britain. Certainly, Perkins, living in Jamaica on half-pay having lost command of his ship *Tartar* in 1804, made a special point of sending interesting shells he had collected to Markham as his friend and patron in 1806.[97] Similarly, Keith sent a box of coral in 1800 to his sister in Scotland to give to his daughter as well as to distribute among the female members of his regional and political network, including the duchess of Montrose.[98] Both coral and shells could be used to make jewellery but were also objects of curiosity and fashionable collecting.[99] Coral necklaces were particularly popular, often either made in Italy or from coral bought and distributed among female connections as Keith had done. The giving of gifts such as these not only consolidated friendships but also acted as reminders of the sender's position in that station and potential access to other goods and networks.

Letters to Markham reveal the benefits of being stationed in the Mediterranean, particularly because of access to wine. As we shall see in Chapter 2, the purser James Saunders curried favour with Markham by sending him sherry.[100] Captain James Bowen also sent Markham a pipe of madeira from on board *Argo* stationed off the island in 1801.[101] On the other hand, John Hunter, the British consul to Lisbon in 1798, acted as Markham's agent and was responsible for sending sherry to Markham and his family.[102] While he was at the Admiralty, Markham relied on this network to provide him with wine from the Mediterranean, drawing on his ties to have it landed out

---

[95] Jones, 'Masculinity, Materiality and Space', 328–329.

[96] NMM, ACG/P/17, Martindale Powell to his mother, 12 June 1805. Quoted in Jones, 'Masculinity, Materiality and Space', 326.

[97] NMM, MRK/102/5/14, Perkins to Markham, 18 May 1806.

[98] BL, Add MS 86496, Keith to Mary Elphinstone, 17 October 1800.

[99] Bettina Deitz, 'Mobile Objects: The Space of Shells in Eighteenth-Century France', *British Journal for the History of Science* 39:3 (September, 2006), 370.

[100] NMM, MRK/104/2/54, Saunders to Markham, 29 November 1802.

[101] NMM, MRK/102/1/84, Bowen to Markham, 17 September [1801].

[102] NMM, MRK/100/2/223, Hunter to Markham, 11 August 1798.

42 PATRONAGE AND THE BRITISH NAVY, 1775–1815

of port to avoid tax.[103] Gift-giving was an essential part of maintaining these local networks of exchange.

Gift-giving was also closely associated with the integration of an officer with established networks on land. Presentation swords are one of the most cogent embodiments of how an officer's service facilitated his integration and are indicative of the subtler patronage relationships that underpinned them. The National Maritime Museum has a large collection of presentation swords. For example, Captain Thomas Stains was presented with a sword from the 'Gentlemen of the Isle of Thanet' for his command of the frigate *Cyane* off Naples in 1809.[104] Similarly, both Admiral Samuel Hood and Admiral John Thomas Duckworth were presented with swords by the white planter elite of Jamaica in honour of their service in command of the Leeward Islands and Jamaica stations respectively in 1791 and 1804.[105]

As the West Indies offered officers an opportunity to mix in established white planter communities and to secure influence, the Mediterranean offered officers access to British networks in Lisbon, Gibraltar and Naples.[106] In the 1780s, Markham made several connections in Lisbon and Gibraltar while stationed in the Mediterranean fleet in command of *Sphinx*. Some of these connections were long-lived. Robert Pringle, Granville Anson Chetwynd-Stapylton and his wife Martha all remained in correspondence with Markham from their acquaintance in Gibraltar in 1785.[107] In 1798, Markham was also approached by Lucy de Kantzow on behalf of her nephew Walter Grossett who had been appointed to *Centaur*.[108] She was the daughter of a wealthy British merchant and married another of Markham's connections from Lisbon, Henry de Kantzow.[109] Her familiarity with Markham, despite their lapsed acquaintance, suggests that she was extremely close with him during his

---

[103] NMM, MRK/102/4/6, Charles Lane to Markham, 8 April 1801; MRK/102/3/1, Benjamin Hallowell to Markham, 30 August 1803.

[104] NMM, WPN1252, Presentation sword belonging to Captain Sir Thomas Stains, 1809.

[105] NMM, WPN1549, Presentation sword belonging to Vice-Admiral Samuel Hood, 1791; NMM, WPN1120, Presentation sword belonging to Admiral John Thomas Duckworth, 1804.

[106] Sara Caputo, a doctoral candidate at Robinson College at University of Cambridge, is currently working on 'Transnational Encounters in the British Navy, 1793–1815', in which she explores the relationship between the Admiralty, the Mediterranean commander-in-chief and the Neapolitan kingdom and navy.

[107] NMM, MRK/108/4/1–6, Pringle to Markham, 5 March 1787–13 October 1788; MRK/108/4/11, Chetwynd-Staplyton to Markham, 23 December [no date]; MRK/107/3/24, Maria to John [no date].

[108] NMM, MRK/108/4/10, Kantzow to Markham, 31 September 1798.

[109] Egerton Brydges, *Collin's Peerage of England: Genealogical, Biographical, and Historical* (London, 1812), v.674.

TIME AND PLACE: THE GEOGRAPHY OF NAVAL PATRONAGE   43

time stationed around Lisbon. Her letter also reveals how being stationed in a location with strong networks facilitated later patronage, despite the removal of a connection from that immediate locale.

The type of service in each station also affected the vacancies available and the type of patronage needed to fill them. In the Mediterranean fleet in 1804, there were thirteen ships of the line, eleven frigates and twenty small vessels including sloops, bombs, gunboats, cutters and schooners.[110] These ships provided ample opportunity for well-connected officers to command large ships they could fill with their followers, as well as for lieutenants to serve in the taking of prizes and battles. However, these vacancies were limited and, as the first section showed, tightly controlled by the Admiralty. Mediterranean appointments were competitive and often went to those officers who were best connected. On the other hand, the varied service of home-waters meant that there were more vessels to serve on. There were more ships serving in the fleets around Britain than anywhere else in the navy. In 1804, ships stationed in home-waters, around Ireland, and the North Sea and Channel fleets, accounted for over half of the ships employed in the navy. Thirty-three ships of the line were stationed in the Channel fleet and twenty-one in the North-Sea, more than any other fleet in the period. The North Sea fleet also had the most small vessels, with twenty-six sloops, twelve bombs, twenty-five gun-brigs, thirty-two cutters and schooners and nineteen armed ships.[111]

Smaller vessels provided opportunities for lieutenants who either through lack of skill or, more commonly, lack of a substantial patronage network had been left languishing on half-pay without promotion. As such, Markham received many requests from lieutenants in cutters and brigs, soliciting him for his assistance with the exchange of men, their prospects for promotion and where their ship would be stationed. Lieutenant Daniel Carpenter, whom we will meet again in Chapter 3, wrote several letters to Markham which illustrate this smaller-scale patronage. Markham secured for him several positions. The first was a small hired vessel called a lugger, the second a leaky but large cutter, *Viper*, and the last a small cutter, *Cheerful*. Each of these vessels served in home-waters.

Carpenter was of that section of the navy that recent statistical studies have demonstrated progressed slowly in their careers through want of opportunity and connection.[112] Carpenter joined the navy in 1779, three years after Markham, however he only made lieutenant in 1798. Admiral Henry Harvey apparently acted as his patron in certain spheres, having been his captain when Carpenter first entered the navy.[113] However, Carpenter also mentioned

---

[110] Rodger, *Command of the Ocean*, 615–617.
[111] Ibid., 615–617.
[112] Wilson, *British Naval Officers*, 38–40, 107–109 and 110.
[113] NMM, MRK/103/1/24, Carpenter to Markham, 5 February 1807.

44 PATRONAGE AND THE BRITISH NAVY, 1775–1815

having to 'obtain friends' to solicit patrons on his behalf in a letter to Markham requesting he be kept in the cutter *Cheerful*, rather than be removed to a position in a larger ship, *Hercule*, where he would earn a smaller wage and be less able to support his family: 'if I should not be fortunate enough to retain the command of the Cheerful I may be afforded time to obtain friends to intercede for a more profitable Employment'.[114] Whether Carpenter meant that he was going to make new friends or draw on those he already had is unclear. Regardless, he was not in a very strong patronage position, reflected in his being given ships that were otherwise unsatisfactory and served in unprofitable stations.

Carpenter frequently requested a more active position or for his commands to be sent on a 'Cruise as may turn out to Advantage'.[115] A more profitable position in Carpenter's mind was one which would allow him to serve in the Mediterranean or West Indies. He expressed concern to Markham about his command of the cutter *Cheerful* because it could not store enough provisions for an extended cruise and he wrote: 'the Sailroom will not contain more than half the Sails, no Gunners Store Room, and with these provisions the Hold will not Store four tons of Water, and the Accommodations are bad in the extreme, all agree, that they never can sail'.[116] In one letter, he directly asked Markham to send him abroad: 'I cannot refrain from presuming further on your goodness, in soliciting your Interest, to obtain for me a foreign station, that of the Lisbon, or Western Islands, I should prefer'.[117] The type of ships available in home-waters gave men in Carpenter's position opportunity for command and a higher wage than on a larger ship where lieutenants with conspicuous skill or connections would be advanced as a priority. However, being given small or badly fitted commands also prevented those with weaker patronage from serving in stations where they could more readily forge profitable connections and prove their skill, further perpetuating their situation. There may have been more patronage available for the unconnected in home-waters but the usefulness of that patronage was limited.

The 1804 fleets in Jamaica and the Leeward Islands also had a comparatively greater proportion of smaller vessels, with only eight ships of the line and eleven frigates but twenty sloops and fifteen cutters and schooners.[118] The need to protect trade interests was similar to the protection of ports in home-waters. These nimble vessels were also better suited to the topography of the West Indies, with its fragmented islands and difficult coastal waters. The difficult waters, however, also made skilled pilots particularly important, and the proliferation of smaller vessels and the frequent conflict meant that

[114] NMM, MRK/103/1/28, Carpenter to Markham, 27 March 1807.
[115] NMM, MRK/103/1/21, Carpenter to Markham, 23 September 1803.
[116] NMM, MRK/103/1/24, Carpenter to Markham, 5 February 1807.
[117] NMM, MRK/103/1/26, Carpenter to Markham, 3 March 1807.
[118] Rodger, *Command of the Ocean*, 616.

TIME AND PLACE: THE GEOGRAPHY OF NAVAL PATRONAGE   45

pilots could make the move from a hired pilot to an officer in the navy in command of their own vessel. Perkins managed to rise to captain because his skill in command of the sloop *Endeavour* secured the interest of Admiral George Rodney while he served in the waters around Sant Domingue.[119] He commanded the private schooner *Punch* in 1778, gathering intelligence of shipping off Sant Domingue, and we can assume that he must have caught the attention of a naval officer because by 1781 he had entered as the lieutenant in command of the sloop *Endeavour*.[120] It was at this time that Perkins most likely forged his connection to Markham, who later proved such an important patron to him. The need for skilled pilots and the availability of smaller ships which Perkins could command himself, therefore, facilitated his rise and was the foundation of a significant part of his patronage network.

The West Indies, therefore, had more small craft suitable for low-level patronage of lieutenants and commanders. The death and sickness rate also meant that there were relatively more vacancies on good ships which could be filled awaiting approval from the Admiralty compared to the pressure on vacancies in the Mediterranean or the competition for leaky ships in home-waters. The West Indies were an attractive option for young lieutenants in Britain, as the high death rate also meant potential for quick promotion within a ship. Securing an Admiralty vacancy before going out to the West Indies was also very attractive. Lieutenant Samuel Chambers asked for Markham's interest in getting him a vacancy on *Blanche*; he wrote:

> Lord St Vincent has promised to send me out to Adml Duckworth, would you Sir be good enough to inform me if there is any likelihood of my getting out, I should esteem it a great favour, having accidently heard that their is a probability of a vacancy in the Blanche.[121]

Previous histories have somewhat inflated death and sickness rates in the West Indies.[122] However, between 1798 and 1803, once active service had increased in the Leeward Islands and Jamaica stations, the mortality rate of seamen serving in the West Indies rose to 9 per cent. The rate of sickness on board ships was much lower, being just above 2 per cent in the Leeward Islands station and only 1–1.5 per cent in Jamaica, where most seamen were discharged to the hospital at Port Royal and so do not appear on the ships' books.[123]

However, yellow fever could devastate an individual ship's crew and is likely the foundation for the West Indies' reputation as an unhealthy station.[124]

---

[119] Hamilton, "'A Most Active, Enterprising Officer'", 5–6.

[120] Ibid.

[121] NMM, MRK/103/1/32, Chambers to Markham, 28 June 1803.

[122] Coriann Convertito, 'The Health of British Seamen in the West Indies, 1770–1806' (unpublished PhD thesis, University of Exeter, 2011), 140.

[123] Ibid., 139.

[124] Ibid., 142–143.

46 PATRONAGE AND THE BRITISH NAVY, 1775–1815

This fear, in turn, drove away the well-connected officers and saved the West Indies from the pressurised patronage of the Mediterranean. Markham's ship *Hannibal* is a good example of this. In 1795, while serving in the West Indies *Hannibal* was ravaged with yellow fever. The muster books show that between 4 March and 27 September 1795 the complement fell from 590 to 519.[125] They lost fifty-eight of the ship's company, eleven marines, and two boys. These are the changes to the number of men borne on the ship, so includes discharge by death, sickness, court martial and desertion but not those who remained sick in the berth. Markham himself was invalided home on 1 October, abandoning his ship and his followers. Frederick Hoffman, who had joined the ship through the patronage of Markham's old captain George Keith Elphinstone, wrote that they 'buried during the cruise forty-three seamen, besides two mids and another of the lieutenants'. He also reckoned that: 'Out of the five hundred and sixty men we brought from England, we had only now two hundred to do the duty of the ship.'[126]

Many junior officers or inferior warrant officers relied heavily on service-based networks, which at the beginning of their career could be centred entirely on their own ship. Although high death rates meant chances for promotion, they also meant the loss of potentially profitable connections. Even where the captain of a ship did not die, a badly connected officer's career suffered. Hoffman joined Markham's ship *Blonde* through a strong connection. However, when Markham quit the *Hannibal* in 1795, another captain took over the ship. Hoffman appears to have had no contact with Markham until a letter in March 1806. He listed four other captains he had served with since *Hannibal* and wrote that he had married and had two children. But he was still a lieutenant and had been for almost seven years.[127] The distance and sickness of the West Indies played a vital role in his losing connection to Markham, despite entering *Blonde* on such strong terms, and it damaged Hoffman's career.

The risk of disease and the perception of the West and East Indies as being particularly hazardous to health also meant that well-connected officers and their families used their patronage to ensure they were kept out of unhealthy stations. Rodger described a patronage of health in the tendency for the well-connected to avoid being sent out to risky stations.[128] Surgeons were approached to provide health certificates which would honourably allow an officer to avoid being stationed in unhealthy stations, and perhaps give them a greater chance of serving in a more desirable station such as the Mediterranean. Those with strong patronage networks could also quickly remove themselves from situations which put them in danger of death by

---

[125] TNA, ADM36/13666–13667, HMS *Hannibal*, 22 August 1794 to February 1796.
[126] Hoffman, *A Sailor of King George.*
[127] NMM, MRK/103/1/64, Hoffman to Markham, [6] March 1806.
[128] Rodger, *Insatiable Earl*, 180.

TIME AND PLACE: THE GEOGRAPHY OF NAVAL PATRONAGE   47

disease. In his semi-fictitious memoir, Hoffman subtly accused Markham of doing just this when he was discharged from *Hannibal* in 1795. Markham spent the next six months recuperating at Dynevor castle in Wales, where he met and became engaged to Maria Rice, the daughter of a family friend.[129] Hoffman, however, painted a very different picture of Markham's quitting *Hannibal*, saying that the first death of the fever on board ship was 'quite sufficient to alarm the nerves of our gallant captain, who never joined the ship afterwards'. Hoffman suggested that Markham used his influence to be sent home as he wrote that Markham 'obtained permission from the admiral to return to England by a lugger going with despatches'. He finished, rather unfavourably, by saying that Markham took his leave of the ship in the French style, 'that is to say by taking no leave at all'.[130]

Whether he was truly invalided by the fever or not, Markham's career did not suffer from his removal from the West Indies. Indeed, he was on half-pay for only two years before he commissioned *Centaur*, a much larger and newly built ship which he then commanded in the Mediterranean and Channel fleets. For Markham, opportunity came from his strong patronage network watched over by his father, the Archbishop of York. The result for those who feared for their health, however, was a significant reduction in their opportunity for appointment and promotion. Perkins lost command of *Tartar* in 1804 because, when ordered to sail to Nova Scotia, he resigned his commission for fear of his health. Perkins suffered greatly from an asthmatic complaint and had until 1804 avoided being sent to colder climates which he wrote 'would be the death' of him.[131] The Admiralty never gave Perkins another command, which Hamilton argues was likely because of his inflexibility.[132]

The opportunities and limitations of each station were determined by environmental factors. However, it was an individual's patronage which affected whether these factors were beneficial or damaged their career prospects. Access to gift-goods helped to strengthen connections at home, and offered some officers network security when their ability to oblige their connections with appointments was limited by Admiralty control. Similarly, access to networks increased an officer's influence in the local area and with his superiors in the fleet or at the Admiralty. However, the necessity of these local networks, and the risk of alienation mentioned in the first section, meant that these connections were often another burden on an officer's already limited patronage. The type of service in each station dictated the patronage that was needed for promotion, as an officer could make their way with few connections in smaller craft, or in larger ships serving in famous actions like Trafalgar.

[129] Markham, *A Naval Career*, 120–122.
[130] Hoffman, *A Sailor of King George*, 30.
[131] NMM, MRK/102/5/14, Perkins to Markham, 18 May 1806.
[132] Hamilton, '"A Most Active, Enterprising Officer"', 16.

48   PATRONAGE AND THE BRITISH NAVY, 1775–1815

However, limited connections also meant that an officer could become stuck in inactive service in a poorly fitted ship which would not offer the opportunities for profit and glory they needed to be recognised for promotion even with connections. The vacancies in the West Indies from the perceived high rate of disease also offered the poorly connected the chance to rise. However, disease could also decimate carefully constructed local networks and remove patrons so that it was only those officers who had strong networks who overcame the misfortune of fever-stricken ships. Looking at naval patronage through the lens of the opportunities and limitations provided in each station reveals the great variety of routes to success as well as the experiences of those less exceptional officers whom Wilson argues made up the bulk of the navy at the end of the long eighteenth century.[133]

Conclusion

Naval patronage was not universal in its operation or entirely rooted in Admiralty control. Environmental factors in each station had a considerable impact on the way patronage was conducted across the global extent of the navy. Distance from Britain limited Admiralty control and meant that commanders-in-chief had greater autonomy in the distribution of appointments. In turn, this meant that they could better satisfy the demands of their own networks. However, many of these networks were still centred on Britain, and the distance which limited Admiralty control also restricted contact with home-networks. The Mediterranean was a popular station because it was close enough to home-networks to maintain connection. It also offered ample opportunity in the form of access to gift-goods, strong local networks in Portugal, Spain and Italy, as well as the chance for active service on larger vessels more likely to engage in battles and take prizes. Unlike the East and West Indies, it was considered a healthy station. Vacancies were limited because the demand was great. Rather than causing all positions to be filled with only those who had strong connections, however, the restrictions meant that the Admiralty and commanders-in-chief sought to fill positions with candidates who both satisfied demands from their networks and political allies, but were also highly skilled.

Looking at naval patronage through a geographical lens provides a clear illustration of its variation. There were certainly trends, but there were also always exceptions which proved the rule. Where others wanted to avoid the West Indies, John Perkins wanted to be kept out there. Of course, his wish to remain in a hot climate was associated with eighteenth-century ideas of acclimatisation and race; he was born in Jamaica and that was where he felt

---

[133] Wilson, *British Naval Officers*, 3.

physically best suited to remain.[134] His wish, and his subsequent misfortune because of it, reveals the importance of an officer's flexibility in where he would serve for success in his career.

Each station may have offered different limitations and opportunities, and some were more competitive than others, but an officer could only be appointed to where the navy needed him, regardless of his skill or connection. The variation of stations, therefore, is an excellent illustration of the balance that every naval patron had to strike in distributing appointments, whether they were a commissioner at the Admiralty, a captain on a ship or an officer in the dockyard. Fundamentally, the job had to be done by someone, and it was often a combination of factors which promoted the filling of a vacancy. In more distant stations, where high death or discharge rates made vacancies more frequent, the factor could be as simple as the candidate was in the right place at the right time. Luck was a significant factor in naval careers. Of course, where an officer could not get an appointment his network solicited patrons to have him moved out to a station where he would be in the way of vacancies when they arose. Patronage, in effect, allowed well-connected officers to create their own luck.

[134] The contemporary medical understanding of warm climates compared to the cold of Britain was that British bodies did not fare well in hot climates while non-British bodies fared poorly in the cold. See David Arnold, *Warm Climates and Western Medicine* (Amsterdam, 1996).

2

Friends and Family: Markham's Network

> Tho personally unknown to you I flatter myself from my relationship to your father his Grace of York and of course to you, to whom I have the honor of addressing this letter for your interest and patronage.
>
> Mrs Gardner, 16 April 1801[1]

Networks defined patronage in the long eighteenth century. By its nature, patronage was personal and usually relied on a relationship between applicant and patron. After all, patrons risked reputational damage if they unknowingly bestowed their favour on someone unsuitable. Personal connection in these exchanges cultivated trust and could act as a kind of guarantee of the applicant's merit or, at the very least, protection for the patron through the benefits of reciprocity. The power of the personal in these requests meant that if an applicant did not personally know their patron it was to their advantage to find a broker who did, to solicit favour on their behalf. At times an applicant might also require another acquaintance to introduce them to a broker with the right connections. The perceived advantage of personal relationships therefore drove the creation of extended chains of connection between recipients of favours and the patrons who had the power to bestow them.

The power of networks, however, did not rest solely in these linear chains of acquaintance. A person's network, which gave them access to patrons and brokers, also gave them licence to approach patrons through virtue of their mutual acquaintances. This was the case for Mrs Gardner quoted above. Though 'personally unknown' to John Markham, Gardner's connection to his father, the Archbishop of York, allowed her politely and directly to solicit Markham's assistance without the need of a broker.[2]

We have seen already how time and place affected the sort of patronage an individual might require or have access to. Location also affected the shape of an individual's network and the sorts of connection that comprised it. Where a person was born and so where their family was based created the foundation for their network. Similarly, where someone was apprenticed or

---

[1]   NMM, MRK/104/4/1.

[2]   NMM, MRK/104/4/1, [H] Gardner to Markham, 16 April 1801.

received their education, if they were of a social level to have access to one, naturally informed the people they knew and the development of their own network, as did their later employment. In a service like the Royal Navy, the location of an individual's service informed their opportunities for patronage whilst it also shaped their network, for better or for worse. The geographical mobility of much naval service granted many the opportunity to expand their pool of connections beyond their family's network. But it also made their relationships with important or hard-won connections at home vulnerable to damage from the difficulty with which they could be maintained at a distance.

Understanding a patron's network is crucial to understanding not only their distribution of patronage, but also who solicited their favour and why. A politician may have had a large, extended network of multiple loose ties whom he would pander to for votes but would not necessarily assist in other instances. A married woman may have styled her connections in terms of familiar friendship and cast her patronage as favours to intimate friends. A shipwright in the Royal Dockyards may have been involved in the local church and taken on the sons of his parish connections as apprentices, consolidating his position in the yard. A strong network with multiple intimate and peripheral ties gave greater opportunities for patronage than a more limited sphere of acquaintances.

This chapter maps a portion of Markham's network from his early career to his time at the Admiralty to understand the subtle workings of his network on his patronage. Establishing his familial and intimate connections helps us to uncover aspects of patronage that are commonly difficult to trace in the historical record. Meetings took place face-to-face or letters of solicitation and approval are lost to us today. Even in those cases where a letter-writer was explicit about bestowing a favour, or in telling a connection who they were to thank for their appointment, the context of the patronage exchange is lost. If a commissioner on the board of Admiralty assisted an ordinary lieutenant without an explicit reason, perhaps that lieutenant had the implicit favour of a large political network. The influence of networks meant that connection facilitated patronage even more than just enabling the direct approach of a broker to a patron.

Of course, personal connection was not the only way an applicant could access patronage. People in positions of significant patronage control, like Markham, received many requests from strangers who drew instead on other possible claims for attention, such as charity and, particularly in the navy, a sense of honour and duty. As we will see below, looser or peripheral ties played an important role within networks, especially in the distribution of favour. Chapter 3 considers the way that patronage operated within these relationships in more depth. In order to understand these peripheral ties and how Markham responded to them in his distribution of patronage, we must

52 PATRONAGE AND THE BRITISH NAVY, 1775–1815

first understand his own network context. And to do that, we must grasp the implicit and explicit influence of his intimate connections.

Mapping Markham's Network

Although the natural variation of friendship and connection largely defies categorisation there are several ways to divide connection to understand the operation of patronage within a network. The first is the proximity to the network's centre judged by the strength of connection through the frequency of correspondence and other sociability.[3] Or, as the sociologist Mark Granovetter framed it, through indications of the relationship's longevity, emotional intensity and degree of reciprocity.[4] Within Granovetter's framework, 'weaker ties' are those lacking in one of these three criteria, including those who lack a personal relationship to the network centre but are connected to it through their strong ties with someone in their overlapping social circles.[5] 'Weak ties' are also much more likely to be geographically dispersed and often connect the central individual to multiple other circles of acquaintance.[6]

Unsurprisingly, 'weaker ties' essentially made up the body of a patronage network. Certainly, historians Lindsay O'Neill and Ilana Krausman Ben-Amos in their respective studies of eighteenth-century trans-Atlantic networks and early modern familial support systems have both identified a tendency for 'weak' or peripheral connections to contact the network's centre only for patronage solicitation. O'Neill called these connections 'ephemeral connections' because of their tendency to appear in the mapping of the network centre's correspondence only when they needed assistance.[7] Ben-Amos, in writing about the support structures of the lower levels of society, coined the term 'problem-anchored networks' to refer to those connections who were contacted only for assistance and were not a part of wider sociability.[8] Both O'Neill and Ben-Amos classify these connections as peripheral because they were not in direct familiar contact with the network's centre by face-to-face visitation or regular maintenance correspondence in the exchange of news or sentiment.

Mapping these 'problem-anchored' networks at a historical distance presents us with several difficulties. What values do we choose to define the connections within the network by? One method is to use a correspondence collection as the basis for setting the parameters of the study, where we can define

---

3   O'Neill, *Opened Letter*; Ben-Amos, *Culture of Giving*.
4   Granovetter, 'Strength of Weak Ties', 1361.
5   Ibid., 1362.
6   Ibid., 1371–1372; Kadushin, *Understanding Social Networks*, 165–168.
7   O'Neill, *Opened Letter*, 79.
8   Ben-Amos, *Culture of Giving*, 46.

connections by the existence of letters to and from the network centre, and establish interconnections through mentions of other correspondents within these letters.[9] However, not all correspondence collections are suitable for this style of mapping, although they may show tantalising glimpses of interconnections that make it tempting to try even when time-constraints or other limitations make doing so unfeasible. The collection of Markham's correspondence from his time at the Admiralty, which forms the basis for Chapter 3, is one such collection. The collection is extremely valuable in showing the action of exactly the kind of problem-anchored network described above, where peripheral ties contacted Markham for his assistance and, often formally-required, approbation. However, the collection itself does not provide enough detail to allow us to consistently and reliably establish the possible interconnections between correspondents in order to make a useful network map, and to do so using more intuitive judgements for each correspondent based on in-depth research into the familial, geographical and emotional factors that inform relationships is far beyond the scope of this study. The implicit influence of overlapping networks on sensitive and easily disrupted patronage relationships is also difficult to capture in a useful way using established methods of social network mapping, especially when we must manually gather and enter all our data drawn from the historical record.

We can, however, build a picture of Markham's network *context* by mapping his 'stronger ties', which helps us to understand the role of networks in his own career and the implicit weight of his connections in his patronage dealings at the Admiralty, even though they may not be so visible in his correspondence collection because of the nature of his position. Of course, the difficulty we are then presented with is how to define his connections without a neat source base upon which to employ a framework like Granovetter's strength of ties based on longevity, emotional intensity and reciprocity. It can be helpful, therefore, to understand eighteenth-century connection as characterised by three principal factors: familial obligation, physical proximity where connections were associated with one another through neighbourhoods or work, and shared values.[10]

The first, familial obligation, was a strong base for connection and relied upon blood and marriage ties to secure friendship. The extended family unit provided a 'ready-made' informal support network for the majority of people in the long eighteenth century.[11] Relations expected the familial provision of

---

[9] O'Neill, *Opened Letter*, 79–82.

[10] The term *homophily* is often used in sociological studies and refers to the tendency of people to group together with individuals of similar interests, ideas and values. See Kadushin, *Understanding Social Networks*, 9.

[11] Ben-Amos, *Culture of Giving*, 47.

charity, mutual support and preferment.[12] The tradition of familial duty and obligation meant that the connections needed less maintenance to receive informal support.[13] However, although familial ties were a very strong base from which to draw on a connection for support, they still required careful maintenance when separated by distance, such as across the Atlantic.[14] Marriages also frequently occurred among the close-knit friendships of the parental network. This was particularly the case for female children who were more restricted in their physical mobility than their brothers. The result was that intimate friendship, as well as friendship connection based on the other factors of physical proximity or shared values, became subsumed within familial obligation.[15]

The second factor, physical proximity, refers to the connection's regional and occupational context. Neighbours and colleagues could establish connection by merit of physical association, if not necessarily social proximity. This was especially true for landowners and members of parliament, who interacted with tenants, neighbouring estates, and voters, and relied upon the support of the community as well as providing support themselves, fostering a culture of mutual obligation.[16] Neighbours and connections in Yorkshire were a central part of Markham's social circle, and were often the foundation for many of his peripheral connections seeking patronage support. Physical proximity was just as important in connections forged in occupations. The navy especially fostered a sense of skill-based separation from wider British society and physically constructed associated company in the ship's crew through messmates on board ship, as well as the formation of squadrons and fleets.[17] These constructed societies were built on the foundation of formal hierarchy and were geographically mobile, bringing individuals into contact with a wider pool of potential connections. Chapter 1 has shown the importance of local networks in foreign stations in the geographical spread of the navy. In many cases, connections were forged first through environmental association and then later strengthened by intimate friendship born out of shared values and similarity. As Ellen Gill puts it, the physical proximity required by naval service instigated 'brotherly' friendships between naval officers who shared similar values and interests.[18]

Shared values worked strongly in combination with familial obligation and physical proximity. Family ties were often strengthened by shared ideas

---

[12] Tadmor, *Family and Friends*, 175–192.

[13] Ben-Amos, *Culture of Giving*, 47.

[14] Pearsall, *Atlantic Families*, 7–11.

[15] Tadmor, *Family and Friends*, 174.

[16] See John Perceval's interaction with his agent in O'Neill, *Opened Letter*, 101–115.

[17] Margarette Lincoln, *Representing the Royal Navy: British Sea Power, 1750–1815* (Aldershot, 2002); Jones, 'Masculinity, Materiality and Space'.

[18] Gill, *Naval Families*, 139–143.

FRIENDS AND FAMILY: MARKHAM'S NETWORK

and values, as were location-focused regional and occupational connections. Scientific or religious networks, such as the Royal Society in the early eighteenth century, or the connections between evangelical naval captains towards the end, are both good examples of connections instigated, moulded and maintained by shared values.[19] The college of Christ Church at Oxford University was a similarly constructed network environment, with deans such as Cyril Jackson purposely selecting from institutions with similar values, such as Westminster school, providing an environmental base of like-minded individuals for much of the Markhams' network.[20] The navy as an institution also, to a certain extent, engendered the creation of these sorts of ties through shared experiences and values of honour and duty.

Most connections were forged through several of these factors, and intimate friendships, based principally on mutual affection, also occurred within these categories. Intimate friendship, however, is difficult to define in the historical record, especially if the connection was taken for granted. Judging Markham's intimate friendships is possible largely through his correspondence, where his physical mobility and that of his friends in the navy fortunately leaves us with the sort of letters which were aimed at maintaining intimate relationships across physical distance.[21] Markham's friend Captain Mark Kerr sent many letters which were explicitly familiar. He addressed Markham as 'My dearest dear Jack' and signed his letters 'Bless you bless you and adieu my Jack your real and affectionate for ever Mark'.[22] In one letter, he even called Markham his 'best friend'.[23] The overtly familiar style of his letters leaves us in little doubt of his intimate friendship with Markham.

However, establishing the existence of an intimate friendship is difficult in instances where no correspondence survives. As we will see in Chapter 6, the reconstruction of the shipwright James Jagoe's network in Woolwich yard between 1782 and 1802 reveals environmental connections which formed the base of his dockyard patronage but can do no more than reveal the framework of his potential intimate friendships. For some of Markham's connections, however, there are many indications that they shared an intimate friendship despite no surviving extended correspondence. Markham's descendant and biographer, Clements Markham, mentioned that Edward Riou was Markham's close friend. Riou joined the navy a year before Markham and they were boys

[19] O'Neill, *Opened Letter*, 157–168; Gareth Atkins, 'Religion, Politics and Patronage in the Late Hanoverian Navy, c.1780–c.1820', *Historical Research* 88:240 (2015), 272–290.

[20] Nigel Aston, 'Markham, William', in H. C. G. Matthews and Brian Harrison (eds.), *The Oxford Dictionary of National Biography* (Oxford, 2004), vol. 36, 697–700.

[21] Pearsall, *Atlantic Families*, 7–11

[22] NMM, MRK/108/2/1, Kerr to Markham, 18 [September] 1799.

[23] NMM, MRK/108/2/2, Kerr to Markham, [1799].

56   PATRONAGE AND THE BRITISH NAVY, 1775–1815

on *Romney* together in 1775.[24] Their careers diverged from there but Riou regularly visited Markham's wife and parents. In the 1790s, Riou and Markham were also both members of the committee for the Naval Society, a sea officers' club which met monthly in a pub in Covent Garden. One of the only letters from Markham to Riou is from this time, and Markham candidly shared his displeasure with certain members of the society.[25] Markham was careful in his correspondence so his frankness with Riou suggests an intimate relationship. Riou died in the battle of Copenhagen in 1801 and it is tempting to envisage a grief-stricken Markham destroying their correspondence. But it is far more likely that the correspondence was simply lost. Certainly, Clements Markham had access to the entire collection and he was sure of the close friendship between the two, so it is possible that he had access to letters which were later separated from the collection. Riou and Markham's relationship, in any case, shows the pitfalls in trying to judge intimate friendship and proximity of connection by frequency of correspondence alone.

There are inherent difficulties in reconstructing individual networks from manuscript material. Authors made mistakes, deliberately masked who their patron had been, or over-emphasised the involvement of celebrities such as Nelson. This was also the case in solicitation letters. One request letter to Markham from John Lake, commander of *Surinam*, mentioned that he had previously found support in the Prince of Wales and Nelson.[26] Neither patron stood Lake in good stead, the first being well-known to be fickle and the second being unable to offer any support having died the previous year at Trafalgar. Applicants could also make mistakes about who had acted in their favour and it was not always clear to applicants who had assisted them, especially if they had large networks or had solicited many patrons. When George Keith Elphinstone got his first command in the navy, his family had plainly drawn heavily on their Scottish networks and were not sure who had finally secured the appointment.[27]

Another problem is that many eighteenth-century diarists and letter-writers couched their patronage in terms of friendship. In her study of a Sussex shopkeeper, Naomi Tadmor found that many of the connections he explicitly called 'friend' in his diary were also those who could offer patronage, such as his family, political connections, and local government officials.[28] However, he rarely called his neighbours 'friends' even though he socialised with them the most frequently. Tadmor suggests that not only was this type of friendship

---

[24] Markham, *A Naval Career*, 27.

[25] NMM, RUSI/235/ER/4/4, Markham to Riou, 3 April 1798.

[26] NMM, MRK/102/4/4, Lake to Markham, 1 November 1806.

[27] UoA, MS3540, George Keith, tenth Earl Marischall to George Keith Elphinstone, 17 October 1772; Marischall to Lady Clementine Elphinstone, 27 October 1772.

[28] Tadmor, *Family and Friends*, 173.

FRIENDS AND FAMILY: MARKHAM'S NETWORK

taken for granted, but that the eighteenth-century conception of 'friend' was a connection who offered something far more substantial than opportunities to socialise.[29]

Friendship, as the language of patronage, was not bound by the intimacy of connection or social proximity. Patronage requests are easier to trace between connections whose relationship was defined by their seeking assistance from the network centre because they were often more explicit about the nature of their relationship and their requests in their correspondence. Intimate friendships, or friendship based on mutual affection and interests, were undoubtedly used to gain advantage, but it is harder to read in the record because the intimacy of the relationship meant that writers took it on trust that their friend would assist them and needed fewer written reminders. The fashion for sensible friendship also meant that many writers were not explicit, perhaps even with themselves, that the exchange of news and favours they performed was a part of patronage. However, close familial connections and especially parents' desire to see their children established in the world often provide a far more explicit outline of the way patronage operated within the network.

Family

Markham's father's friends and his siblings' spouses formed the core of his familial network. Figure 2.1 illustrates a simplified version of the interconnected web of his family and family friends through the means of an elaborated family-tree. His parents, William Markham and Sarah, née Goddard, form the centre while his siblings and their marriage connections, as well as three important friend connections, radiate out. The siblings are arranged in the order of their birth from left to right, with John's elder brother William beginning the top row on the left and ending with John's youngest sister on the bottom row at the right.[30] His brother David, who died unmarried as we shall see below, is depicted on the middle level with his friend connection John Perkins, whom we encountered in Chapter 1. Each male connection in this simplified family network is also marked by whether he attended Westminster school and Christ Church at the University of Oxford, as a way to show the influence of Markham's father's connections throughout the family.

William Markham had an extended network with multiple powerfully positioned connections, as well as several location- and value-based connections who formed his close social circle, visiting his family and assisting his children. William Markham was originally from Kinsale, Ireland. He was educated at Westminster school between 1733 and 1738, and then entered

[29] Ibid., 174.
[30] See Appendix II for more details of the Markham children including their birth dates.

58   PATRONAGE AND THE BRITISH NAVY, 1775–1815

Christ Church college at Oxford, where he studied until 1752. He became the Archbishop of York in 1776, having served in various roles including the headmaster of Westminster school 1753–1764, Dean of Christ Church 1767–1777 and Bishop of Chester 1771–1776. His patronage network included very influential figures such as the Prince of Wales and Thomas Pelham-Holles, duke of Newcastle, whom he was connected to through Westminster school.[31]

Westminster school and Christ Church college formed the location and value base for William Markham's closest connections.[32] William Murray went to Westminster and Christ Church between 1719 and 1724, as did nephew David Murray between 1739 and 1748.[33] Another important connection to the Markham family in the later eighteenth century, Granville Leveson-Gower, the first marquess of Stafford, was also a contemporary of William Markham's at both Westminster and Christ Church.[34] George Rice and David Murray, both depicted in Figure 2.1, as well as another family friend, John Skynner, similarly studied at Christ Church with William Markham, Murray and Gower between 1739 and 1752.[35] Many of these connections became embedded in the Markham network through frequent visits to the Archbishop's Yorkshire residence of Bishopthorpe, and as we can see in Figure 2.1, formed the basis for many of the Markham children's marriages.

Throughout much of this period David Murray served in influential government roles including as secretary of state and ambassador to Vienna and France, and the intimacy of his connection with William Markham is apparent in their correspondence.[36] Murray often asked for the Archbishop's advice in affectionate terms. In a letter in 1783 asking for advice about a tutor for his son, he wrote: 'I have too many proofs of your constant and affectionate friendship to make any apology for troubling you upon a subject in which my Happiness is materially concerned'.[37] He also shared family news, including the birth of his children, and news of their mutual acquaintances. In 1786, he wrote reassuring the Archbishop that he would 'send Lady Dynevor the letters

---

[31]   Aston, 'Markham, William', *ODNB*, vol. 36, 697–700.

[32]   See Appendix II for a chronological list of William Markham's Westminster-Christ Church circle.

[33]   James Oldham, 'Murray, William, first earl of Mansfield', *ODNB*, vol. 39, 992–1000; H. M. Scott, 'Murray, David, seventh Viscount Stormont and second earl of Mansfield', *ODNB*, vol. 39, 884–887.

[34]   William C. Lowe, 'Gower, Granville Leveson-, first marquess of Stafford', *ODNB*, vol. 23, 116–117.

[35]   Peter Thomas, 'Rice, George', *ODNB*, vol. 46, 649; David Lemmings, 'Skynner, Sir John', *ODNB*, vol. 50, 890–891.

[36]   Scott, 'Murray, David', *ODNB*, vol. 39, 884–887.

[37]   Scone, NRAS776/Box110/Bundle1, David Murray to William Markham, 3 September 1783.

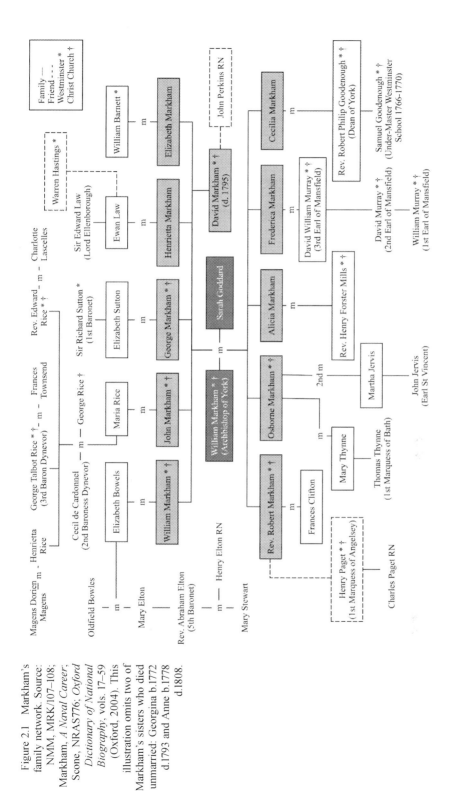

Figure 2.1 Markham's family network. Source: NMM, MRK/J07–108; Markham, *A Naval Career*; Scone, NRAS776; *Oxford Dictionary of National Biography*, vols. 17–59 (Oxford, 2004). This illustration omits two of Markham's sisters who died unmarried: Georgina b.1772 d.1793 and Anne b.1778 d.1808.

60   PATRONAGE AND THE BRITISH NAVY, 1775–1815

for Vienna'.[38] Lady Dynevor was Cecil de Cardonnel, the wife of George Rice and the mother of John Markham's future wife Maria. The intimacy of David Murray and William Markham's acquaintance is best reflected in a letter from June 1767, in which Murray sent instructions to Markham for an epitaph to be added to his late first wife's urn, which he finished: 'adieu my dear friend, my best comp[ts] to Mrs M and a kiss to little David who I rejoice to hear is so fine a Boy'.[39] The intimacy of Murray and Markham's connection bound the two families together, despite the geographical distance between the two. William Murray, the first earl of Mansfield, spent much of his time in greater physical proximity to the family in London where he lived next door to them in Bloomsbury Square. Indeed, after the Gordon Riots, William Markham wrote to John detailing how he had sheltered Mansfield and his grand-nieces after they had been forced to leave their house by the mob.[40]

The Markhams and the Murrays' close, almost familial, connection was reflected by their involvement in John's patronage, as we shall see below. The children of the two families were also closely connected. John gave advice in candid, familiar letters to David William Murray, the son of David Murray and eventually the third earl of Mansfield.[41] Markham's younger sister Frederica also had a very close connection with the third earl. One of Markham's letters to Murray in 1796 refers to his affair with Frederica, which Markham firmly advised against: 'had you stayed in England [would] have rendered it highly improper in me to suffer you to keep dallying on with my sister for two years in secret'.[42] David William and Frederica married in 1797, ultimately tying the two families together.

George Rice's connection to William Markham from their time at Christ Church together also resulted in the marriage of their children. Maria Rice, George Rice's daughter, married John in 1796. George Rice was related through his mother to the duke of Newcastle and although he entered Christ Church in 1742 he never graduated, instead becoming an active political agent for Newcastle in South Wales.[43] Maria's mother, Cecil de Cardonnel, second baroness of Dynevor, corresponded with William Markham, and used his connection to David Murray to have her letters sent safely to Vienna.[44] The

[38] Scone, NRAS776/Box110/Bundle1, David Murray to William Markham, 11 September 1786.

[39] Scone, NRAS776/Box110/Bundle1, David Murray to William Markham, 17 June 1767.

[40] Markham, *A Naval Career*, 35.

[41] Scone, NRAS776/Bundle579, Markham to David William Murray, May–November 1796, April 1797; NMM, MRK/108/1/1–17, David William Murray to Markham.

[42] Scone, NRAS776/Bundle579, Markham to David William Murray, 9 May 1796.

[43] Thomas, 'Rice, George', *ODNB*, vol. 46, 649.

[44] Scone, NRAS776/Box110/Bundle1, David Murray to William Markham, 11 September 1786.

FRIENDS AND FAMILY: MARKHAM'S NETWORK

association of Rice and de Cardonnel with William Markham meant that Maria was close friends with the younger Markham girls. Maria was twelve years younger than John and much closer in age to his sisters Alicia, Georgina and Frederica. In a letter to the third earl, Markham described Maria as 'a very great friend of my sisters'.[45] As a family friend, Maria had often visited Bishopthorpe, the Markham family home, and Markham wrote that he had 'known her from her childhood, and was ever partial to her'.[46] John had also gone to Westminster with her brother, George Talbot Rice, also depicted in Figure 2.1, further cementing the families' connection.

The youngest Markham daughter, Cecilia, also married the son of a connection from Westminster, Robert Philip Goodenough, who became Dean of York and was the son of Samuel Goodenough.[47] Samuel Goodenough had been educated at Westminster and Christ Church but had not been a contemporary of William Markham, rather becoming connected to him when he served as undermaster at Westminster school between 1766 and 1770 just after William Markham had been headmaster.[48] The Westminster-Christ Church 'hub' provided the Markhams with a pool of connections and it is not surprising that several of the children married within this circle.

Other Westminster and Christ Church connections became frequent features of the Markhams' family life. Granville Leveson-Gower's daughter Louisa was a friend of Markham and Maria. She married Archibald MacDonald, who also studied at Westminster and Christ Church although not at the same time as John and his brothers. MacDonald likely entered the Markhams' social circle because of his connection to William Murray at Lincoln's Inn. As Lord Chief Justice, William Murray had a reputation for preferring lawyers who had come through both Westminster and Christ Church.[49] John asked after 'Mr and Lady MacDonald', referring to Archibald and Louisa after their marriage in 1779, in familiar letters to his father that year.[50] The MacDonalds' integration with the Markhams' network is illustrated in Archibald's support of Warren Hastings during his impeachment trial between 1787 and 1795.[51] Hastings had assisted Markham's elder brother William, as well as his sister Henrietta's husband, Ewan Law, when they served under him in India.[52] He is illustrated in Figure 2.1 as a friend connection to Ewan Law. Maria Markham also mentioned a 'young MacDonald' in a letter to Markham in 1798 where she asked after

[45] Scone, NRAS776/Bundle579, Markham to David William Murray, 5 October 1796.

[46] Ibid.

[47] See Appendix II for list of Markham's siblings. Markham, *A Naval Career*, 265.

[48] James Price, 'Goodenough, Samuel', *ODNB*, vol. 22, 772–774.

[49] Oldham, 'Murray, William', *ODNB*, vol. 39, 993.

[50] NMM, MRK/107/1/4–5, Markham to William Markham, 28 September 1779 and 30 October 1779.

[51] Thorne, *House of Commons 1790–1820*, iv.486.

[52] Markham, *A Naval Career*, 83.

62 PATRONAGE AND THE BRITISH NAVY, 1775–1815

his other young protégés on *Centaur*. This may refer to Fred MacDonald, who served on *Centaur* as a '1st Class' boy, a position many boys hoping to become officers entered the navy at before being rated midshipmen.[53] Maria asked after young MacDonald because, as she wrote, 'I daresay I shall see Ly Louisa'.[54] This suggests that Fred MacDonald was, if not a son, then a kin connection of Louisa and Archibald MacDonald and that he secured his position through their friendship with Markham.

John Skynner and his family also frequently visited the Markhams at Bishopthorpe. John Skynner and William Markham had been contemporaries at Christ Church between 1742 and 1751.[55] Skynner then moved into the law at Lincoln's Inn and William Markham remained at Oxford but familiar letters to John mentioned in Clements Markham's biography suggest that the Skynners and the Markhams stayed in close acquaintance. In the letter William Markham wrote to Markham about the Gordon Riots he mentioned that John Skynner also sheltered in his house with two of his servants.[56] In a letter from 1757, David Murray asked William Markham to pass on his best compliments to John Skynner as well as their other friends from Christ Church.[57] Just as with the Murrays, the Skynners were incorporated into a kinship role in their intimate connection to the Markhams. Both Frederica Markham and Maria mentioned the Skynners visiting Bishopthorpe in their correspondence. Frederica wrote several letters to Murray during their long engagement in 1797. In one from August she mentioned Lady Skynner and Frederica Skynner looked well and 'that it is not an easy matter to sit down composed to answer a letter with *your* sisters and Fred Skynner in my room'.[58] The mention of Murray's sisters shows the level of intergration between the families.

Like the Murrays, the Skynners had a strong supporting role in the Markham family, in much the same way that Ben-Amos outlined occurred in extended familial networks.[59] In a letter from August 1797 Frederica mentioned walking in the garden with Skynner and she wrote of him: 'I do not know anyone whose judgement I have greater reliance on or whose opinion I would sooner take in any difficult situation where I wanted impartial advice.'[60] Skynner's patronage connections were mainly based in his position as Chief Baron of

---

[53] TNA, ADM36/14162–3, HMS *Centaur*, April 1797–September 1798.

[54] NMM, MRK/107/3/14, Maria to John, 14 February 1798.

[55] Lemmings, 'Skynner, Sir John', *ODNB*, vol. 50, 890–891.

[56] Markham, *A Naval Career*, 60.

[57] Scone, NRAS776/Box110/Bundle1, David Murray to William Markham, 30 July 1757.

[58] Emphasis in original. Scone, NRAS776/Bundle579, Frederica Markham to David William Murray, 25 August 1797.

[59] Ben-Amos, *Culture of Giving*, 45.

[60] Scone, NRAS776/Bundle579, Frederica Markham to David William Murray, 13 August 1797.

FRIENDS AND FAMILY: MARKHAM'S NETWORK   63

the Exchequer between 1777 and 1787. Although Skynner does not seem to have directly assisted Markham in his career, his influence was probably vital in the career of Markham's younger brother Osborne Markham, who began at Lincoln's Inn in 1790.[61]

Cyril Jackson also played a prominent role in the Markhams' familial network through his connection to William Markham. Cyril Jackson owed his career to William Markham, having come to Westminster school in 1760 when William Markham was headmaster, and managing to get into Christ Church in 1764. William Markham appointed him as his sub-preceptor when he served as preceptor to the two eldest sons of George III, granting Jackson access to royal favour and further patronage.[62] Jackson frequently corresponded with Markham and his siblings and took on an almost parental role. In one letter to Markham, Cyril Jackson addressed him with the familiar 'My dear Jack' and wrote 'I love still to call you so now and then'.[63] In another to Frederica, when she had married Murray and had become the countess of Mansfield, he signed off his letter with 'Adieu, duck – every affectionate remembrance to Lord Mansfield and all the little animals about you'.[64] Frederica even wrote to Murray about Jackson's pet names: 'you may give the Duck's love to the Dean when you write next to him and tell him that tho' she does not care how soon he gives her a new title, she hopes he will never make use of it to her, but keep to the old one of "dear duck" which she shall always prefer to any other from him'.[65] Maria often mentioned Jackson visiting the family at Bishopthorpe and at her house in Portugal Street in London in 1797 and 1798.[66] Cyril Jackson acted as a broker in the Markham network, moving between families like the Skynners, Murrays and Markhams who were all mutual acquaintances. He passed on news and best wishes, carried letters and visited children when they went to school, joined a profession or married into a new family. The subtler forms of patronage recommendation which came to both William Markham as Archbishop and also John as a naval captain and at the Admiralty would most likely come from someone in a position in the network like Jackson.

The most significant connections in Markham's parental network for his career were the earls of Mansfield. William and David Murray secured Markham's entry to his first ship *Romney* as a boy and his appointment to

---

[61] Thorne, *House of Commons 1790–1820*, iv.548.

[62] W. R. Ward, 'Jackson, Cyril', *ODNB*, vol. 29, 470–473.

[63] NMM, MRK/108/4/29, Jackson to Markham, 20 July [unknown year].

[64] Scone, NRAS776/Box95/Folder2/5–6, Jackson to Frederica Markham, 24 [unknown month] 1811.

[65] Scone, NRAS776/Bundle579, Frederica Markham to David William Murray, 1 August 1797.

[66] NMM, MRK/107/3/1 and MRK/107/3/19, Maria to John, 14 September 1797 and 20 May 1798.

64   PATRONAGE AND THE BRITISH NAVY, 1775–1815

Sphinx as captain in 1783. The Murrays likely had a regional connection to the family of Markham's first captain George Keith Elphinstone, through Lord Kintore, who assisted David Murray in his political presence in Scotland.[67] There is no direct correspondence between the Murrays and the Elphinstones in the family papers held at Scone Palace, Perthshire. However, there are two letters in the correspondence of the family of George Keith, tenth Earl Marischall, which reveal that his nephew George Keith Elphinstone received his first ship after making post-captain through the influence of the first earl of Mansfield.

The first is a letter from Marischall to his nephew in 1772, in which he congratulated him on getting a ship and apologised for not knowing who had recommended him to the Admiralty: 'by whom I can not tell you, I suppose by Sir John Lindsay or Admiral Dennys'.[68] John Lindsay was William Murray's nephew, and Marischall's guess suggests existent patronage ties between the families. The second letter explicitly states that the patron was William Murray, as Marischall wrote to his niece Lady Clementine Elphinstone: 'I wish you joy, Dear niece, of little Ben's having got a ship; its owing to Ld Mansfield's favour'.[69] Given the explicit acknowledgement of Mansfield's involvement in securing Keith his post-captaincy, it is very likely that Keith acted on this debt by entering John aboard *Romney* in 1775. Mansfield's connection to the First Lord of the Admiralty and the obvious power of his recommendation also probably played a crucial role.

Later correspondence between Markham's father and David Murray, who at that time was Viscount Stormont, reveals the Murrays' continued interest in John's career, albeit perhaps not a very close attention to detail. In a letter from August 1781 Murray was surprised to find John no longer in the ship he thought he was serving in: 'When I heard of the arrival of the *Roebuck* I was in great hopes of seeing your son but I hear he has got a promotion tho' not such a one as I wish him and he most certainly deserves.'[70] This comment acted as an offer of support and illustrates some of the nuances of his position in William Markham's social circle and his connection to John. First, he appears to offer support without the Archbishop soliciting him directly. The intimacy of their connection meant that interest in one another's sons was implicit. However, Murray's surprise at finding Markham already promoted suggests that patronage between intimate connections was not as pressurised as patronage between weaker ties, where the applicant continued to remind their patron or broker of their need for interest.

---

[67] Scone, NRAS776/Bundle1235, David Murray to Charles Cathcart, 14 January 1788.

[68] UoA, MS3540, Marischall to Keith, 19 October 1772.

[69] UoA, MS3540, Marischall to Elphinstone, 27 October 1772.

[70] Scone, NRAS776/Box110/Bundle1, David Murray to William Markham, 22 August 1781.

FRIENDS AND FAMILY: MARKHAM'S NETWORK

David Murray acted as the Markhams' principal connection to well-placed naval patrons such as George Rodney, commander-in-chief of the Leeward Islands. Murray's disapproval at the progress of John's promotion suggests his assuredness that his connection with Rodney could achieve a greater promotion. Certainly, Murray acted upon his offer of support when next he met with Rodney. In a letter from September 1781, Murray mentioned meeting with Rodney where he pressed for the admiral's interest in Markham:

> The first time I saw S[r] George Rodney ... I mentioned your son to him. He immediately answered in the handsomest manner that he ... would take the first opportunity of making him Post ... if this arrangement meets with your Grace's approbation I will put it when Rodney returns to town.[71]

The form of Murray and Rodney's connection is unclear. They corresponded on government business in dispatches when Murray was secretary of state.[72] The meeting referred to here suggests a more familiar acquaintance and stronger tie alongside this official connection. Of course, dining together is not a good indicator of affective friendship but it does suggest a closer connection than if they had merely been in contact via letter. Regardless of the emotional nature of their connection, Murray was a high-profile patron that Rodney would have been eager to please.[73] Murray's recommendation of John reinforced the good impression he had already made on Rodney as a lieutenant and Rodney's interest assisted Markham when he was court-martialled in 1780 for attacking a French ship sailing under a flag of truce while he was in command of the sloop *Zebra*. It is also likely to have prompted his promotion of Markham to post-captain in 1782. Whether Murray explicitly requested Rodney's involvement at each juncture or not, Markham's connection to him alone made him a valuable officer for Rodney to advance. The Murrays' connection to the Markhams therefore neatly illustrates the power of connection beyond even the direct act of solicitation.

Sibling Connections

Markham's siblings and their marriage connections also formed a central part of Markham's network in the 1790s, providing routes for their extended connections to Markham's patronage. We have encountered some of their marriages already above and illustrated in Figure 2.1. The siblings' families

---

[71] Scone, NRAS776/Box110/Bundle1, David Murray to William Markham, 26 September 1781.

[72] See Scone, NRAS776/Box15, Letters to David Murray, Viscount Stormont, 1779–1781; NRAS776/Bundle1384, Miscellaneous Correspondence of David Murray, Viscount Stormont, 1779–1781.

[73] Rodney had a reputation for pleasing his friends in high places a little too much during the American Revolutionary War; Rodger, *Command of the Ocean*, 344.

66   PATRONAGE AND THE BRITISH NAVY, 1775–1815

formed a major part of the social circle centred on Bishopthorpe in the 1790s and Frederica Markham's detailed correspondence with Murray in the summer of that year recorded many of the visitors. Frederica mentioned that her sister Elizabeth and her husband William Barnett, another alumnus of Westminster school, visited frequently throughout June and August, as well as her eldest brother William Markham and his wife Elizabeth Bowles whom she called the 'Williams'.[74] Both siblings lived in Aberford near Leeds, easily within reach for a short visit to Bishopthorpe just outside York. They also brought extra connections with them. The 'Williams' brought Elizabeth Bowles's sister with them whom Frederica called 'Mrs Palmers'.[75] They also brought a pair whom Frederica always referred to as 'the Lady Hays'.[76] The Hays sometimes also visited with the Barnetts and spent time with siblings in Aberford.[77] Frederica also mentioned Lord and Lady Errol visiting Aberford on 29 August, so the 'Lady Hays' were most likely the unmarried sisters of George Hay, fourteenth earl of Errol.[78] Maria also mentioned having met Lady Errol while at Bishopthorpe in October 1797.[79] The Errols were Scottish peers and a good example of the extent of the Markhams' familial network which is not otherwise shown in direct correspondence.

Frederica's other siblings from further afield also visited Bishopthorpe in the summer of 1797, including Alicia and her husband Henry Forster Mills. Henrietta, her husband Ewan Law and her brother-in-law Edward Law, first earl of Ellenborough, also dined at Bishopthorpe on 6 August.[80] They brought with them connections from their own social circle including Sir Frederick Eden, who had just published *The State of the Poor* (1797), and some young lawyers, including two whom Frederica referred to as 'Fandango and Fantastick'.[81] Her brother George and his wife Elizabeth Sutton do not seem to have visited, but his father-in-law Sir Richard Sutton certainly did.[82] Maria

---

[74] Scone, NRAS776/Bundle579, Frederica to Murray, 25 June, 28 June, 8 August, 10 August, 11 August and 23 August 1797.

[75] Scone, NRAS776/Bundle579, Frederica to Murray, 23 August 1797.

[76] Scone, NRAS776/Bundle579, Frederica to Murray, 28 June 1797.

[77] Scone, NRAS776/Bundle579, Frederica to Murray, 25 June, 28 June, 11 August 1797.

[78] She refers in particular to a 'Lady M Hay' dining with them at Bishopthorpe on 11 August, who was possibly Lady Maria Elizabeth Hay, Hay's second youngest sister; Scone, NRAS776/Bundle579, Frederica to Murray, 11 August, 29 August 1797; John Burke, *A General and Heraldic Dictionary of the Peerage and Baronetage of the British Empire* (London, 1837), i.360.

[79] NMM, MRK/107/3/5, Maria to John, 14 October 1797.

[80] Scone, NRAS776/Bundle579, Frederica to Murray, 6 August 1797.

[81] Donald Winch, 'Eden, Sir Frederick Morton, second baronet', *ODNB*, vol. 17, 682–683; Scone, NRAS776/Bundle579, Frederica to Murray, 1 August 1797.

[82] Scone, NRAS776/Bundle579, Frederica to Murray, 2 August 1797.

FRIENDS AND FAMILY: MARKHAM'S NETWORK 67

also mentioned Lady Sutton visiting in July 1798.[83] Frederica's brother Robert was also absent because he was trying to arrange his marriage to Frances Clifton, another local Yorkshire connection.[84]

Local connections understandably made up the central part of the Markhams' social circle at Bishopthorpe. Regional connection to the family gave acquaintances access to Markham and his patronage on board *Centaur* between 1797 and 1801. He took on Henry Elton, aged fourteen, as a volunteer boy in 1798 at the behest of his brother's new wife Elizabeth Bowles. Henry Elton was her cousin. His father Abraham Elton was part of the Westminster-Christ Church network and frequently solicited Markham's attention for his son.[85] Other Yorkshire connections asked after Henry Elton via Maria including a man she referred to as 'Old Garthshore', who visited Bishopthorpe in September 1799.[86] Frederica also mentioned the Garthshores in her letters in 1797, and on one occasion mentioned that Mrs Garthshore had a long talk with her father in the 'summer house', something which Frederica wrote she was made aware of because of the 'uncommon strength and power of Mrs G's lungs, who without any exertion ha[d] informed the *whole house*' that it was raining heavily outside.[87] Although the correspondence does not survive, we can assume that Markham's father and perhaps his mother wrote to him while he served at sea in the late 1790s. Frederica herself mentioned writing to him throughout the summer of 1797. The recommendation to appoint Elton to his ship therefore could have come from multiple points in his intimate network.

There are other less certain connections to Yorkshire among the young boys Markham appointed to *Centaur*. He took on Jonathan Kelly as a volunteer boy in 1799 who is described in the muster book as having been born in Yorkshire.[88] Kelly was probably the son of Markham's old school friend and a regional connection, George Kelly.[89] Maria mentioned the Kellys visiting Bishopthorpe on 16 and 17 August 1798, so the request to have Kelly entered on *Centaur* most likely came through a family connection.[90] Markham's protégé William Croft probably also secured his appointment through his connection to Markham's family at Bishopthorpe. Certainly, his father Stephen Croft wrote to Markham from Stillington in Yorkshire about William's promotion

---

83 NMM, MRK/107/3/22, Maria to John, 24 July 1798.
84 Scone, NRAS776/Bundle579, Frederica to Murray, 1 August 1797.
85 R. K. Webb, 'Elton, Sir Charles Abraham, sixth baronet', *ODNB*, vol. 18, 342; NMM, MRK/108/4/33–38 and MRK/108/4/41, Abraham Elton to Markham, 25 February 1796 to 19 February 1807.
86 NMM, MRK/107/3/36, Maria to John, 25 September 1799.
87 Scone, NRAS776/Bundle579, Frederica to Murray, 1 August 1797.
88 TNA, ADM36/14163, HMS *Centaur*.
89 Markham, *A Naval Career*, 24.
90 NMM, MRK/107/3/27, Maria to John, 14–16 August 1798.

68   PATRONAGE AND THE BRITISH NAVY, 1775–1815

after Markham left *Centaur* in 1801.[91] William Croft also wrote to Markham several times after 1801, and twice from Stillington.[92]

Markham was able to oblige other connections in his command of *Centaur*. He took on Roddam Augustus Read as lieutenant who was the eldest son of the former secretary of Admiral Roddam and Admiral Sir Peter Parker.[93] He also had Charles Paget as his lieutenant briefly for a month in June 1797, before he made the step to the command of the *Martin* sloop.[94] Charles Paget was the younger brother of Henry Paget, first marquess of Anglesey, who had attended Westminster and Christ Church with Markham's younger brother Robert. Charles Paget also entered the navy under Andrew Snape Douglas in 1790, who had served with Markham on *Roebuck* and later in the Mediterranean fleet between 1783 and 1786.[95] Paget continued to correspond with Markham on naval matters when Markham joined the Admiralty in 1801, although not with the familiarity of some of Markham's other *Centaur* connections such as William Croft, Henry Elton and Jonathan Kelly.[96]

Markham's siblings also brokered Markham's Admiralty patronage. His brother William certainly had connection to some of the youngsters on *Centaur*, such as Thomas John Williamson, mentioned in the Introduction, who was likely the son of one of William's connections in Bengal when he served in the East India Company in the 1780s.[97] William also wrote more directly to access his Admiralty patronage in 1806 to recommend the son of a neighbour of his Yorkshire connection Sir Thomas Slingsby: 'Sir Tho' is a very worthy man and one I should much wish to gratify by a compliance with the spirit of his application'.[98] He showed an awareness of the constraints of Markham's patronage, as Sir Thomas wished the boy to be placed in a rating better than a common seaman but William wrote that 'I know that you can not make him a midshipman, as he has not ever served.'[99] His awareness

[91] NMM, MRK/104/1/82 and MRK/103/1/47, Stephen Croft to Markham, 26 December 1801 and 28 April 1804.

[92] NMM, MRK/103/1/42 and MRK/102/1/161, William Croft to Markham, 5 July 1802 and 19 October 1804.

[93] TNA ADM36/14165 and 'Naval History of the Year 1805: Obituaries', in *Naval Chronicle*, vol. 14 (July–December 1805), 512.

[94] TNA, ADM35/14163–5, Muster Books: HMS *Centaur*.

[95] John Knox Laughton, 'Paget, Charles (1778–1839)', in *Dictionary of National Biography, 1885–1900* (43), 49, accessed via https://en.wikisource.org/wiki/Dictionary_of_National_Biography,_1885-1900/Paget,_Charles_(1778-1839)

[96] NMM, MRK/102/5/2–5, Paget to Markham, 26 May 1801 to c. September 1803.

[97] NMM, MRK/107/4/8. William Markham to John Markham, 9 August 1803; TNA, ADM 36/14167 and 14168, Muster Books: HMS *Centaur*, 1 December 1800–30 April 1801. See Introduction, note 57.

[98] NMM, MRK/107/4/9, William to John, 26 June 1806.

[99] Ibid.

FRIENDS AND FAMILY: MARKHAM'S NETWORK 69

reflects a degree of experience with naval patronage which in turn suggests that he brokered more requests either by letter or in person than survive in the collection.

Markham's brother Robert also brokered requests although with less certainty of the system's pressures. In March 1807, he passed on the request of his wife's cousin, Lady Almeria Carpenter, who was the mistress of Prince William Henry, duke of Gloucester and Edinburgh.[100] He wrote: 'I was applied to some time ago by Lady Almeria Carpenter to recommend a young man now serving on board a sloop (which I have forgot) to your protection'. Unlike William, he did not enclose the letter of the brokered connection, but rather, because he could not remember the details of the application, he brokered their acquaintance via letter: 'As I really do not recollect what it precisely was she esteemed for, tho I think it was to get him exchanged into a frigate, I shall desire her to make her request to you, and we shall *both* be much obliged to you if you will pay attention to it.'[101] Markham's brother-in-law Ewan Law also brokered requests. In 1803, he brokered the request of his friend Walter Wilkins, the MP for Radnor, who in turn requested Markham's interest in Captain Thomas Walbeoff.[102] His letter shows a reluctance, however, to overburden Markham with requests from his extended network, as he wrote: 'I can compute the number of applications you must receive of this nature and among them excuse this from me. I never pretend to judge of the propriety of such representations.'[103] Markham managed to make the appointment and Walbeoff sent him a letter thanking him for his interest in July 1803.[104]

Those of Markham's siblings who did not get married, such as his brother David, still brought him connections who later drew on his patronage. David Markham rose to the rank of colonel in the army and served in India as well as the West Indies in the 1790s at the same time as Markham. He died at Sant Domingue in 1795, but it seems that before his death he was introduced to John Perkins. Perkins, mentioned in Chapter 1, was already an acquaintance of John from the early 1780s when they served in Jamaica together. Perkins only included his connection to David in his applications to Markham's favour in 1806, perhaps when he felt that Markham's interest in him was waning after he gave up *Tartar* in 1805. He wrote: 'knowing the goodness of your hart towards me, which I have all ready had a Prove of, and the regard your Brother had for me during his time at Port au

---

[100] Matthew Kilburn, 'William Henry, Prince, first duke of Gloucester and Edinburgh', *ODNB*, vol. 59, 121.

[101] NMM, MRK/107/4/13, Robert to John, 1 March 1807.

[102] Thorne, *House of Commons 1790–1820*, v.565.

[103] NMM, MRK/108/4/19, Law to Markham, 2 June 1803.

[104] NMM, MRK/102/6/13, Walbeoff to Markham, 1 July 1803.

70   PATRONAGE AND THE BRITISH NAVY, 1775–1815

Prince, givs me agrater Clame to request still your interest'.[105] Markham was greatly affected by David's death and Clements Markham suggested that his grief was what invalided him from *Hannibal* and sent him home when his crew was struck with yellow fever. Perkins emphasised his connection to Markham by mentioning his previous relationship with David, and this perhaps strengthened his application. However, the Admiralty did not give Perkins another command, so either Markham was not in a position to give another ship to Perkins after he had already resigned a good commission to stay in Jamaica, or the use of his dead brother's connection was too much in what was so plainly a solicitation letter.

Markham's many siblings and their partners provided an intimate centre to an extended network of multiple weaker ties. Their connections provided the pool from which Markham selected the young 'gentlemen' of his ship, those boys destined to become commissioned officers. An officer's network is perhaps best represented by his selection of these boys but the convoluted ties that connected many of them to Markham illustrate the difficulty Evan Wilson and S. A. Cavell encountered in distinguishing patrons behind individual appointments in their quantitative surveys of officers' careers.[106] Markham's familial network reveals that he made appointments from the regional locales of his family in Yorkshire and Maria's family in Pembrokeshire. Many of the initial patronage solicitations, therefore, took place face-to-face and without the passing mentions of his 'young friends' in his wider correspondence the initial connection between Markham and those he assisted would be invisible.[107]

Social Circle

Maria's letters to Markham and his to her between 1797 and 1805 mentioned many acquaintances of Maria's in London as well as Markham's in the navy. They provide us with an impression of Markham's social circle, or familiar network, and the number of acquaintances who could access his patronage on *Centaur* and at the Admiralty from 1801 via face-to-face solicitation.

As at Bishopthorpe, Maria's social circle in London was principally formed around her siblings and in-laws. She often dined with her sister Henrietta Magens, her brother George Talbot Rice and his wife, and other members of her extended familial circles such as her sister-in-law Henrietta Law. At one such dinner at the Laws in March 1799, Maria mentioned the other guests, including Edward Law who was Henrietta's brother-in-law and 'the Thynnes', who were most likely the widow and children of Thomas Thynne, first

---

[105] NMM, MRK/102/5/14, Perkins to Markham, 18 May 1806.
[106] Wilson, *British Naval Officers*; Cavell, *Midshipmen and the Quarterdeck Boys*, 37–41.
[107] NMM, MRK/107/3/14, Maria to John, 14 February 1798.

FRIENDS AND FAMILY: MARKHAM'S NETWORK

marquess of Bath.[108] Markham's brother Osborne married Lady Mary Thynne in 1806 and Maria mentioned Thynne frequently in her letters to Markham so it is reasonable to assume that the Thynne family were a frequent feature of their social circle between 1797 and 1805.[109] At this same dinner, Maria also mentioned her sister and a Mr Thomas Hope, presumably Markham's cousin by the marriage of his mother's niece, Ann Goddard, in 1782 to John Williams Hope, the adopted son of the wealthy Dutch merchant, Henry Hope. The Hopes feature elsewhere in Maria's correspondence to Markham, hosting apparently 'dull' parties which she attended dutifully along with her husband's other siblings and their spouses, as well as in connection to friends she frequently visited such as the Curzons.[110] There also seems to have been a possible further connection with Markham's sister Anne, whom Maria potentially dissuaded from marrying Thomas Hope in 1799 after writing to Markham that she thought him unsuitable and 'not a man that I think any woman could be in love with'.[111] Maria also mentioned two other diners at the Laws in March 1799: William Burns and Mr Giles. She gave no further detail on who they were, however, and never mentioned them again in her correspondence with Markham, suggesting they were part of the Laws' social circle rather than her own.[112] Their proximity to Maria's intimate connections, however, gave them an associated connection to herself and Markham and potentially provided access to patronage if they drew upon that tie. Their presence gives a glimpse of the number of acquaintances who could approach Markham who otherwise have left little trace of their connection in the written record.

Maria also dined frequently at Markham's parents' house in South Audley street, and her father-in-law's friends were a frequent part of her social circle in London. Benjamin Langlois, who was an old friend of David Murray's and by extension William Markham's, often dined with the Markhams in London as well as at Bishopthorpe. In one letter to Markham, Maria wrote that she dined at the Archbishop's with Langlois who 'enquired much after you'.[113] By moving between these circles Maria provided a point of familiar contact for Markham within his extended familial network.

Maria shared more detail of her social activities in some letters than in others. Her letters from late 1797 and 1798 are particularly detailed because it was her first time in London by herself since marrying Markham in 1796.

---

[108] NMM, MRK/107/3/32, Maria to John, 25 March 1799.

[109] Markham, *A Naval Career*, 256.

[110] NMM, MRK/107/3/28 and 33, Maria to John, 27 February–1 March 1799 and 1 April 1799; Scone, NRAS776/Box 95/Folder 2, Mrs Sarah Markham (née Goddard) to Frederica Murray (née Markham), c.1813; Markham, *A Naval Career*, 15–16.

[111] NMM, MRK/107/3/33, Maria to John, 1 April 1799.

[112] NMM, MRK/107/3/32, Maria to John, 25 March 1799.

[113] NMM, MRK/107/3/19, Maria to John, 20 March 1798.

72   PATRONAGE AND THE BRITISH NAVY, 1775–1815

Maria spent much of 1798 with Frederica attending parties or other social meetings.[114] Frederica's social circle was far larger than Maria's because of her marriage to Mansfield who had considerably more connections among the Scottish elite than Markham. Maria was invited to multiple events with Frederica, including breakfast with Henry Scott, third duke of Buccleuch, and dinner with Louisa Murray (Cathcart), the dowager countess of Mansfield and Frederica's mother-in-law.[115] Alone in London, Maria moved between the extended social circles of her intimate connections, which meant that her network was made up of many weaker ties who, by virtue of their connection to her extended family, also had access to herself and Markham.

However, many connections visited Maria directly. Augustus Pechell, a contemporary of Markham's from Westminster, visited Maria on multiple occasions and Maria called him 'your friend ... for such I must consider him, no man can seem more heartily interested for you than he does'.[116] Many of her visitors were connected to Markham from his schooling or his time at sea. Maria explicitly mentioned Captain Edward Riou visiting her on several occasions and initially his visits to Maria seem to have been frequent. In a letter to Markham in 1798 she wrote: 'you ask if Riou repeats his morning visits'. However, she goes on to say that he stopped because she felt it was indecent for him to meet her so often in the morning without Markham there and 'it was very evident by my manner that I did not like it'.[117] Riou also frequently visited Markham's parents at South Audley street and Maria seems to have been happier to meet him there. His visits reveal his intimate position in Markham's network. Certainly, Maria supposed that the appointment of Walter Grossett as a lieutenant on *Centaur* was through Riou's interest, as she wrote: 'I fancy by Capt Riou that this young man has been appointed thro' his interest at least that he is a friend of his.' Riou had sent a note to her to tell her that Grossett was going out to *Centaur* and so could carry any letters or gifts she wished to send to Markham.[118]

Thomas Richbell, first lieutenant of *Centaur*, also remained an intimate connection of Markham's for the rest of his life. He sent Markham multiple pictures of actions on board *Centaur*. He also took Markham to Europe on board his ship when Markham's health was failing at the end of his life in 1826.[119] There are only two letters from Richbell in the Markham collection. However, Maria frequently mentioned him. In one letter from 1797, she wrote

---

[114] NMM, MRK/107/3/28, Maria to John, 27 February–2 March 1799.

[115] NMM, MRK/107/3/19, Maria to John, 20 March 1798.

[116] NMM, MRK/107/3/30, Maria to John, 15 March 1799; Markham, *A Naval Career*, 24.

[117] NMM, MRK/107/3/18, Maria to John, 9 April 1798.

[118] NMM, MRK/107/3/21, Maria to John, 20 July 1798.

[119] Markham, *A Naval Career*, 136 and 218.

FRIENDS AND FAMILY: MARKHAM'S NETWORK 73

that she missed Markham so keenly that she could imagine eating bread and cheese with Markham and Richbell on *Centaur*.[120] In 1800 after Richbell had left *Centaur*, he wrote to ask Markham to draw on his connection to Archibald MacDonald to get a nephew of his placed in Christchurch school in London. He also wrote of Maria: 'I feel myself much flattered by being so particularly remembered by Mrs Markham to whom I beg my most respectful compliments and beg leave to remain with the utmost esteem'.[121]

Markham's close naval connections formed part of his and Maria's social circle and although the letters exchanged between himself and his naval friends dealt largely with naval matters, their embeddedness in his network suggests familiarity, friendship and perhaps even affection. Markham mentioned awaiting letters from Maria via his commanding officer, Admiral Charles Pole, while he was at Portsmouth in 1797.[122] There are a few letters from Pole to Markham in the collection but Pole was also married to Markham's cousin Henrietta Goddard, so their naval connection was strengthened by familial bonds.[123] There are also 125 letters from Admiral Bartholomew Rowley in the collection and Markham mentioned dining with him at Torbay in 1800.[124] Rowley's sister, Philippa, married Admiral Charles Cotton who has thirteen letters in the collection. Lady Philippa Cotton also wrote directly to Markham herself in 1803, soliciting his patronage.[125] She did not excuse her lack of connection, which suggests that they were acquainted and perhaps part of the same social circle. The wife of Captain Thomas Wells, serving beside Markham in the Channel, was also possibly part of Maria's social circle. In a letter of 27 February 1799, Maria mentioned that she attended one of Mrs Hope's 'dull' parties with 'Mrs Wills'.[126] Markham mentioned Thomas Wells in many of his letters, perhaps because of his proximity to him in the squadron or because Maria's possible connection to his wife meant that she would want to hear news of him. Markham also often dined with Wells when he went ashore to dine with Rowley at Torbay in 1800.[127] Of course, it is also possible that the 'Mrs Wills' Maria referred to was not the wife of Captain Thomas Wells at all. Perhaps it was a shorthand way of referring to her sister-in-law Elizabeth, married to Markham's elder brother William. Or perhaps Maria was referring to the wife of Thomas Willes, the surgeon on board *Centaur*. Markham mentioned Willes in other letters, including one where he shared

---

[120] NMM, MRK/107/3/7, Maria to John, 27 October 1797.
[121] NMM, MRK/108/4/30, Richbell to Markham, 28 May 1800.
[122] NMM, MRK/107/2/4, John to Maria, 6 December 1797.
[123] Markham, *A Naval Career*, 194.
[124] NMM, MRK/107/2/15, John to Maria, 1 February 1800.
[125] NMM, MRK/104/4/43, Cotton to Markham, 17 July 1803.
[126] NMM, MRK/107/3/28, Maria to John, 27 February 1799.
[127] NMM, MRK/107/2/15, John to Maria, 1 February 1800.

how impressed he was with the recovery of a member of the crew who had recently fractured his skull, something which Markham attributed directly to the 'persevering skill and humanity' of Mr Willes, whom he also stressed 'I esteem more and more daily'.[128] Although Willes himself was not mentioned by Maria, her possible connection to his wife and Markham's references to him in his letters suggest that their connection may have become closer than a merely professional connection aboard *Centaur*.

Maria socialised with several of the wives and female relations of Markham's naval connections in a way that was typical of naval wives at the end of the eighteenth century.[129] In a letter from 1797, while at Bishopthorpe, Maria mentioned a 'Miss Pasley', who told her that the wife of Captain William Pierrepont had to live with a brother who hated her, while Pierrepont served at sea. Maria was writing to Markham about the difficulty of being separated but how comfortable she felt living with his family at Bishopthorpe.[130] Maria's use of 'told' suggests that either she was in face-to-face contact with Pasley in Yorkshire or that they were corresponding with one another. Certainly, John mentioned Admiral Thomas Pasley in his letters to Maria which suggests the family was part of their social circle.[131] There is no correspondence between Maria and Miss Pasley in the collection but there is between Markham and Thomas Pasley.[132] Pasley's correspondence with Markham was principally about the running of the navy but Maria's oblique reference to her familiar relationship with his daughter suggests that his connection to Markham may have been closer than a peripheral occupational tie. William Pierrepont certainly corresponded with Markham and sent several letters between 1801 and 1807, suggesting a stronger than peripheral position in his network, which was perhaps why Pasley mentioned his wife to Maria.[133]

Markham mentioned Maria corresponding or socialising with the wives of several other of his naval connections. He often mentioned her spending time with 'Mrs Sutton', presumably Frances Sutton, the wife of John Sutton who served in the Channel fleet with Markham in 1800 and 1801. Markham himself had a strong connection to Sutton through their service together and mutual acquaintances, and forty-three letters from Sutton survive in the Markham collection.[134] The subjects of his letters are mainly naval rather than

---

[128] NMM, MRK/107/2/33, John to Maria, 1 June 1800.

[129] Gill, *Naval Families*, 69–74 and 171–172; Lincoln, *Naval Wives*, 56–71.

[130] NMM, MRK/107/3/3, Maria to John, 8 October 1797.

[131] NMM, MRK/107/2/29, John to Maria, 27 April [1800].

[132] NMM, MRK/101/7/38–50, MRK/104/5/38, Pasley to Markham, 29 March 1801–8 July 1807.

[133] NMM, MRK/102/5/20–35, Pierrepont to Markham, 9 August 1803–29 March [1806].

[134] NMM, MRK/101/6/80–122, Sutton to Markham, 12 April [1801]–13 April [1807].

FRIENDS AND FAMILY: MARKHAM'S NETWORK 75

familiar but Maria's association with Frances Sutton shows how ties forged in the service were often reinforced with familiarity elsewhere in a network. Certainly, Markham often mentioned Sutton in his letters to Maria with the apparent expectation that she would share her news with Frances. In a letter from September 1800 he mentioned that Sutton had had a minor accident on board his ship and that he was 'rather displeased' to see that Markham was writing to Maria and that he told Markham 'you must not write those things to the cottage'. Markham did, although he also urged Maria, 'do you only keep them to yourself, for though he has perhaps persuaded her that no harm can ever happen to his ship yet if she hears anything by chance which he so stridently conceals from her, will she ever have confidence in what he says again?'[135] The exchange of news strengthened both Maria's connection to Frances but also Markham's connection to Sutton. Naval wives were vital in the maintenance of naval familiar connections which also often underpinned much of naval patronage.

Certainly, forging a connection with Maria seems to have been the object of some of Markham's more peripheral or lapsed naval connections. The wives of some of Markham's connections at sea approached Maria to renew or strengthen their husbands' connection. In 1799, she wrote that she had returned the visit of 'Lady Orde', who had called on her while she was out. Lady Jane Orde was the wife of Admiral John Orde, who had served aboard *Roebuck* in the same squadron as Markham aboard *Perseus* in 1776 to 1778, and she appears to have sought Maria out to establish a familiar acquaintance.[136] Orde was serving alongside Markham in the Mediterranean fleet between 1798 and 1799 and so was probably already acquainted with him at an occupational level. Maria wrote to Markham that when he returned he would wish to see both Lady Jane and Sir John Orde. Certainly Maria's letter suggests that her introduction to Lady Jane was because of Orde's desire to be better connected to Markham, as she wrote: 'I am sure he is partial to you by the pains she took to come to me'.[137]

The invitations Maria received to gatherings held by other naval wives may have been further attempts to bring her into their social circles and to therefore strengthen their husbands' ties to Markham as well as offer opportunities for face-to-face patronage. She received one invitation from a 'Mrs Montagu', who was probably Charlotte Montagu, married to Captain George Montagu, whom Markham mentioned in his letters as he served off the coast of Ireland in 1797.[138] Maria also spent time with Lady Caroline Warren, taking her lead

---

[135] NMM, MRK/107/3/38, John to Maria, 3 September 1800.

[136] Markham, *A Naval Career*, 26–30 and 49–50; Denis Orde, 'Orde, Sir John, first baronet', *ODNB*, vol. 41, 920–921.

[137] NMM, MRK/107/3/31, Maria to John, 17–18 March 1799.

[138] NMM, MRK/107/3/19, Maria to John, 20 March 1798; MRK/107/2/1, John to

76 PATRONAGE AND THE BRITISH NAVY, 1775–1815

at many social events.[139] Warren was married to Captain John Warren who also served with Markham in the Channel fleet. She seems to have been acquainted with Markham directly and her two letters to Markham in the collection suggest a familiar relationship. She signed off one letter about arranging travel on board a ship to Sheerness with: 'How angry you ought to be, at being so plagued! Adieu'.[140] In a sense, Maria's association with the wives of naval officers was partly based on shared values or at the very least the shared experience of being separated from their husbands while they served at sea.[141] The connections, in some ways, were also referred environmental connections because of their husbands serving in the same fleet. Categories aside, the connection of the wives of naval officers to each other suggests that familiarity in social circles strengthened connection forged through mutual service. Partly, this stemmed from Maria's need for advice and condolences about her situation.[142] In other ways, however, we can read these connections as part of the subtle establishing of ties which they could draw on for future patronage.

Certainly, Markham advised Maria against becoming too friendly with certain women in case they overburdened him with requests. In a letter from 1800, he advised her not to attend a party being held by a 'Mrs Cary' even if Warren was going.[143] He stressed that as Warren was older she was less vulnerable than Maria who might ruin her reputation or be taken advantage of by those trying to make a closer connection to Markham through her. 'Mrs Cary' may refer to Sophia Cary, married to the geographer John Cary. Both were mentioned in the correspondence of Charlotte-Georgiana Jerningham, Lady Bedingfield, as being familial ties and members of Bedingfield's social circle.[144] Markham wrote to Maria: 'I am not fond myself of making new acquaintance, particularly in the Cary stile and I shall be sorry to pass much time with them when we are in, or that they should importune me'.[145] Markham worried that Maria expanded her social circle too far in London with

---

Maria, 21 January 1797.

[139] NMM, MRK/107/2/28, John to Maria, 23 March 1800.

[140] NMM, MRK/104/4/47, Warren to Markham, [undated].

[141] Lincoln, *Naval Wives*, 65.

[142] Ibid., 65–66.

[143] NMM, MRK/107/2/28, John to Maria, 23 March 1800.

[144] CRL, Jerningham Letters, JER/407, JER/810, JER/813, JER/816, Lady Frances Jerningham to Lady Charlotte Bedingfeld, 4 June 1806, 29 October 1814, 31 October 1814, 10 November 1814; JER/870, John Cary to Lady Charlotte Bedingfeld, 2 June 1815; Edgerton Castle (ed.), *The Jerningham Letters (1780–1843): Being Excerpts from the Correspondence and Diaries of the Honourable Lady Jerningham and her Daughter Lady Bedingfeld* (London, 1896), i.174, 191 and 200.

[145] NMM, MRK/107/2/28, John to Maria, 23 March 1800.

FRIENDS AND FAMILY: MARKHAM'S NETWORK

acquaintances who would then have access to him and request patronage favours. He also, however, seems to have principally objected to them because they were Catholics; he stated in the rest of his letter that he distrusted all 'confessors' because he felt that the act of absolution gave them licence to behave badly. Nonetheless, his advice to Maria highlights the importance of their familiar network in facilitating requests to Maria for Markham's naval and Admiralty patronage.

Maria's social circle and Markham's connections at sea reveal the potential for the subtler patronage conducted between familiar connections, often face-to-face, providing a counterpoint to the more easily distinguishable transactions apparent in direct solicitation letters. Of course, Maria and Markham's letters expose only a very small portion of their relationships, and the examples given here open only a small window into this network of weaker ties. There are many connections in Maria and John's correspondence which are too obscure to trace. Maria called one connection only 'Mrs L' and in other cases Markham wished her to pass his compliments on to 'Lady L and the commissioner's family'.[146] We can guess at who connections like these were, and several deductions have been made in this chapter. Even without being able to identify every passing mention, however, they reflect the number of potential routes that weaker ties within Markham's extended network could take to approach him for his patronage assistance. Maria and Markham's correspondence also shows how familiar connections on shore, by socialising with Maria, could enhance connections at sea.

Naval Connections

Markham had a strong network of friendships and weaker ties within the navy. Certainly, some of Markham's naval connections strengthened their ties by visiting Maria, but many seem to have relied on their connection to Markham forged by their mutual service. As we shall see in the following chapter, Markham's naval correspondents were numerous. Although we have a wealth of material in the form of individual letters, it is often difficult either to establish the exact nature of each individual correspondent's relationship with Markham, or hope to sketch the complexity of their interconnections with each other and wider society. In his role as a lord commissioner of the Admiralty, Markham received letters from a large range of relationship types: from complete strangers all the way to his intimate friends. Our understanding of his friendships is gleaned from biographies and the style of the surviving letters themselves. But even with these aids, it is not always clear.

---

[146] NMM, MRK/107/3/19, Maria to John, 20 March 1798; MRK/107/2/15, John to Maria, 1 February 1800.

78   PATRONAGE AND THE BRITISH NAVY, 1775–1815

One way to gain an idea of Markham's naval circle, then, is to consider his correspondents in terms of the number of their letters which survive in the collection. The frequency of their correspondence, as well as associations aboard ship and in social clubs, builds a picture of Markham's naval circle and those officers he respected, or felt affection for, as well as those who could solicit him directly. This approach does, of course, present inevitable methodological issues, not least because the survival of correspondence creates a biased data set. Markham certainly did not retain all the letters he received at the Admiralty. Historians working on the epistolary collections of politicians or merchants who diligently kept detailed letter-books can offer an insight into the sheer amount of correspondence received by a man in Markham's position.[147] Thomas Grenville in his brief time as First Lord of the Admiralty received an average of twenty-one letters a day from outside of government, roughly two-thirds of which concerned appointments.[148] The Markham collection certainly does not contain Markham's entire correspondence. Several of the letters to Markham obliquely refer to previous correspondence which has not survived. In a dedicated qualitative study of his epistolary network, such references could be used to mediate the incomplete data set. However, there is always the difficulty presented by not knowing why Markham kept the letters he did or what correspondence may have been discarded or destroyed under the care of his descendants.

Equally, not all high-frequency correspondence reflects the longevity of a connection's relationship with Markham. Some correspondence occurred over a short space of time and on a single issue, meaning frequency reflects the connection's persistence rather than the strength of their tie to Markham. It is important to stress, therefore, that frequency of correspondence was not necessarily an indicator of patronage success. After all, persistent applications in a short space of time were sometimes the result of a failed request and applicants successful in their first approach were not as likely to risk irritating Markham by following their requests with further correspondence. However, there were certainly correspondents who used the success of one request to apply for further assistance, in some cases to strengthen that connection to Markham by reminding him of their presence in his network.

Figure 2.2 illustrates the correspondents in the collection who wrote four or more letters to Markham between 1801 and 1807. The central band have more than twenty letters to Markham in the collection, the second band shows those with ten to nineteen letters, and the third all of those who wrote between four and nine. Those with less frequent correspondence in the third band were the most numerous, which reflects how Markham's time at the Admiralty

---

[147] See Whyman, *Sociability and Power*, 184–187; and O'Neill, *Opened Letter*, 9–17 and 78–112.

[148] Knight, *Britain Against Napoleon*, 235–236.

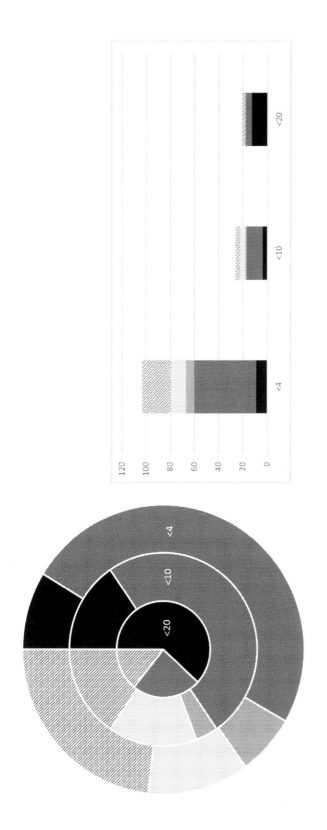

Figure 2.2 Correspondents by frequency in Markham Papers 1801–1807. Source: NMM, MRK/101–106.

80 PATRONAGE AND THE BRITISH NAVY, 1775–1815

prompted many of his peripheral connections to approach him, as we shall explore further in the following chapter.

As a way to provide context for Markham's naval circle, this illustration is helpful at the very least for demonstrating the centrality of the senior ranks of the navy in his possible network. As we can see, admirals made up the greatest proportion of Markham's most frequent correspondents, accounting for roughly two-thirds of those for whom twenty or more letters survive in the collection. The majority of these letters were, of course, official correspondence about naval organisation and Admiralty concerns. Many of the admirals included in this illustration, however, also appear among Markham's familiar connections that we have already explored, suggesting that his relationships with them were not entirely dependent on his position at the Admiralty. For example, twenty-nine of the forty-three letters that survive in the collection from John Sutton, who served with Markham in the Channel fleet and whose wife was close to Maria, are from after he made rear-admiral in April 1804.

The formation of the committee of the Naval Society in 1792 is helpful for understanding how Markham may have formed these connections, even before he joined the Admiralty in 1801. From 1792 Markham was a committee member for the Naval Society, or Naval Club of 1765, a subscription society that met every month and dined in a Covent Garden tavern in London.[149] Among those on the committee with Markham in 1793 were Captain John Dalrymple (promoted to admiral 1795), Admiral Sir Peter Parker, Admiral John Jervis (the future earl of St Vincent), Captain George Keith Elphinstone (admiral 1794) and Captain Edward Riou.[150] The committee had originally consisted of just three sea officers and a secretary, but upon his joining the committee in 1792 Markham introduced a scheme to use the surplus subscription fee, a guinea per year, to assist the widows and orphans of men killed in the service.[151] The committee increased to fourteen men to enforce this new measure and to collect the subscriptions from the 305 members of the society.

A common ground of *shared values* likely acted as an important factor in the selection of these committee members. The newer members supported Markham's scheme for the widows and orphans, which suggests they were selected, at least in part, because they shared his ideals. Certainly, a letter from Markham to Riou reveals that not all members of the society approved of Markham's plan. In the letter, Markham asked Riou to read out a speech in defence of his scheme, and to make a note of Admiral Mark Milbanke's

---

[149] Markham, *A Naval Career*, 93.

[150] NMM, RUSI/235/ER/4/4, Printed Letter to Subscribers, 20 March 1793. The committee also included: Richard Brathwaite, Richard Kingsmill, Charles Buckner, Skeffington Lutwidge, Francis John Hartwell, Harry Burrard and George Stewart, Lord Garlies.

[151] NMM, MRK/100/2/201, Markham to Navy Society, 3 April 1797.

FRIENDS AND FAMILY: MARKHAM'S NETWORK 81

reaction as 'he always hoped to be able to get at the money by a vote, to fill that insatiable paunch of his with champagne, and beef stakes fried with onions'.[152] There are no letters from Milbanke to Markham in the collection, even though Milbanke served as the port-admiral for Portsmouth when Markham was MP, which certainly reinforces the conclusion that he and Markham were not particularly close, perhaps specifically because they did not share common values.

Despite his lack of affection for some members, Markham's involvement in the Naval Society is useful in mapping his naval circle. During the period of peace and low employment until 1793, he potentially maintained as many connections through the Naval Society as when he was employed in active service. He may have forged or strengthened his connection to Jervis while they both served on the committee, which later proved profitable when he went to the West Indies with Jervis later that year as well as when Markham commissioned *Centaur* in 1796, and joined the Mediterranean fleet under Jervis in 1799, following him to the Channel fleet in February 1800 and of course to the Admiralty in 1801.[153] Equally, we can see his continued association with George Keith Elphinstone. There are over 200 letters from Keith in the collection. Many were to Markham in his capacity as Admiralty commissioner and relate to the organisation of appointments, stores and ships rather than the familiar exchange of sentiment and news. However, serving on the Naval Society committee together in 1793 reflects their continued connection outside their mutual service and that they shared at least one social circle.

The appointments Markham made to his commands between June 1793 and February 1801 also give an impression of his naval circle. He saw to his friends on the Naval Society committee when appointing officers to *Blonde* in 1793. He took on Frederik Hoffman as a midshipman, whose mother was a friend of Keith's.[154] He also obliged Sir Peter Parker, by appointing Joshua Behenna, listed in the muster book as having been appointed 'per order of Sir Peter Parker'.[155] Of course, Parker as admiral had technical prerogative over appointing lieutenants to Markham's ship. As we shall see in Chapters 3 and 4, the official use of patronage in some ways lessened the reciprocal obligation but did not remove it entirely. The previous chapter also showed how obliging requests from hierarchical seniors allowed for a measure of autonomy as cooperation built trust and obligation between officers. Markham accepted men from his other naval connections, including John Thomas Duckworth,

---

[152] NMM, RUSI/235/ER/4/4, Markham to Riou, 3 April 1798.

[153] Markham, *A Naval Career*, 173.

[154] A. Beckford-Bevan and H. B. Worlyche-Whitmore (eds.), *A Sailor for King George: The Journals of Captain Frederik Hoffman R.N. 1793–1814* (London, 1901), 1–2.

[155] TNA, ADM36/11389, HMS *Blonde*.

82 PATRONAGE AND THE BRITISH NAVY, 1775–1815

whom Maria referred to as having been particularly 'pleasant' to Markham, suggesting their close connection.[156] He took on Thomas Sargent as an acting-lieutenant of *Hannibal* per Duckworth's acting order on 31 May 1795.[157] He also obliged connections on his ships including obliging his carpenter on *Hannibal* by making John Webster, his relation and previous servant on the *Blonde*, a midshipman.[158]

Markham also used his naval network to place his protégés in more advantageous positions. When he joined *Blonde* in 1793 he had appointed William Durban, who had served as midshipman on *Sphinx*, as his second lieutenant.[159] In 1794 he managed to get William Durban appointed to *Barfleur*, a much larger ship and a better position for a well-connected lieutenant to rise in.[160] *Barfleur* was under Keith's command and although there is no explicit reference to the transfer being a favour between him and Markham, it is very likely to have been the case, especially as Markham had just taken Hoffman on as midshipman on *Blonde*. Certainly, Keith continued to look out for Durban and took him with him to *Monarch* in 1795 and wrote to Markham about him in 1804, which suggests that he saw him as a protégé of Markham's.[161] Durban also remained in correspondence with Markham, although did not often solicit him for favours.[162] His frequency of correspondence shown in Figure 2.2, however, reflects the longevity of his relationship to Markham and perhaps a stronger tie, if not an overly familiar one.

This was not necessarily the case for Markham's other protégés. William Croft, who joined *Centaur* in 1796, remained in correspondence throughout 1801 to 1807.[163] While a lieutenant, he often asked for Markham's continued interest and couched his letters in familiar terms. In one letter of thanks from 1804, he addressed Markham with the familiar 'My Dear Captain Markham'. He also wrote openly and even apologised for not stating his gratitude more formally, writing:

> I *am* so much over joyed at my fortune that I really cannot sufficiently collect myself to make you a suitable acknowledgement for so great a favour but from the length of our acquaintance I trust you have found my disposition sensible of obligation.[164]

[156] NMM, MRK/107/3/30, Maria to John, 15–16 March 1799.

[157] TNA, ADM36/13666, HMS *Hannibal*.

[158] Ibid.; TNA, ADM36/11389–90, HMS *Blonde*.

[159] TNA, ADM36/10595, HMS *Sphinx*, 28 June–3 October 1783.

[160] TNA, ADM36/11389, HMS *Blonde*, 1 July 1794.

[161] TNA, 36/11749, Muster Book: HMS *Monarch*, entered 23 March 1795; NMM, MRK/101/3/172, Keith to Markham, 8 April 1804.

[162] NMM, MRK/102/2/41–47, Durban to Markham, 14 March 1801–31 December 1806.

[163] NMM, MRK/103/1/42–45 and MRK/102/1/161–163, Croft to Markham, 5 July 1802–20 February 1807.

[164] Letter torn in places. NMM, MRK/103/1/45, Croft to Markham, 11 March 1804.

FRIENDS AND FAMILY: MARKHAM'S NETWORK   83

Henry Elton, a protégé from Markham's familial network (see Figure 2.1), also wrote to Markham in familiar and sentimental terms. In a letter in 1806 he wrote that Markham's kindness had 'resembled more the affection of a father than the approbation of a commanding officer'.[165] Elton did not write with the frequency of Durban or Croft so does not appear in Figure 2.2. This may partly be because he did not become a commander of a small ship, as Croft and Durban did, until 1814, and so he had far less to offer Markham in return for his repeated solicitations and corresponded less often with him in his Admiralty capacity. In many ways, Elton reflects how an applicant could be well-embedded within their patron's network and still not advance quickly in their career. As Gill argued, an officer needed more than just strong connections to further his career, he also needed to please his immediate superior officers with his good reputation and character.[166]

Certain connections from Markham's commands also remained strong connections in his naval circle. Thomas Richbell, whom we encountered earlier because of his visits to Maria, forged a close friendship with Markham but did not correspond frequently with him at the Admiralty. Similarly, Edward Riou appears to have forged a strong connection with his first lieutenant, Bendall Robert Littlehales, aboard the *Beaulieu* in 1794. Littlehales was then introduced to Markham's familiar circle, possibly leading to Markham recommending him to replace him in command of *Centaur* when he joined the Admiralty in February 1801.[167] Markham's brother William also appears to have been acquainted with Littlehales, as he mentioned to Markham in a letter that Littlehales had ill-advisedly brought one of Markham's protégés to London where he could get into trouble.[168] It is possible that Littlehales visited Maria and Markham's family with Riou in the late 1790s, and William perhaps made Littlehales's acquaintance in this period. This also suggests a more familiar tie with Littlehales. Certainly, of all Markham's correspondents below the rank of admiral, Littlehales was the most frequent writer. There are twenty-three letters to Markham from Littlehales in the collection. He passed on news of Markham's protégés and the state of *Centaur*.[169] He also arranged for the shipment of wine to Markham and passed on news of his family and compliments to Markham's extended familial network. Later in his career he also asked for Markham's influence with Thomas Grenville, the First Lord, in 1806.[170]

Figure 2.2 includes other connections from *Centaur* who remained in correspondence with Markham. Robinson Kittoe, Markham's purser from

---

[165] NMM, MRK/108/4/42, Elton to Markham 22 July 1806.

[166] Gill, *Naval Families*, 137.

[167] TNA, ADM 36/11919, HMS *Beaulieu*, August 1794–June 1795; ADM36/14168, HMS *Centaur*; NMM, MRK/102/4/26, Littlehales to Markham, 6 May 1801.

[168] NMM, MRK/107/4/8, William Markham to Markham, 9 August 1803.

[169] See NMM, MRK/102/4/25, Littlehales to Markham, 20 April 1801.

[170] NMM, MRK/102/4/41–42, Littlehales to Markham, 7 and 27 December 1806.

84 PATRONAGE AND THE BRITISH NAVY, 1775–1815

Centaur, remained a strong connection. There are fourteen letters from Kittoe in the collection from 1801 to 1809.[171] The surgeon Thomas Willes stayed in correspondence and requested Markham's assistance several times.[172] Walter Grossett who had been recommended to Markham by Riou also wrote to Markham asking for assistance.[173] Both Willes and Grossett were connected to others in Markham's network. The previous section has already explored the potential connection of Willes's wife to Maria in 1798. Grossett, as well as being connected to Markham's good friend Riou, was also the nephew of Lucy Kantzow, who applied on his behalf for Markham's continued interest in 1798.[174] Kittoe, however, had more correspondence with Markham and this perhaps reflects the fact that he was not so integrated into Markham's familial and familiar networks, but rather maintained the connection forged on *Centaur* directly by letter himself. Markham also seems to have assisted Kittoe more than either Grossett or Willes, which suggests that affectionate connection carefully maintained by letter could in certain cases outdo embedded familiar connection in gaining Markham's patronage.

There are certainly letters in the collection from Markham's former crew or messmates who were not frequent enough correspondents to be represented in Figure 2.2, nor did they appear in Maria and John's correspondence, suggesting that neither were they embedded in his social circle. There are three letters from Russel White, who was carpenter of *Perseus* and Markham's mentor and messmate in 1776.[175] William Trounsell, carpenter of *Centaur*, also wrote to Markham at the Admiralty, drawing on his more recent connection for assistance.[176] The wording of these letters suggests that there was more correspondence that has not survived and Markham's notes on the letters show that he was ready to oblige both men when opportunity arose, which reflects the strength of former ship-based connections unrepresented in Figure 2.2.

We could expect to see a correlation between high-frequency correspondence and Markham's distribution of patronage. In some cases of greater correspondence frequency, Markham certainly seems to have lent his assistance readily. James Saunders, a purser, wrote to Markham several times between 1801 and 1806. On two occasions Saunders wrote to request a move into a different ship, the first into *Dragon* and the second into *St George*. Markham

---

[171] NMM, MRK/102/3/90, MRK/104/2/6–10, MRK/104/5/4, MRK/105/11/12–14 and 24, MRK/105/12/7–8, Kittoe to Markham, 1801–[1809].

[172] NMM, MRK/104/3/59–61, MRK/105/8/5–6, Willes to Markham, 21 April 1802–27 July 1807.

[173] NMM, MRK/102/2/114–116, MRK/104/5/3, Grossett to Markham, 3 June 1803–13 February 1807.

[174] NMM, MRK/108/4/10, Kantzow to Markham, 31 September 1798.

[175] NMM, MRK/104/3/48–50, White to Markham, 29 April 1801–30 June 1802.

[176] NMM, MRK/104/3/18, Trounsell to Markham, 21 April 1801.

FRIENDS AND FAMILY: MARKHAM'S NETWORK   85

seems to have secured the moves because Saunders gained both appointments.[177] Saunders also arranged the transport of sherry for Markham in 1802 which suggests the strengthening of the connection.[178]

As Chapter 1 has shown, the transport of wine was a valuable method of maintaining distant connections. Gift-giving played an important role in eighteenth-century society in securing relationships which could be drawn on for patronage, similar to the familiar maintenance achieved by socialising in the same circle.[179] Saunders's transportation of the wine was an act of reciprocity for Markham's interest in his career. It may not have been equal in form but offering something in return for Markham's assistance strengthened connection where familiar maintenance was not available. Saunders's multiple requests and his reciprocal offers certainly suggest that high frequency of correspondence was associated with strengthening connection and that Markham assisted those who maintained their connection to him.

Captain Robert Corbet similarly secured Markham's attentions. He strengthened his connection by offering the vacancies on his sloop *Bittern* for Markham's patronage, which in terms of reciprocity set him above many other officers who were restricted to obliging their own followings, especially when vacancies for lieutenants were scarce. In one letter, Corbet passed on news of a midshipman Markham had placed on the *Bittern*, and asked whether he had meant this boy to fill the vacancy he had 'set aside' for Markham or if he had another in mind. Markham made a note on the reverse of the letter: 'I did not mean him to take more, but will perhaps ... ask him to take another.'[180] Whether Corbet intended to or not, his willingness to oblige Markham made him a valuable connection whom Markham was readier to assist in return.

Frequency of correspondence is a useful tool to understand Markham's naval circle and his distribution of patronage within it, because, in many cases, it does not illustrate Markham's strongest connections but rather those who had most cause to write. Of course, considering the frequency of correspondence alongside Markham's familial and familiar networks reveals the overlap with his more intimate circles. Although his close connections such as Riou or Richbell are not well represented in Figure 2.2, others such as Littlehales are. Those who served alongside Markham or under his command on *Blonde*, *Hannibal* and *Centaur* were also frequent correspondents. Figure 2.2 represents Markham's naval circle in its broadest sense including those environmentally and occupationally associated with him, not just the intimate

---

[177] NMM, MRK/104/2/82, Saunders to Markham, 22 October 1801; MRK/104/2/84, Saunders to Markham, 9 June 1803; TNA, ADM 36/15344, HMS *Dragon*, August 1801–June 1802; ADM 36/16530, HMS *St George*, December 1804–June 1805.

[178] NMM, MRK/104/2/54, Saunders to Markham, 29 November 1802.

[179] Ben-Amos, *Culture of Giving*, 80–81.

[180] NMM, MRK/102/1/152, Corbet to Markham, 6 June 1802.

86 PATRONAGE AND THE BRITISH NAVY, 1775–1815

naval connections and 'brother officers' who may have otherwise formed the centre of his naval community.[181] But emotional or social proximity does not seem to have consistently affected Markham's distribution of patronage within his network. Markham's family and the friends of his social circle certainly accounted for part of Markham's distribution of patronage, but these peripheral, naval connections made up a far larger and more diverse section, as we shall see in the following chapter.

Conclusion

Mapping Markham's familial, familiar and naval correspondence networks illustrates the breadth of connections who could draw on his patronage but also the methods used to strengthen and secure their connection to him. Granovetter's factors of connection, emotional intensity, reciprocity and longevity, each allowed an applicant access to Markham's patronage.[182] Intimate friendship strengthened a tie and granted a secure and unpressurised form of patronage support that is reflected in the requests from Markham's family and his father's friends' support of his early career. Reciprocity from naval connections in the form of offering vacancies and transporting wine also strengthened connections and secured Markham's assistance. The subtleties of Markham's familiar networks surrounding Maria in London also reflect the importance of reciprocity. Lady Jane Orde approached Maria to renew her husband's connection to Markham, but Maria also benefited by surrounding herself with respectable connections who extended her social circle and provided more support for Markham, while also protecting her from undesirable connections. Markham's network shaped his patronage because it determined who could contact him but also who he was obliged to assist because of their previous assistance to him, their position in society or their connection to his other friends.

Patronage, however, also shaped Markham's network. Many of those who approached Maria did so because it strengthened their connection to Markham and gave access to his patronage. Similarly, every one of his high-frequency naval correspondents requested his assistance. Those who made the most requests also ensured their connection to Markham through reciprocity or by their familiar connection to Maria and his social circle.

Patronage was not only a tool that connections utilised in the pursuit of promotion, advancement and position; it was also a tool of social maintenance. It bound connections together through mutual obligation and facilitated the opening of new or lapsed acquaintance. The composition of an individual's intimate circle certainly affected who asked them for patronage

[181] Gill, *Naval Families*, 139–144.
[182] Granovetter, 'Strength of Weak Ties', 1362.

and the construction of intimate circles such as family and intimate friends was motivated primarily by other factors such as physical proximity and shared values. However, patronage as social necessity motivated the construction of wider networks of peripheral ties who had as great a claim to Markham's patronage as his intimate connections.

3

Followers and Strangers: Markham's Admiralty Correspondents

> … as I know these appointments are generally left to some one of the Lords to arrange, and you are the only one with whom I have any old acquaintance, the plague of my application (the advantage attending acquaintance with any of those 560 mendicants called Post Captains) falls to your lot
>
> Captain Charles Herbert to Markham, c.2 July 1803[1]

Looking at Markham's intimate connections is just one way to understand his patronage. In his position as a lord of the Admiralty, Markham was solicited by hundreds of applicants, not least some of the 560 begging post-captains, referred to somewhat ironically by Captain Herbert in the above quote, who plagued him with their applications through virtue of his being their only 'acquaintance' on the board. Certainly, plenty of those who wrote to Markham while he served at the Admiralty were well embedded in his network, via their connection to his family or social circle. However, from a network perspective many of Markham's correspondents who applied for his patronage could be considered to be 'weaker ties'. They were not necessarily embedded in his network, or if they were, it was via myriad weaker links.

Multiple types of connection carried weight in naval patronage. An individual's network, who they knew, who they were related to and their social position, was a vital part of accessing patronage. But it was not the only factor that determined the quality of an individual's connection with their patron or that, in turn, influenced the bestowal of favour. Similarly, the influence of *network* in patronage should not be read as analogous to the privilege those with connections among the highest levels of society and government are sometimes assumed to have enjoyed.[2] The social elite and 'well-connected' did not necessarily fare better in individual patronage exchanges, especially if they misjudged the tangled web of priorities, fashions and expectations that underpinned them. Equally, those from lower down the social scale were not

---

[1] NMM, MRK/102/3/30, Charles Herbert to Markham [postmark 2 July 1803].
[2] Lewis, *A Social History of the Navy*, 202.

excluded from Markham's assistance just because they did not maintain their connection to him by having tea with his wife or being friends with his father.

The above quote is taken from a letter written to Markham by Captain Charles Herbert in July 1803 asking for two lieutenants to be appointed to his ship *Uranie*. It incidentally and evocatively captured some of the complex interplay of factors which surrounded the role of connection in naval patronage. He opened his letter by apologising for taking the liberty of directly writing to Markham when he was uncertain if it was a subject 'in the department of the Admiralty business' with which Markham concerned himself. He then emphasised that Markham was the only member of the board with whom he had 'any old acquaintance' whilst simultaneously acknowledging the volume of applications which Markham must receive in his position. In doing so, Herbert navigated the administrative necessity of writing to Markham in his professional capacity as a lord of the Admiralty, while also drawing on his existing relationship to act as excuse, and potentially surety, of his request.

Later in the letter, Herbert shared his concerns for his own career prospects. He complained that although he had commanded frigates for the last seven years, he had never 'had the chances of the service as others have', namely, cruises where he could hope to capture prizes and consequently boost his reputation in the navy. To this, he added: 'as I have no interest, perhaps never shall have'. Perhaps to avoid coming across as overly entitled or self-pitying, he then finished his letter by again apologising: 'but on these scores you probably can only recommend patience therefore with apologies for having spun out a letter so long which was only meant when began to trouble you with a simple request'.

From our perspective, it seems unlikely that Herbert had 'no interest'. He was the son of an earl and both he and his family were politically active. He also had a level of connection with Markham, as a member of the board of Admiralty, that prompted him to address him as 'Dear Sir' and speak fairly candidly about his hopes for profitable employment and the burdensome nature of the 'Admiralty business' in which Markham was involved.[3] A year earlier, he had perhaps damaged his 'interest' when ill health prompted him to leave his command without seeking official permission from the Admiralty, thereby going directly against St Vincent's wishes and earning the First Lord's displeasure. However, even this damage did not prevent his being given the command of another frigate in 1803, at a time when other officers were being turned away.[4] Furthermore, despite having 'no interest', Herbert was also

[3] R. Thorne (ed.), *The History of Parliament: the House of Commons 1790–1820* (1986), http://www.historyofparliamentonline.org/volume/1790-1820/member/herbert-hon-charles-1774-1808

[4] *The Letters of Admiral of the Fleet The Earl of St. Vincent whilst First Lord of the Admiralty, 1801–1804*, ed. David Bonner Smith, vol. 1 (Navy Records Society,

90   PATRONAGE AND THE BRITISH NAVY, 1775–1815

successful in his request for lieutenants, at least for one of them.[5] It is likely that despite Herbert's claims, Markham was just one of many potential patrons or brokers that he had access to. The same was also true of many of those who solicited Markham's favour at the Admiralty.

'Interest' was a term that seemed to carry both a very specific meaning in the eighteenth-century navy, while also remaining fairly vague and flexible. On the one hand, many writers used it to refer to the direct intervention of brokers, who had social or political power they could lever in a patronage exchange on the applicant's behalf. On the other, many used 'interest' to more widely refer to the general weight of connections within an individual's network, or rather the weight of obligations attached to connections within that network, that acted implicitly as levers within an exchange. Network certainly facilitated access to patronage, and the weight of connections could boost or strengthen patronage relationships, both directly and implicitly, through this amorphous idea of 'interest'. But 'interest' was not synonymous with connection. Nor should we take it as an alternative term for patronage as a whole. Because, as we will see, despite the anxieties voiced here so explicitly by Captain Herbert, many officers lacked the 'interest' they felt was required in their patronage dealings with the Admiralty. And yet, many were still successful.

This chapter drills down into Markham's correspondence from the time he served as lord of the Admiralty between 1801 and 1807, to understand why this was. Looking at Markham in his role as patron, or perhaps more accurately, as a broker of Admiralty patronage, reveals a more complex picture than the one of direct reciprocity and network obligation we have encountered so far. It also exposes the strange place patronage occupied between the formal and informal, the explicit and implicit, the administrative and personal.

Markham's Correspondents

The collection of Markham's correspondence housed in the Caird Library at the National Maritime Museum, Greenwich, contains over 4,000 letters written to him during the years he served as a lord of the Admiralty. Letters from admirals alone account for 1,487 of these. Compared to the letters from the ranks of post-captain and below, the admirals' correspondence contains a much higher proportion of logistical and strategic communications interspersed with both notices of appointments made using the admiral's prerogative as fleet or station commander-in-chief, as well as scattered recommendations of

---

1927), 361; Rif Winfield, *British Warships in the Age of Sail, 1793–1817* (Barnsley: Pen and Sword Books, 2014), 246.

5   TNA, PROB 11/1493/281 Will of Meabron otherwise Meaban Holmes, formerly First Lieutenant belonging to His Majesty's Ship Amelia but late First Lieutenant belonging to His Majesty's Ship Uranie 28 February 1809.

individuals to Markham's favour. Chapter 1 has already touched on some of the nuances of station patronage compared to the kind managed centrally at the Admiralty. We have also seen the prominence of admirals among Markham's most frequent correspondents in Chapter 2. Other studies have also dealt well with the particular nature and pressures of admirals' patronage.[6] This chapter focuses instead on the part of the collection containing letters from correspondents below the rank of admiral as well as members of the public, in which have survived the majority of Markham's patronage dealings in his position at the Admiralty.

Within this part of the collection there are 1,601 letters representing 657 individual correspondents. Trying to build a relational database of Markham's applicant network based on his correspondence is something of a thankless task or at least one that was beyond the scope of this study. Social network mapping tools can reveal clusters and trends in connection, and can be useful in some cases to understand the overall picture of an individual's correspondence network. However, the difficulty we face with Markham's collection is one created particularly by his role as an Admiralty patron. Of the 657 identifiable correspondents who wrote to Markham at the time he served as a lord of the Admiralty, 311 have only one surviving letter in the collection. Many of these offer glimpses at the nature of their relationship with him, as a patron, friend or colleague. Some even offer some clues to their other connections and, by extension, their position within both Markham's network and their own networks that threaded through the navy and wider society. However, the majority do not provide enough detail to make it possible to reconstruct these networks reliably.

It is possible, however, to reveal broader trends in the collection by grouping the correspondence and correspondents by certain characteristics. Some of these trends are not at all unexpected. For instance, if we split the correspondents broadly along the lines of 'Naval' and 'Non-Naval', then requests from naval connections by far dominated, with 469 correspondents writing 1,175 of the letters. In this instance, 'Naval' includes those on active service, the retired or unemployed, as well as immediate female relations such as wives and sisters whom we could consider 'naval women'.[7] 'Non-Naval' includes other extended family members of naval personnel, political connections, members of wider government and the military, as well as Markham's extended network of family friends.

It may seem unsurprising that this part of Markham's correspondence was dominated by naval connections. But in many ways, it flies in the face of ideas laid down by outspoken critics of the influence of nobility and politics on naval patronage in this period. St Vincent, for instance, was extremely vocal in

[6] Morrow, *British Flag Officers*.
[7] Lincoln, *Naval Wives*; Gill, *Naval Families*.

his disapproval of what he saw as the abuse of patronage from this section of society. In a letter to George III, St Vincent expressed his deep concerns that the navy was 'so overrun by the younger branches of nobility, and the sons of Members of Parliament' who 'so swallow up all the patronage, and so choke the channel to promotion, that the son of an old officer, however meritorious *both* of their services may have been, has little or no chance of getting on'.[8]

Recent demographic studies of officers' backgrounds have already challenged this idea. Evan Wilson has demonstrated with his statistical analysis of commissioned officers' careers that the sons of 'nobility' did not fare better in their promotion to post-captain than their peers from other social backgrounds. In fact, they were about as successful as the officers who came from 'Business and Commercial' backgrounds, which largely included the sons of merchants and tradesmen. Both categories were comparatively less successful than the sons of 'Landed Gentry' and 'Professional Men', the category that included the sons of the old officers whom St Vincent was so concerned about.[9] By dividing this section of Markham's correspondents by their professional and social rank, we can see a similar trend.

Although St Vincent may have felt beset by the family and friends of nobility and MPs, if anything, Markham was beset by post-captains. Far more post-captains than any other category wrote to Markham, whereas the titled and MPs made up a comparatively very small proportion of his correspondents. Post-captains made up nearly a third of correspondents in this part of the collection. Lieutenants and commanders were the next highest category, followed by the broad category of 'civilians' which includes all of those non-naval correspondents who are not readily identifiable as either someone with a title, a profession (such as magistrate, doctor or reverend), a position as MP or in local politics (such as mayor, alderman, or town clerk), or in government. It included members of the landed gentry or upper merchant classes, who readily related to Markham and his family in his familiar circles, as well as those further down the social scale such as Mary Higg, who ran a lodging house on Plymouth dock.

St Vincent's perception of naval patronage being 'choked' by the sons of nobility and members of parliament probably had much more to do with the way those from the highest levels of society approached their role as brokers for their friends and relations, than a reality where connection to the social elite was the defining characteristic of naval patronage. In his position as both First Lord and an earl, St Vincent certainly received the majority of the requests from the weightier, socially powerful connections and 'friends' of

---

8 Quoted in Rodger, *Command of the Ocean*, 513; Jedediah Stevens Tucker, *Memoirs of Admiral the Right Hon. The Earl of St Vincent* (London, 1844), vol. II, 267.

9 Wilson, *British Naval Officers*, 109–110.

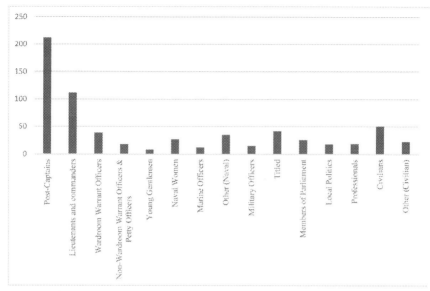

Figure 3.1 Markham's correspondents grouped by their rating, social rank and position. Source: Markham's Correspondents Database.

government, which were difficult to ignore; a pressure which we will explore more thoroughly in the following chapter. Among Markham's correspondence, though, they are under-represented. Even if we look at the distribution of letters across these groupings, post-captains still represented the greatest overall amount of correspondence. A greater proportion of these post-captains also wrote to Markham multiple times, with almost a fifth of individual post-captains having more than five letters surviving in the collection, compared to less than a tenth of titled correspondents and no MPs.

Of course, geography had an influence here. As we saw in Chapter 1, the social elite or London-based civilians and professionals had the opportunity to solicit Markham in person at the Admiralty itself. Whereas most naval connections relied heavily on letters to conduct their patronage through virtue of being on active service at sea or, as in the case of naval women, based in port-towns away from London. It therefore makes sense for naval groupings such as post-captains to have dominated his patronage correspondence. It is also important to recognise the pivotal time that Markham served at the Admiralty in terms of the transformation of the navy's administration that had led to the increasingly centralised nature of appointments and patronage control. There are more letters from post-captains in this part of the collection simply because much of their correspondence was taken up with the routine business of filling the vacancies on their ships and recommending those in their command to positions elsewhere.

94 PATRONAGE AND THE BRITISH NAVY, 1775–1815

These routine requests perhaps do not fit so easily within the conception of patronage as a reciprocal system of favours and obligation. On the surface, they appear to draw very little on the sorts of social ties and connection maintenance described in Chapters 1 and 2. However, many factors came into play in Markham's response to routine appointment requests that brought them within the complex web of expectation and connection that defined patronage. Although many of the post-captains' requests were routine, their applications still rested on the nature of their connection with Markham. This was itself informed by several factors including their position within his wider network, their social position and power, their ability to reciprocate his support in other arenas such as politics, as well as a larger set of hard to define motivations such as Markham's sense of duty and charity to those who needed his support.

This implicit influence is significant when we consider the apparent gap in the volume of post-captain letters compared to non-naval titled and MPs. The gap appears drastic when we categorise the correspondents purely by their professional and social rank. However, the categories of MP, titled and post-captain were not mutually exclusive. There were officers within the large post-captains group who came from the nobility or who stood as members of parliament. For instance, Captain Charles Herbert, whom we met at the beginning of this chapter, was a post-captain, an MP and the son of an earl. Here he is categorised simply as a post-captain.

Fourteen of the post-captains in this part of the collection were either the sons of nobility, and therefore could be styled 'Honourable', or they had inherited titles themselves.[10] Another two were the illegitimate sons of earls. Therefore, 7.5 per cent of Markham's post-captain correspondents were titled or the sons of nobility, approximately twice the proportion that Wilson found made it to the rank of post-captain in his randomised demographic study of officers' careers. The prevalence of MPs is slightly more difficult to quantify, partly because of the differences in the lengths of time members retained their seats. However, at least five held their seats from 1802 to beyond 1807 when Markham left the Admiralty, such as Edward Buller, who served as MP for Looes 1802–1820. Another eight captains had a significant political dimension to their correspondence with Markham even if they did not hold a parliamentary seat during this time, such as William Lukin who offered Markham his political support in Norfolk.[11] Beyond this number, there were also those who were politically connected within their immediate familial network, such as Charles Ryder, whose father-in-law was William Baker, MP for Hampshire.[12] The key point here is that even if they did not leverage the

---

[10] At least another twenty were also the sons of baronets and so sat at the upper end of the landed gentry.

[11] NMM, MRK/104/5/11, William Lukin to Markham, 2 March 1806.

[12] NMM, MRK/102/5/63–67, Charles Ryder to Markham, 3 May 1802– 27 October

weight of their connections and position in the letters to Markham directly, the influence was implicit, in both how they approached Markham and how he dealt with their requests.

We should not, therefore, underestimate the possible influence of these socially elite or politically well-connected officers. However, we should also not be too quick to assume that they were guaranteed preference. Certainly, the handful of titled officers accounted for 12.5 per cent of post-captain letters to Markham, which suggests that they exerted some influence with him. However, almost half of these were from two of his most frequent correspondents: his intimate friend Lord Mark Kerr, and Robert Stopford, who wrote to Markham frequently on political matters to do with Yarmouth elections.[13] In comparison, most of Markham's titled post-captain correspondents wrote to him fairly infrequently. This may have been because, despite how 'friendless' Charles Herbert presented himself as being, most socially elite officers made use of networks that would allow them to put their requests directly to the First Lord himself. This was a trend that almost certainly contributed to St Vincent's feeling of being hounded by the sons of nobility. To Markham, they mostly made brokered requests, rather than requests for themselves as the recipient of his favour. Interestingly, the requests they made were also predominantly routine requests for the appointment of officers or assistance of warrant officers like gunners or boatswains, rather than requests on behalf of their relations.

Brokers: Relationships, Routine and Reputation

This is an important point when we look at the distribution of correspondents across the collection who made requests primarily for themselves as recipients compared to those who acted as brokers, as well as the patterns that emerge when we look at the relationship between brokers and those they recommended. Unsurprisingly, the majority of the titled, political, professional and other civilian correspondents from outside the navy only made requests on behalf of others and so can be classed as brokers. A slightly greater proportion of naval women wrote to Markham with requests for themselves, but otherwise they follow a similar trend, with sixteen of the twenty-two correspondents only ever writing on behalf of their husband, brother or son serving in the navy.

The naval correspondents, however, generally show the opposite trend. The ranks below post-captain mostly wrote to Markham as recipients, without brokering any other requests. Lieutenants and commanders were the largest in

---

1806; MRK/104/1/15, William Baker to Markham, 7 April 1806; Portsmouth History Centre, CHU 3/1D/9 Charles Ryder married Jane Baker 19 September 1799, witnessed by Wm Baker jnr and Susana Peakes.

[13] NMM, MRK/108/2/1–18, Mark Kerr to Markham; MRK/102/5/103–122, Robert Stopford to Markham, 31 May 1803–29 June 1807.

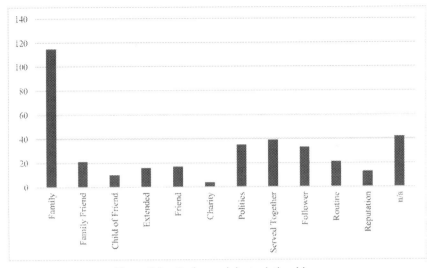

Figure 3.2   Broker-recipient relationships.
Source: Markham's Correspondents Database.

this category with 91 out of 112 correspondents only ever writing to Markham directly for his support or appointments for themselves. Warrant and petty officers had a similar distribution, with roughly 5–6 per cent of writers acting solely as brokers, 17–19 per cent writing a mixture of requests and 75–76 per cent only ever making requests for themselves as the recipient. On the other hand, only fifty-six, or just under a third of post-captains, wrote solely as recipients, whereas sixty only ever made brokered requests and a further seventy-three made a mixture of brokered and personal requests. The importance of captains in navigating the strange space between the personal and the impersonal in their routine requests for lieutenants to fill their commands accounts for some of this greater proportion of brokered requests, but not all.

Figure 3.2 shows the relationships that the 341 named individuals from these brokered requests had with their brokers. Just over a tenth of all relationships here defied categorisation or are not readily identifiable from the information included in the letters or biographical details of the applicant and broker (marked as n/a in Figure 3.2). When we look at the group of brokered candidates as a whole, the most common type of relationship was a familial one, with 115 recipients being recommended to Markham by a relation. This broad trend supports the general view of patronage in this period. As we saw in Chapter 2, family played an important role in the eighteenth-century networks of employment and support. Markham's own family was crucial in his career. Parental brokers held a unique position in their bargaining power, because of the social expectation that family members had a duty to provide

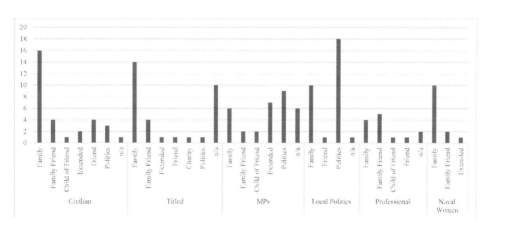

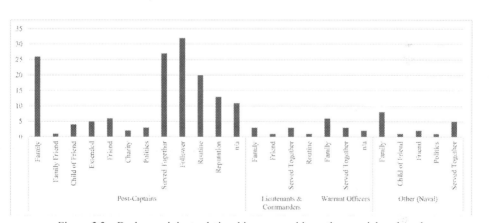

Figure 3.3 Broker-recipient relationships grouped by rating, social rank and position of the broker. Source: Markham's Correspondents Database.

for their relations and immediate dependants with their patronage support.[14] Chapter 5 looks at the aspects of this in more detail.

When we break down the relationships by the rank of the broker, a slightly different picture emerges (Figure 3.3). Naval women, the titled and the broader category of civilians all still predominantly brokered applications on behalf of their relations. Those within the 'professional' category, however, made more applications on behalf of family friends or the children of their friends, than their own family members.[15] Those tagged as 'local politics', which included Markham's constituents in Portsmouth and members of the town's political corporation, made a high number of requests on behalf of family members, which we will consider in more depth in the following chapter. However, the majority of their requests, usually from the members of the corporation itself, were on behalf of those connected to them more broadly through the town's local politics. Similarly, despite St Vincent's claims about being plagued by the sons of MPs, most of the identifiable relationships MPs had with those they recommended were political. Indeed, roughly only a fifth of MPs' requests were on behalf of family members, with the greater majority made on behalf of political connections such as constituents, or connections from their extended networks including family friends and their children.

There are of course inevitable difficulties in categorising these sorts of relationships in such simplistic terms but, because of the nature of some of the overtly political relationships Markham had with his correspondents, some were quite explicit in their reasons for recommending someone to his attention. For example, Jervoise Clarke Jervoise, MP for Yarmouth between 1801 and 1808, wrote to request a promotion for a Lieutenant Richard Power whom he described as: 'A friend of mine whose connections are good and at my request came and voted for the returned members for Han[ts], hath desired me to serve him to be made a Master and Commander.'[16]

There are 148 named individuals recommended by captains in the collection, accounting for 150 of the relationships depicted here. The majority of these relationships were broadly service-based. Like the other categories, post-captains made a high proportion of requests on behalf of family members, particularly sons, but they made slightly more on behalf of candidates with whom they had previously or were currently serving and an even greater number on behalf of those whom we could consider to be their followers. The distinction between the 'served together' and 'follower' categories is somewhat subjective. Relationships categorised here as 'follower' were those

---

[14] Ben-Amos, *Culture of Giving*, 197–199.

[15] This category included bishops and reverends as well as doctors at university within Markham's extended familial and Christ Church network (e.g. Bishop of Durham).

[16] NMM, MRK/104/1/189, Jervoise Clarke Jervoise to Markham, 30 November 1806.

that showed evidence in the broker's letter or in the candidate's career history of a prolonged connection between the two, such as the candidate having followed their broker between commands, or the broker showing repeated interest in the candidate's success. Those simply marked as 'served together' were a mixture of those who had served with their broker as equals such as shipmates or messmates, directly under his command but not to the extent of following directly from ship to ship, or those for whom there is not enough evidence to establish a relationship beyond the captain mentioning in the letter that the candidate had previously served, or was currently serving, with him. As such, both types of relationship reflected a strong basis in the service.

However, as we saw in the previous chapter, the reasons why an officer took someone on as a follower were varied. Certainly, some 'follower' relationships were born of shared service and having impressed the broker while under his command. But other followers came as favours to friends within and without the service, as well as from their extended familial networks.[17] There was also a strong familial aspect to followings, with many fathers taking their sons and immediate young relations on board their own ships.[18] Therefore, many of those that appear in the 'family' category could also appear in the 'follower' category, although the distinction between familial and non-familial followers is worth preserving for our purposes here.

With the caveat that it is not feasible to try to establish the exact nature of each follower's relationship with their broker, the dominance of service-based relationships in the post-captain brokered requests reflects something of the norms of naval patronage and, by extension, the expectations that governed the manner and style of requests and Markham's response to them. If we assume that the same kinds of connection were involved in the creation of these follower relationships as we have already seen existed between Markham and his followers, then it is striking how few repeated requests there are for the named candidates in this part of the collection from their family or political connections. This suggests that either captains were self-motivated to recommend their followers, without the constant solicitation of whatever initial connection had forged the relationship, if one existed beyond simply shared service; or that these connections solicited captains to make the applications on their behalf directly to Markham, rather than approaching him themselves. Either option suggests that captains' requests were the preferred form of recommendation, both by applicants and by Admiralty patrons, like Markham.

---

[17] Within the constraints of this project it has also proved easier to trace the careers of lieutenants than marines or warrant officers, meaning that, undoubtedly, some of those within the 'served together' or 'n/a' category could also be categorised more suitably as 'follower'.

[18] Wilson, *British Naval Officers*, 14, 85; Gill, *Naval Families*, 87–91.

100   PATRONAGE AND THE BRITISH NAVY, 1775–1815

This apparent preference for service-based recommendations was likely partly motivated by the strange place that officer appointments occupied between administration and personal favour at this time. Although technically anyone serving or connected to the navy had licence to write to Markham in his role at the Admiralty, captains had even more reason to do so for the practical need of requesting officers to fill the vacancies on board their ships. A captain's request, therefore, could come across as less demanding, because of the Admiralty's ability to deny it on the impersonal grounds of the constraints or the good of the service. No small point, in a time where the centralisation of appointments had caused officers like Markham to be inundated with requests from all sides.

The preference for service-based recommendations is also evident in the next highest categories of captain-brokered relationships: 'routine' and 'reputation'. Relationships marked as 'routine' here were those with very little other information about the connection between the broker and candidate other than the request, usually for a lieutenant but also commonly for a warrant officer, to fill a vacancy directly on board the broker's own ship. This category in itself is not representative of the total number of this type of request. Some of those within the other categories, particularly 'follower', also appeared in these 'routine' requests, but the broker either made it clear to Markham that they were his follower and therefore his preferred candidate, or he also made other applications for them at different times which allows us to define the relationship in some other way.

The relationships marked as 'reputation' were requests where it was clear from the letter that the captain did not personally know the candidate he recommended, but that he had heard good things about them. For example, Robert Stopford, in writing to Markham to try to change one of his current lieutenants, first asked if either Markham or his fellow Admiralty lord, Thomas Troubridge, had anyone he could exchange him with, and, if not, he requested Lieutenant George Hewson: 'I do not know him personally but the recommendation I have had of him warrants me in wishing his appointment'.[19] Many of those in the 'routine' category may have been recommended because of their reputation, and presumably some of those marked as 'n/a', for whom it is not possible to establish the nature of the relationship between broker and candidate.

These requests reveal the results of recommendations, if not the actual network, that occurred between captains as well as others whose recommendation of technical skill and character could be trusted (in other words, not family or political connections). It is likely that some of the relationships in the smaller categories such as 'extended' or 'child of friend' were similar

---

[19] NMM, MRK/102/5/105, Robert Stopford to Markham, 27 June 1803.

in the sense that the broker made an application on behalf of someone he did not personally know. The relationships marked as 'extended' included requests made on behalf of candidates who were the followers of others in the broker's network or through other convoluted chains of recommendation. Similarly, brokers who recommended a 'family friend' and 'child of friend' did not always know them directly. However, these recommendations were strengthened by the personal connection of the familial or follower relationship higher up the chain, meaning they carried a different weight than simply the candidate's good 'reputation' to bolster a request.

The 'routine' and 'reputation' relationships highlight the more impersonal side of naval patronage that is sometimes difficult to grasp. Combined together, these categories accounted for more relationships than 'followers', which perhaps more accurately reflects the prominence of requests where the nature of the broker's connection to their candidate was not clear or absent entirely. Alongside the more impersonal style that was often present in the applications on behalf of those whose primary connection to their broker was that they had 'served together', these relationships give an overall impression of the significance of merit- and obligation-based service recommendations above all other kinds from post-captains. In contrast, familial relationships were proportionally much more common in the comparatively much smaller number of brokered requests from lieutenants and commanders as well as wardroom and non-wardroom warrant officers.

In this context, it is striking that the handful of titled post-captains, like Charles Herbert, made very few requests for themselves and even fewer on behalf of family members. Instead, they mostly made requests on behalf of their followers or routine requests for lieutenants or warrant officers. Even Robert Stopford, who spoke at length with Markham in his letters about his political concerns in Yarmouth and Ipswich, made primarily routine requests for lieutenants to fill the vacancies on his ship. This may partly have been because the political nature of his interest in them was implicit and he did not feel the need to spell it out to Markham. But it is possible he found that this style of politically motivated recommendation did not succeed, at least in filling the positions on board his own ship.[20] Or perhaps he drew more on his service connections to find lieutenants to recommend to the vacancies because the uncertainty of whether his request would be obliged was too risky for his political connections to withstand, a point which we will explore

---

[20] He only made two explicitly politically motivated requests: one on behalf of a lieutenant to secure a position on a prison ship where he could still be involved in the Ipswich election in which Stopford was hoping to stand, and another for the discharge of a seaman whose connections seemed to command a lot of votes. NMM, MRK/102/5/109, Stopford to Markham [undated]; MRK/102/5/113, Stopford to Markham [postmark: 9 August 1806].

102   PATRONAGE AND THE BRITISH NAVY, 1775–1815

more in the following chapter. Either way, Stopford couched his requests in the very simple, impersonal style of routine requests, which made it appear as though his position as a politically active son of an earl had very little to do with his naval patronage.

Equally, Charles Herbert, who had made it so clear to Markham that he felt he had 'no interest', made requests only on behalf of his followers, one of whom was the son of a retired purser who had served with him for a long time.[21] In light of St Vincent's vocal disapproval of the disproportionate influence he ascribed MPs and the nobility, it was likely no coincidence that those who we would assume had plenty of 'interest' styled themselves firmly in the contexts of their service-based relationships. Herbert may have had these defining characteristics, but he couched his patronage communications with Markham firmly in the context of obligation to the service, which suggests *this* was what he felt, or perhaps wanted Markham to feel, was the primary characteristic of their connection.

The lack of personal information about the candidates in many of the letters from post-captains certainly gives the impression that the normal requirement for personal connection that underpinned preferment was not so important in naval patronage. However, there is a need for caution in understanding these more impersonal requests. If it was so usual to write to a lord of the Admiralty to arrange the routine appointment of commissioned and warrant officers to ships, then we would expect to see more brokered requests from the thirty-five commanders among Markham's correspondents. Instead, Markham's commander correspondents overwhelmingly made applications only for themselves as the recipients. Those that did make brokered applications mainly did so on behalf of their sons or warrant and commissioned officers they had served with and with whom they had strong relationships or charitable reasons to recommend them.

Alexander Saunderson Burrowes, for instance, asked that his old shipmate Lieutenant Stephen Perdriau be appointed to his new command *Pylades* in place of his current lieutenant who had requested to be superseded for family reasons.[22] Thomas Gordon Caulfield, commander of *Aurora*, made a request for a less active position for his purser, 'a worthy good man who has been a long time in the service' and who was now too infirm to go to sea again. He wrote that

> if it comes in your way and you could with Convenience to yourself assist him it would be doing a truely meritorious deed which would give a competency for Life to an honest deserving Old Man, whose youth has been spent in the service of his country.[23]

[21] NMM, MRK/102/3/29, Charles Herbert to Markham, 29 March [1801].
[22] NMM, MRK/102/1/126, Burrowes to Markham, 25 September [1803].
[23] NMM, MRK/102/1/133, Caulfield to Markham, 24 March 1801.

MARKHAM'S ADMIRALTY CORRESPONDENTS 103

The one request categorised here as routine, for lack of any other information to define it, was from Donald McLeod, commanding *Sulphur*, who requested the removal of his current gunner to a less active ship, and asked for a 'Mr Taylor', who was on the spot, to replace him.[24] Interestingly, the one request on behalf of a friend came from John Astley Bennet, who was not only firmly connected to Markham as one of his followers, but was also the son of an earl. However, he went to some pains to carefully explain that he made the recommendation based on his own friendship with the candidate as well as with his patron, and also finished his letter with a strong emphasis on merit: 'But I should not have presumed to offer him to your notice was not I satisfied that Every one who knows him will bear testimony to his being one of the best officers of his rank.'[25]

The impersonal styles of request were not without risk, despite the apparent distance between the broker and candidate that the lack of personal information in the letters suggests was present. They also did not operate entirely outside the expected conventions of patronage. In fact, Markham's response to some brokered applications suggests that, despite an apparent emphasis placed on the more impersonal style of recommendation, he still expected a level of personal connection to exist between the broker and the person he recommended. Failing that, he expected the broker to be aware that by requesting an officer to fill a vacancy in his ship, he took on the role of broker and the consequent responsibility for protecting his candidate's reputation, as well as his own.

In 1801, soon after coming to the board, Markham replied to a request from Captain Peter Turner Bover chastising him for having made an application on behalf of a lieutenant seemingly without his knowledge. Bover had written on 16 May about one of his current lieutenants wishing to be superseded: 'I shall therefore esteem it a particular favor, if you would be good enough to appoint Lieut Wm Hellard to the Blenheim in Mr Fulton's vacancy'.[26] Markham, and by extension the Admiralty, approved Bover's request and sent Hellard orders accordingly. However, Hellard was not in a position to take up the appointment and was forced to turn it down in a public letter to the Admiralty. Markham made a note on Bover's original letter of the reply he sent:

> When you requested my assistance in the appointment of Lieut Hellard to the Blenheim I took it for granted that you had this officers consent to your application, but I cannot sufficiently express my surprise at reading a public letter from him this morning desiring leave to decline employment. The censure to which you have exposed this officer from the Board needs no comment to point out the impropriety of the proceeding.[27]

---

24 NMM, MRK/102/4/76, Donald McLeod to Markham, 6 October [no year].
25 NMM, MRK/102/1/45, Bennet to Markham, 26 August 1803.
26 NMM, MRK/102/1/80, Peter Turner Bover to Markham, 16 May 1801.
27 NMM, MRK/102/1/80, Markham reply, 20 May 1801.

104   PATRONAGE AND THE BRITISH NAVY, 1775–1815

The problem here, rather than the lack of a personal connection exactly, was more likely that the language Bover used made it sound like Hellard was a close connection of his, which misrepresented the nature of their relationship and therefore the level of priority that Markham should give to his recommendation.

Certainly, as with the 'reputation' category, it was not unusual for captains to make requests on behalf of lieutenants whom they did not know. The entire system of extended recommendation rather relied on it. The nature of centralised Admiralty appointments also meant that they were often landed with multiple lieutenants whom they neither knew nor even particularly liked.[28] But even so, making requests for lieutenants entirely unknown to them carried risks when this was not explicitly stated. Captain Edward Buller, for example, wrote to Markham in 1803 requesting the removal of a lieutenant whom he had previously requested but now found unsuitable because his angry temperament and aggressive style of dealing with the crew made Buller's command of the ship exhausting. Perhaps feeling the awkwardness of his request he added a note to the end of his letter by way of an explanation: 'You will very likely ask whether Lt Harris was not appointed by my request, he was, but it was by the recommendation of an navy agent. I never saw him before.'[29]

Some captains were slightly more cautious in their approach to recommending strangers and preferred instead to take the strangers offered them by the board. Robert Barton wrote to Markham in January 1804 to fit out his command of *Goliath*. Thanking Markham for 'the offer of getting anyone I might wish', he added only that: 'a Lt Ferritor has apply'd to me, I did not object to his writing, but as I have no sort of knowledge of Him, I should be just as well pleased with any other it might suit the board to appoint'.[30] Others were explicit about the risk and responsibility they felt in making a recommendation, especially if the candidate was not well-known to them. In response to a question Markham had previously put to him about a midshipman currently under his command, whom Markham had received other requests on behalf of, Captain Richard King wrote: 'he has behaved well since in the Sirius, and I am told he is perfectly Honest, further I cannot say, as its proper to be very Cautious in Recommendations'.[31]

Brokers had power in naval patronage, despite the hurry of Admiralty business and the personal distance in recommendations that the practical

---

[28] See for example John Whitby's repeated requests for lieutenants who had some 'personal attachment' with him, rather than the strangers appointed by the Admiralty, who he felt were jeopardising the smooth running of the ship: NMM, MRK/102/6/26–28, John Whitby to Markham, [postmark: 23–30 April 1802].

[29] NMM, MRK/102/1/116, Captain Edward Buller to Markham, 6 October 1803.

[30] NMM, MRK/102/1/18, Captain Robert Barton to Markham 28 January 1804.

[31] NMM, MRK/102/3/83, Richard King to Markham, 3 September 1801.

requirement to fill positions sometimes caused. This was partly because of the space it gave lords like Markham to refuse requests when it was not possible for him to fulfil them. But it was also because when brokers made requests on their candidate's behalf they effectively gave their candidate connection to Markham through virtue of their own relationship with him.

In this context, the tendency of socially influential and well-connected officers like Herbert to minimise the power of their network connections and disproportionately favour impersonal-style requests reads more as privilege. Many may have opted for this more impersonal approach to try to make themselves appear less demanding. The implicit weight of their other powerful connections could make a well-connected broker's request on behalf of a favoured candidate heavier than from other types of broker, because of the risk turning it down presented to someone in Markham's position. But equally, if personal connection was nevertheless still important in impersonal-style requests, then those who did not emphasise their connection to their candidate must have been confident that they did not need to give Markham extra information. Perhaps this was because he already trusted their recommendations or maybe wanted to fulfil their requests to nurture his own connection with them and by extension their influential network and so was less interested in the virtues of the candidate themselves as a result. In that case, the high proportion of routine requests from titled officers reflects the implicit, if not direct, strength of their connection with him. Well-connected officers could essentially afford to be *less* pushy in their requests, which could make them more successful in the long run, because they did not need to risk damaging their connection to Markham by making requests that could be deemed demanding or entitled.

Of course, some of those who did have both a strong connection with him and were well-connected elsewhere, such as John Astley Bennet, were extremely careful to only recommend candidates with whom they had a very strong relationship and reason to recommend them. Although he had many factors in his favour, Bennet was only a commander and was already greatly indebted to Markham as his follower. The implicit influence of his social position could well be the reason he felt able to make his recommendation at all, when most commanders and Markham's other followers never made brokered requests. However, there was still an inherent power imbalance in their connection, because of Bennet's level of obligation towards Markham. This meant that he was unable to make the more impersonal-style requests because, in the context of their power imbalance, the requests would appear entitled simply because of the presumption of unstated personal connection.

However, he also did not need to draw on the semantics of the impersonal requests because the nature of their relationship meant he could make requests on behalf of others as a part of an obligation to himself, as long as he embedded them firmly in the language of merit-based recommendation and the good

106   PATRONAGE AND THE BRITISH NAVY, 1775–1815

of the service. Many captains viewed brokered requests in the same way they viewed the requests they made for themselves as the recipient, whereby Markham obliging their brokered or direct request confirmed an obligation of reciprocity primarily on them, as the one who made it. This seems particularly to have been the case with requests on behalf of family members, as we saw at the beginning of this book with Edward Pellew's framing of the inherent reciprocity of naval patronage as a 'wheel' of returned favours.[32] The same distance that allowed for the recommendation of unknown candidates seems to have stretched this reciprocity but the expectation of conferred obligation was not entirely absent.

Of course, not all kinds of recommendation neatly followed a linear chain of requests between a candidate, their connections, the broker and the patron. Rather some recommendations took the form of introducing a candidate directly to Markham either by letter or in person. In this sort of recommendation, the broker acted as a conduit in forging the initial connection, but not necessarily in the continued maintenance of the brokered relationship. On the one hand, this meant that it did not contribute to developing their own relationship with Markham, in the sense of Pellew's 'wheel' of reciprocity. On the other hand, this sort of recommendation potentially carried less risk, as the broker became less directly involved in any future successful or unsuccessful requests or connection. At the very least, it was less work for them in seeing directly to their candidate's patronage needs.

In many ways, this sort of recommendation could prove to be very successful for the candidate. It is possible that many of the correspondents in the collection, for whom it is difficult to establish the origins of their relationship with Markham, were initially recommended in this way. They effectively were able to forge their own personal connection with him by temporarily relying on their broker's existing connection. However, recommendations of this sort were not always a reliable substitute for developing a personal connection with Markham as their patron.

Some applicants certainly seem to have overestimated the strength of connection that a brokered introduction gave them with Markham, especially in their ability to make more demanding or difficult requests. John Walker, a purser who was recommended to Markham via a letter of introduction from the prominent naval physician Thomas Trotter, wrote in May 1802 thanking Markham for appointing him to *Gelykheid*. However, it seems that he did so primarily to be able to obliquely ask for his support in getting him a position on a bigger ship:

> ... yet as a young man it is natural to wish to obtain such a situation as shall enable me to provide a comfortable support for my Wife and little

---

[32] NMM, MRK/101/13/100, Pellew to Markham, 15 August 1806.

MARKHAM'S ADMIRALTY CORRESPONDENTS 107

Boy. I need not inform you of the pay of a Purser of sixty four in ordinary, which even with our own little private property, is a very limited income.[33]

Markham's note on the letter gives us his reaction to Walker's request: 'a polite refusal. neither know the drift of his application or if I did could I give a preference to his [while there] are those who have naturely [sic] a claim upon me and of whom I have perfect knowledge'.[34]

Markham's response underlines the importance of personal connection in these relationships, regardless of the apparent preference for service-based recommendations and the acceptance of the more impersonal ones. Despite his successful recommendation from Thomas Trotter, which was effective at securing him employment in advance of the impending peace, Walker was in no position to make these sorts of demands of the relationship. He had no 'natural' claim on Markham and was essentially a stranger.

Interestingly, perhaps sensing his mistake, Walker drew on his service credentials in his reply as he tried to salvage the fledgling relationship: 'I flattered myself alltho I owed the honor of an interview with you solely to my letter of introduction from Doctor Trotter, yet my conduct should prove me not undeserving, if you would condescend to favour me with your patronage.' He also fell back on his need to support his family as a way to excuse his being so demanding:

I am well aware of the numerous claims upon your benevolence, and far is it from my wish to appear importunate, as it would give me real concern if you sir, concluded from my address I infringed too much on your goodness, and that my zeal of serving my family had led me beyond those bounds of Respect, which I must ever feel from your Character, and elevated station in Life.[35]

Dr Trotter's letter of introduction does not seem to have survived in the collection. It is possible that his recommendation of Walker was in the same impersonal style as many service requests, which gave Markham very little idea of the strength of their connection and therefore the reliability of Trotter's recommendation. Or perhaps Trotter gave the impression that his recommendation was one of obligation, from having served with Walker, which suggests that despite shared service being one of the largest categories of relationship between brokers and candidates, patronage relationships born of obligation could only go so far.

33 NMM, MRK/104/3/31, John Walker, purser, to Markham, 14 May 1802.
34 NMM, MRK/194/3/31, Markham's note, 20 May 1802.
35 NMM, MRK/104/3/32, John Walker to Markham, 6 June 1802.

Flexibility and Obligation

We have already seen some of the relationships Markham had with his correspondents. Many of the civilian correspondents wrote to him as family friends, through their connection or friendship with his father or other family members. Others, we shall see in the following chapter, were defined by their connection to him in local politics when he won his seat as MP for Portsmouth in 1802. Of his service-based relationships, we have already seen some of his closer or more intimate relationships, like the connection he had with Captain Mark Kerr, or the relationship that existed somewhere between friend and follower that he had with Captain Bendall Littlehales who took over his command of *Centaur* when Markham joined the Admiralty. Some of his other followers were also drawn from his extended family and friend networks, such as William Croft or Walter Grossett. There were also those who were connected to him through more extended ties, such as Captain John Perkins whom we met in Chapter 1, or those from lower down the social scale who wrote to him from having served together, such as the carpenter Russel White whom we met at the beginning of this book.

However, many of Markham's correspondents have left us few clues to be able to make a clear judgement about the nature or origin of their relationship with him beyond the context of their social or professional position. It is possible that many of his naval correspondents began their relationship with him via recommendations or introductions, like John Walker. Others may have made his acquaintance through having served together in a way that is not obvious to us now, or perhaps through some other sort of social or political context, as could well have been the case with a captain like Charles Herbert. There were also some who wrote to him directly without any prior acquaintance, simply through virtue of his public position as a lord of the Admiralty and his reputation for fairness and justice. Even without the sort of personal information that can shed light on the deeper nature of a correspondent's relationship with Markham, the style of their requests offers some clues about the expectations that surrounded naval patronage and Markham's particular approach to distributing his favour.

One of the defining features of most of his correspondence was that it was crucial for all applicants to Markham's favour to appear undemanding, regardless of the nature of their connection to him. The increasing centralisation of naval appointments saw the collision of old manners and expectations with the practical realities of having the people with the power to make appointments inundated with requests from every part of their network, as well as from the connections of their colleagues on the board and those who had no connection but still needed assistance. Many applicants showed an awareness of the limits of his patronage and the great number of applications he must have received in his position. Captain George Jones, in writing to ask

MARKHAM'S ADMIRALTY CORRESPONDENTS 109

for Markham's help in getting a lieutenancy of marines for his connection's son, spelled it out quite clearly:

> I shou'd not attempt thus to trouble you but from the great kindness I have ever experience'd from you, as well as being well aware that you will be solicited on the same subject by those who have a much greater influence with you than I possible [sic] can have.[36]

When Captain George Cockburn asked Markham to appoint his preferred lieutenants to his new command *Phaeton* in 1803, he was fairly practical about the limits there might be on Markham's patronage and stressed his flexibility several times.[37] He opened his letter as such: 'If it does not interfere with your arrangements and you have not any Body that you wish to place as Lieuts of the Phaeton will you allow me to name Mr Clement Milward [...] and Mr Ralph Standish.' He further emphasised his flexibility by explicitly stating his preference that 'should you only be able to give me one of them I prefer the former'. He laid out his perception of Markham's position quite clearly: 'I take the liberty of making the request to you under the supposition that it is indifferent to you which Lieutenants are appointed provided they are of proper standing on the List to hold the respective stations.' As an added security he finished his request by offering the vacancies up to Markham, should he need them: 'should there however be any Body concerning whom you are interested and wish to place in the Phaeton I beg to assure I shall with great Pleasure give up this application'. Cockburn's flexibility seems to have paid off, because at least one of the lieutenants he recommended was appointed to *Phaeton*.[38]

Alongside being undemanding, then, another key characteristic of successful connections was their ability to be flexible in their requests. Many applicants stressed their awareness that Markham might not be able to fulfil their requests, opening their requests with phrases such as the one used by Captain George Johnstone Hope in May 1803: 'If it does not interfere with any appointments you may have already made I have to beg Mr Thos Janveron may be appointed Lieut of the Defence.'[39] This was also true of those outside the service. In fact, some letters suggest that officers felt the need to impress upon their

---

[36] NMM, MRK/102/3/77, Captain George Jones to Markham, 16 July 1803.

[37] NMM, MRK/102/1/143, Captain George Cockburn to Markham, 12 July [1803].

[38] TNA, ADM 9/3/675 Captains' Services: Clement Milward, post-captain, seniority 28 May 1813; William O'Byrne *A Naval Biographical Dictionary* (London: John Murray, 1849), 764, accessed via https://en.wikisource.org/wiki/A_Naval_Biographical_Dictionary/Milward,_Clement

[39] NMM, MRK/102/3/56, Captain George Johnstone Hope to Markham, 3 May 1803.

110   PATRONAGE AND THE BRITISH NAVY, 1775–1815

civilian brokers the need to be flexible and grateful in their dealings with the Admiralty lords. John Hoper, a lawyer and one of Markham's neighbours and political connections from his new home in Lewes, wrote in May 1803 to recommend Lieutenant Henry Hume Spence. Spence, Hoper wrote, had served in the navy for thirteen years and spent nearly six years on active service in the West Indies and was now looking for employment. Hoper also reported something that Spence had told him: 'Do not rest upon this with Capt[n] Markham for there are many who have much better pretensions than I have.'[40] This self-effacing style seems to have stood Spence in good stead, because two months later Markham received a letter from Spence's father thanking him for his favour in securing his son a position.[41]

It was, however, possible to be too flexible. Or rather, the need to be undemanding could be problematic for some, especially those candidates who relied mainly on service-based relationships with their brokers to secure appointments. A broker's flexibility and undemanding style could make a candidate seem less of a priority, even if multiple brokers made requests for him to join their ships. In 1803 Markham received requests from two different captains to have Lieutenant Robert Yule take up one of the lieutenant vacancies in their ships. The first was made by Captain Henry Blackwood, who wrote to Markham in that unassuming style typical of these routine service requests:

> When I had a conversation with you some time ago about Lieut[s] you was so good as to say, you would accommodate me as far as you could, under this impression I shall be much obliged to you (whenever I am appointed) to allow me to name Mr Goddard Blennerhassett as first lieut and Mr Robt Y[u]le as either 2d or third whichever is most convenient.[42]

The second request for Yule came a month later, this time from Captain William Broughton who, similar to Blackwood, asked for Yule alongside making a request for another officer:

> Having a vacancy for a Lieut I have this day made application for one to be appointed and have to request you will again excuse my troubling you in favor of Lieut Richard Delves Broughton of the Autumn Sloop or Lieut Robert Yule shou'd he still remain unemploy'd.[43]

Yule's connection to both captains appears to have been primarily based on having served with them. He had served under both consecutively during his

---

[40] NMM, MRK/104/2/96, Mr John Hoper to Markham, 30 May 1803.

[41] NMM, MRK/104/2/105, Henry Spence to Markham, 20 July 1803.

[42] NMM, MRK/102/1/68, Henry Blackwood to Markham, 10 June 1803.

[43] NMM, MRK/102/1/110, William Robert Broughton to John Markham, 29 July 1803.

time on *Penelope*, first as master's mate between 1797 and 1802, then as an acting-lieutenant for the final two months of the ship's commission.[44]

However, Yule remained unemployed. Although he was requested by two captains, who had served with him and whom he could be considered a follower of, neither was particularly forceful in his request for him. Markham was likely aware that despite the unassuming style of Blackwood and Broughton's letters, the first officers they mentioned in each case were those that they had a greater interest in seeing placed, and so took priority. Although they recommended Yule, the lack of any factors beyond their having served with him and knowing him to be a capable officer, meant he fared less well in this particular exchange. From our perspective, this reflected more on Yule's ties to his brokers, being primarily ones of service rather than politics or family, than it did on Blackwood and Broughton's relationships with Markham.

The need for flexibility is important to consider when gauging patronage success in the particular context of naval appointments in this period. The hurry of Admiralty business that so many correspondents acknowledged in their applications meant that they also did not always get exactly what they requested. Captain John Kidd wrote to Markham on 29 November 1803, recommending one of his followers, Lieutenant Edward Hall, for active service after a period of sickness had required him to give up the position in a frigate that Markham had previously secured for him at Kidd's request. Kidd's letter was brief and to the point, finishing with: 'If you will again have the goodness to favour me by giving him another ship in active service you will lay me under more than double obligation.'[45] The following month, Hall was appointed to a signal station in North Yarmouth.[46]

The partial success of Kidd's request could reflect the strength of Kidd's relationship with Markham and the consequent context of his application. Kidd's request on behalf of Hall is his only surviving letter in Markham's papers. There are no other clues to the nature of their relationship other than his reference to Markham's previous attention to his request, his addressing Markham as 'Sir', and the fact that he included no other familial news or best wishes to Maria Markham or other family members; all of which suggests that their connection was primarily based on Markham's role as a public lord of the Admiralty, or perhaps another kind of service-based relationship steeped in the naval fashion for brief and impersonal requests. In this context, Kidd's request may simply have been of lower priority to Markham. However, this period was also a tough time for lieutenant appointments to active service, so an appointment to a signal station was a mark of some favour, or at the

---

[44] TNA, ADM 9/7/2411 Lieutenants' Services: seniority 2 October 1802.

[45] NMM, MRK/102/3/81, John Kidd to Markham, 29 November 1803.

[46] O'Byrne *A Naval Biographical Dictionary*, 441, accessed via https://en.wikisource.org/wiki/A_Naval_Biographical_Dictionary/Hall,_Edward_(a)

112   PATRONAGE AND THE BRITISH NAVY, 1775–1815

very least, it suggests that Markham obliged Kidd's request as much as he could. Certainly, there were other captains with apparently much stronger relationships or claims on his attention who were not at all successful in their requests at this time.

We could assume that certain characteristics granted a correspondent a closer connection to Markham and therefore more access to his support. We have already seen the prevalence of familial and political links in the brokered requests, as well as how a basis of shared service accounted for a large proportion of naval broker relationships. Certainly, shared service is one type of relationship between Markham and his correspondents which we can determine with some reliability. At the very beginning of this book we met the carpenter Russel White, whose applications to Markham's favour based on their shared service over thirty years earlier when Markham first entered the service are an evocative example of the way the obligation from shared service shaped connection and by extension patronage in the navy. Shared service was also a solid foundation for some of Markham's closest friendships in the service. As noted in the previous chapter, his friendship with Edward Riou likely began when they both entered the navy aboard *Romney* in 1775. His close friendship with Lord Mark Kerr seems to have begun, or was at least strengthened and made more intimate, during their shared service in the Mediterranean in 1798–1799.

As an obligation, shared service certainly seems to have played a role in how Markham distributed his patronage among his correspondents. Fifty-five of Markham's correspondents in this part of the collection served with him, either alongside him in his early career as a youngster, or directly under his command once he made post-captain. Roughly half of these could be considered followers because of the way Markham had continued to support them after they had left his command. It is not possible to definitively judge the success of every application to Markham in a way that would allow us to establish an overall accurate success rate, not least because many applicants likely did not solicit Markham alone and rarely do we have explicit evidence that he was directly responsible for an applicant's success. However, these follower requests were by far the most likely to be successful from among the requests for which it is possible to establish success with any degree of confidence. This was partly because the nature of their relationship with Markham meant that most of their requests to him were straightforward and easily achievable. As we have already seen with John Astley Bennet, the level of obligation followers felt towards their patron made them disinclined to overburden him with difficult requests, whilst simultaneously being confident that he would oblige them when and wherever he could.[47]

[47] See also NMM, MRK/102/1/162, William Croft to Markham, 20 February 1807; MRK/102/3/35, Thomas Hill to Markham, 25 March 1807.

MARKHAM'S ADMIRALTY CORRESPONDENTS 113

The obligation born of shared service also defined a high proportion of the relationships Markham had with those of his correspondents whom we could consider to be from lower down the social scale. Of his twenty correspondents from the lower ratings, mostly non-wardroom warrant officers such as carpenters, gunners and boatswains, nearly half had served either with him or directly under his command. For those like the carpenter Russel White, their shared service conferred a long-standing sense of obligation upon him for the care and support they provided at the very beginning of his career. John Simpson, who was carpenter on board *Roebuck* in 1779 while Markham was an acting-lieutenant, also received Markham's unequivocal support both for himself and his son, of the same name, whom Markham appointed to the profitable position of first lieutenant aboard *Camilla* in March 1801.[48] For others who had served directly under his command on board *Hannibal*, *Blonde* or *Centaur*, Markham's sense of obligation, or perhaps more specifically his sense of duty towards them, was more recent but no less powerful. William Wright, who had been under Markham's command as boatswain of *Hannibal* in 1795, wrote in 1801 soon after Markham joined the Admiralty to request his help getting him a position on board a larger ship, so that he could better support his family: 'I humbly beg your Intrest [sic] to get me a rate higher the Dreadnaut [sic] his [sic] now vacant and will be launchd in a short time Sir my family his [sic] so large my pay will do little moar [sic] at present than find Bread'. Markham noted his reply on the letter, showing his ready support: 'can't promise Dreadnaught, but do promise not to forget him at a proper opportunity'.[49] Just over a year later Wright wrote again to thank Markham after he had received orders to join *Union*, an appointment which he was 'confident' he owed to Markham's 'interest' in his favour:

> Permit me to say, I consider it as my *indispensable Duty* to acknowledge *your* goodness on many Occasions, and particularly so on my *present appointment*, which while I have breath I shall with true heart felt gratitude consider and also to subscribe myself.[50]

For the lieutenants among his correspondents who had served under his command, but who were not close enough to be one of his followers, their shared service gave them a reliable route to seeking his assistance once he was

---

[48] NMM, MRK/104/2/93, John Simpson, carpenter, to Markham, 5 June 1802; MRK/103/2/32, John Simpson to Markham, 5 March 1801; TNA, ADM 29/2/326 Service of John Simpson, carpenter; ADM 9/7/2075 Lieutenants' Services: John Simpson, seniority 31 May 1798.

[49] NMM, MRK/104/3/54, William Wright, boatswain, to Markham, 10 April [1801].

[50] NMM, MRK/104/3/55, William Wright to Markham, 8 May 1802. Emphasis in original.

114   PATRONAGE AND THE BRITISH NAVY, 1775–1815

at the Admiralty. Lieutenant Frederick Hoffman wrote to him on 6 March 1806 to request his 'Interest for another step', having been serving as a lieutenant for the last seven years without any apparent prospects of promotion:

> as I had the honor of serving under your command on my first entrance into the service, in the Blonde, and Hannibal and having experienced your humanity, and feeling, indices me to use my present plea; trusting I have not too much intruded on your time, which I know is materially engaged, and requesting a further indulgence of a few lines.[51]

He appears to have been successful as a few days later he was appointed to the frigate *Diamond*.[52]

However, past shared service was by no means a guarantee of intimacy or even connection and support. Captain David Stow wrote to Markham in July 1803 to ask for his assistance in securing him a place in the sea fencibles: 'After a lapse of twenty years I ought perhaps to apologize for attempting to renew an acquaintance which you may possibly have almost forgotten, particularly when it was with a view to solicit a favour.'[53] Similarly, Captain Isaac Schomberg's letter to Markham in June 1803, writing to ask for some inside knowledge on the likelihood of achieving his hopes of getting an active vessel, reveals the fraught web of expectations that surrounded the relationship between old shipmates:

> I write this letter my dear Sir, in confidence, on the recollection of what I might term our former friendship – which length of years and absence may leave in some measure softened down to acquaintance, but be assured that this is not the case with, yours faithfully, I Schomberg.

By stating his own continued sense of connection to Markham, Schomberg effectively managed to acknowledge the lapse in acquaintance while also reaching out to establish the friendship.

It is not clear whether Stow was successful in his attempt to renew his connection with Markham. However, despite the acknowledgement that such connections could 'soften' from friendship to 'acquaintance' without the maintenance or embedded connection mentioned in the previous two chapters, Schomberg's bid for reconnection seems to have been effective. Four letters from him survive in the collection, in which he made two direct requests for Markham's assistance. His next letter apologised for taking up Markham's

---

[51] NMM, MRK/103/1/64, Frederick Hoffman to Markham, 6 March 1806.

[52] O'Byrne *A Naval Biographical Dictionary*, 526, accessed via https://en.wikisource.org/wiki/A_Naval_Biographical_Dictionary/Hoffman,_Frederick

[53] NMM, MRK/102/5/123, David Stow to Markham, 16 July 1803.

time and asked instead for a position in the sea fencibles, which seems to have been successful.[54]

There seems to have been a general impression among Markham's connections that being an 'Old Messmate' carried some weight with him, even for more awkward situations or requests. Captain John Oakes Hardy apparently recommended his friend Commander Goodwin Colquitt write to Markham in May 1803, after a brain injury eight years earlier had prevented Colquitt from directly seeking active employment. In his letter Colquitt wrote that Hardy had suggested 'he thought I had some claim to promotion and by explaining the Reasons for not soliciting for Employment might have some weight with an Old Messmate'.[55] Colquitt had served with Markham on *London* nearly twenty-two years earlier. The lapse of acquaintance however seems to have played on Colquitt's mind, as he opened his letter with an effusive apology:

> I feel myself much embarrassed in addressing you on a subject which I have much at Heart. So long a distance of Time has elapsed since I had the pleasure of being with you in the London, that it renders it the more difficult for me to apologise in requesting your aid and assistance in getting me put on the Post List.

The spy and journalist, William Augustus Miles, also gave Markham's reputation for assisting 'old shipmates' as his reason for being so forward in his somewhat awkward and unusual request in March 1807. He wrote inviting Markham to a 'plain family dinner' with the hope of talking about getting an appointment as the agent for prisoners of war in Holland or Spain, where he might be able to be 'useful' from an intelligence perspective.[56] He excused himself for being so 'explicit' in his purpose before being 'honor'd with an interview', by having heard it mentioned much to Markham's credit that he had 'invariably shewn a very friendly disposition' to all his 'old shipmates'.

Despite his reputation for assisting old shipmates, however, Markham did not oblige either of these more awkward requests. To Colquitt he wrote back apologising that although he had favoured 'two or three old friends' where he could, 'the door is now shut to promotion' and so application was 'fruitless'.[57] In May 1803, Markham was turning down many of the requests that came his way, although adding one more name to the post list as an act of charity for an officer who would likely not ever actively serve seems like it could have been achievable. With the end of the Peace of Amiens, the navy was mobilising

---

[54] NMM, MRK/102/5/82, Isaac Schomberg to Markham, 26 June 1803.

[55] NMM, MRK/102/1/148, Commander Goodwin Colquitt to Markham, 2 May 1803.

[56] NMM, MRK/104/2/33, William Augustus Miles to Markham, 20 March 1807.

[57] NMM, MRK/102/1/148, Markham's note, 3 May 1803.

116   PATRONAGE AND THE BRITISH NAVY, 1775–1815

once again, and perhaps assisting a disabled commander to the post list was too great a stretch of obligation to be approved by St Vincent. Markham had certainly helped get positions for others of his old messmates disabled in the service. Lieutenant Thomas Williams wrote to him in September 1803 with a request for his son, but also to thank Markham for his favour the previous year in getting him his current position as lieutenant of Haslar Hospital. Williams had served with Markham when they were both lieutenants on board *Roebuck* between 1780 and 1781, but he had lost his leg the following year, which had made it difficult for him to accept active, and therefore advantageous, service that could have given him the next step needed for promotion to post-captain.[58] His reputation for assisting old shipmates, or those who had served under his command, therefore, was likely born in truth, at least for the earlier part of his time at the Admiralty.

To Miles, Markham also apologised for his 'engagements' preventing him from accepting his 'kind invitation', but he was a little more forceful in turning him away than he was Colquitt. In his drafted response on the reverse of Miles's letter he wrote that, despite how his 'civility due to' Miles may have led him to assist, his 'official business' meant he was unable 'to spare any portion' of his time in a discussion which in the 'present situation' would be 'altogether unproductive of any result which can tend to forward your plans'.[59] It is unclear exactly how Markham and Miles had been 'old shipmates'. Miles mentioned in his letter first having met Markham in 1776, so it was presumably when he served in a civil appointment under Admiral Rodney while Markham was a youngster on board *Perseus*.[60] So perhaps this connection was too tenuous for Markham to feel a strong enough sense of obligation to assist him, especially at such a precarious time for his own influence, with the change of government beckoning within the next few days and thus the end of his time at the Admiralty.

Generally, however, Markham's sense of obligation towards those who had served under his command was consistent and seems to have been one of the most powerful forms of obligation he felt towards his applicants. At times, it even challenged the otherwise prevailing naval emphasis on merit as a priority in the distribution of appointments, because he seems to have taken it into consideration even when an applicant's service had not overly impressed him. Joseph Elias, a twenty-six-year-old midshipman who had first entered the service as a first class boy on board *Centaur* under Markham's command in 1797, wrote to beg for Markham's assistance in 1802 when he

[58] NMM, MRK/103/2/40, Lieutenant Thomas Williams to Markham, 15 September 1803; TNA, ADM 9/6/1676 Lieutenants' Services: Seniority 15 May 1780.

[59] NMM, MRK/104/2/33, William August Miles to Markham, 20 March 1807, Markham's drafted response [no date].

[60] Gerald le Grys Norgate, 'Miles, William Augustus', *ODNB*, vol. 37, 379.

faced being unemployed once *Centaur* was finally paid off.[61] He apologised to Markham for taking the 'liberty' of addressing him with a private letter, but that he had 'lost my Relations on whom I had Dependance am left Destitute of Friends to Provide for myself'. He feared that he had 'incurr'd' Markham's displeasure from his time on board *Centaur* because he had 'Enemys' on the ship who had represented him poorly despite his always striving to do his duty to the best of his power. He asked if Markham would give him 'another trial', and send him to a smaller ship where he promised: 'I will Pay every atention [sic] in my Power to merit your favours.'[62]

Elias's father seems likely to have been a cordwainer or some other kind of artificer in Kent, so perhaps this difference in social status, as well as his relatively advanced age upon entering the service, affected his patronage relationships.[63] He could not boast the same level of intimacy as a follower like Henry Elton or William Croft that we met in the previous chapter. However, although it seems to have damaged his relationships with some on board *Centaur*, it did not prevent Markham from favouring him, even though he saw him as otherwise unexceptional as an officer. In his note on Elias's letter, Markham wrote that he was 'by no means prejudiced against him', he just felt that 'he had never life enough to carry on the duty to my satisfaction, and came to sea too late to make a seaman'.[64] Despite this he put Elias forward to be 'considered for another ship', and Elias was appointed to *Eugenie* the following month.[65] He then remained employed throughout the subsequent short peace and the resumption of hostilities, under a series of captains who had close ties to Markham of either friendship or obligation.[66] So it seems likely that Markham continued to look out for him. He did not make lieutenant until 1806, at thirty years old, and he can perhaps be considered as one of the more unsuccessful 'young gentleman', well above the average age for 1801 that S. A. Cavell noted in her analysis of young gentlemen's careers.[67] But he was not without patronage. In fact, given the various apparent impediments to his

---

[61] TNA, ADM 36/14165 Muster Book: HMS Centaur 1 June 1799–31 January 1800; Jos Elias, Boy 1st Class, entered 21 April 1797, Woolwich Vol. Born Maidstone, age on entry 21.

[62] NMM, MRK/104/1/104, Joseph Elias to Markham, 15 June 1802.

[63] Kent History and Library Centre, P18/1/A/3, Kent Baptisms: Joseph Elias son of Samuel and Ann Elias, baptised 24 September 1775, Bearsted, Holy Cross, Kent; TNA, IR 1/52 fl61, Samuel Elias, apprentice to Robert Hewey, cordwainer, in Hawkhurst Kent, 1756, premium £2.2s.0d.

[64] NMM, MRK/104/1/104, Markham's note, 15 July 1802

[65] TNA, ADM 9/8/2686 Lieutenants' Services: Joseph Elias, seniority 15 August 1806.

[66] See correspondence with Captain George Hope Johnstone, MRK/102/3/56–59, and Captain James Hardy, MRK/102/3/18–23.

[67] Cavell, *Midshipmen and the Quarterdeck Boys*, 218.

118   PATRONAGE AND THE BRITISH NAVY, 1775–1815

success, his age, his social level and the death of his 'friends', his continued connection with Markham can perhaps better be seen as a rousing success.

Elias illustrates an important part of naval patronage in this period that is easy to skim over if we focus too narrowly on the role of family connections in the creation of followers. Certainly, we saw in Chapter 2 that many of the 'young gentlemen' and junior officers whom Markham supported, both as a captain and during his time at the Admiralty, came from his familial network or were the children of his close acquaintances. But there are also many correspondents in the collection whose initial connection to Markham is less obvious but whose letter-writing and careers fit the profile of follower. From the pattern in Markham's followers we saw in Chapter 2, we could assume that Elias, or his relations, had some connection to Markham in 1797 that secured his entry to *Centaur* as a first class boy. The nature of these connections, however, is not clear. Yet, Markham still treated Elias as a follower, and it was not even because of his exceptional talent for the service.

Obligation from shared service was one factor that defined correspondents' relationship with Markham and his distribution of Admiralty patronage. But Markham also had a reputation for fairness and justice, and seems to have gone out of his way to help those he judged deserving, from merit or obligation, regardless of their position in his network. In fact some of Markham's correspondence suggests that having a prior connection with him actually was not a prerequisite to securing his support.

Strangers

Given the size of the navy and the difficulty of getting positions, it is not surprising that some of those who wrote to Markham for his assistance did so without any prior connection to him. Indeed, it seems likely that most of the lower-frequency correspondents in the collection began as strangers, although only a small proportion gave any indication in their letters that makes it possible to categorise them as such with confidence. The practical need to write to some lord of the Admiralty to ask for employment or the appointment of lieutenants, however, did not make the reality of doing so any less awkward, especially because of the strange place between personal favour and administration naval patronage occupied in this period.

Captain William Granville Lobb wrote to Markham in June 1803 requesting a lieutenant's appointment for his nephew to a frigate, after being told by Markham's fellow board member, Thomas Troubridge, that Markham had control over the appointment of officers. Despite Troubridge's direction, Lobb was plainly uneasy with writing to Markham directly, leaning on his concern for his young nephew as an excuse for taking the liberty of writing to him without prior acquaintance: 'shou'd there be any impropriety in my making [the request]; independent of being unknown to you, you will have

MARKHAM'S ADMIRALTY CORRESPONDENTS

the goodness to impute it, to my anxiety about a young man, so newly arrived, and who was bro't up with me'.[68]

Others felt reassured that Markham's reputation for even-handedness would outweigh any impropriety from writing to him directly with no prior connection, or at least chose to present themselves as such. Captain Woodley Losack wrote requesting a replacement for his second lieutenant whose health was badly impaired by service in the East Indies. Such a request may seem fairly straightforward, but Markham's patronage was likely necessary to perform the exchange delicately and avoiding any potential damage to the young officer's reputation that could arise from a public letter asking for him to be superseded. It seems to have been Markham's reputation in this regard that spurred Losack to take the risk in applying to him directly:

> I have many apologies to make for the liberty I assume in addressing myself to you, not having the Honor of being personally Known, but from the several acts of Kindness which I am aware of your having confer'd upon officer's [sic] I feel embolden'd to become under an obligation to you of which I shall sensibly consider myself by your acquiescence.[69]

Despite being 'personally unknown' to Markham, two more letters from Losack survive in the collection, in which Losack also acted as broker for others under his command. In these requests, he particularly emphasised their merit above all other considerations, such as in his recommendation of George Jeffries, his boatswain, of whom he wrote: 'If Merit Sir will entitle him to your favor I can assure you he deserves it most fully as being a very good, active, zealous officer.'[70]

These other considerations of duty and fairness are potentially how some of the correspondents for whom the exact nature of their relationship with Markham is unclear forged their connection. Being able to write directly without prior acquaintance was also not something reserved for commissioned officers, or those with the social bearing and strong social connections to give them the confidence that their unsolicited acquaintance would be acceptable. William Rule, boatswain of *Santa Dorotea*, wrote to Markham in April 1802, asking to be placed on a larger ship. In style, his letter was virtually indistinguishable from those of many commissioned officers, including opening by excusing himself for taking the 'liberty' of addressing Markham directly:

> Hoping you will excuse the liberty I have taken in thus addressing you, but well knowing your goodness, I am induced to trouble you with a Statement

---

68 NMM, MRK/102/4/46, William Granville Lobb to Markham, 10 June 1803.
69 NMM, MRK/102/4/52, Woodley Losack to Markham, 22 September [no year].
70 NMM, MRK/102/4/51, Woodley Losack to Markham, [no date].

120   PATRONAGE AND THE BRITISH NAVY, 1775–1815

> of my present situation, trusting you will render me what Assistance and Patronage you may think me deserving of.[71]

There was, of course, no guarantee that their bid for connection would result in a successful ongoing patronage relationship, in much the same way as those who drew on lapsed acquaintances took a chance in trying to re-establish their relationship with Markham to access his Admiralty patronage. Some were certainly unsuccessful, especially at times where Markham was largely unable to oblige any applicants, such as in the final weeks of his time at the Admiralty.[72] Generally, though, applicants who explicitly presented themselves as strangers to Markham seem to have fared better than his shared service connections, who drew on his reputation for helping old shipmates.

Rather than a direct sense of obligation or direct reciprocity, in the style of Pellew's wheel, Markham seems to have judged stranger connections by other prioritising factors. For some, these were factors such as his sense of duty to the applicant's long service, or a sense of charity towards their having a large family to support. Captain John Carter Allen, for instance, couched his request firmly in professional obligation, drawing on both his own and his late father's service: 'Sir, as an officer in His majesty's Service and the son of an Old and much respected Officer (Late admiral John Carter Allen) I trust you will excuse me in troubling you ...'; and appealing to Markham's sense of duty: 'it is for this Sir I have now taken the liberty of addressing you, trusting sir as a professional man, you will not overlook old services'.[73] Lieutenant Thomas Lowton Robins employed not only his sense of duty to the country but also his need to support his family as his excuse for writing without acquaintance to request a position as the commander of a prison ship:

> I have not the Honor to be personally known to You: but, I hope your Goodness will excuse my thus introducing myself to your Notice, soliciting Employment; Being urged thereto, as well on account of the nature of the present Contest which calls forth every officer and Man, as by a wish to reduce the number of Difficulties I contend with in the Supporting of my large Family of Seven Children.[74]

Some strangers, although personally unknown to Markham, were otherwise fairly well-embedded within his wider network. However, rather than drawing on a brokered connection to establish a relationship with him, they drew

---

[71] NMM, MRK/104/2/76, William Rule, boatswain, to Markham, 23 April 1802.

[72] See for example NMM, MRK/102/1/5, John Carter Allen to Markham, 14 March 1807.

[73] NMM, MRK/102/1/5, John Carter Allen to Markham, 14 March 1807.

[74] NMM, MRK/103/2/30, Thomas Lowton Robins to Markham, 13 July 1803.

instead on these more abstract obligations of duty and charity for his support. Captain Phillip Somerville, for example, wrote to Markham without any prior acquaintance but captured his attention and established a strong connection of his own. He first wrote in April 1802, in the 'utmost anxiety' about his son's commission as a lieutenant, who despite being placed as an acting-lieutenant on board *Dragon*, had still not been confirmed. Hearing from his agent that Markham had interested himself in his son's promotion several months earlier, Somerville begged his interference again, asking him to 'excuse the anxiety of a father' who had 'seven other children to provide for, and I fear little or no chance of employment after the wind up tho' I most ardently wish it'. These 'urgent reasons' he hoped would 'tempt' Markham to 'forgive this intrusion from a stranger'.[75] His approach seems to have been effective, or at the very least, Somerville's son's lieutenancy was quickly confirmed and dated to the same date as his letter.[76] In his following letter, he again emphasised his position as a 'stranger' to Markham as he expressed his gratitude and that of his son for the 'very great interest you have taken in our concerns tho' total strangers to you'.[77]

Somerville, however, may have had more claim on Markham's interest than he thought. He appears to have been loosely connected to Admiral Keith whom he mentioned in his first letter as having been the one who gave his son his acting commission. He also obliquely mentioned having Nelson's support in explaining his fears about not being able to support his family without employment: 'Lord Nelson gives me every reason to hope my Promotion is certain but that you well know will not add to my half pay'.[78] In his second letter, alongside thanking Markham for his support, he made a slightly riskier direct request for himself, asking if it may not be 'presuming if I further intreat [sic] you to use that interest you so kindly promise me in endeavouring to procure me employment'.[79] In doing so he also asked for Markham's advice on a 'peculiar situation' he found himself in. He had learned from a private letter that he was to be promoted to post-captain, but was unsure if he could write to St Vincent immediately to ask to be continued in commission before the news had been made official. His concern was that he had only a 'trifling claim' on St Vincent, having entered the service under his command on board *Foudroyant* in 1777. We have already seen how Markham prioritised this type of shared service connection among his other correspondents, so it seems strange that Somerville would downplay this connection.

[75] NMM, MRK/102/5/88, Somerville to Markham, 24 April 1802.
[76] *The Commissioned Sea Officers of the Royal Navy, 1660–1815*, ed. R. L. DiNardo and D. Syrett (Navy Records Society, 1994).
[77] NMM, MRK/102/5/89, Somerville to Markham, 1 May 1802.
[78] NMM, MRK/102/5/88, Somerville to Markham, 24 April 1802.
[79] NMM, MRK/102/5/89, Somerville to Markham, 1 May 1802.

122 PATRONAGE AND THE BRITISH NAVY, 1775–1815

Somerville was either guileless and underestimated his connection to Markham via these indirect ties, or he expertly employed these expectations of charity and duty to excuse his forging a more direct connection with Markham for himself. Strangers like Somerville were in a similar position, in a network sense, to those who made his acquaintance via a brokered introduction, such as John Walker. As we saw in Walker's case, however, these relationships could be extremely fragile and seemingly difficult to navigate. The more abstract factors of duty and charity seem to have been more successful and, therefore, writing as a stranger could counter-intuitively be a safer option for applicants whose only other means to establish an acquaintance with Markham was via a weak recommendation.

Regardless of how deliberate Somerville was in styling himself as a stranger, the complex spread of factors, from duty and charity, to his ties of obligation to many of Markham's strong connections, seems to have encouraged Markham to take Somerville under his protection. In the coming years Somerville looked to Markham for further support and candid advice. He also, crucially, readily obliged Markham in return by taking the sons of other brokered connections he needed to get employment.

Lieutenant Daniel Carpenter is another correspondent who secured Markham's consistent support without having any prior acquaintance. His initial connection to Markham seems to have come via George Tierney, a politician who was appointed Naval Treasurer in 1803. Carpenter first wrote to Markham in August that year, acting on Tierney's advice to introduce himself and gently remind him of a verbal recommendation Tierney had made on Carpenter's behalf at some point in the previous couple of months, which from 'the length of time that has elapsed and the numerous applications you must consequently have, I am led to believe his application must have escaped your memory'.[80] Markham seems to have responded positively, offering his support. Over the next four years, Carpenter wrote to Markham at least another ten times. His surviving correspondence is a mixture of requests for employment and effusive thanks for appointments that Markham secured for him: the first being to *Viper*, a rather leaky cutter, in December 1803, and the second to the more profitable cutter *Cheerful* in January 1807.

In the grand scheme of brokered connections, Carpenter's relationship with Markham does not seem particularly unusual. But the consistency of Markham's interest in him is striking because other than an unclear connection to George Tierney, he did not have many of the other characteristics that could distinguish him as a profitable person to patronise. His career had not been particularly successful. He joined the navy in 1779 on board *Convert* under the command of Captain Henry Harvey, whom he served under twice more in his early career. Unlike Markham, he was not lucky enough to make lieutenant

---

[80] NMM, MRK/103/1/19, Carpenter to Markham, 10 August 1803.

during the American War of Independence. Instead, he served throughout the 1780s and early 1790s as a midshipman or master's mate until he finally got a step as an acting-lieutenant in 1796, eventually being confirmed as lieutenant of *Champion* in 1798. In 1800, he met with a further setback when he was court-martialled for disobedience and disrespect to his captain while serving as lieutenant of *Expedition*, resulting in his being dismissed from the ship.[81] He was fortunate however to remain employed, albeit not in a very lucrative position, as commander of the hired lugger *Speculator*, in which he still served when he first wrote to Markham in August 1803.[82]

His role as the sole earner for a fairly large family, who seemed to be at permanent risk of destitution if his letters are to be believed, also made his requests at times somewhat awkward. In March 1807, after being so effusively thankful to Markham for his appointment to *Cheerful* a few months before, Carpenter was arrested while he was in the process of fitting out the ship. Facing the prospect of being superseded from his command, Carpenter's wife, Harriet, discovered that he had since been appointed as one of the lieutenants of the third rate *Hercule*, repairing at Chatham. As a result, Carpenter wrote to Markham in some distress, asking him to again intervene and allow him to retain his command, so that he could support his family: 'You know Sir! my situation. You know that they have no other dependence in the World but on me.' He stressed that 'if their Lordships still persist in my Appointment to the Hercule, I shall be under the unavoidable necessity of resigning my Commission as such an Appointment, will not be sufficient to support [them]'.[83] Once again, Markham seems to have been able to assist Carpenter, as two days later he wrote to thank him for allowing him to keep command of *Cheerful*:

> Sir! our Family is indebted for affording me the means for their support. Without your very friendly interference, we must have been plunged into the Abys and Distress, and Indigence, your Humanity have again placed me in a Situation, that bade us to hope, for a Change of our fortune, and for which we are in Duty bound to be grateful to you, and to pray for your Health and Prosperity.[84]

Carpenter does not appear to have had any close ties to Markham. Even if his connection was initially forged via George Tierney, then their relationship hinged primarily on second-hand ties to politics and government, rather than

---

[81] TNA, ADM 12/27C 'Black Book Vol II': digest of convictions of officers at court martial, arranged chronologically, f.24.

[82] TNA, ADM 9/7/2066 Lieutenants' Services: Daniel Carpenter, seniority 21 February 1798.

[83] NMM, MRK/103/1/28, Carpenter to Markham, 27 March 1807.

[84] NMM, MRK/103/1/29, Carpenter to Markham, 29 March 1807.

124 PATRONAGE AND THE BRITISH NAVY, 1775–1815

the deeper ties of family or professional friendship we have seen in the brokerage of other followers so far. Yet, despite the difficulties that surrounded Carpenter, not least his previous court martial and his difficult family and financial situation, Markham frequently offered his support and sometimes direct intervention in his circumstances. This suggests that Markham's interest in Carpenter rested in some other motivating factors.

One of these may have been Carpenter's wife, Harriet. Carpenter frequently mentioned his wife in his correspondence with Markham. She also wrote directly to Markham for his assistance during a particularly difficult situation Carpenter found himself in while trying to fit out and command the leaky cutter *Viper* in 1804. We will explore the action of gender in her taking on this more direct patronage role in Chapter 5. Here, the aspect of her position that is particularly interesting for understanding Markham's response to Carpenter is that Harriet was a 'child of the service'.[85]

In two of his letters, Carpenter mentioned his wife's deservingness of support explicitly because of her late father, who had died in the service. In the first he listed it amongst his other reasons for needing support:

> I trust Sir, when you consider the very serious loss Mrs Carpenter sustained in the Death of her Father in the Service of his Country, while She was an Infant, and my being very much involved from Mercantile transactions, a large family to support with no other means than my pay and what chance may throw in my way, you will be inclined to Serve her by favouring me with such a Cruise as may turn out to Advantage.[86]

In the second, he laid it out even more clearly: 'you have taken Mrs Carpenter by the Hand and honoured Her with Unprecedented Friendship, and have assured Her that you never would lose sight of me, for the Loss she sustained in Her Father, and for the Sake of Her and Her family'.[87] It is likely that Harriet's father was Captain Henry Bryne, who died while in command of *Andromeda* in a hurricane in October 1780.[88]

---

[85] Cavell, *Midshipmen and the Quarterdeck Boys*, 119–120.

[86] NMM, MRK/103/1/21, Carpenter to Markham, 23 September 1803.

[87] NMM, MRK/103/1/24, Carpenter to Markham, 5 February 1807.

[88] London Metropolitan Archives, ACC/0891/02/06/0515, Bond in £400 to secure an annual payment of £40: Henry Bryne of Portsea, Hants., Captain of his Majesty's Frigate Andromeda to Mary Maria Wady of Portsea, spinster; England Births and Baptisms 1583–1975; 'Portsea, Hampshire, England, Harriet Bryne, daughter of Henry and Maria Bryne, baptised 6 Mar 1781', *Family Search* accessed 16.08.23 at https://www.familysearch.org/ark:/61903/1:1:QLYH-LVTV; 'Surrey Marriages: Southwark, St George the Martyr' (Parish Register Transcripts, West Surrey Family History Society), *FindMyPast* accessed 25.06.20 via https://www.findmypast.co.uk/transcript?id=SURR EY%2FFHS%2FMAR%2F0060845%2F1, marriage of Daniel Carpenter and Harriet

Damage and Risk

We have already seen that most requests made to Markham were flexible and undemanding, both from those who seemed to have strong relationships with him and from those with looser ties. The more difficult a request, the greater the chance that it would be refused and potentially damage the relationship. However, Markham's support of Carpenter suggests that flexibility was not always the reigning factor in his decision to lend his assistance.

Carpenter's court martial is interesting here. Some officers personally requested a court martial to exonerate themselves in situations where they felt their judgement or character was being unfairly tarnished.[89] It was also standard practice to call a court martial on commanding officers to investigate the loss of a ship, and sometimes in cases of significant damage, but if the court saw no fault in their actions, they were typically honourably acquitted. However, many officers suffered significant damage to their careers or were forced to retire from the service entirely as a result of charges brought against them, especially in cases of insubordination, disrespect or disobedience.[90] Even in cases where an officer was acquitted or the charges brought against him were found to be unreasonable, being brought to one at all could still be a reputation-killer.

Of course, being well-connected gave some young officers the chance to avoid a reputation-ending court martial entirely. One of Markham's political connections, Thomas Assheton Smith, wrote to him in 1803 asking for his help getting his son removed from his ship, *Lark*, when it arrived in the Downs because the ship's commander had advised him that it was the only way to avoid bringing his son to a court martial for his 'improper behaviour' while on board.[91] It is not clear exactly what Smith's son had done to place him at such risk of disgrace, but he told Markham that *Lark*'s commander, John Tower, suggested that allowing his son to go to a court martial 'must be fatal to Him'.[92] Markham obliged him and not only removed Smith's son but also

---

Bryne, 1795; Plymouth and West Devon Record Office, 166/9 Baptism registers, Stoke Damerel: baptism 26 March 1806, f.54, Arabella Eliza, daughter of Daniel and Harriet Carpenter, born 9 January 1800, Amanda Ann, daughter of Daniel and Harriet Carpenter, born 14 December 1802, Henry Daniel, son of Daniel and Harriet Carpenter, born 7 November 1805; Rif Winfield, *British Warships in the Age of Sail, 1714–1792: Design, Construction, Careers and Fates* (Barnsley: Pen and Sword Books, 2007), 235.

[89] *Naval Courts Martial, 1793–1815*, ed. J. D. Byrn (Navy Records Society, 2009), 76.

[90] Wilson, *British Naval Officers*, 52–54.

[91] NMM, MRK/104/2/98, Thomas Assheton Smith to Markham, [1803].

[92] In a separate letter to Markham, Admiral Keith also mentioned a possible incident as 'that infamy in the Lark': Keith to Markham, 22 December 1803, in Markham (ed.), *Selections from the Correspondence of Admiral John Markham*, 123.

126 PATRONAGE AND THE BRITISH NAVY, 1775–1815

got him another appointment very shortly afterwards, on board *Nemesis* under the command of Phillip Somerville, who we saw above felt deeply indebted to Markham and so perhaps could be safely trusted with taking on such a potentially risky request.[93] Regardless of whether Smith meant fatal in the sense of his career and reputation or in reference to a charge that could carry a death sentence, he and Markham moved quickly to protect his son. Their efforts seem to have been effective too, or at least, Smith appears to have avoided any charges being brought against him and went on to serve aboard *Temeraire* at the battle of Trafalgar.[94]

But what of those who were not so lucky as to have their connections intervene and prevent the court martial taking place? Lieutenant John George Nops was court-martialled in March 1803 having been accused of treating a midshipman while he was third lieutenant on board *Determinee* 'in a manner unbecoming the character of an officer and a gentleman by pulling his ears and felling him to the deck'.[95] In his defence, Nops admitted that he had light-heartedly taken the midshipman by the ear 'in order to lift him up as a youngster', which he did not see as an impropriety at the time.[96] Ultimately, the court judged the charge that had been brought against Nops to be 'trifling' and so he was fortunately acquitted. However, without an honourable acquittal Nops risked carrying the stigma of the charge forward with him in his career, a point that he was acutely aware of in his statement to the court: 'a bare acquittal for want of evidence will not by any means take away the stigma the accusation has lain me under'.[97]

After the court martial, he was moved from *Determinee* to *Dreadnought* where he served until January 1804 when he moved to another acting-lieutenant position on board *Neptune*, until he secured command of the gun-brig *Defender* on October 1804 where he remained for two years until the ship was paid off in November 1806.[98] He wrote to Markham in the following January. Only one letter from Nops survives in the collection, but his opening to it suggests there had been some previous correspondence.[99] He began by apologising for being troublesome by 'intruding' on Markham again so soon, but he felt he could not 'pass over' the letter Markham had sent him without some explanation.

---

[93] NMM, MRK/104/2/100, Thomas Assheton Smith to Markham, 17 September 1803.

[94] TNA, ADM 36/15851 Ship: TEMERAIRE 1805 Sep–1806 Jan, Lt. William Smith entered 1 September 1804.

[95] *Naval Courts Martial* (NRS), 538.

[96] *Naval Courts Martial* (NRS), 542.

[97] *Naval Courts Martial* (NRS), 543.

[98] TNA, ADM 196/5/427 Officers' Service Record (Series III): John George Nops, Commander, Date of Appointment: 28 September 1802.

[99] NMM, MRK/103/2/13, John George Nops to Markham, 13 January 1807.

'No man is more ready to allow', he wrote, 'that there are many Officers much more deserving, than I can be.' It seems, then, that Markham initially gave him the usual polite brush off, reminding the applicant that there were many deserving officers to be seen to; not unusual in the context of January 1807 when Markham was facing signs of a likely change of administration and an end to his time at the Admiralty.

However, in this instance Markham seems to have lent his support. Nops was appointed to *Princess Augusta* some time between 19 February and 3 March 1807, moving to the command of another gun-brig, *Turbulent*, shortly after on 7 May 1807.[100] Like the others who were not well-known to him, Nops emphasised Markham's reputation for fairness in his request: 'I do not pretend to any claim, but on that justice for which you are so remarkable and forms so distinguishing a part in your character'. But, interestingly, he also actively used the stigma he struggled against as a result of his court martial as the reason why he needed Markham's support, because unlike the many other 'deserving officers', he could not risk waiting his turn. He wrote: 'those officers lye under no stigma, they can make use of the influence of their friends, therefore a little delay can be but of little consequence to them'.

Nops's court martial had undoubtedly damaged his reputation and by extension his patronage and career. It did not, however, prevent him from approaching Markham or accessing his support. In fact, rather the reverse. Whereas Markham seems to have initially set him aside, along with the numerous other 'deserving officers' with whom he had no prior or close connection, Nops's disadvantaged position seems to have changed his mind. Perhaps his own experiences with being court-martialled, as we saw in Chapter 2, made Markham sympathetic to seemingly blameless officers like Carpenter and Nops who faced the disadvantage without the strong connections that Markham himself had benefited from. Or perhaps his position as an Admiralty patron, in the ambiguous space between the administrative and the personal, placed enough distance between himself and those who carried the reputational damage of the court martial that he could afford the risk of supporting them.

He certainly helped others in the aftermath of courts martial. For example, Gertrude Buller, wife of Captain Edward Buller who wrote several friendly letters to Markham himself, wrote in January 1804 recommending her brother-in-law Augustus Buller, who had been dismissed from the service in a court martial the previous June for having 'absented himself from his duty frequently without leave'.[101] He was reinstated to his rank and his name erased from the navy's 'Black Book' in February 1804.[102] The Bullers were well-connected:

[100] TNA, ADM 196/5/427 Officers' Service Record (Series III): John George Nops.
[101] NMM, MRK/102/7/39, Gertrude Buller to Markham, 12 January 1804; MRK/102/1/115–118, Edward Buller to Markham, 1803–1806.
[102] TNA, ADM 12/27C Black Book Vol II, f.111v.

128   PATRONAGE AND THE BRITISH NAVY, 1775–1815

Gertrude was the daughter of Colonel Philip Van Cortlandt, a prominent North American family, and Edward was himself from a prominent Cornish family and had been MP for East Looe since 1802.[103] So it may not have been Markham directly who assisted them in this instance, but it is also equally possible that it was.

His assistance was also not limited to well-connected commissioned officers. The boatswain James Morgan was court-martialled and dismissed from his ship *Isis* when he hurt his ankle on shore and was unable to get back in time to sail.[104] He was sentenced to be dismissed from *Isis* and to serve before the mast, but a month after his letter to Markham he was serving as boatswain once again, on board *Beaulieu*.[105] On the day of the court martial he wrote to Markham for his help:

> I have now Sir, to implore your protection (for the sake of my Wife and Family, I have three small Children one of whom is at the breast, and are at present with me) and hope from your known generosity, I hope you will have the goodness (on their accounts) to use your interest, and rest assured that my future conduct shall be such as to meet your approbation, and make up for my late neglect.[106]

Morgan's invocation of his need to protect his wife and family may well have been significant in Markham's decision to assist him despite the court martial, as we have seen with other kinds of requests. Or perhaps Markham had a particular soft spot for assisting those whose position he felt had been unfairly damaged by being brought to a court martial in the first place.

He did not, however, help everyone who applied to his assistance in the aftermath of a trial. Lieutenant John Sibrell requested Markham's assistance in getting him employed in a better command than the hired cutter *Duchess of Cumberland* in February 1804, almost a year after he had been court-martialled for disrespect towards the commander of another vessel and dismissed from his own as a result.[107] He languished on *Duchess of Cumberland* for at least another year until he was given a slight step to the gun-brig *Piercer* in 1805, under the first lordship of Henry Dundas, Viscount Melville.[108] In general,

---

[103] *The History of Parliament: The House of Commons 1790–1820* (1986), ed. Thorne, https://www.historyofparliamentonline.org/volume/1790-1820/member/buller-edward-1764-1824

[104] NMM, MRK/105/3/31, James Morgan to Markham, 3 May 1803; TNA, ADM 12/27C Black Book Vol II, f.49v.

[105] TNA, ADM 48/64/110 Will of Morgan, James Rank/Rating: Boatswain's Mate Ship Name: Beaulieu 04 June 1804.

[106] NMM, MRK/105/3/31, James Morgan to Markham, 3 May 1803.

[107] NMM, MRK/103/3/8, John Sibrell to Markham, 15 February 1804; TNA, ADM 12/27C Black Book Vol II, f.111.

[108] Winfield, *British Warships in the Age of Sail, 1793–1817*, 340.

MARKHAM'S ADMIRALTY CORRESPONDENTS

Markham also did not make a habit of overstepping his purview by intervening after courts martial. In response to Captain William Kelly's request for his advice and support following his court martial over his behaviour during a mutiny on board his ship, Markham wrote unequivocally that 'it would be highly improper for me to offer any private opinion upon a subject which belongs to the Board'.[109]

Of course, Markham may have helped some of his connections because of their position in his network and ability to return the favour, like Thomas Assheton Smith, who was MP for Andover in Hampshire, or the Bullers.[110] However, connection alone was also not enough to encourage his assistance in the risky situation that followed a court martial. Indeed, in some cases, the use of the usual patterns of brokered support and application to his patronage actually seems to have damaged an individual's connection to him, and perhaps that of the broker too.

In March 1807, Samuel Best, who had been a surgeon on board the sloop *Hazard* before he was dismissed by a court martial in February 1807 for a prolonged absence from his ship in the previous December, wrote to Markham for his assistance in getting him reinstated to his former rank. Alongside his own polite letter, he enclosed one from his relation, Joseph Hepworth, a landed gentleman in Yorkshire, who seems to have been known to Markham via his family connections there.[111] Hepworth enacted all the usual, and often effective, forms of a brokered request. He apologised for the 'necessity of addressing' Markham on Best's behalf, but in the absence of Thomas Troubridge, whom Best had served under on board *Culloden* for several years, Hepworth was his 'only recourse'. He also vouched for Best's character, writing 'I have known him ever since he was a Child and his Character has been irreproachable', as well as mentioning his 'dutyful' behaviour towards his widowed mother who was surviving on 'a very small income'. Best also finished his own letter by requesting 'a few minutes conversation to explain particulars that you may be satisfied you do not employ your influence in the behalf of a person unworthy thereof'.[112]

Despite the politeness of both Best and his relation's letters to Markham, his drafted response makes it clear that he was not at all inclined to intervene on Best's behalf, regardless of his connections:

---

[109] NMM, MRK/102/3/79, Markham's note dated 31 August on William H. Kelly to Markham, 28 August 1803.

[110] Thomas Assheton Smith, MP for Caernarvonshire 1774–1780; MP for Andover, Hampshire 1797–1821, https://www.historyofparliamentonline.org/volume/1754-1790/member/assheton-smith-thomas-1751-1828.

[111] NMM, MRK/105/8/16, Joseph Hepworth to Markham, 1 March 1807.

[112] NMM, MRK/105/8/15, Samuel Best to Markham, 5 March 1807.

130 PATRONAGE AND THE BRITISH NAVY, 1775–1815

> Adm¹ M is sorry that his occupation does not permit of a personal interview with Mr Best, nor can the Adm¹ use his influence in favour of any individual on account of that person being patronised by the Adm¹ˢ friends, but due attention will be paid to any circumstances attending the trial should His Majesty in council think fit to refer it to the Board of Admᵗʸ for their consideration and opinion in mitigation of the sentence.

The refusal of a personal interview because of his being so occupied with his Admiralty business, and the promise that the *board* would consider the case should it merit it, read in many ways as the usual sort of brush off Markham gave to people he could not help. But the line about his being unable to use 'his influence' is particularly damning. Markham may well have been offended that Best had laid out the typical mechanism of patronage so explicitly in a situation where the usual reciprocity was not really possible, given Best's bad position and the risk it would pose to Markham to intervene. His firm refusal at the very least indicates that Markham would not be drawn into lending his support and risking his *own* reputation in such a murky situation, simply because of Best's connections to someone in his extended network.

This may partly have been because the situation surrounding Best's court martial was different from some of the other cases presented here. A series of letters in the correspondence of the navy's Transport Board, the medical department at this time, reveal that there was some question over Best's sanity when he was absent from *Hazard*.[113] Now, a judgement of mental derangement was not necessarily as destructive to an individual's reputation as might first appear. Markham certainly helped others who had been found to be insane, or had even spent time in Hoxton house, the private asylum the navy contracted for the care of 'lunatic seamen'.[114] However, the situation for Best soon became murkier. Failing to hear from the Transport Board about what best to do, the admiral in charge of Best ordered that he be surveyed by the surgeons at Plymouth hospital, who reported back that they found 'no symptom of insanity about him'.[115] Best was then court-martialled on 9 February and he was sentenced to be dismissed from the service. A Transport Board note about

[113] NMM, ADM/ET/53 Affidavit of John Lower, Surgeon and Apothecary that surgeon Samuel best 'laboured under Mental Derangement', 15 January 1807; William Young to Admiralty, 15 and 28 January 1807; William Marsden, admiralty secretary, to Transport Board, 2 and 11 February 1807.

[114] Catherine Beck, 'Patronage and Insanity: Tolerance, Reputation and Mental Disorder in the British Navy 1740–1820', *Historical Research* 94:263 (February 2021), 92.

[115] TNA, ADM 1/5379, letter from Admiral William Young to William Marsden, Admiralty, 30 January 1807, enclosed in the minutes of the court martial of Samuel Best, 9 February 1807.

Best on 23 March reveals the severity of his situation: 'The Board under all the Circumstances of the Case do not think proper to employ Mr Best again.'[116]

The amount of back and forth between the Admiralty and the Transport Board suggests that Markham was most likely aware of the strange circumstances surrounding Best's case, when Best wrote to request his assistance on 5 March 1807. Surgeons also fell into a difficult space in terms of who was in charge of their appointments. Best was sent between the Transport Board and the Admiralty several times offering his memorial of service to appeal to be reinstated after his court martial. Both boards asked the other for their opinion on how to proceed.[117] But ultimately the control over surgeons' appointments rested with the Transport Board. So it is possible that Markham simply did not want to risk overstepping his purview in this case, especially given the murky waters that surrounded Best's mental state, and more importantly his character, as his supposed insanity had not been satisfactorily proven.

Best's letter and Markham's response ultimately reveal the importance of the somewhat ephemeral role of *expectation* in the style of patronage that Markham performed. The standard rules of engagement, that connections and especially brokered connections were the way to secure assistance, did not necessarily work in the pressured circumstances that a lord of the Admiralty found himself. Any sense of expectation or entitlement to his assistance because of these factors could actually serve to damage a person's request and as a result their relationship with Markham as their patron and supporter. Here the weight of connections, therefore, could actually serve to damage an individual's position. Whereas Markham seems to have actively helped those without friends, his threshold for offence with officers of a higher social status with many connections within elite society, seems to have been extremely low. Especially if they showed any signs of an entitlement to his attention for having played the game of reciprocity, or Pellew's wheel, correctly.

Captain Albermarle Bertie angered Markham in 1803 by complaining that his first lieutenant had been transferred to another ship by the request of a less senior officer, while his request to have his own candidate made his first lieutenant had been ignored: 'you have taken Mr Sharpe from me at the request of a very junior officer without my knowing any thing of the Circumstances'.[118] Markham drafted two replies on this letter, and the difference in the two reflects his anger as well as his careful framing of the response. He was visibly affronted in the first draft and sarcastically offered to never promise to help Bertie again to avoid future offence: 'the complaint you make however is

---

[116] NMM, ADM/ET/53 William Marsden, admiralty secretary, to Transport Board, 23 March 1807.

[117] NMM, ADM/ET/53 Samuel Best to Admiralty, 16 and 21 March 1807; Admiralty clerical note forwarding letters to Transport Board, 22 March 1807.

[118] NMM, MRK/102/1/55, Bertie to Markham, 27 June [1803].

132 PATRONAGE AND THE BRITISH NAVY, 1775–1815

sufficient warning to me when future applications may be made not to attend them by which means I shall be certain of not giving offence, although I may not be able to give satisfaction'. His second draft, which was probably his actual reply, was far more formal and correct, but no less firm: 'If you have any thing to say in future on the subject of appont⁵ of off⁵ to the Windsor Castle, I request that the letter may be addressed through Sir Evan Nepean.'[119] Nepean was the Admiralty secretary and, by suggesting this, Markham effectively severed the connection which allowed Bertie to solicit him directly.

Bertie may have felt he had a fairly strong claim on Markham's attention. Two years earlier, when fitting out his new command *Malta* in 1801, he had accepted two young officers whom Markham was interested in: Lt Richard Maundrell and Lt Donald Fernandez, who had both served with Markham on *Centaur* between 1799 and 1801.[120] However, Markham may not have seen it this way. Donald Fernandez, for instance, had certainly served with Markham but he had also spent most of his early career following Bertie from ship to ship,[121] which suggests that he was more Bertie's follower than Markham's. Markham, then, may have seen accepting him on *Centaur* in 1799 as a favour to which Bertie was in his debt, rather than the other way around.

The case with Maundrell is a little less clear. He seems to have been favoured by Markham, and, interestingly, had also previously been court-martialled.[122] So Bertie may have seen accepting Maundrell onto *Malta* in 1801 as quite a large favour to Markham's interests. In a letter a few weeks before the one that offended Markham in 1803, Bertie had made a request for Maundrell to replace the lieutenant who was removed against his wishes. The way he made the request suggests he thought that he was ingratiating himself to Markham by favouring Maundrell once again:

> I have no wish to Object to [Sharpe's] removal, should the Board think proper to replace him by Lieut Richard Maundrell, who is a person you spoke very highly of to me when you put him into the Malta, and who in my opinion deserves every Thing that can be said of him.[123]

If anything, however, Markham seems to have read this more as a demand, than anything close to resembling a favour.

Perhaps this was connected to the way that Markham viewed the reputational effects of courts martial, as we have seen already. Or perhaps it had

---

[119] NMM, MRK/102/1/55, Bertie to Markham, 27 June [1803].

[120] NMM, MRK/102/1/59, Bertie to Markham, 26 March [1801].

[121] TNA, ADM 9/6/2000 Lieutenants' Services: Donald Fernandes, seniority 9 February 1797.

[122] TNA, ADM 12/27C Black Book Vol II, 30 May 1795; *Naval Courts Martial* (NRS), 544–551.

[123] NMM, MRK/102/1/55, Bertie to Markham, 1 June [1803].

more to do with Bertie's professional position, on the cusp of becoming a rear-admiral, and social position, as the illegitimate son of an earl. Like St Vincent, perhaps Markham felt any hint of demand or entitlement much more acutely in this context than if the criticism had come from an officer in a less privileged position. After all, Pellew's wheel of reciprocal favours had a negative edge to it. The same web of powerful connections that provided access to a patron could also be brought against that patron if they neglected or offended an applicant. Reciprocity in this sense, therefore, was less about what gifts or favours could be directly reciprocated, and more about what damage a refusal could do to Markham and his family's reputations if the snubbed applicant was well-connected enough to make their lives difficult once he was out of the Admiralty.

We will also see in the following chapter how those with political connections could lever the weight of their influence against someone in Markham's position. Perhaps even more so than someone like Bertie, Markham's constituents had both a duty-bound claim on his attention and a kind of power over him. After all, his seat in parliament and his consequent ability to assist the government who supported his position at the Admiralty depended upon his constituents and the Portsmouth corporation remaining satisfied with him. The reciprocity of their position was an incentive for him to look to their needs but it was also in many ways a threat. Those who overstepped the faint line of politeness by accusing him of neglecting them or prioritising others, or even just stating their expectations too explicitly, met the same rebuff and damage to their connection with him as others like Best and Bertie.

This may be why Markham so often fell back on the less personal structures of Admiralty business when refusing requests. Employing the language of duty to the service and the pressure of Admiralty appointments allowed Markham and others on the board to place distance between themselves and demanding applicants by making a refusal less personal. It may also be why he seems to have been so willing to help those who presented themselves as 'friendless'. The strangers among his correspondents who emphasised his reputation for fairness and duty, or those in his network who stressed that he was their 'only friend', in effect emphasised that there would be no push back if he was unable to fulfil their request.

Typically an applicant needed a strong personal connection with Markham to make a demanding or risky request, as we saw when he rebuffed the purser John Walker because he had no 'personal knowledge' of him. But in this context, perhaps counter-intuitively, having no strong connections and being in an otherwise weak patronage position from factors such as reputational damage, actually made an applicant more likely to succeed in securing Markham's favour. They may not have been able to reciprocate his support directly, in the sense of Pellew's 'wheel', but they were also less able to reciprocate negatively. Furthermore, when his support put them in a position

134 PATRONAGE AND THE BRITISH NAVY, 1775–1815

where they were finally able to reciprocate, Markham could trust that they would remember his assistance and could be relied upon to help him, as Phillip Somerville did.

Reciprocity and Trust

This chapter has somewhat complicated the idea of reciprocity as a defining factor within the patronage exchange. The nature of Admiralty patronage and its somewhat ambiguous position between the formal and informal, the administrative and the personal, stretched the usual rules and expectations of the exchange, making direct reciprocity less possible and consequently less important. Reciprocity, however, remained closely connected to the role of *trust* in naval patronage. Trust in patronage relationships went both ways. An applicant trusted that their broker or patron would have their best interests at heart, either because of personal affection, previous obligations or because of other incentives they offered the patron to fulfil their request. The patron, in return, trusted that the applicant would be a credit to their favour and not damage their reputation, would be satisfied by their support and would reciprocate the favour given the opportunity. For someone in Markham's position, this trust also included the expectation that the applicant would understand that it was not always possible to fulfil their request.

The apparent entitlement in the requests or behaviour of well-connected applicants could just as easily be read as the great amount of *trust* they had that their request would be readily obliged because of their status. Yet, the lack of a personal relationship with Markham or the presence of other factors that damaged their reputation in his eyes made him reluctant to prioritise their requests above others he deemed more deserving of his assistance or to trust that they were worth the risk in more difficult requests. We could read his response to complaints like Bertie's as a lack of trust that his effort on his behalf would be reciprocated. If someone had so many good connections, would they remember Markham when *he* needed support and no longer had the gift of Admiralty patronage in his possession?

In contrast, whereas applicants like Bertie perhaps expected too much in their requests of Markham, those lower down the social scale seem to have expected too little, especially when it came to their expectation of being secure in his attention to them at all. In part, this reflects a pattern that the larger the social gap between applicant and patron the less incentive there was for the patron to take care of the applicant. Those lower down the social scale are typically excluded from discussions of patronage and credit, partly because the power imbalance between patrons like Markham and lower-level applicants made direct reciprocity unrealistic. Typical modes of reciprocity were in many ways missing in these sorts of relationships, meaning that individuals had fewer ways that they could foster obligation and bolster trust. It was also more

MARKHAM'S ADMIRALTY CORRESPONDENTS

difficult to access the patronage networks of people like Markham from this level of society. However, as Chapter 6 will explore in more depth, personal connection, trust and reciprocity, all key defining features of patronage among the elite, also defined relationships and employment among the lower levels of society. Equally, this chapter has shown that success in requests was not strictly determined by an applicant's ability to directly reciprocate Markham's support. We have also seen that lower-level applicants were by no means excluded from his patronage. In fact, they used many of the same styles of approach as those above them on the social scale.

Nevertheless, some of Markham's lower-level correspondents seem to have been aware that his support of them was by no means guaranteed. Even the carpenter Russel White, whose relationship with Markham had an originally much more reciprocal basis than most lower-level correspondents, was unsure of his connection and Markham's willingness to assist him, despite Markham's assurances that he would help him and his sons when the opportunity presented itself.[124] In his last surviving letter in the collection, White requested Markham's support once again to help him secure a position on *Royal George* because his current ship *Salvador del Mundo* was going into dock and he feared would be broken up, leaving him unemployed. His anxiety, most likely fuelled by Markham's apparent failure to help him before, prompted White to make an even deeper appeal to Markham's charity and sense of duty:

> I shall be much Distrest to provide for my family as No part of it is provided for and if any thing should happen to you I have No other frind to asist me or famely wich is the Reason of my trubling you so offten wich I hop you will forgive one for Duing But my famely is the Ocasion if I should be out of Bread I have No means to support my family.[125]

Markham's noted reply suggests that White was once again disappointed: 'There is no vacancy made but he may depend upon it that I will attend to his interests when opportunity offers.'

White was lucky, however, in the sense that *Salvador del Mundo* was not broken up as he feared. He remained employed in his position on board until June 1808 when he finally retired from the service.[126] One of his sons also joined him on board in the March following his last surviving letter to Markham. He was rated as a first class volunteer and a month later as a

---

[124] NMM, MRK/104/3/48, Russel White to Markham, 30 April 1801, Markham's noted reply, 30 April 1801; MRK/104/3/49, White to Markham, 19 June 1802, Markham's noted reply, 21 June 1802.

[125] NMM, MRK/104/3/50, White to Markham 30 June 1802.

[126] TNA, ADM 29/1/254 Navy Pay Office: Entry Books of Certificates of Service (Warrant Officers).

136   PATRONAGE AND THE BRITISH NAVY, 1775–1815

midshipman, which suggests that his initial entry to the ship was secured by his captain, Charles Henry Lane, rather than Markham's direct intervention.[127] However, Lane was one of Markham's trusted connections and *Salvador del Mundo* was also the flagship of Admiral George Keith Elphinstone, so despite his concerns White was well within Markham's sphere of connection and influence. Nevertheless, he seems to have not trusted that Markham would remember him if the ship had been broken up. For a warrant officer like White, laying so much hope on the support of a patron at such distance and under such pressure as Markham could seem like too great a risk.

A letter from Captain Robert Keen about the potentially damning behaviour of his boatswain represents this vertical lack of trust well. Keen wrote to Markham in December 1801 to inform him of the disappearance of Thomas Robinson, the boatswain whom Markham had recently appointed to his ship.[128] Robinson had served under Markham's command as boatswain of *Centaur* between 1798 and 1801, and it seems that he drew on this connection either actively or passively in securing Markham's favour.[129] Keen told Markham that Robinson had joined the ship with his chest and bedding and had spent some time speaking to Mr Bonner, the boatswain he would be replacing. After a few hours of talking with Bonner, Robinson asked for leave to go ashore and never returned. Keen believed his old boatswain had 'prejudiced' Robinson against the ship and was 'desirous to find out if possible the true reason that has induced Mr Robinson to have acted so unthinkingly'. He urged Markham: 'should he ever make another application for your patronage, I hope you will induce him to explain his Conduct'.

Although Keen by no means condoned Robinson's behaviour, he seems to have understood, or perhaps even expected, that Robinson would believe the late boatswain more readily than he would trust Markham. Keen finished his letter explaining his reason for writing to Markham privately rather than reporting Robinson's absence via more public channels: 'I do not make a public application, not wishing to injure the present Boatswain, whose only fault that I know of has been too much Credulity'. Robinson's behaviour could have severely damaged his reputation and relationship with Markham, and Keen seems to have been aware of this. In stressing the previous boatswain's possible influence in 'prejudicing' Robinson against the ship, Keen perhaps hoped to show that his behaviour was not born out of disrespect or ingratitude to Markham, but rather a *natural* trust in his peers over his superiors; even if that trust may have been misplaced or was a product of Robinson's naivety in apparently failing to consider that Bonner may have had ulterior motives

---

[127] O'Byrne *A Naval Biographical Dictionary*, 1281–1282, accessed via https://en.wikisource.org/wiki/A_Naval_Biographical_Dictionary/White,_Mark

[128] NMM, MRK/102/3/80, Robert Keen to Markham, 9 December 1801.

[129] TNA, ADM 36/14164–7 Ship: CENTAUR Mar 1798–Jul 1801.

in persuading him to desert his post. In relation to Mr Bonner's behaviour, Keen stated the point more explicitly. While acknowledging that Mr Bonner's 'large Family of Six Children claims great compassion', Keen stressed that if he could be convinced of Bonner's 'ingratitude in this Instance' he would not hesitate in recommending him for 'punishment instead of promotion'.

If we read Robinson's behaviour from outside the paternalistic and slightly condescending lens of his superior officer's description, then we can begin to see the priorities that helped him navigate his career, employment and connections. In listening, even perhaps naively, to the other boatswain on the ship, Robinson showed that connections to his peers were potentially more important to him than his supposedly more strategic connections to officers he had served under like Markham. Certainly, Robinson could benefit by pleasing connections like Markham, as others of his rating did. But Robinson's willingness to believe the other boatswain also suggests that he felt there was no guarantee of Markham's continued support and assistance to him, or that Markham would be ready to assist him if he ended up employed in a potentially harmful situation. His claim to Markham's attention from having served under him was useful for securing employment, but was not worth risking serving on a bad ship, which could damage his reputation and even his health. Rather than being at the mercy of Markham's potential disregard, de-prioritisation or even straightforward neglect, Robinson acted in what he felt was his own best interest.

Robinson's lack of comparative power made him less able to reciprocate Markham's patronage support directly. This lack of reciprocity meant that Markham likely gave his support primarily out of a sense of duty or paternalistic responsibility to the lower-ranking men who served under his command. In turn, this kind of exchange carried less of a burden of trust on Robinson because the ripples of poor behaviour or reputation would have to travel further up the social scale to affect Markham, who still appeared to be charitable and magnanimous for assisting men of 'good character' who had worked well under his command in the past, and whom he supported for the 'good of the service'. Inherent in this style of connection was the implication that there was little the lower-level applicant could do to boost their connection to Markham, to make it more secure or to enhance its longevity and the likelihood of success. We have seen, however, that even if there was no guarantee of longevity in this sort of connection, the same was also true of relationships with more strengthening factors, such as similar social status, network embeddedness and direct reciprocity. So lower-level connections were not necessarily in a worse off position than their superiors higher up the social scale.

Robinson's actions also show that connection to the social elite was not necessarily the greatest priority for those lower down the social scale. This was not because they were excluded from patronage, rather the mechanisms of trust and guarantee were stretched too taut at this social distance. Robinson's

138 PATRONAGE AND THE BRITISH NAVY, 1775–1815

lack of power may have made him a less important connection to Markham and therefore a lower priority in his bestowal of favour, but, from the other side, Markham's lack of embeddedness in Robison's network made him less trustworthy as a patron.

Conclusion: 'my only friend'

When we look at naval patronage beyond a focus on 'strong ties' we can piece together a more complex picture, but one that, on the surface, also appears to be full of contradictions. Markham's responses to his Admiralty correspondents can seem alarmingly inconsistent at times. On the one hand, he would rebuff a slightly presumptuous request like John Walker's on the grounds that he was otherwise unknown to him, while on the other, he would seem to readily help those who couched their requests firmly in the semantics of being a stranger, like Phillip Somerville. It is not surprising that applicants to his favour sometimes fell afoul of this tangled web of expectations.

These apparent inconsistencies have been previously understood as symptoms of the underlying, sometimes overriding, power of connection and *interest* in the distribution of Admiralty favour.[130] As John Morrow noted in his study of the careers of admirals: 'When claims of merit were part of an overt bid for favour, they were frequently advanced to support cases that rested to some degree on interest.'[131] We have seen here the role that an emphasis on merit played in requests, especially from well-connected officers whom we could expect to have a great deal of *interest*. We have also seen the way that these sorts of applicants were conscientious in their employment of the naval fashion for flexibility and an impersonal style in requests, often in a way that was not so possible for the less well-connected or those lower down the social scale.

Connection was vital in naval patronage and so was *interest*. But the way that individuals cultivated *interest* was not only through the weight of their network connections and the reciprocity associated with them. Relationships could be moulded and defined instead by other factors of duty and charity, which were sometimes rooted in the personal connection created in situations like shared service and other times were employed on a more abstract level, especially when no prior acquaintance existed. Equally, the utility of flexibility and an impersonal style came from the awkward position between the personal and the administrative which naval patronage occupied because of the practical requirements and pressures of the navy's growing bureaucracy. It was not *just* a style to be used by the well-connected and elite to make them appear less demanding or to politely hide the teeth of their expectations. It was also necessary because the volume of appointments and applicants stretched the usual norms of direct reciprocity.

[130] Lewis, *A Social History of the Navy*, 202.
[131] Morrow, *British Flag Officers*, 159.

As such, being well-connected did not necessarily carry any extra weight for individuals in their applications to Markham's patronage. In fact, sometimes the implicit pressure and *threat* of these connections could work against an applicant. However, the combination of the fashion and preference for flexible impersonal requests with the necessity of approaching patrons like Markham either without prior acquaintance or through tenuous, unstable and weak brokered links, created a situation where, for a proportion of Markham's correspondents, he was their 'only friend'.

In May 1804, Markham received a flurry of letters from lieutenants and commanders fearing that his leaving the Admiralty would dash their hopes for advancement. Lieutenant John Pearkes, the son of a London merchant who had served under Markham on *Hannibal* and *Blonde*, asked him to make a final appointment for him to a small vessel or tender in the West Indies.[132] As Markham was 'the only friend in the service to whom I can with confidence look for support', he hoped that his ample experience in that station would give him a better chance for continued employment once Markham was out of the Admiralty.[133] Another of his followers, William Wooldridge, who had served with him on *Centaur*, shared with Markham his doubts that St Vincent would give him a better ship than his current command, a leaky blockship in Margate Roads, where he feared he would remain 'to the end of the Chapter' without Markham's assistance. He also stressed to Markham that: 'I have no other person to look up to, but yourself'.[134] Two days later, he wrote again, this time begging to be placed in the sea fencibles rather than remain in a ship where he had no hopes of gaining credit or promotion: '[a]s I fear my prospects in the service will end on your removal from the Admiralty'.[135] Markham seems to have been unable to achieve this for him either. Instead, Wooldridge ended up overseeing the fitting out of two new, speedily built sloops, *Elk* and *Harrier*, and then sailing the latter out to the East Indies, perhaps where he hoped his Cornish family's connections might put him within the influence of Edward Pellew.[136]

Unlike Pearkes, who died of apoplexy while a lieutenant on the frigate *Mermaid* in 1812, Wooldridge did finally make post-captain in June 1807.[137] His

---

[132] TNA, ADM 48/71/97 Will of John Pearkes, Midshipman, Hannibal, no. 180, 14 March 1795.

[133] NMM, MRK/103/2/17, John Pearkes to Markham, 7 May 1804.

[134] NMM, MRK/102/6/39, William Wooldridge to Markham, 10 May 1804.

[135] NMM, MRK/102/6/40, William Wooldridge to Markham, 12 May 1804.

[136] Winfield, *British Warships in the Age of Sail, 1793–1817*, 294; Kresen Kernow (formerly Cornwall Record Office), GR/554 marriage settlement: James Wooldridge, Penzance, Esq., Captain R.N. and Caroline Treweeke, Penzance, spinster. Witnesses: Mary Treweeke, Penzance, widow (mother of C.T.), William Wooldridge, Trevalyer, Esq., Captain in R.N., George Treweeke, Penzance, Esq., Captain 7th Reg. Light Dragoons.

[137] TNA, ADM 102/296 Royal Hospital Haslar May 1812; ADM 9/2/400 Captains'

140 PATRONAGE AND THE BRITISH NAVY, 1775–1815

removal to the potentially more friendly networks of the East Indies seems to have served him well, at least to begin with. After *Harrier* he gained command of the frigate *Psyche* as well as the approval of Pellew as the commander-in-chief. However, he still struggled to get the step to post-captain and he wrote to Markham once again asking for his help in December 1806. In his letter he stressed that he had seen multiple younger lieutenants make post-captain ahead of him, some of whom had even been promoted while commanding the very same sloop he had sailed out there in.[138]

It is not clear who helped him achieve the step to post-captain in the end. His seniority was dated from three months after Markham had left the Admiralty for a second time. His letter from December 1806 also did not arrive in London until June 1807, where it was redirected to Markham at his home in Lewes. However, given Pellew's reputation for speedily advancing the careers of his favoured candidates and that Wooldridge had struggled to make the step even after two years within his influence, it seems just as possible that Wooldridge owed the step once again to Markham who may well have put his name on the list of lieutenants for promotion as a final gesture before leaving the Admiralty. His worries in 1804 that he would be left without 'prospects' were not completely unfounded, even though he was in a slightly better position than Pearkes from the slim potential of gaining Pellew's, albeit possibly half-hearted, support.

Being well-connected may not have necessarily helped correspondents in individual applications to Markham's favour. It did, however, give them more options than were available to struggling lieutenants like Wooldridge or Pearkes. Captain Thomas Louis, for example, was disappointed in his applications to St Vincent and appeals to his friendship with Markham for the promotion of his son in 1803 and 1804.[139] But this was not a problem for long because he soon managed to have his son sent out to the Mediterranean fleet where he could be within the influence of his friend Admiral Nelson instead.[140] Using this other channel of support, Louis secured his son's promotion by February 1805 and thanked Nelson firmly for it.[141] The reality for the less well-connected was not that they were excluded from patronage but that they could not be so flexible. Turbulent years like the early 1800s which saw a high rate of turnover in government may have been helpful for some, because it meant they did not languish on the outside of a faction for too long. But on

---

Services: William Wooldridge, Post Captain, seniority: 10 June 1807.

[138] NMM, MRK/102/6/41, William Wooldridge to Markham, 18 December 1806.

[139] NMM, MRK/102/4/55–56, Thomas Louis to Markham, 15 September 1803 and 9 July 1804; MRK/102/7/35, Thomas Louis to Markham, 19 January 1804.

[140] NMM, CRK/8/110–111, Thomas Louis to Nelson, 4 January and 20 May 1804.

[141] NMM, CRK/8/117, Thomas Louis to Nelson, 6 April 1805.

the other hand, it also did not give them much time to capitalise on the periods when their connections were in positions of patronage control.

There is also another strange nuance to this. Some applicants, like Pearkes and Wooldridge, needed Markham, and their acknowledgement of being dependent and otherwise 'friendless' was unlikely to be a gambit to make themselves appear more favourably. But others, who presumably did have other options because of the nature of their connections, also stressed to Markham that he was their only friend, the only one they could look up to, and similarly lamented him leaving the board. One of his followers, Commander Thomas Brown, wrote: 'My hopes of getting a sloop or a Promotion are now at an End.'[142] Yet, Brown made his step to post-captain in January 1806 anyway, under Charles Middleton, Lord Barham, as First Lord.[143] He was apparently not as bereft of connections as he thought. Similarly, Lieutenant Michael de Courcy wrote in the same period: 'You are the only person I have to look up to.'[144] As the son of the Irish aristocrat Lord Kinsale, nephew of Captain Michael de Courcy and brother-in-law to Captain Charles Dashwood it seems unlikely that Markham was the *only* person he could look to for assistance.

As we saw at the very beginning of this chapter, other seemingly well-connected and well-positioned applicants like Charles Herbert also presented themselves as without 'interest' or without 'friends' in their correspondence with Markham. If we assume that his position as the son of an earl and an MP meant that he actually had multiple possible profitable connections he could draw on, then his approach seems stridently tactical. His level of connection if leveraged could implicitly translate a request into a demand, which would put Markham in a difficult and even dangerous position if the hurry of Admiralty business made him unable to fulfil it. Although the weight of his connections loomed behind his positioning himself as 'friendless', it was a way to make his commitment to the navy's stretched norms and expectations of reciprocity even clearer than a simple adherence to an impersonal style of request.

However, perhaps the claims of the apparently well-connected to being 'friendless' were not entirely strategic. Unlike Brown, De Courcy did not make the step to post-captain, even after Markham returned to the Admiralty in 1806. As Evan Wilson has shown, plenty of lieutenants like De Courcy from the upper levels of society also never made post-captain. Having lots of options was not the same as having a guarantee of success. For someone in Markham's position it was easier to retreat behind impersonal refusals on the grounds of 'duty to the service' than to make it obvious that he took the weight of connections into account when fulfilling requests. It would seem to

---

[142] NMM, MRK/102/1/19, Thomas Brown to Markham, 13 May 1804.

[143] *The Commissioned Sea Officers of the Royal Navy*, ed. DiNardo and Syrett.

[144] NMM, MRK/103/1/36, Michael de Courcy to Markham, 3 May 1804.

142   PATRONAGE AND THE BRITISH NAVY, 1775–1815

follow that the risks of these weighty connections made less well-connected but otherwise deserving applicants a more attractive option for his favour.

One way to understand the apparent inconsistencies in naval patronage, then, is to consider the applicant's network position not just in terms of the power of their connections but also the scale of their *expectations*. This chapter has shown the considerable variability and individuality of success. For someone like Pearkes, success in the aftermath of losing his best patron at the Admiralty simply meant continued employment. For Wooldridge, it was continued employment *and* promotion. For Daniel Carpenter, it was remaining in command of the small ships that gave him slightly more pay to support his family, but less chance to impress a commander-in-chief like Nelson who could promote him. For someone like the purser John Walker, securing the support of a new patron and an appointment was not enough, he also needed a bigger ship with more of an income. For the boatswain Thomas Robinson, receiving an appointment at the hands of his patron through ties of obligation and duty was not necessarily a success, because he could not entirely trust that the position would be good for him.

These highly individual contexts are not only vital in how we read patronage success, they also surrounded Markham's understanding and response to requests. What meant success for one of his correspondents could mean failure for another. Someone like Bertie felt neglected when his requests for lieutenants, carefully couched in the flexible and accommodating tone of the favoured naval style, were apparently rejected. His use of the flexible impersonal style was a self-conscious fashioning, that overlaid his expectation that his requests deserved to be obliged. Consequently, a failed request meant that he had been disregarded, rather than the more likely practical reality that it was simply not possible for the Admiralty to fulfil his request at that time.

Markham was sensitive to these different demands and expectations. However, just as there were limits on his ability to oblige a request, there were also limits on his ability to interpret the exact context in which the applicant made it. This was especially true for those whose network position and power were not so heavily implied as someone like Bertie, as was often the case for those with fewer options available to them. Someone in a vulnerable network position but who could leverage the obligations of duty and charity instead, needed to make this clear to Markham while avoiding the pitfalls of appearing either presumptuous or over-demanding. If they managed to navigate their initial connection with him well, then they could be fortunate to be fairly secure in continuing to receive his favour in the future.

Yet many of Markham's correspondents who were in this position were conservative and practical in their use of his patronage, requesting appointments that may not be their best hope of gaining accolades and speedy promotion but would see that they stayed employed or able to support their families without being at the mercy of capricious captains or a change of government. It seems they did not entirely trust that they could rely on him or that the next Admiralty lord would be as receptive to strangers. Rather than risk being left on the outside of a patronage network in a position which may have carried the hope of speedy advancement, but consequently also needed the protection of an attentive patron to ensure they were not replaced by someone else's protégé, many instead seem to have opted for these less ambitious but potentially more secure appointments.

We may be able to see with the benefit of distance that interest with Markham was made up of multiple factors beyond being well-connected among the social elite. Also, that the pressures of the navy's growing bureaucracy, increasing centralisation of appointments, and war were eroding the need even for prior acquaintance and reciprocity in the distribution of Admiralty favour. At this time of transition, where naval patronage existed awkwardly in the space between the personal and administrative, the doors to patronage and career success may have been open to everyone with merit and the obligation of duty. However, that did not mean that everyone *trusted* that they could step through them.

4

Constituents and Corporations:
The Expectations of Political Connection

> ... I fear your Portsmouth friends must have anticipated much of your patronage. But I am willing to hope it may still be possible to squeeze my Nephew in somewhere into some gunboat or some hole or corner of some kind. Perhaps Sir Thomas Troubridge may be less fettered ...
>
> Lieutenant-Colonel William Frankland, 3 May 1804[1]

Patronage wove the naval and political together in the fabric of eighteenth-century society. Political considerations, such as securing support for government from members of parliament and an MP's duty to his constituents, affected an officer's patronage but it is simplistic to frame the distribution of naval appointments merely as political rewards. Some aspects of promotion were inherently political as officers came from well-connected families who exerted power over admirals, commanders-in-chief and the Admiralty lords. On the other hand, naval position gave some officers more power in the political sphere because power in promotions and appointments made naval candidates more attractive in certain boroughs than civilian opponents. The fundamental operation of patronage was the same in both a naval and political context but, as officers like Markham discovered, the pressures and priorities of each sphere affected the subtle manners and expectations of the exchange.

Chapters 1 and 2 have illustrated the fluid boundaries between civilian and naval circles. Individuals rarely conceived of the two as distinct and most occupied more than one sphere of influence, especially in politics. Approximately ninety members in the House of Commons between 1790 and 1820 were naval officers; a comparatively small amount compared to the 300 members who were barristers and the 400 members who had at some time served in the army.[2] Unlike the army, many naval MPs between 1790 and 1820 actively served in the navy while they held their seats and consequently maintained influence over naval appointments. They were also

---

[1]   NMM, MRK/104/5/25.
[2]   Thorne, *House of Commons 1790–1820*, i.313.

THE EXPECTATIONS OF POLITICAL CONNECTION 145

well-connected in civilian circles. The great compiler of biographies for members of parliament, Roland Thorne, estimated that sixty-eight naval MPs won their seats through the civilian influence of their families and less than fifteen came in on the direct interest of the Admiralty.[3] However, naval MPs were numerically few and had little intersectional impact on wider politics or the navy. They were not hugely influential in the House of Commons, most rarely sat in parliament at all, and those who did, spoke little or passively supported the government.[4] Evan Wilson also demonstrated that MPs made up only 2 per cent of the wider body of commissioned naval officers at the end of the long eighteenth century.[5]

Of course, these estimates do not account for the numerous officers, seamen and dockyard workers who had familial connections in the House of Commons and the House of Lords as well as those who themselves were constituents and freemen or had connection to others with the power to pressure MPs. Regardless of whether naval MPs sat in the House, they secured their seats through their wide-ranging networks of support and their position gave them access to appointments in the navy as well as governmental influence. Political connections such as these and the middling borough elite who supported them gave individuals with weak or non-existent ties to the navy access to naval patronage, and vice versa. The role of politics in naval patronage was not corrupt in the sense Michael Lewis frames it, nor is it effective to cast politics simply as the bridge between the naval and civilian worlds.[6] Rather, the impact of naval connection on borough politics and the pressure exerted on the Admiralty by non-naval MPs and their connections reflect how deeply integrated the navy was in British society in the long eighteenth century.

This chapter focuses first on the effect of party politics on the distribution of Admiralty patronage. The first section compares St Vincent and his fervent disavowal of promoting for political reasons with Markham's more delicate approach in the few applications which can be identified as politically motivated in the collection. As we have already seen, the Markham collection consists mainly of the applications he received and we catch glimpses of how he responded through the notes he wrote to himself on these letters or his drafted replies. St Vincent's letter-books, on the other hand, include his responses to requests, giving us another perspective of a more complete patronage exchange and the priorities of applicants and patrons within that. The second section of this chapter explores how Markham distributed patronage as MP for Portsmouth between 1801 and 1818. The request for naval favour was not always as clear cut as the buying of votes on behalf of the

3   Ibid., 314.
4   Ibid., 315.
5   Wilson, *British Naval Officers*, 118.
6   Lewis, *A Social History of the Navy*, 226–227; Rodger, *Wooden World*, 333.

146 PATRONAGE AND THE BRITISH NAVY, 1775–1815

political corporation. However, the pressures and priorities of patronage in borough politics had a lot in common with patronage at the Admiralty. This was particularly true of the corporation's ambition that patronage would tie individuals to the institution, which collided with the reality that patronage fundamentally relied on personal connections.

Politics at the Admiralty

The Admiralty was a political body at its heart. The First Lord and the board of commissioners were appointed by the political interest of the party in power and as such their fortunes were tied to that political group. The First Lord sat in cabinet and commissioners were encouraged to participate actively in the House of Commons through securing seats in government boroughs or on their private interest.[7] The opportunity to serve the crown when the country was at war made the navy an increasingly popular career for the younger sons of the aristocracy as well as the extended families of politicians. The distribution of appointments was, therefore, a vital and time-consuming part of the First Lord's responsibility. Not only did he have to satisfy the demands of the party's political allies in the aristocracy and borough political elite, he also had to answer to the pressures of the service, securing the support of admirals and crafting a strong, talented navy through promotion.[8]

Unsurprisingly, both civilian and naval First Lords made it plain that their decisions were firmly in the good of the service and not in making political friends or enemies. Declining requests from clients in politically powerful positions was a reality which had to be dealt with carefully. Being such a high-profile member of government with access to the patronage of appointment and promotion in the entire navy meant that First Lords were open to application from acquaintances of even the slightest professional or political degree. Being an MP gave a broker licence to approach a member of the board on behalf of their constituents' personal connections and every officer in the navy was entitled to solicit the interest of the board. First Lords, therefore, were inundated with requests for preferment, and the ability to oblige their own connections, let alone those of the party, was not always possible.

N. A. M. Rodger discusses the pressures exerted on a civilian lord in his focused study of John Montagu, earl of Sandwich, during his time at the Admiralty between 1771 and 1782.[9] Sandwich was enthusiastically accused of jobbery by factions within the navy and of only pleasing his friends by those

---

[7]   Lincoln, *Representing the Royal Navy*, 42.

[8]   Morrow, *British Flag Officers*, 141–147.

[9]   Rodger, *Insatiable Earl*, 172–191. For a similar discussion of Earl Spencer's time at the Admiralty see Moira Bracknall, 'Lord Spencer, Patronage and Commissioned Officers' Careers, 1794–1801' (unpublished PhD thesis, University of Exeter, 2008).

THE EXPECTATIONS OF POLITICAL CONNECTION 147

civilian and political connections outside.[10] The plight of a naval First Lord
was not much different.[11] St Vincent, when he came to the board in February
1801, spent much of the first six months declining requests for his patronage.
He was determined to promote from his list of commanders and post-captains
on half-pay, of which there were well over a hundred; a point he was fond
of telling unsuccessful applicants. He followed a standard pattern in making
these rejections. In refusing the request of the earl of Chichester, he wrote:

> the fact is, that the list of Commanders, and Post Captains so far exceeds
> the number of ships and sloops, one third of the officers of those ranks are
> out of employment, and it has been a maxim with the present Admiralty
> Board not to add to the number excepting in reward of meritorious services
> in arms, insomuch that I have not advanced any of the officers who served
> with me in the Ville de Paris.[12]

However, St Vincent also doubted his ability to please the political elite.
In a letter to the duke of Grafton, he confessed his concerns:

> the confidence which your Grace reposes in my Zeal and assiduity is well
> founded, but I have seen so many good and gallant Admirals make a very
> contemptible figure at this Board, that I do not feel so bold on the score of
> abilities as my Friends are disposed to be.[13]

Certainly, he seems to have been more likely to explicitly offer his patronage
support in exchange for political ties when he was out of the Admiralty than
when he served as First Lord. In 1806, when St Vincent was out of government
and in command of *Hibernia* and the Channel fleet, he wrote offering his
support to Filmer Honywood, MP for Kent.[14] He wrote:

> Remembering as I do that old Baker who is gone, was a staunch Friend and
> Supporter of yours, and that your Friends are my Friends I have applied for
> Lieutenant Henry Baker to fill a vacancy in the Hibernia, and happy shall
> I be if it leads to his promotion.[15]

The pressure of the numerous applications to his favour from the politically powerful as well as his own friends, and those officers he felt deserved
promotion, meant that St Vincent's distribution of Admiralty patronage

---

[10] Rodger, *Insatiable Earl*, 174–175.
[11] Morrow, *British Flag Officers*, 147.
[12] BL, Add MS31170, St Vincent to Chichester, 22 September 1801.
[13] BL, Add MS31170, St Vincent to Grafton, 26 February 1801.
[14] Thorne, *House of Commons 1790–1820*, iv.221–222.
[15] BL, Add MS31167, f.239, St Vincent to Honywood, 1 August 1806.

148 PATRONAGE AND THE BRITISH NAVY, 1775–1815

appears inconsistent. His correspondence suggests firmly that St Vincent's two principal motivators in the distribution of Admiralty patronage were long, meritorious service alongside political support.

Applicants to Admiralty patronage were not overt in their offers of political support in exchange for naval preferment. Rather, their support was an implicit part of the long eighteenth-century style of political friendship, in which, Naomi Tadmor has argued, the use of the language of friendship encouraged reciprocity in otherwise utilitarian relationships.[16] Support in the House or in securing a borough for a favoured candidate was not offered in direct exchange for Admiralty patronage, but obliging the request of a connection in a position to assist the Admiralty politically strengthened a bond which could be drawn upon later. We can assume that those with more distant connections, however, had to make explicit offers of political support in their applications for Admiralty patronage because the convoluted route to their support meant it was not guaranteed and was not implicit in the exchange. However, explicit offers of political support rarely appear in the Markham collection, and St Vincent was cautious not to promise too much in his responses to applicants.

Most First Lords obliged party recommendations. Lewis described politics as the 'crux' of the patronage system and he considered that no other form of eighteenth-century patronage operated on a greater quid pro quo, reciprocal exchange, than political patronage.[17] This was in operation in full force at the Admiralty where the First Lord's position relied on his keeping his party in power by offering promotion and appointment as direct reward for political support. Roger Knight calculated that Thomas Grenville made 889 appointments in the twenty-one weeks he was First Lord, roughly eight a day.[18] Grenville kept good notes of the applications he received during his brief time at the Admiralty between 1806 and 1807. For part of 1806, leading into 1807, he even noted down where the support for applications for admirals had come from and whether he fulfilled requests or not.[19] Most of the clients were recommended by the 'party'. Two of the three admiral appointments that he made were from party recommendations: John Holloway and Isaac Coffin.[20] The third apparently 'non-party' appointment was Vice-Admiral Rowley for command at the South Downs.[21]

The higher an officer rose in the service, the more opportunities he had for political engagement as well as connection to those also politically engaged.

---

[16] Tadmor, *Family and Friends*, 236.

[17] Lewis, *A Social History of the Navy*, 209.

[18] Knight, *Britain Against Napoleon*, 236.

[19] HL, Stowe Papers, ST102, Thomas Grenville: Promotion Books. My thanks to Roger Knight for giving me access to his notes on these papers.

[20] Coffin was a close connection of St Vincent and Markham.

[21] Rowley also featured prominently in Markham's network described in Chapter 2.

THE EXPECTATIONS OF POLITICAL CONNECTION   149

There will always be a difficulty in establishing what exactly merited a 'party' recommendation in the eyes of contemporaries, as well as to what extent the original client believed they were drawing on political, rather than familial or regional, connections. The appointment of admirals was inherently political but simply because at that level of the navy the political, service-based and personal were enmeshed to such a degree they were largely inseparable. An admiral had more autonomy in making appointments, and therefore was an alternative route to naval patronage for the political elite.[22] Appointments to command were also offered to admirals as reward for political support, or to remove troublesome members from the House of Commons. Lewis suggested that Edward Pellew's position in the East Indies was a prime example of 'political interest'. Throughout 1801 to 1804, Pellew had supported St Vincent as First Lord, and by extension Addington's ministry. He was awarded his flag and command of the East Indies just as Addington fell from power and Pitt formed his new ministry. Rather than awarding the command to his own supporter, Pitt allowed Pellew to keep it on the condition that he in future support the Pitt administration. He consequently bought Pellew's support and removed him from home politics where he could be troublesome.[23] Henry Dundas, first earl Melville, and First Lord of the Admiralty under Pitt, pulled a similar trick by then splitting the command of the East Indies and awarding half to Thomas Troubridge in 1804.[24] Troubridge was a strong supporter of St Vincent and Addington, and although he did not speak in the House of Commons as much as Markham, he acted as a vote in support of St Vincent's reforms.[25] As with Pellew, his appointment to the East Indies removed him from his seat at Great Yarmouth and silenced him in the House. It also had the added benefit, as N. A. M. Rodger puts it, of setting 'two anti-Pittite political admirals at one another's throats'.[26]

Both Grenville and Dundas were civilian First Lords who came from large established political families and founded their careers on party politics. Their prioritisation of political applications is no real surprise.[27] St Vincent, on the other hand, has a very different historical reputation. Lewis argued that St Vincent made a 'gallant' attack on patronage as part of corruption and attempted to 'loosen the indiscriminate grip of the octopus of Interest'.[28] However, historians who have focused on the course of Addington's

---

[22] Morrow, *British Flag Officers*, 129–133.

[23] Lewis, *A Social History of the Navy*, 209–210.

[24] This episode is also mentioned in Chapter 1.

[25] Thorne, *House of Commons 1790–1820*, v.416–417.

[26] Rodger, *Command of the Ocean*, 547.

[27] Knight argues that Grenville also went to great pains to promote from the half-pay list: Knight, *Britain Against Napoleon*, 236.

[28] Lewis, *A Social History of the Navy*, 226.

150 PATRONAGE AND THE BRITISH NAVY, 1775–1815

administration accuse St Vincent of being unnecessarily antagonistic and Addington himself reportedly called St Vincent a 'political liability' after the ministry fell in 1804.[29] Lewis perhaps took St Vincent too much at his word when he described him as 'attacking' the patronage system. When St Vincent assumed power in 1801 he repeatedly told correspondents that politics would have little to do with his distribution of Admiralty patronage. To his friend, John Lloyd, he wrote: 'I never will mix in Politics', but added the caveat 'farther than is necessary to acquit myself to the persons I act with'.[30] This sentiment perhaps best reflects St Vincent's distribution of patronage and the way he responded to the numerous applications he received.[31] He did oblige political connections, where necessary.

He used his personal interest to ensure that both Markham and Troubridge sat in the House of Commons. For Markham, he drew on his connection to Sir John Carter, who, as we will see in the following section, was the informal patriarch of the Portsmouth corporation. In 1801, when he was frequently turning down other applications to his interest, St Vincent promised assistance to Carter. In August 1801, he promised Carter his candidate would 'fill the next Vacancy' in his nomination.[32] In October, he promised that he had given directions to promote another candidate, Lieutenant George Butterworth, and that he was looking to assist another, writing: 'for the interests of any one, connected with your Family cannot be indifferent'.[33] By November, St Vincent had secured Markham one of the seats at Portsmouth, made vacant on the death of Lord Hugh Seymour.[34]

St Vincent similarly used his connections at Great Yarmouth to have Troubridge placed there alongside his brother Thomas Jervis. He solicited the support of both Sir Thomas Gooch, the future MP for Suffolk, as well as other Yarmouth connections including George, Marquis Townshend.[35] St Vincent's disapproval of John Robinson, MP for Harwich, who had numerous familial connections in that corporation, most likely led to Addington replacing both MPs at Harwich with his own candidates, namely James Adams, another commissioner at the Admiralty, and his brother John Hiley Addington.[36]

---

[29] C. Fedorak, *Henry Addington, Prime Minister, 1801–1804: Peace, War, and Parliamentary Politics* (Akron, 2002), 109–110.

[30] BL, Add MS31170, f.3, St Vincent to John Lloyd, 19 February 1801.

[31] For years 1801–1804 see BL, Add MS31168–70.

[32] BL, Add MS31170, f.36, St Vincent to Carter, 11 August 1801.

[33] BL, Add MS31170, f.100, St Vincent to Carter, 24 October 1801.

[34] Thorne, *House of Commons 1790–1820*, iv.546–548.

[35] BL, Add MS31170, f.100, St Vincent to Gooch, 23 October 1801; Thorne, *House of Commons 1790–1820*, iv.34–36; BL, Add MS31170, f.78, St Vincent to Townshend, 19 September 1801.

[36] Thorne, *House of Commons 1790–1820*, iii.37 and 47–50.

THE EXPECTATIONS OF POLITICAL CONNECTION   151

Robinson had written to St Vincent in some anger when St Vincent took control of appointments made to Harwich packet ships in spring 1801. It was an unwise point to argue. St Vincent replied sternly that he thought it appalling that 'Borough influence should ever be exercised in such very important concerns' and 'no wonder that so many of [the packet ships] have failed in their duty'.[37] Even so, St Vincent was perhaps unwise in alienating Robinson with this style of rebuff. Robinson was also the Surveyor-General of Woods and Forests after 1786 and had considerable control over the timber supplies to the Royal Dockyards.[38] This later proved fatal to St Vincent's ambitious scheme of reforms in the yards and of private contractors.[39]

What St Vincent designated as politically necessary confused his contemporaries. He did not necessarily oblige even those who believed they had a strong claim on his patronage because of their position, such as Sir Richard Hill, MP for Shropshire, to whom he wrote:

> No man has better claim upon me, either in my public, or private capacity, than you have, and it is altogether unnecessary to call any other Person whatever to your aid. In the distribution of the patronage of the Admiralty, I am endeavouring to do strict justice.[40]

He similarly gave Lord Kensington the brush off while also acknowledging his political obligation to him through virtue of Kensington's position:

> My respect for your Lordships character and very long services in the House of Commons, where I had the honor to sit with you, would prompt me to an instant compliance with your wishes, was it in my power, I have so many engagements for commissions in the Marines, that I can only place your Friend Mr John James at the end of a long list.[41]

However, giving the appearance of putting a stop to promotion above commander and yet obliging certain connections met with disapproval from members of the political elite who felt that naval appointments were owed them by their government support. One example of this type of refusal was St Vincent's dealing with Captain William Allen Proby. Proby, otherwise known as Lord Proby, was the son of John Proby, first earl of Carysfort, a Whig who had significant political influence in County Wicklow, Ireland, as

---

[37] BL, Add MS31170, f.24, St Vincent to Robinson, 30 March 1801.

[38] Thorne, *House of Commons 1790–1820*, v.29.

[39] Knight, *Britain Against Napoleon*, 320–324; Roger Morriss, *The Foundations of British Maritime Ascendancy: Resources, Logistics and the State, 1755–1815* (Cambridge, 2011), 142 and 177.

[40] BL, Add MS31170, St Vincent to Hill, 17 April 1801.

[41] BL, Add MS31170, St Vincent to Kensington, 13 June 1801.

152   PATRONAGE AND THE BRITISH NAVY, 1775–1815

well as being brother-in-law to both William Grenville and George Grenville, first marquess of Buckingham, who in 1802 formed the centre of the new opposition.[42] Proby had been on half-pay since he lost his ship to mutiny in 1800 and was taken prisoner. After failing to take the seat at Wicklow in early 1801, he wrote to St Vincent, presumably requesting active service, but also suggesting that St Vincent believed he did not want employment. St Vincent gave a polite general answer of promised support in return: 'I have always considered your Lordship as most sincerely attach'd to the profession, and I shall have great pleasure in placing you in a situation to do equal honor to your country, and to your family'.[43] His empty promise was a concession made to the political power wielded by Proby's family. Certainly, St Vincent was not nearly so careful with less weighty applicants and often outright refused to enter into any 'engagement'. His refusal of William Elford, MP for Plymouth, was typically blunt: 'With every disposition to shew attention to your recommendations, I cannot possibly enter into an engagement for the promotion of Lieut[t] W B Hunt'.[44]

Proby languished on half-pay for another two years before finally being appointed to the frigate *Amelia*. Three years between losing a ship and being placed in a newly commissioned frigate was not a long wait for most officers in the navy. As Wilson has shown, promotion was grindingly slow for the majority of officers.[45] The relatively few officers whom he identified as politically well-connected had an extremely high, and often speedy, success rate in promotion.[46] Certainly, the wait did not please Carysfort. Grenville ascribed his displeasure to 'wishing that Lord St Vincent may terminate this embarrassment by giving [Proby] a tight frigate, instead of leaving him to provide himself with a pretty wife'.[47] To prevent his son from being idle, Carysfort pressed to get him in the House of Commons, first for County Wicklow and then securing the seat for Buckingham at the general election on his brother-in-law's interest. Proby then voted with the new opposition and moderately spoke against St Vincent's reforms in the dockyards, contributing eventually to the fall of the ministry in 1804.

St Vincent's supposed failure to appoint Proby to a frigate in 1801 may well have been because of Proby's having lost his ship in 1800, which put an indelible mark on his reputation.[48] Certainly, in other instances, St Vincent

---

[42] D. Fisher, 'The New Opposition, 1801–1804', *History of Parliament Online*, http://www.historyofparliamentonline.org/periods/hanoverians/new-opposition-1801-4 (accessed 10 September 2016).

[43] BL, Add MS31168, St Vincent to Proby, 22 April 1801.

[44] BL, Add MS31170, St Vincent to Elford, 7 October 1801.

[45] Wilson, *British Naval Officers*, 37–41.

[46] Ibid., 115 and 119.

[47] Thorne, *House of Commons 1790–1820*, iv.898.

[48] Lewis, *A Social History of the Navy*, 217.

THE EXPECTATIONS OF POLITICAL CONNECTION   153

was happy to oblige political connections with weak candidates who had not made such severe mistakes in the service. To John Fane, earl of Westmorland and the Lord Privy Seal, he promised to add his candidate's name to his list of commanders awaiting promotion, despite the fact that his 'services are not brilliant'.[49] Of course, this promise was likely just as conciliatory as his one to Proby, the crucial difference being Fane's Tory but otherwise fairly neutral political position virtue of his role as Lord Privy Seal, and that St Vincent seems to have felt more able to stress in his reply that Fane's candidate was essentially unsuitable. Perhaps St Vincent hoped that stressing this point would emphasise how big a favour he was bestowing on Fane even if no appointment materialised, and thus protect himself from any backlash, similar to the way Markham navigated politically weighted requests as we saw in the previous chapter. The fact that he was not so direct with Proby suggests the influence that political pressure from within his own party had on him, and the conflict it caused when it ran counter to his personal principles of what was right for the service.

St Vincent was not immune to the pressure to oblige political connections. In fact, he most consistently obliged applicants who supported Addington's administration and he often promised to assist current and previous members of cabinet. He promised to assist a relation of John Mitford who was secretary of the Treasury, writing 'I have suitors innumerable and very small means, but I will not forget that Captain Mitford is a near Relation of yours'.[50] He also placed in a gun-brig a candidate of Charles Long, the previous secretary of the Treasury under Pitt and who still sat in the House as MP for Midhurst.[51] Where he could not promote at home he sometimes offered to send the candidates of the politically powerful abroad where they could then draw on the patronage of commanders-in-chief such as George Keith Elphinstone. In this way, he obliged Thomas Parker, the brother of the earl of Macclesfield and supporter of Pitt, as well as George Boscawen, Viscount Falmouth, to whom he wrote that 'the steady and uniform support your lordship has given to His Majesty's Government, justly entitles you to ask any thing, I can consistently grant'.[52]

Many of the applicants he promised to oblige without offering anything substantial were politically well-connected. He gave similar promises to look out for the candidates of both Charles Bragge, who was Addington's brother-in-law and treasurer of the navy, as well as Charles Yorke, who was secretary at war and MP for Cambridgeshire.[53] He also offered support to political families

[49] BL, Add MS31170, St Vincent to Westmorland, 29 April 1802.
[50] BL, Add MS31170, St Vincent to Mitford, 27 February 1801.
[51] BL, Add MS31170, St Vincent to Long, 14 September 1801; Thorne, *House of Commons 1790–1820*, iv.448–452.
[52] BL, Add MS31170, St Vincent to Parker, 18 April 1801; St Vincent to Falmouth, 4 May 1801.
[53] BL, Add MS31170, St Vincent to Bragge, 12 August 1801; Thorne, *House of*

154 PATRONAGE AND THE BRITISH NAVY, 1775–1815

whose allegiance was primarily to Addington and himself. In April 1801, he promised Jane Bastard, wife of Edmund Bastard, MP for Dartmouth, that he would promote the interest of her nephews Edward and Philemon Pownoll in the marines.[54] It was not an empty promise. In June 1801, St Vincent wrote to John Pollexfen Bastard, brother of Edmund and MP for Devon, that he had managed get a place for Edward: 'I do assure you I received the greatest satisfaction, in being so soon able to place Mr Pownoll advantageously'.[55] Unfortunately, Edward's appointment in the marines seems to have later fallen through, but St Vincent had offered much more substantial support than he did to other applicants. He did, however, in 1804 manage to secure a promotion for Lieutenant John Bastard, Edmund's son.

Despite being strongly independent, Edmund Bastard and his brother consistently supported Addington and St Vincent during their time in office, refusing to move against them in 1804 when the Grenvillite opposition toppled their ministry. Of course, John Bastard and the Pownoll brothers suited St Vincent's style of patronage. Their father was the much-respected Captain Philemon Pownoll and as 'children of the service' they met St Vincent's criteria for being worthy of assistance.[56] They were also friends of Edward Pellew, whom St Vincent championed and later promoted to admiral in 1804.[57] The strength of the Bastards' service connections and independent style of politics is most likely what attracted St Vincent to favour them and, in doing so, he bought strong supporters for himself and Addington in a time of great faction and in-fighting in parliamentary politics.

Those applicants that St Vincent declined to favour were, for the most part, either lacking in political connection, or were generally known to be passive in the House and therefore neither a threat nor potential supporters of St Vincent and Addington. He refused both James Hamlyn, MP for Carmarthenshire, and John Clevland, MP for Barnstaple, most likely because they were quiet in parliament.[58] St Vincent gave a particularly harsh rejection to Clevland

---

Commons 1790–1820, iii.242–247; BL, Add MS31170, St Vincent to Yorke, 2 September 1801; Thorne, *House of Commons 1790–1820*, v.665–673.

[54] BL, Add MS31170, St Vincent to Jane Bastard, 27 February 1801; Lewis Namier and John Brooke (eds), *The History of the House of Commons 1754–1790* (Woodbridge, 1964), ii.64.

[55] BL, Add MS31170, St Vincent to John Pollexfen Bastard, 10 June 1801; Thorne, *House of Commons 1790–1820*, iii.153–155.

[56] Gill, *Naval Families*, 87.

[57] Tom Wareham, 'Pownoll, Philemon', *ODNB*, vol. 45, 167.

[58] BL, Add MS31170, f.4, St Vincent to Hamlyn, 22 February 1801; Thorne, *House of Commons 1790–1820*, iv.139.

THE EXPECTATIONS OF POLITICAL CONNECTION   155

as he wrote that he 'will never endure to be told, to whom Promotion is due, for Services performed'.[59]

However, St Vincent was also accused of rejecting applications because of political differences. His reply to Anne Piggott suggests that she had sent an aggrieved letter about the board's failure to promote Lieutenant William Bennet, brother-in-law of Lady Charlotte Wrottesley and son of Charles Bennet, fourth Earl Tankerville.[60] He wrote:

> Although I cannot subscribe to the reasoning of Lady C Wrottesley upon the subject of the ill treatment her Ladyship conceives her brother has received, you may venture to assure her that the Politics of Lord Tankerville have not operated, nor can they in the smallest degree, to the prejudice of Mr Bennett, as far as relates to me.[61]

Similarly, he seems to have alienated William Elford, MP for Plymouth, with his refusals, as when Elford regained his seat in the general election in 1802, St Vincent wrote to him that 'The fortunate circumstances which attended your Election at Plymouth will I am persuaded convince you that Government has no Enemies in that borough.'[62]

He was not alone in being accused of refusing an appointment based on political difference. Certainly, other sea officers felt that their political position alienated them from Admiralty favour. This is shown clearly in an earlier exchange of letters between Admiral George Collier and his broker the duke of Portland detailing Collier's attempts to gain the First Lord of the Admiralty, Lord Chatham's approbation to raise his flag at Chatham. When Chatham refused Collier's request, he wrote to Portland complaining that it must have been down to his politics: 'I am afraid, my Lord, that my Sins have arisen out of my political Character; the part I took when the Prince of Wales Debts was to be agitated in the House of Commons'.[63]

---

[59] BL, Add MS31170, f.62, St Vincent to Clevland, 7 August 1801; Thorne, *House of Commons 1790–1820*, iii.450.

[60] Wife of William Piggott of Doddershall Park, Buckinghamshire. Borough connection of George Grenville, first marquess of Buckingham; John Burke, *A Genealogical and Heraldic History of the Commoners of Great Britain and Ireland* (London, 1838), iv.646; David Fisher (ed.), *The History of Parliament: The House of Commons 1820–1832* (Cambridge, 2009), vi.777–779.

[61] BL, Add MS31170, f.102, St Vincent to Piggott, 27 October 1801.

[62] BL, Add, MS31170, f.228, St Vincent to William Elford, 25 August 1802; Thorne, *House of Commons 1790–1820*, iii.679–680.

[63] UoN, Portland Manuscripts, PwF 3.007, Collier to Portland, 24 October 1794. My thanks to Dr Reiter for sharing her research; Jacqueline Reiter, *The Late Lord: The Life of John Pitt 2nd Earl of Chatham* (Barnsley, 2017), 29.

156   PATRONAGE AND THE BRITISH NAVY, 1775–1815

Ironically, politics did have an extra influence on St Vincent. He was so keen to make sure that political opposition would not affect his distribution of patronage that he went out of his way to promote the interests of his political enemies. In one case, he deliberately promoted the interests of the son of John Fisher, a long-standing opponent in Yarmouth. Before he came to the Admiralty, St Vincent requested that Captain John Aylmer place Lieutenant William Fisher in *Dragon*.[64] A letter to Townshend in December 1801 suggests he made this first appointment without an eye to winning Fisher's favour because he wrote that as soon as he had found out that William Fisher was John Fisher's son he told Captain George Campbell to ensure that Fisher passed his lieutenant's exam, and then he promoted Campbell to admiral as a reward. His scheme initially backfired and the Fisher family gave the credit to Campbell instead, a point which St Vincent was keen to stress to Townshend: 'It is evident the Fisher family did not give me credit for so much liberality by ascribing to Adm¹ Campbell which I know he disclaims.'[65] When he wrote to Townshend he was explicit that he had supported Fisher because his father was a political opponent: 'I felt a pride in serving a Member of a worthy family whose Borough Politics had been adverse to me'.[66] St Vincent made sure that Townshend knew he had acted apolitically so that even if the Fishers did not realise he had acted in their interest, he could make sure that everyone else in the borough and in elite circles knew. The appointment and promotion was, undoubtedly, primarily politically motivated. By making it appear that the appointment was based on merit rather than politics, St Vincent tried to ensure that his opponents could not refuse to accept his influence on the grounds of their political opposition.

Certainly, he obliged other political connections, but argued he had done so for merit alone and no credit was due to him. In those instances, he stressed that the appointment was made for merit or on someone else's behalf, therefore, removing the need for reciprocal exchange and consequently couching the exchange in terms of friendship, which was a stronger bond than one of direct debt. He wrote to Colonel John Leveson-Gower, who was MP for Truro, that

> I should have apprized you of the promotion of your Brother, but that I did not wish to affix a merit to an act of Friendship in favor of a family I have long held in the highest respect and esteem, therefore strove to avoid receiving the acknowledgments conveyed in your obliging letter.[67]

---

[64] BL, Add MS31167, f.170, St Vincent to Aylmer, 8 January 1801.

[65] Ibid.

[66] BL, Add MS31170, f.134, St Vincent to Townshend, 31 December 1801.

[67] BL, Add MS31170, St Vincent to Leveson-Gower, 12 February 1802; Thorne, *House of Commons 1790–1820*, iv.430.

THE EXPECTATIONS OF POLITICAL CONNECTION   157

Similarly, he wrote to Charles James Fox that 'Capt Campbell was promoted to the Rank of Commander by a Commission from this Board dated the 6th July, which was not communicated to you, because I wish'd not to make a merit of what I really felt was due to you'.[68] In favouring them, he strengthened the connection which facilitated patronage. But by making it clear the promotion was apolitical he also protected himself from having to oblige party connections in the future. St Vincent spent much of his time trying to deflect applications to his patronage and his disavowal of supporting political claims most likely came into that. He often advised his closest connections to turn away applications, as he did to Lady Elizabeth Fane, the wife of John Fane, MP for Oxfordshire:

> My dear Madam, I must entreat you to turn the back of your hand to all applications for promotion to any rank higher than a Lieutenant, the lamentable profession of preferment having saddled me with at best fifty meritorious Post Captains and as many commanders on half Pay, and until they are provided for I will not listen to any recommendations whatsoever.[69]

And to Anne Piggott, mentioned above, he ended his letter with the same phrase: 'I hope you will turn the back of your hand to every application you receive, for the compliance with one, will produce a dozen.'[70]

In comparison to St Vincent, Markham received very few requests from supporters of Addington or Pitt. Partly, it may have been because there were other commissioners on the board who were more deeply embedded in parliamentary networks, such as James Adams, or William Garthshore. The offer of political support was implied and rarely explicit in the application letters Markham received. The complicated nature of individual networks means that political obligation can be sometimes difficult to trace in a collection of correspondence such as St Vincent's or Markham's. After all, most applicants were connected to at least one person who was involved, sometimes intimately, in borough politics. Despite this, political connection was not commonly alluded to in requests made to Markham, although in some cases, the ability to return a favour from Markham with political support was implied. A female applicant might not offer the support of her brother in her request for her son's preferment, but if she was of high enough social standing, then her family connection was well-known and her political support, therefore, implicit. Sarah D'Oyly had strong political connections through her late husband Christopher D'Oyly, and her sister's marriage to Welbore Ellis, the late Lord Mendip. D'Oyly wrote to Markham on behalf of her late brother's illegitimate

---

[68] BL, Add MS31170, St Vincent to Fox, 9 October 1801.
[69] BL, Add MS31170, St Vincent to Fane, 22 February 1801.
[70] BL, Add MS31170, f.102, St Vincent to Piggott, 27 October 1801.

158 PATRONAGE AND THE BRITISH NAVY, 1775–1815

son, Captain George Blake.[71] Markham obliged her request, as shown in her letter of thanks of 18 August where she included George Blake's own words of gratitude:

> Believe me Madam, that at a time like the present, I shall feel, (as I have before had the honour to tell you) happy to serve my King and County in any shape. And I shall therefore, most thankfully accept an appointment to the Sea Fencibles whenever a vacancy may take place.[72]

Markham may, however, have been a conduit for those politically connected applicants who wanted to avoid St Vincent's more opaque distribution of patronage. General Thomas Maitland, MP for Haddington in Scotland, requested Markham to actively employ Captain George Stuart, who had just been made a commander. Maitland's request was unusual because he clearly stated his political debt to Stuart as well as the strength of Stuart's naval service: 'Independent of his merit as an officer I am under particular obligations to him in Politics.'[73] Thomas Maitland and his brother James Maitland, eighth earl of Lauderdale, were keen supporters of the Addington administration, and access to Admiralty patronage should have been a ready boon for them.[74] However, the rest of Maitland's letter suggests that St Vincent had already given Maitland the brush off, as he wrote: 'I feel disinclined to Press on Lord St Vincent with my application particularly as … he has treated me with unremittent attention.' If St Vincent's attention had really been 'unremittent', it is unlikely that Maitland would have been so reluctant to approach him himself. The letter was undated, but Maitland's reluctance to make a political request for someone so newly promoted to commander suggests it was written between late 1801 and April 1802. St Vincent had sharply declined assisting Maitland's cousin earlier in the year, simply writing: 'Sir, Neither importunity nor influence will accelerate your being employed, there are many with superior claims who must be first taken care of.'[75] Maitland, therefore, was reasonably hesitant to approach St Vincent himself on this track. The rest of his letter suggests that Markham acted as a conduit for requests which sought to appease political connections. Maitland wrote: 'if however you think you could mention it without interfering with any engagement of [St Vincent's] it would be rendering me a most singular favour and giving to the service I

---

71 NMM, MRK/104/4/11, D'Oyly to Markham, 1 August 1803; Namier and Brooke, *House of Commons 1754–1790*, ii.336 and 397.

72 NMM, MRK/104/4/12, D'Oyly to Markham, 18 August 1803.

73 NMM, MRK/105/3/41, Maitland to Markham, [Winter 1801].

74 Thorne, *House of Commons 1790–1820*, iv.528–529.

75 BL, Add MS31170, St Vincent to John Maitland, 26 March 1801.

THE EXPECTATIONS OF POLITICAL CONNECTION

believe a truly valuable officer'.[76] Markham most likely obliged Maitland. Stuart received command of the sloop *Albatross* in April 1802, confirming his rank as commander.[77]

Given the importance of maintaining the support of politically powerful individuals and St Vincent's eagerness to limit requests to himself, we would expect to see many requests in the Markham collection which openly state their political obligations or desires as Maitland's did. However, the requests Markham received while he served on the board rarely included even the subtlest reference to political support in return for Admiralty favour. Of the few that did mention political ties, two were MPs from Yorkshire who presumably had regional connections to Markham's family.

James Archibald Stuart Wortley of Wortley Hall in Yorkshire and member for Bossiney in Cornwall, wrote to Markham in 1803 requesting a lieutenant's commission for William Edwards, the nephew of one of his constituents.[78] Wortley emphasised his political obligation to his constituents as a point of common understanding with Markham:

> I am very well aware that persons in your situation are very much tormented on subjects of this sort but you will easily understand that making one's constituents contented is of some consequence otherwise I can assure you, you should not have been troubled with this.[79]

Although Wortley was apologetic for taking up Markham's time and patronage he was confident that making the request on behalf of his constituents would meet with success, which suggests Markham's understanding of the plight of MPs meeting the naval needs of their constituents. Wortley also implicitly offered his support to Markham and by extension the Addington administration. By satisfying his constituents he could further secure his seat at Bossiney which meant he in return could offer his political support to the Addington administration. Wortley stood as an independent MP, his seat in Bossiney deriving from his family property in the area. Consequently, party politics had less control over him and the bestowal of favours bound him to an individual in government rather than the party. However, he supported Pitt's return to power in 1805, toppling the Addington administration and removing St Vincent and Markham from the Admiralty, which reveals the power an independent MP, like Wortley, could wield.[80] Markham did not immediately

---

[76] NMM, MRK/105/3/41, Maitland to Markham, [Winter 1801].
[77] TNA, ADM 196/68/349, Officers' Service Records (Series III): George Stuart.
[78] Most likely David Edwards, referred to simply as Edwards in the letter; Thorne, *House of Commons 1790–1820*, v.310–313.
[79] NMM, MRK/103/2/48, Wortley to Markham, 6 August 1803.
[80] Fisher, *House of Commons 1820–1832*, vii.326–333.

160 PATRONAGE AND THE BRITISH NAVY, 1775–1815

oblige the request. Edwards remained in *Prince of Wales* as a midshipman, then a master's mate, until he finally passed his lieutenant's exam formally at home and was promoted in August 1806.[81] However, the delay does not seem to have been negligence, or indirect refusal, on Markham's part. A letter in 1806 from Lord Frederick Campbell, another political connection, suggests that Markham had had some difficulty in seeing to Edwards, as he wrote: 'I take the very first opportunity of thanking you for your very kind attention to my wishes in favour of William Edwards which you seem to think at last may be successful.'[82]

In January 1807, John Wharton, the MP for Beverley in Yorkshire, requested Markham's assistance with his constituents' various naval applications. However, unlike Wortley, Wharton particularly requested that Markham frame replies for each constituent so that Wharton would have proof that he had acted on their behalf:

> I avail myself of your kind permission to lay before you the cases, and to state the wishes of some of my constituents in the navy, and shall be much obliged to you to give orders that I may have separate official answer to each application, that I may be able to show the friends of each that I have endeavoured to accomplish their wishes, and to convince some of them that what they desired was unattainable.[83]

By phrasing his request this way, Wharton forestalled Markham's potential refusal. His request also reveals a subtlety in the patronage exchange, that the mere act of asking could be enough to satisfy an MP's constituents. A change in the interest at Beverley upon the rumoured death of a major patron meant that Wharton's seat would be contested within the next few months.[84] It was in his favour, therefore, to show his constituents that he was working on their behalf among his connections.

Obliging political connections to the government was a vital part of the distribution of Admiralty patronage. However, the expectations of those connections were as much a hindrance to First Lords as they were a help. St Vincent spent much of the early part of his time as First Lord refusing requests or making empty promises to those he needed to. However, to meet his own political ends, such as placing Markham and Troubridge in important boroughs, St Vincent did circumvent his own declaration that he would not promote from outside his list of commanders on half-pay. This inconsistency

---

[81] TNA, ADM 9/8/2681 Lieutenants' Services: William Edwards, seniority 15 August 1806.

[82] NMM, MRK/102/1/128, Campbell to Markham, 10 June [1806].

[83] NMM, MRK/104/3/46, Wharton to Markham, 18 January 1807.

[84] Thorne, *House of Commons 1790–1820*, v.521–524.

THE EXPECTATIONS OF POLITICAL CONNECTION   161

contributed to his fall into disfavour with the new opposition and Addington's eventual abandonment of him as a 'political liability'.[85] Troubridge suffered a similar fate, although his death in 1807 when he left the East Indies for the Cape of Good Hope perhaps has made his removal from Britain appear more of a political exile than it was.[86] Markham, however, did not get tarred quite so heavily with the same brush. Thomas Grenville did refer to the 'enemies' Markham had made under St Vincent when he was considering keeping him on his board of Admiralty but, crucially, Markham continued to be an effective commissioner in 1806 and 1807 as well as an MP until 1818.[87] Perhaps this was partly owing to the fact he could take a subtler approach to political applications than St Vincent could as First Lord. Obliging political connections at the Admiralty was certainly a double-edged sword.

Naval Favours and Portsmouth Politics

Markham's distribution of naval patronage played a vital role in his security at Portsmouth between 1801 and 1818.[88] At the beginning of his career as MP, his access to Admiralty, and, by extension, government favour, forged personal ties in the borough and constructed the complicated network of dependency and obligation which underpinned political patronage. He used his influence in the borough to surround himself with his own naval connections and to give St Vincent greater control of the dockyard and customs of the port. In 1803, George Grey, St Vincent's good friend and protégé, was appointed as commissioner of Portsmouth dockyard. Markham's friend George Murray was also the admiral of the port between 1803 and 1809, replacing admirals who were more hostile to Markham such as Mark Milbanke, mentioned in Chapter 2. His success was based firmly on his connection to the Portsmouth corporation, who maintained his seat until his political and naval influence waned in the 1810s and the electorate were tempted by a more attractive Admiralty candidate in 1818.

Markham won his seat at Portsmouth in 1801 when St Vincent solicited Sir John Carter, the mayor for 1797 to 1798 and 1800 to 1802, and unofficial head of the Portsmouth corporation.[89] Carter was the head of the family which effectively controlled the corporation, and consequently most Portsmouth elections,

---

[85] Fedorak, *Henry Addington*, 109–110.

[86] Rodger, *Command of the Ocean*, 547.

[87] Markham (ed.), *Selections from the Correspondence of Admiral John Markham*, xii.

[88] Markham lost his seat in 1818 but regained it in 1820, retaining it until he retired in 1824.

[89] HRO, Bonham Carter Papers, 94M72/F31/2, John Bonham Carter Election Notebook [1818].

162 PATRONAGE AND THE BRITISH NAVY, 1775–1815

political and civil patronage appointments. The corporation was made up of a mayor, three magistrates, several aldermen and a cohort of burgesses of the borough drawn from the mercantile elite of the city and surrounding districts including Portsea, Gosport and Petersfield. The corporation had the leasehold for large parts of the city as well as the right to make freemen of the borough who then in turn had the right to vote, so it was essential to have the support of the corporation to win one of the two Portsmouth seats. Between 1785 and 1798 Carter's son John recorded an average of eleven aldermen sitting in the corporation meetings, voting in replacement aldermen to the vacancies of those that died and in the annual mayoral election.[90] After 1798 the number rose to twelve.[91]

At times Markham's role at the Admiralty collided with his obligations as an MP and he was not afraid to ignore requests from his constituents on the grounds of his duty to the service. The way Markham reconciled his personal obligations to constituents, the wishes of the corporation and his own sense of naval duty reveals the differing expectations for naval and political patronage and how Markham conceived of his honour within each. The central difference was who held the most power in the patron-client exchange between a naval patron and a political patron. Constituents had, in some ways, more bargaining power than naval officers because their votes directly impacted their MP's position. On the other hand, patrons in the navy like Markham had recourse to honourable naval duty which allowed them to refuse troublesome requests and extricate themselves from difficult personal obligations.[92]

The Portsmouth corporation tried to achieve much the same protection by encouraging all patronage to be filtered through its members and fostering the practice that favours were distributed by the corporation rather than by individuals. John Gaselee, a prominent member of the corporation who was mayor several times, outlined how the corporation dealt with its patronage and applications when he wrote to Markham in June 1802: 'All Corporate applications are to be made through the Mayor, and those which are not so, should not implicate the Corporation.'[93] This spread both the burden of risky applications

---

[90] John Carter became John Bonham Carter in 1827 when he inherited property from his cousin Thomas Bonham. Fisher, *House of Commons 1820–1832*, iv.587–591.

[91] HRO, Bonham Carter Papers, 94M72/F31/2, Election Notebook [1818]. See Appendix III for full list of mayors, magistrates and aldermen who were elected each year.

[92] Rodger argued that the navy was uniquely positioned to lead the change in late eighteenth-century honour from 'personal, interested, egotistical service of one's king and one's honour' to 'disinterested duty to God, the Crown, and the good of the Service'; N. A. M. Rodger, 'Honour and Duty at Sea, 1660–1815', *Historical Research* 75:190 (November, 2002), 446–447.

[93] NMM, MRK/106/3/8, Gaselee to Markham, 20 June 1802.

THE EXPECTATIONS OF POLITICAL CONNECTION 163

and the reward of successful ones, but it also allowed the corporation to satisfy more requests. Rather than splitting a constituent's obligation between multiple individual patrons, a constituent was tied to the whole corporation and consequently was far more likely to follow the corporation's political line. This stabilised the political patronage of the borough and enabled oligarchies, like the Carter family, to wield considerable control.

Of course, many members of the corporation and constituents solicited Markham directly, as an insurance against their falling into disfavour with the corporation. A letter of thanks from Richard Calloway for Markham's assistance to his son is typical of personal letters of thanks:

> Your very obliging Favor of Yesterday's date I duly received: and I beg to say that for the appointment of my son as mate to the Aurora, you have my grateful acknowledgements and I am persuaded he, as well as myself, will ever be most strongly impressed with a true sense of the marked indulgence granted him.[94]

Some corporation members also encouraged Markham to create personal ties of obligation amongst his constituents and corporation members, so he was not solely reliant on Carter as his main supporter. The most explicit example of this was from Reverend George Cuthbert, Carter's brother-in-law and a prominent corporation member who was mayor several times.[95] Cuthbert, in a letter from 1806, after suggesting Markham assist a young lieutenant from a large family with many borough votes, stressed that this future interest would protect Markham 'if any accident should happen to Sr John'.[96] Cuthbert's willingness to undermine the corporation potentially helped Markham to establish himself in Portsmouth and to maintain his position as MP after he left the Admiralty in 1807 and Carter's death in 1808. However, Cuthbert's self-serving approach to patronage eventually rebounded on Markham in 1818, as we will see later in this section.

The tension surrounding the corporation's reliance on personal obligation, while promoting a veneer of non-partisan decision making and their duty to the borough, is strikingly similar to the operation of Admiralty patronage. However, the corporation saw their patronage as distinct and markedly different. William Goldson, the newly elected mayor in 1806, wrote to Markham to ask for his influence at the Treasury to secure customs appointments in the port. However, once the preliminary moves were made, Goldson told Markham he would instead go through Thomas Erskine, who was the other member for Portsmouth. He wrote that Erskine was 'more at leisure'

---

94 NMM, MRK/106/3/4, Calloway to Markham, 20 June 1802.
95 HRO, Bonham Carter Papers, 94M72/F31/2, Election Notebook [1818].
96 NMM, MRK/106/2/8, Cuthbert to Markham, 21 September 1806.

164   PATRONAGE AND THE BRITISH NAVY, 1775–1815

than Markham, but Goldson was most concerned with Markham's official position at the Admiralty which he felt meant 'sometimes soliciting a quid pro quo, which is what we protect against, as it is always considered attached to the Corporation'.[97]

Indeed, the corporation were suspicious of the priority Admiralty concerns took in Markham's dealings with them, as revealed in a letter from Calloway, who was the town clerk, in 1803. Calloway originally wrote to Markham in June 1803 to request his interference at the Admiralty on behalf of a leasee of the corporation who was being prosecuted by the Court of Exchequer. In his second letter replying to Markham's response, Calloway hinted that Markham could have gathered more information about the case from the Admiralty: 'they beg me to say they had entertained hopes that you would have been more explicit as to the Knowledge the Admiralty might have of the Merits of the case'.[98] To further emphasise the point, Calloway ended his letter: 'As a Representative of the Borough you are considered as one of the Guardians of its Rights and for which Reason I am directed to write to you on this subject', although he did soften it by adding: 'At the same time, I am authorized to say, the Corporation by no means wish to have any other Favour shown them on the Occasion, by the Board of which you are one of the members.'[99]

Certainly, Markham's drafted replies to his constituents and less prominent corporation members suggest he valued naval merit over political connection, or at least wished to represent himself as doing so. John Merritt, a burgess of the corporation, wrote to Markham to request assistance of his father's petition for superannuation from his position as steward at Haslar Hospital, Gosport. Merritt led with his Portsmouth connection:

> The circumstance that induced me to trouble you, is my being an Inhabitant of Portsmouth and a Burgess of its Corporation, by whom you have been returned as their Representative in Parliament, which will ever do them credit in electing a character of your reputation as an Officer and of great esteem and moderation in private life.

Merritt further emphasised Markham's good character, as well as his father's long service, particularly in reference to St Vincent's reputation for favouring this:

> Having lightly stated these circumstances I should esteem it a particular favour if you could be so good, Sir, as to forward his plea and petition, when he should send it, and to inform me what encouragement ... an old servant of the Crown may expect. I trust the Earl of St Vincent (from his

[97] NMM, MRK/106/4/1, Goldson to Markham, 27 February 1806.
[98] NMM, MRK/106/4/5–6, Calloway to Markham, 30 June 1803 and 2 July 1803.
[99] NMM, MRK/106/4/6, Calloway to Markham, 2 July 1803.

THE EXPECTATIONS OF POLITICAL CONNECTION

well known character) and their Lordships in general will no doubt listen to the Petition of a Man who has passed the whole active part of his life in the service.

Markham only highlighted the naval call for his favour in his note on the letter, as he wrote: 'will give my assistance in support of his claim on the public for his long service'.[100] This, of course, may have merely reflected St Vincent's influence at the Admiralty, where Markham made sure to stress that he favoured the naval merit of the application rather than Merritt's claim on him as a member of the corporation.

Certainly, other civilian applicants also acknowledged St Vincent's public patronage style. Martin White, a well-connected Portsmouth constituent, was relatively tentative in pressing Markham's political obligation to him in 1802 and he acknowledged that Markham's position at the Admiralty restricted his ability to satisfy his request because of St Vincent's public stop on promotion: 'I own I feel myself much mortified at not seeing his Name in the list of Commanders, but as Lord St Vincent has declared that the door to promotion is shut I must submit'.[101] This in turn suggests White's awareness that his political credentials would have little effect under St Vincent's administration, as opposed to under Charles Grey, Lord Howick in 1806, who was a civilian First Lord.

Indeed, when Markham failed to satisfy White's son's request for promotion in 1806, White took full advantage of his political connections to pressure Markham. The son, Lieutenant Martin White, had written to Markham in June but did not mention his political claims on Markham's patronage.[102] But when this failed to provoke a response, the elder Martin White wrote and stressed his connection to the corporation and his family's standing within the borough:

> My father and Mr White of Islington are the oldest Aldermen of the Corporation, and I am inclined to believe are entitled to a part of the patronage of the Boro', having uniformly this a long period strenuously supported the Independence of the Corporation, and very materially contributed to effect the Freedom, which it now possesses.[103]

White even suggested that his going through another political channel might be detrimental to Markham's position, although it is unclear whether the implied damage would be done to Markham's position at the Admiralty or in Portsmouth:

---

[100] NMM, MRK/106/3/7, Merritt to Markham, 14 June 1802.
[101] NMM, MRK/104/3/51, White to Markham, 24 June 1802.
[102] NMM, MRK/103/2/38, White (Lt.) to Markham, 10 June 1806.
[103] NMM, MRK/104/3/53, White to Markham, 17 November 1806.

166   PATRONAGE AND THE BRITISH NAVY, 1775–1815

Should you not have the power of doing something for him soon, I hope you will not stand in his way should he be inclined to make use of other Interest to succeed; I had much rather have it effected this by your means, but I feel an imperious necessity to get something immediately done.[104]

Despite these strong political claims, Markham did not oblige the request and seems to have placed his duty to the navy, or at least his reputation at the Admiralty for being even-handed, above pleasing his Portsmouth constituents. In the draft of his reply on the reverse of White's letter from November 1806, Markham wrote:

It was at the expense of all my other engagements that I obtained the promotion of your son from Lord Howick. Which is so recent this I do not perceive there is any hardship in his waiting while I pay attention to some claims which press upon me.[105]

Markham further protected himself, either consciously or unconsciously, by deliberately taking White's comment at face-value and treated it as a request for permission to solicit elsewhere, rather than engaging with the veiled threat: 'I can certainly have no objection to your using any interest for the welfare of your son which I shall always feel pleasure in promoting to the utmost of my power.'[106] Despite the usefulness of Admiralty patronage to secure his position in Portsmouth, Markham did not necessarily prioritise his political connections over his Admiralty concerns. As we have seen, many officers and their families had a keen sense of the patronage they were entitled to, but it was difficult for them to honourably criticise a patron's refusal of their request if that patron, like Markham, couched it in terms of his duty to the service.

The cases of Sir Robert Chalmers and Captain Thomas Searle best represent these tensions between Markham's Admiralty and political obligations. Both men sought naval appointments through their strong connections to the corporation. And both men did not initially meet Markham's standards of behaviour for naval appointment but his Portsmouth connections persuaded him to assist them.

Various members of the corporation recommended Chalmers to Markham to be placed as the superintendent of *Alexander* at Motherbank, Portsmouth. *Alexander* was a type of quarantine ship called a lazaretto, and the less active position suited Chalmers's age, at 57, and his rank of captain in the Royal Marines. The position lay in the hands of the Treasury, and the corporation needed Markham to use his governmental position to interfere on Chalmers's

[104] Ibid.
[105] Ibid., Markham's drafted reply on reverse of letter.
[106] Ibid.

THE EXPECTATIONS OF POLITICAL CONNECTION

behalf. Goldson, elected mayor in 1805, recommended Chalmers to Markham on strong terms: 'I am requested by my Colleagues to desire that you will recommend to the Treasury, Sir Robert Chalmers to the command, or chief superintendence of her, under whichever denomination it might come. His character and knowledge must strongly recommend him.'[107] Cuthbert also recommended him: 'I know him to be a man of honor in every respects but has brought himself low in the world by thinking others as honorable as himself'.[108] Goldson arranged for Markham to meet with Chalmers to secure his support:

> We much wish you will press this, and get an answer to the application as soon as you can. By our desire Sir Robert Chalmers will wait on you in a few days when we wish you to point out any way he can individually assist in accomplishing an answer.[109]

However, another letter from Cuthbert in April 1806 suggests that this meeting was not successful, and Markham had consequently refused to appoint Chalmers to *Alexander*: 'I am much concerned to find, (by a side wind) that the visit of my worthy friend Sir Robert Chalmers has not impressed you with the Idea of his being able to undertake the command of the Lazaretto at this Port'. Cuthbert's next line hinted at what possibly went wrong: 'he is certainly, subject to a nervous affliction, which in being introduced to a stranger has a strong effect on him'.[110] Cuthbert rallied to Chalmers's support, writing: 'but be assured he is in every respect equal to the station we wish you to intercede for' and 'the care of a Lazaretto cannot require any exertion he is not equal to in every respect, and if Honor, integrity and attention can be a recommendation, I will pledge myself for him in every point'.[111]

A letter in October from John Adams Carter, Sir John Carter's cousin, shows that Markham obliged Cuthbert and Goldson despite his misgivings.[112] Carter also bluntly requested that Markham help Chalmers secure his half-pay as a captain of marines: 'Sir Robert Chalmers having obtained the appointment of Superintendent of the Lazaretto at the Motherbank, will petition for a dispensing order to retain his Half-pay as Captain of Marines for procuring which I have to request your assistance.'[113] Chalmers's connection to the corpo-

---

[107] NMM, MRK/106/3/16, Goldson to Markham, 23 March 1806.
[108] NMM, MRK/106/2/7, Cuthbert to Markham, 29 July 1806.
[109] NMM, MRK/106/3/16, Goldson to Markham, 23 March 1806.
[110] NMM, MRK/106/2/6, Cuthbert to Markham, 9 April 1806.
[111] Ibid.
[112] NMM, MRK/106/3/24, Carter to Markham, 6 October 1806.
[113] Ibid.

168 PATRONAGE AND THE BRITISH NAVY, 1775–1815

ration, therefore, secured his position on the lazaretto rather than Markham's own good opinion of his character and skill.

The case of Captain Thomas Searle was different. Rather than failing to impress Markham, Searle outright offended him by accusing him of obliging St Vincent's connections before his duties at Portsmouth and to the navy. Searle had Carter's support, but he overestimated his political position. Carter wrote to Markham in 1804 to recommend Searle: 'I have been informed that strong recommendations are gone from this place of Capt. Searle of the Fencibles. I am desired to say that his conduct has been very correct, diligent and proper, but his wishes are for more active employment.'[114] However, Carter had no personal connection with Searle and he outlined this in his letter, albeit as a subtle recommendation of Searle's merit. He wrote: 'He was a stranger to me till he was appointed, but I can say he is deserving.'[115] Searle had already approached Markham once before in 1803, after being told by Benjamin Tucker that St Vincent had suggested he solicit Markham for his position in the sea fencibles.[116] In this letter, he also referred Markham to Captain Thomas Richbell for a character reference, which certainly had strength to it as Richbell was one of Markham's old lieutenants from *Centaur*, mentioned in Chapter 2.

In 1804, Markham removed Searle from his position at the sea fencibles and placed him in *Perseus*, satisfying Carter's request. *Perseus* was an old frigate in poor condition which had been converted to a bomb vessel in 1798 and so was not likely to offer opportunities for achieving future promotion. Searle wrote to Markham to request a sloop of war or a better position, this time emphasising his connection to the corporation:

> Should I not be fortunate enough to get the Other step through your Interest at present, I shall esteem it a particular favor if you will be pleas'd to get me mov'd to a Sloop of War being convinc'd my Friends at Portsmouth will feel equally Obliged to you.[117]

His next letter stressed that he had only wanted to quit the sea fencibles on the promise of members of the corporation that he was to receive a better position, rather than a ship in an unfit state to sail. He wrote: 'I had no wish whatever to quit that Situation had it not been with a prospect of promotion held out to me by Sir Jno Carter, Mr Goldson etc who wrote you on that subject.'[118] He requested that Markham remove him from *Perseus* and place him back in the sea fencibles. However, in his third letter, presumably in response to Markham's failure to satisfy his request, he gave voice to a rumour that Markham was obliging St Vincent by making space in the sea fencibles

---

[114] NMM, MRK/106/1/7, Carter to Markham, 25 April 1804.
[115] Ibid.
[116] NMM, MRK/102/5/69, Searle to Markham, 9 June 1803.
[117] NMM, MRK/102/5/70, Searle to Markham, 9 May 1804.
[118] NMM, MRK/102/5/71, Searle to Markham, 12 May 1804.

THE EXPECTATIONS OF POLITICAL CONNECTION 169

and accused Markham in strong language which very nearly severed his connection. He wrote:

> I was inform'd immediately after seeing you, that I was appointed to the Perseus Bomb for no other *purpose* than to make a vacancy in the Portsm[th] Sea Fencibles for a *Particular Friend of Lord St Vincent*, which I think was rather unfair as I can with pleasure say I gave satisfaction to Cap[t]. O'Bryan the Gentlemen of *Portsmouth* and the Sea Fencibles *could I do more*.[119]

Markham's drafted reply reveals the level of his offence at this accusation. First, Markham stressed that in this case he had prioritised his Portsmouth connections above the wishes of St Vincent: 'It was at the particular request of Sir J Carter that you was appointed to the Perseus Bomb, and I obtained this as a favour of Lord St Vincent at a moment when he was pressed to put another captain into her.' Then he stressed that, by listening to rumour, Searle levelled a personal attack on both himself and St Vincent: 'I am sorry that you should lend your belief to a tale calculated to calumniate Lord St Vincent and myself, who had no other view in moving you than to gratify the wish expressed by Sir John Carter to put you afloat.' He finished the letter with the strong words: 'you have however Sir given me sufficient caution never to interfere in your concerns in future'.[120] There are no replies in the collection from Searle in 1804 to such strong admonishment.

Searle did not, however, lose his supporters in Portsmouth. By 1806, he was once again recommended and obliged as Markham appointed him to the sloop *Grasshopper*. William Goldson, the new mayor, wrote in September 1806 to join his support and recommendation for Searle with Carter, who was in retirement. He wrote:

> Sir John Carter to join me in requesting your attention to Cap[t]. Searle of the Fury he has a large family and we are confident his merits as an officer will justify our intercession for his being removed into an active Brigg or Sloop of War.[121]

And they recommended him again a few weeks later:

> Sir J Carter joins with one in pointing out to you that the Grasshopper Brig is launched at Hythe to Day, we both think it would be furthering the service were Cap[t] Searle of the Fury to be appointed to her as from his character he would be able to man her with very little trouble.[122]

---

[119] Emphasis in original. NMM, MRK/102/5/72, Searle to Markham, 16 May 1804.
[120] NMM, MRK/102/5/72, Markham's drafted reply, 18 May 1804, Searle to Markham, 16 May 1804.
[121] NMM, MRK/106/3/21, Goldson to Markham, 7 September 1806.
[122] NMM, MRK/106/3/22, Goldson to Markham, 22 September 1806.

170 PATRONAGE AND THE BRITISH NAVY, 1775–1815

Carter then mentioned Searle once more in his letter to Markham in October, writing:

> I believe Mr Goldson sometime since mentioned Cap[t] Searle to you wishing he may be appointed to the Grasshopper fitting at this Port, which will be pleasing to us. His merit put him forward and while at this place he gained the goodwill of the magistrates by his conduct.[123]

In both instances, as well as when Carter originally recommended Searle in 1804, the recommendation was one based on his perceived naval merit, rather than his ability to oblige Markham politically. Certainly, Searle's letter of thanks to Markham mentioned the quid pro quo obligation of naval patronage, rather than offering his support in any future borough elections: 'I at the same time beg to observe should you have a Friend that you would wish to send with me I shall feel great pleasure in paying him every attention in my power'.[124] The request for naval favour was not always as clear cut as the buying of votes on behalf of the corporation and situations such as Searle's reveal the complicated net of obligations produced by Markham using his Admiralty position to gift appointments through the corporation.

However, his role at the Admiralty between 1801 and 1807 helped him oblige both the corporation and some individuals within the borough. He built his reputation for fair dealing on this foundation, as well as creating strong personal ties of patronage obligation and friendship, which supported him once he left the Admiralty in 1807. His situation in Portsmouth after he left the Admiralty, however, was more precarious. He could not so readily oblige his constituents with naval favours and despite the corporation's avowal of independence, having an MP who was also a member of the government was an attractive option for a borough so much at the whim of the administration.

Of course, just because he had lost the influence he held as an Admiralty commissioner did not mean Markham was completely without means to please his constituents and tie them to him. From July 1807, Markham drew most heavily on the patronage of his family connections, particularly his younger brother Robert, Archdean of York, and his old family friend David William Murray, third earl of Mansfield. Cuthbert, once again without subtlety, outlined Markham's position in Portsmouth once he left the Admiralty. In asking for Markham's assistance for his son, Cuthbert wrote: 'You, my dear Sir, at present have not much in your power, but no doubt you have many friends, tho' perhaps not in a Political sense, who are ready and willing to accede to any request you may think right to make them.'[125] His emphasis on

[123] NMM, MRK/106/1/14, Carter to Markham, 19 October 1806.
[124] NMM, MRK/102/5/73, Searle to Markham, 7 November 1806.
[125] NMM, MRK/106/4/3, Cuthbert to Markham, 5 July 1807.

THE EXPECTATIONS OF POLITICAL CONNECTION

having a lack of 'Political friends' was either heavy-handed or a veiled threat. Cuthbert certainly reckoned himself as a major player in the corporation, who garnered much personal interest. The rest of the letter reveals more of Cuthbert's heavy-handed approach as he unusually suggested that Markham apply to Mansfield on his behalf:

> I see by the paper that Ld Mansfield is with the present ministers, his interest must command at this time anything he would ask, and cannot easily persuade myself, that he would deny any assistance to a person you would be pleased to interest yourself about.[126]

Most letters to Markham were not as confident or direct in seeking his influence with his intimate friends and family. Cuthbert's manner was, perhaps, a personal quirk, but he reflects the change in Markham's position from one of power through his access to Admiralty patronage, to a far more precarious position where he had to please his corporation connections more readily to maintain his position. His patronage context changed and he made some adjustments to his new situation, but he largely carried on as he had as a naval captain and Admiralty commissioner. The subsequent difficulties he faced highlight the subtle differences between naval and political patronage pressures and priorities.

His position in the borough is best represented by correspondence from 1816 and 1818 when the Portsmouth seats were contested and a canvass was undertaken. In 1816, Markham's fellow MP, Thomas Miller, died, leaving his seat open. Two new candidates stood, opening the borough to a general canvass for both seats including Markham's. The first was John Carter, Sir John Carter's son, who had just returned to Portsmouth from practising the law at Lincoln's Inn. He was opposed by John Wilson Croker who was the secretary of the Admiralty from 1809. As the incumbent seat, Markham was not obliged to canvass or even appear for the election. In fact, James Carter, his supporter and the mayor of the corporation in 1816, suggested that his coming to Portsmouth for the election might be seen as his having 'doubt' in the strength of his interest in the borough.[127] Markham and Carter had the support of the Carter faction in the corporation and John Wilson Croker withdrew before it came to a vote.[128]

The bestowal of past favours carried a lot of weight in electors' decisions to support Markham, as did access to his family patronage and connections. Politic ideals also played a significant role as many supported Markham to

---

[126] Ibid.

[127] NMM, MRK/106/3/45, James Carter to Markham, 3 October 1816.

[128] NMM, MRK/106/3/41, Croker to Edward Carter, 14 September 1816; MRK/106/3/42, Croker to James Carter, 25 September 1816.

172 PATRONAGE AND THE BRITISH NAVY, 1775–1815

defend the corporation's independence from Robert Jenkinson, the second earl of Liverpool's self-proclaimed Tory government. The alderman Sir Henry Featherstone wrote that he had a 'a considerable share ... in rescuing the Borough of Portsmouth from the grasp of Government' and that he 'must always feel an interest for its continued independence'. Consequently, he wrote that he would 'readily offer you my vote, on the occurrence of a general election, should you require it'.[129] Henry Taylor, a burgess, was explicit about offering his support on party terms as he wrote: 'Be assured that, not any man of principles contrary to those whig principles on which you have acted, will ever supplant your claim in my opinion to the preference to which you are so greatly intitled by your parliamentary conduct.'[130] Croker had clashed frequently with Markham in parliament as secretary of the Admiralty, particularly in discussions about St Vincent's reforms, as well as reducing or freezing officer's pay while raising the pay of the Admiralty secretary.[131] The effects of many of these would have been felt keenly in Portsmouth and 1816 was perhaps an ill-judged time for a government candidate in opposition to the politics of the largely Whig Carter faction to try for the vacated seat.

Equally, Markham's bestowal of new patronage favours was vital in securing votes and could counter many political differences. Edward Carter wrote to Markham in October 1816 about securing a vote from an elector named William Harward: 'Perhaps you may be able to make an application to obtain Mr Harward's vote, through Lord Stanhope. For although Harward is decidedly against us in politics, Lord S (I am informed in a very handsome manner) gave his son a living.'[132] Carter later wrote that Harward would give his vote to Markham if he would 'do anything for his son'.[133] Harwood himself had written to Markham to state his situation, namely that he could not interest himself in Portsmouth while his son was without a secure position. Tellingly, Harwood sought Markham's family patronage in his brother's influence as Archdean of York:

> I had allowed my Son to indulge to hope with me, that from your present Interest in the Diocese of York there might be great probability of your procuring him some little preferment, or some ecclesiastical office in the Cathedral, through your Connection and relatives in that Diocese.[134]

---

[129] NMM, MRK/106/3/47, Featherstone to Markham, 6 October 1816.

[130] NMM, MRK/106/3/49, Taylor to Markham, 9 November 1816.

[131] Hansard, *Parliamentary Debates*, 1st Series, 25, cols. 91–98, Commons debate, 12 March 1813; 33, col. 223, Commons debate, 13 March 1816; 35, cols. 385–403, Commons debate, 17 February 1817.

[132] NMM, MRK/106/1/34, Edward Carter to John Carter, 13 October 1816.

[133] NMM, MRK/106/1/36, Edward Carter to Markham, 26 October 1816.

[134] NMM, MRK/106/3/44, Harwood to Markham, 3 October 1816.

THE EXPECTATIONS OF POLITICAL CONNECTION 173

His request was also based in previous favours which he had received from
Markham via Sir John Carter:

> I am indeed to remind you of the Letters you favored me with some few
> years ago on that subject, my application to you met with that indulgence
> for which I felt duly gratefuly, and that highly respected Sevensman and
> Magistrate Sir John Carter, approved of the motives which urged me to make
> the request, and readily seconded, my application, which was obligingly
> answered by yourself.[135]

However, Markham's use of his personal, familial patronage connections
was fraught with risk once he was no longer protected by the veneer of naval
duty he had had as a serving officer and at the Admiralty. Carter's suggestion
that Markham oblige Harward with his familial patronage rather than using
Stanhope's interest did not seem to have met with Markham's approval as
Carter wrote: 'I certainly agree with you – that it would not be very encouraging to you to lay yourself, under obligations to your relatives after (I may
say) the base conduct you have met with from persons you have privately
obliged'.[136] Offering private favours could put the candidate in a difficult
position, particularly if they reneged on the obligation. All favours, after all,
were gained through drawing on an individual's network and the bestowal
of favours on those undeserving of them would ruin a patron's reputation in
the eyes of his network, who might be less inclined to assist in the future.

It turned out that Stanhope had favoured William Harward's son, but the
church living he had given him was not in his gift so, as Edward Carter wrote:
'Mr H's son was turned out'.[137] Carter wrote that Stanhope had not been a
'loyal patron to the advowson', the ecclesiastical broker with the church living
in his gift, which highlights the vulnerability of patronage networks to offence
and the importance of principle and trust. He wrote:

> But nevertheless had Stanhope equally conferred the obligation and therefore
> if any application could be made through him, it might have effect. Perhaps,
> if any *small* thing in the way of preferment should happen to be in the gift
> of any of your relatives, it might be worth your while to make an offer of
> it to Mr H.

Although he was cautious in suggesting this: 'I beg you to understand it is by
no means a thing any of us make a point of with you'.[138] In doing so, Carter
emphasised that this would secure Markham's position but that if he did not

---

[135] NMM, MRK/106/3/44, Harwood to Markham, 3 October 1816.
[136] NMM, MRK/106/1/36, Carter to Markham, 26 October 1816.
[137] Ibid.
[138] Ibid.

174   PATRONAGE AND THE BRITISH NAVY, 1775–1815

want to risk a dangerous patronage connection then the corporation would still support him.

Failure to satisfy a request from a constituent could provoke their removing their support and ruffle egos, which the election agent then had to carefully smooth over. In another letter in 1816, Edward Carter mentioned the alderman Thomas Sharp, whom Markham had accidently offended previously by promising to assist a relation in the navy and then not fulfilling the request. Carter wrote:

> I understand the ground of offence (or of fancied offence) arose from your telling once when he made an application for Mr Chaldecott (his brother in law) to be appointed Surgeon to a prison ship– that you would speak to *Sir John C* about it as Mr S thought it … to have been done for *him* without speaking to anyone else.

However, the removal of support could be provoked by a simple social mistake, as Carter went on to say: 'you also (I understand) passed him once in going into the George Inn here without speaking'.[139] Carter also stressed, however, that he did not think that Sharp had any 'just reason' to be offended with Markham or to refuse his vote on those grounds.[140]

Sharp eventually offered his support in December but primarily because of Markham's previous work in the House of Commons, as well as it being the wish of his constituents:

> be assured Sir of my support as I have attended to your Parliamentary conduct and have the pleasure to say that it has met my approbation as well as that of a very great majority of your constituents and while you continue to act on independent principles I think you may be certain of receiving the Suffrages of the Electors for the Boro– of Portsmouth.[141]

There was no mention of insult or offence and the issue appears to have been neatly sidestepped by the strength of Markham's connection to the corporation and the obligations between his constituents and himself. Markham held his seat in 1816 because of the weakness of the proposed opponent as well as Markham's strength of connection to the Carter family and a lingering sense of obligation within the corporation and several constituents.

However, things were quite different in 1818. Markham lost his seat to the government candidate, Admiral George Cockburn. Unlike Croker, Cockburn had a reputation as a dutiful and honourable admiral, who, much like Markham

---

[139] NMM, MRK/106/1/35, Carter to Markham, 20 December 1816.
[140] NMM, MRK/106/1/36, Carter to Markham, 26 October 1816.
[141] NMM, MRK/106/3/50, Sharp to Markham, 17 December 1816.

THE EXPECTATIONS OF POLITICAL CONNECTION   175

in 1801, was recommended because of his new position at the Admiralty. Timothy Jenks argues that political admirals had a particular strength because they co-opted the image of the plain-speaking, heroic naval officer and mediated 'class tensions' within a 'conservative concept of the national will'.[142] The landscape of connections in Portsmouth had also changed. John Godwin and William Goldson, the last of Sir John Carter's original supporters in the corporation, died in 1817. There was also a rift in the corporation between those that now followed the younger John Carter and those who supported the government. A vital player in this rift was Cuthbert. In 1818, Cuthbert supported Cockburn rather than Markham and the corporation's reaction to his betrayal reveals how the corporation had prioritised previous obligation in their patronage dealings, as well as revealing the risk of personal favours to both the corporation broker and the MP.

The exchange of letters between Markham and Cuthbert relating to the split suggests that Markham believed that his bestowal of favours on constituents or corporation members created a bond of trust, which Cuthbert then broke. In the first letter, Cuthbert stressed that he supported Cockburn because he was the government candidate, just as he had lent his support to Markham in 1803:

> this place connected as it is with Government, ought to bring in one member for its support, that is *still the* opinion of *Mr Temple* and *myself*, and if you recollect, on that ground and *that ground only*, you yourself were chosen under the express auspices of Lord St Vincent.[143]

But Cuthbert also revealed his ulterior motive in splitting with Markham in his letter from 2 June:

> I have often wished I never had had any connection with the Corporation, it has been constantly a *Mill Stone* about my neck even during the life of Sir John Carter, and the source of constant uneasiness and insult from the moment of his death. Things have strangely changed, since I last conversed with you on the subject of Election.[144]

Cuthbert represented his split from Markham as one of his duty to support the government, but also as a reaction to his perceived mistreatment at the hands of the Carter family. Markham was insulted by Cuthbert's lack of principles regarding supporting a friend, particularly as Markham felt Cuthbert was indebted to him because of his previous assistance in promoting Cuthbert's

---

[142] Timothy Jenks, *Naval Engagements: Patriotism, Cultural Politics, and the Royal Navy 1793–1815* (Oxford, 2006), 72–73.

[143] NMM, MRK/106/2/17, Cuthbert to Markham, 2 June 1818.

[144] Ibid.

176 PATRONAGE AND THE BRITISH NAVY, 1775–1815

son and obliging his many requests. In his heated reply to Cuthbert's letter of 5 July, Markham wrote: 'I have fulfilled every duty to my friends, those especially which regard yourself'.[145] Rather than being chastised, as were other connections who overstepped their position, Cuthbert countered that their patronage relationship was on a more equal footing: '*The favour* you conferred on me was in return for *those* I had *previously* conferred on *you*. Had the *obligations* been otherwise than *mutual*, your insulting reply would have *cancelled* them.'[146]

The argument was very much a public one, with the strongly worded letters being copied and passed among the politically engaged of the borough, and appearing in a collection of John Carter's personal political papers.[147] Cuthbert's rivals in the corporation also did not consider his supporting Cockburn an honourable act motivated by political difference or pragmatism. A poem from 1818 about the election instead suggests that his opponents thought his split from Markham was because of the death of Markham's father, the Archbishop of York, and Markham's consequently restricted ability to satisfy any ecclesiastical favours Cuthbert might ask of him:

> But were the Archbishop still alive
> Or had his son aught else to give
> You would have rested quiet.[148]

The poem implies that Cuthbert only remained loyal to Markham while he had access to Markham's naval and his family's ecclesiastical patronage. In the eyes of Markham's supporters in Portsmouth, his past favours to Cuthbert should have been enough to hold Cuthbert's support in face of the contest with Cockburn. Thomas Bonham, a prominent corporation member who assisted Markham with canvassing for his seat in 1818, outlined the importance of pleasing constituents as well as the reputation Cuthbert gained by the way in which he abandoned Markham: 'Mr Temple has surprised me much joining Cuthbert, who's conduct has been so very ungrateful that he is not worthy our *Notice* as a man, as a Christian or a Clergyman'.[149]

Certainly, other members of the corporation thought the favours Markham had shown Cuthbert previously would securely tie him to Markham. Thomas Erskine, the other MP for Portsmouth, wrote to Markham in 1805: 'Cuthbert dined with me yesterday. He is very much obliged with what you have done

---

[145] NMM, MRK/106/2/19, Draft letter, Markham to Cuthbert, 30 July 1818.

[146] NMM, MRK/106/2/20, Cuthbert to Markham, 2 August 1818.

[147] HRO, Bonham Carter Papers, 94M72/Z3, copy of a letter, Markham to Cuthbert, 5 July 1818.

[148] HRO, Bonham Carter Papers, 94M72/Z3, Election 1818 Skit Rev G Cuthbert.

[149] NMM, MRK/106/3/63, Bonham to Markham, 31 May 1818.

THE EXPECTATIONS OF POLITICAL CONNECTION 177

for him, and I am confident he'll always feel as he ought to do regarding you.'[150] Thomas Waller also stressed his principles in giving Markham his vote in 1818, hinting at Cuthbert's betrayal:

> Give yourself no trouble abt writing to me or waiting on me. I will stick to my principles, and while the Carters stick to theirs, I will act with them. *You may depend on my vote.* Interest I have none, but you have my best wishes. Principles with me are *everything*, and all other considerations nothing. Not all the patronage of the Treasury or Admiralty shall buy or sell me.[151]

However, honourable allegiance to previous patronage favours could also work against Markham, especially when faced with Cockburn as a candidate, who had had a longer and more glamourous sea career than Markham. This in turn allowed him to draw on naval 'heroic identities' and encourage constituents to renege on previous obligations in the name of duty to the nation.[152] William Grover Carter apologised that he would support Cockburn rather than Markham:

> I am favord with your letter of the 28 instant and beg to assure you that nothing should prevent my giving you my Vote at the ensuing election, but my having known Sir George Cockburn many Years and a branch of my family being under obligations to him at this present time.[153]

Equally, Markham lost many of the burgesses' votes who wavered between the corporation and the government. Without the steady hand of Sir John Carter's old supporters, Godwin and Goldson, or the personal favours Cuthbert had encouraged Markham into securing back in 1806, many burgesses supported the more attractive government candidate, who gave them access to Admiralty patronage. George Soaper wrote to Markham to let him know that he would vote for neither Markham nor Cockburn, to extricate himself from this difficult situation. He wrote:

> I beg to inform you that my opinions and Feelings are decidedly favourable to his Majesty's present Government and that I wish to see the Borough represented by Members who will support that Government but who at the same time stand quite independent of it. You will easily perceive that consistently with those Principles I can neither vote for you or your Colleague Mr Carter nor for Sir George Cockburn.[154]

---

[150] NMM, MRK/106/3/15, Erskine to Markham, 13 June 1805.
[151] NMM, MRK/106/3/56, Waller to Markham, 30 May 1818.
[152] Jenks, *Naval Engagements*, 264–265.
[153] NMM, MRK/106/3/57, William Grover Carter to Markham, 30 May 1818.
[154] NMM, MRK/106/3/62, Soaper to Markham, 31 May 1818.

178 PATRONAGE AND THE BRITISH NAVY, 1775–1815

These sentiments were later reported in the *Hampshire Telegraph*.[155] Soaper's refusal to endorse Markham damaged Markham's standing in the election more than it did Cockburn's. After all, Cockburn came with the promise of Admiralty and government patronage. Cuthbert's betrayal of Markham's interest and confidence may have also damaged his reputation as a capable patron.

Markham defended his position in Portsmouth for seventeen years by his use of patronage and the bestowal of both naval and familial favours among his constituents and the corporation. But once a better Admiralty alternative presented itself, in the form of Cockburn, Markham's support base failed. Markham's naval networks were also fragile, having not served at sea since he first joined the Admiralty in 1801. In the House of Commons, he had consistently stood against the successive boards of Admiralty. With the death of the last of Sir John Carter's allies in 1817, the Portsmouth corporation lost some of its independence and could not control the electors or schisms within the borough. Faced with these difficulties, many electors reverted to the 'duty' of supporting the administration and, as with First Lords claiming they did not distribute patronage on political grounds, Markham's supporters could forget their obligation to him on grounds of their principle and duty. Nowhere is this clearer than Cuthbert calling Markham unprincipled in 1818. Markham's failure at the complicated game of favours necessary to secure himself at Portsmouth once he lost his Admiralty patronage reflects the difference between naval and political patronage. However, it also illustrates how vital active naval position was for a sea officer to hold a large port-town borough such as Portsmouth.

Markham's assistance to political allies whilst at the Admiralty, and his use of both naval appointments and political favours in securing personal ties and obligations, reveal the complexity of eighteenth- and early nineteenth-century patronage. Markham's position was not as simple as a hierarchy of priorities, with the navy and the nation's security on top, and the independence of the Portsmouth corporation below. In some instances, his naval concerns clearly won out, while in others he was happy to oblige rude and overbearing connections, such as Cuthbert, to secure his position. He did continue to defend St Vincent's reforms in the House throughout his time as an MP, but he never stood up in the House to tackle any issue particularly relating to Portsmouth. Nevertheless, his constituents often claimed he had their interests at heart and his use of patronage to oblige them personally was fundamental in his reputation for supporting Portsmouth more broadly.

[155] 'Portsmouth Saturday June 20 1818', *Hampshire Telegraph and Sussex Chronicle*, 976 (June, 1818).

Conclusion

Naval appointments and political favour were tools within the broader context of eighteenth- and early nineteenth-century social machinery. However, Markham himself would perhaps not have seen such a distinction between his naval and political acquaintances. He certainly does not seem to have been particularly overt in why or how he distributed his patronage. Unlike other patrons, Markham often couched his favours in terms of friendship, obligation or duty to the navy. Perhaps because of this, his use of patronage at the Admiralty and at Portsmouth was neither overtly naval nor political in tone. Markham, as a case study in the patronage relationship between politics and the navy, is a perfect example of the difficulty in treating the two as separate in the eighteenth and early nineteenth century. Markham occupied both spaces and used his naval and political position to enforce his own agenda and maintain his social position.

However, Cuthbert's betrayal of Markham in 1818 suggests that constituents approached the patronage of their MP differently than how naval officers applied to the Admiralty. Initially, Markham's involvement in the Admiralty gave him distance from the demands of his constituents, which suited his hands-off style of patronage better than when he had to canvass support after 1807. Markham styled his distribution of favours in terms of duty and friendship but, underneath, he strongly believed that the favours he bestowed tied the applicant to him in obligation. In the navy, duty and honour masked the inherent inequality of requests made to the Admiralty. A captain of middling connection and skill had very little with which to pressure a commissioner into providing for him. The commissioner, on the other hand, had access to vacancies spread across the entire navy, and little was lost if one officer out of a thousand was offended. Of course, St Vincent applied this to all requests, including those from the ministry's political allies, and the result was a political backlash which toppled Addington's administration. Constituents had far more bargaining power than captains, and this fundamentally changed their approach to patronage. They demanded rather than solicited.

Members of the corporation saw themselves as Markham's equal in patronage, not his client. In the equal patronage relationships between Markham's intimate connections, described in Chapter 2, recommendations were passed on as affectionate favours between close friends. Markham did not see Cuthbert as an equal. Perhaps this was because they did not share affective friendship, or because Cuthbert was not Markham's equal in the navy. Perhaps it was because Cuthbert asked Markham for multiple favours, and so he felt that Cuthbert was in his debt. Intimate connections and affective friendship did not operate with the same quid pro quo as relationships with weaker ties. However, the line between what was considered an affective friendship and what was considered a 'friend', in the sense Tadmor tells us that Turner described his political allies, was indistinct even to contemporaries.[156]

Markham couched his patronage in terms of duty and friendship but Cuthbert was far more explicit. This in turn gave Cuthbert licence to ignore the reciprocal obligation he was under to Markham when it suited him to change political allegiance. Markham's lack of clarity about his patronage came from his experience distributing naval favours. It allowed him to participate in the culture of sensible stoicism. When he was at the Admiralty, he had great access to patronage favours and so it was not so important to be clear with those he favoured that they were tied to him in obligation; he could always secure new connections and he was overburdened as it was. His position in Portsmouth, however, was far more vulnerable.

The greatest difference between political patronage and naval patronage, therefore, was that honour and duty in the navy regulated patronage reciprocity. As Rodger has argued, the navy in many ways led the transition of honour in the late eighteenth century from 'personal, interested, egotistical service of one's king and one's honour' to 'disinterested duty to God, the Crown, and the good of the Service'.[157] Officers were honour-bound to feel obliged because this new form of *duty* attached them to the nation as a whole. Constituents and members of political corporations, however, felt that the MP was obliged personally to them for their vote. They held the power in the exchange and if an MP like Markham was not explicit about what he was owed when he bestowed favours, then constituents could easily break his trust. Demands of this sort rarely went down so well in the navy. This is best reflected in the requests of those whose lives intersected both naval and political circles, such as Martin White, who was particularly cautious in soliciting Markham's patronage, or Thomas Searle, who was not, and suffered the consequences.

[156] Tadmor, *Family and Friends*, 216–236.
[157] Rodger, 'Honour and Duty at Sea, 1660–1815', 446–447.

5

Gender and Parenthood: The Power of Brokers

> ... the Viper's state is such that without compleat repair she will not last another winter, she is leaky and sails badly, but Mr Carpenter do not like to complain fearing she might be paid off which would be depriving him of the chance of having it in his power to provide for his family ...
>
> Harriet Carpenter, 26 April 1804[1]

Harriet Carpenter wrote to Markham from on board her husband's ship *Viper* docked at the South Downs. She thanked Markham for the previous favours he had bestowed on her and her husband Lieutenant Daniel Carpenter. She also indirectly requested his influence in ensuring that *Viper* was entered to be refitted before winter and that Lieutenant Carpenter would secure a new position if it was. As a broker and a woman, she was better able to emphasise the distress of Carpenter's position and the need for their application to Markham. Daniel Carpenter had already applied to Markham for a better ship but made no mention of the poor state of *Viper*, perhaps to avoid seeming self-serving and ungrateful.[2] Harriet Carpenter's letter illustrates how a person's gender, and their consequent position in society, shaped their patronage.

The patronage exchange, the act of solicitation and the distribution of favours, was not inherently gendered. Men and women could act as patrons, brokers or clients, and there was a large variation in the way people of both genders performed their patronage. However, a person's gender informed their position in society, which, consequently, affected their behaviour, as well as their ability to take an active role in certain spheres. Women's involvement in occupational spheres like the Royal Navy was limited.[3] Many officers such as Edward Pellew engaged in a quid pro quo style of naval patronage which he called the 'wheel' of favour.[4] Women would naturally, therefore, seem to be

---

[1] NMM, MRK/104/4/14.

[2] NMM, MRK/103/1/19–22, Carpenter to Markham, 10 August, 23 September 1803 and 27 November 1804.

[3] Lincoln, *Naval Wives*, 16.

[4] NMM, MRK/101/13/100, Pellew to Markham, 15 August 1806.

182 PATRONAGE AND THE BRITISH NAVY, 1775–1815

excluded from naval patronage. After all, they had little naval, governmental or political power to offer in return for patronage favours.[5] However, patronage was a much wider system than simply the direct reciprocal exchange of favours between equals. Men may have dominated positions of great patronage control, but the system relied on a wide array of brokers of both genders from across the social spectrum. These brokers fielded formal requests from their extended networks but they also conducted the more informal side of patronage in passing on the wishes of friends and maintaining connections through visits and correspondence.

Despite the restrictions of their gendered position, women were not limited to informal patronage. Elite women acted as patrons because of the power they held in property and in securing political votes and many also applied for sinecures and positions for themselves.[6] Widows and unmarried women across the social scale acted with a greater autonomy because they could not rely so readily on male connections. On the other hand, they may simply be more visible in the historical record when their machinations were not directed through male counterparts.

Most women, restricted as they were in the positions that were available to them, engaged in patronage through brokering the requests of their male relations and acquaintances, as well as their female friends. This was particularly true of naval wives, who had to act independently while their husbands served at sea. Historian Margarette Lincoln argued that through the absence of their husbands, brothers or fathers, women took on much more responsibility in managing the family and by extension patronage, stepping outside what was considered to be 'conventional female activity'.[7] Elaine Chalus also demonstrated that elite women often took over the patronage of military or naval husbands serving abroad.[8] Although Ellen Gill does not frame her discussion of female involvement in the 'naval community' as their participation in patronage, she has demonstrated that the wives of officers were fundamental junctures in correspondence networks, vital for the maintenance of naval friendships and the organisation of the intimate patronage of boys' entry to the service.[9] She also illustrates the active role women took in the patronage of the lower levels of society through writing petitions and letters on behalf of sailor or dockyard worker husbands, although she again couches their activity in terms of community support.[10] Women maintained familiar

[5]   Chalus, *Elite Women*, 108.

[6]   Ibid., 107–110.

[7]   Lincoln, *Naval Wives*, 15.

[8]   Chalus, *Elite Women*, 131–132.

[9]   See particularly the role of Louisa Bowes Vere Broke in Gill, *Naval Families*, 67–74, 100–103 and 145–179.

[10] The difficulty in separating the processes of lower-level patronage from elite patronage is discussed in Chapter 6. Ibid., 195–199, 203 and 210–217.

GENDER AND PARENTHOOD: THE POWER OF BROKERS

and political networks in their husband's absence, they cultivated new connections and they approached the Admiralty in their husband's favour.[11] Their role in patronage, however, was not necessarily beyond conventional. Rather, female brokerage of connection in extended familiar networks was an ordinary part of naval patronage and, indeed, of eighteenth-century society.[12]

Women also held a particular power in solicitation letters. An increase in the popularity of sensibility at the end of the long eighteenth century left some patrons suspicious of the cynical uses of friendship for advancement. Markham seems to have viewed self-serving requests with distaste and many men who could have solicited him personally went through brokers instead. When they did approach him for themselves, they often gave the poverty of their family or their eagerness to serve the crown as reasons for their wish for advancement rather than personal aggrandisement. However, Daniel Carpenter's desire to not complain directly to Markham, for fear of seeming ungracious or undutiful, reveals the gendered position which restricted male patronage. For those without brokers and extended networks, often the only option was to apply directly to the Admiralty for favour. But this also meant that they could be less candid about their need for promotion because it ran counter to masculine naval ideals of duty as well as stoicism. Brokered letters, on the other hand, could draw on ideals of charity and altruism, meaning that larger appointments or favours could be requested under the guise of being a dutiful friend. This was particularly true for female brokers who could also draw on gendered stereotypes of anxiety, ignorance and female duty, to excuse their solicitation.[13]

This chapter explores how gender shaped brokers' management of patronage requests as well as the tendency towards gendered tropes in solicitation letters. The first two sections consider gendered position in brokerage and parenthood. The first section discusses the effect of female gendered position, where women provided stability in familiar circles while their male counterparts were absent at sea. Maria Markham's role in her marriage to John forms the spine of this chapter as an in-depth case study of an individual's experience. Gender norms and the sensible ideal shaped Maria's perception of her position, role and duties. Close reading of her letters to John while he served in Ireland, the Mediterranean and the Channel fleet between 1797 and 1801 reveals Maria's involvement in patronage recommendations as well as her maintenance of their familiar connections. However, she was never explicit in her management

---

[11] Lincoln, *Naval Wives*, 16 and 56–64.

[12] Chalus, *Elite Women*, 155–156; Lincoln, *Naval Wives*, 61–64.

[13] Joanne Bailey, *Parenting in England 1760–1830: Emotion, Identity and Generation* (Oxford, 2012), 38; for analysis of the feminine-associated 'soft virtues' see Vivien Jones, *Women in the Eighteenth Century: Constructions of Femininity* (London, 1990), 1–13; for discussion of female 'duty' see Gill, *Naval Families*, 145–179.

184 PATRONAGE AND THE BRITISH NAVY, 1775–1815

of patronage requests. This makes her case an important counterpoint to the direct solicitations other women made to Markham.

The danger in isolating female patronage from male in a discussion of this sort is that the temptation to ignore those cases which suggest a lack of female involvement in favour of those which do creates a distorted picture of the wide variation in patronage engagement at the end of the long eighteenth century. The previous chapters in this book have already shown that women were a part of naval patronage networks and their presence and activity within them was unremarkable to those at the time. Separating patronage by gender is, to some extent, an artificial distinction. However, the informal nature of much of female patronage means that historians such as J. M. Bourne sidelined female participation in wider works on advancement and promotion.[14] This section consequently uses Maria's self-styled disengagement as a counterpoint to the more obvious role of women in brokering requests to Markham at the Admiralty, to understand the subtlety of informal patronage as well as the extent of individual variation.

Some applications also suggest that many women acted more explicitly as brokers for their families and networks in the absence of their husbands, either through service abroad or by their death. Maria's subtle involvement shows that women could be active in patronage without being explicit, which in turn suggests that their more obvious patronage engagement in the absence of their male counterparts was an extension of established informal mechanisms to incorporate the more obvious mechanism of direct appeal. Female participation in naval patronage, therefore, was far more extensive than the form represented in available examples of direct female application.

Discussion of gendered position naturally focuses on women. The male gendered position, being less restricted, is harder to define but in the case of the navy was largely caught up in occupational priorities and expectations. Duty and fatherhood shaped male patronage. Service history and a desire to perform their duty were central features of male requests. Fatherhood, however, gave male applicants greater licence to use anxiety and fears of ill health as reasons for the fulfilment of their request. Male gendered position is also difficult to define because men were not restricted to their occupational spheres, but were culturally encouraged to be active in the domestic sphere. Philip Carter argued that men were encouraged, not only to regulate, but also to participate fully within the household by the end of the eighteenth century.[15] Consequently, the male gendered position was more flexible and varied than the female position. Elin Jones has recently argued that naval masculinity was modified by the pressures of service and was distinct from the polite 'man of feeling' proposed by authors such as Carter or the evangelical father mentioned

---

[14] Bourne, *Patronage and Society*, 82.
[15] Carter, *Emergence of Polite Society*, 100.

GENDER AND PARENTHOOD: THE POWER OF BROKERS   185

by Joanne Bailey.[16] It is perhaps not unsurprising that male naval applicants did not always invoke their role as father in their requests. Because of their restricted position, however, most female requests invoked their position as mother, sister or daughter.

The third section of this chapter considers gendered trends in the language and style of patronage applications. After all, letters were social performances, designed to succeed with their intended recipient.[17] Therefore, they tell us as much about Markham's public figure as they do about the intentions and preoccupations of the sender. Requests to Markham at the Admiralty were, of course, heavily affected by gendered position. Women, generally, had little cause to ask for positions for themselves and so the majority of female applications were brokered requests which in turn allowed for a greater expression of need or anxiety. Serving officers, on the other hand, often had greater recourse to request advancement, interest or position for themselves. However, they were also restricted by their need to seem both dutiful and the capable head of their family, able to provide through their meritorious service.[18] There were some requests, therefore, that male applicants seem to have been reluctant to make. Some women framed their brokered requests in terms of a service to themselves and some men framed their requests as service to their family or friends, so the gendered aspects of the letters are complex and difficult to define. Other factors such as the social status of the correspondent, their level of intimacy with Markham and the state of naval promotion in war and peace also had a considerable effect on the way applicants formed requests.

Female Brokerage

Maria Markham was apart from her new husband from September 1797, when Markham joined *Centaur* at Spithead, until August 1799. John was then at sea in the Channel fleet until January 1801.[19] During this time Maria lived with John's family at Bishopthorpe, her own family at Dynevor castle and spent much time with both families in London at her house on Portugal Street. Maria was Markham's point of contact within his familiar network during his absence and their correspondence highlights her perception of her role and duties as well as some of the realities of her position. There are thirty-six letters from Maria to John in the Markham collection and seventy-eight from John to Maria.[20] Maria's letters cover the first three years of their separation from 1797

---

[16] Jones, 'Masculinity, Materiality and Space'; Carter, *Emergence of Polite Society*, 88–125; Bailey, *Parenting in England*, 71.

[17] Brant, *Eighteenth-Century Letters*, 24–27.

[18] Bailey, *Parenting in England*, 38.

[19] Markham, *A Naval Career*, 136–153 and 180.

[20] NMM, MRK/107/3/1a–36b, Maria to John; MRK/107/2/1–83, John to Maria.

186 PATRONAGE AND THE BRITISH NAVY, 1775–1815

to 1799.[21] There are no letters from Maria to John for any of the following years of their marriage until her death in 1810. John's letters cover mainly his periods of absence.[22] There are few from 1797 to 1799, during which time he served off the coast of Ireland, where bad weather made the transportation of letters unreliable, or he was on frequent cruises in the Mediterranean, where he had little time to write. However, there are twenty-three from 1800 when he was stationed in the Channel fleet blockading Brest. There were still difficulties sending letters, which depended on his being close to the admiral's ship to send out his correspondence with the captain taking dispatches to the mainland. In 1800, Maria took up residence in Liversmead, near Plymouth, which made a more frequent correspondence possible, as well as the sending of gifts for the ship such as fresh fruit and vegetables.[23]

The lack of letters from 1801 is explained by the pair's reunion when John took up his position at the Admiralty. During this time, they lived together in the apartments in Whitehall provided for lord commissioners.[24] The letters in 1802 reflect Maria's absence from Whitehall upon the birth of their first child in October 1801 and their moving the family home to Ades in Lewes.[25] During this time, John spent much of his time in London at the Admiralty, or in Portsmouth attending to his duties as MP. The twenty letters from 1805 reflect Maria's confinement to her duties as a mother at the house in Ades while John remained in London sitting in parliament and defending St Vincent from attack by their political enemies.

This is, by no means, a complete correspondence. Maria commented to John in one letter that she had 'never written less than twice every week', since they parted in summer 1797.[26] The letters in the collection, therefore, are only a snippet of a much larger correspondence, although it does provide glimpses into their familiar network, as illustrated in Chapter 2, as well as into Maria's perception of her position. John's letters to Maria illuminate a little more of her role in patronage beyond that of a 'friend' to his following of young officers. Possibly either Maria's letters passing on requests were lost or she was never explicit about her role as informal patron in their familiar circle.

Certainly, Maria passed on very little in the way of patronage requests to John between 1797 and 1798. When Maria married John, she entered fully into his intimate circle of acquaintance as well as his familial network. It is difficult for this reason to trace her role and involvement in the patronage that

[21] Thirteen in 1797; thirteen in 1798; six in 1799.

[22] Seven in 1797, seven in 1798, twenty-three in 1800, thirteen in 1802, twenty in 1805, one in 1806, one in 1807, nine in 1809.

[23] NMM, MRK/107/2/34, John to Maria, 4 June 1800.

[24] Markham, *A Naval Career*, 244.

[25] Ibid., 244.

[26] NMM, MRK/107/3/21, Maria to John, 20 July 1798.

GENDER AND PARENTHOOD: THE POWER OF BROKERS 187

placed William Croft, Henry Elton, John Kelly and Fred MacDonald on board *Centaur*, all youngsters from John's Yorkshire and Christ Church networks mentioned in Chapter 2. However, she was instrumental in the maintenance of these connections while Markham was away. Kelly's mother explicitly hoped to be remembered to John upon dining at Bishopthorpe with Maria in August 1798.[27] The same summer, Maria also passed on news of Croft's father.[28] One letter from John to Maria passed on news of the health of McDonald, Croft and Elton, which implies Maria's interest in their wellbeing, news of which she would pass on to their familiar network through visits or letters. Her interest in the boys also suggests her possible involvement in their initial appointment.

Maria may not have brokered the appointments of John's other protégés but she was certainly involved in the maintenance of their parents' connection to herself and Markham. In one letter in 1798 she asked for news of 'young MacDonald' because 'I daresay I shall see L^y Louisa'. She also mentioned other youngsters including Croft, saying: 'I do hope all my other young friends go on well.'[29] Her familiar air implies an informality to her involvement in John's patronage. Certainly, other letters suggest her perception of her position being less formal than that of broker to John's naval patronage. When John asked Maria whether a friend of his had visited her, she assured him that 'I have always mentioned to you I have met him, or any other of the party I think you know'.[30] This neatly represents how Maria viewed her letters, as a way of remotely keeping John informed of the movements, news and wishes of his friends in Britain. Maria seems to have considered the sharing of news about John's 'young friends' a part of her sensible affection for him rather than a means of managing patronage connections.

John passed news to Maria of other connections whom he appointed to his ship from the recommendations of their familial network. In 1798 he told Maria that 'Thomas the sailmaker of Carmarthen does very well.'[31] The initial recommendation for this appointment probably came from Maria's brother, George Talbot Rice, who was MP for Carmarthenshire, although it may have also come via Maria who was also part of the Welsh network which secured Rice his seat.[32] Even if she did not broker the sailmaker's appointment, John passing on news of him suggests Maria was important in the maintenance of his network through the sharing of that news. Certainly, he passed on news of men who had been recommended by their Welsh network and expected Maria to share that news. In a letter from December 1798, Markham wrote:

---

[27] NMM, MRK/107/3/27, Maria to John, 14 August 1798.
[28] NMM, MRK/107/3/22, Maria to John, 24 July 1798.
[29] NMM, MRK/107/3/14, Maria to John, 14 February 1798.
[30] NMM, MRK/107/3/18, Maria to John, 9 April 1798.
[31] NMM, MRK/107/2/13, John to Maria, 22 December 1798.
[32] Thorne, *House of Commons 1790–1820*, v.13.

188   PATRONAGE AND THE BRITISH NAVY, 1775–1815

'as you are in Wales you may tell Mr H Lloyd that D Davies about whom he interested himself is well'.[33] Whether she styled herself as such, Maria was John's point of contact in their familiar network which he was not in direct correspondence with and this included patronage connections.

Maria's tendency to align herself with informal modes of social maintenance may have meant she simply did not emphasise or acknowledge her involvement in brokering patronage in her letters. Certainly, her letters show a fondness for the fashion of sensibility. The backlash against Lord Chesterfield's *Letters to His Son*, published in 1774, reveals how deliberate use of friends for advancement became tainted as deceitful and untrustworthy.[34] Those who subscribed to the romantic ideal of 'feeling', therefore, emphasised the role of friendship in their patronage instead. Maria styled herself in her letters as a champion of sensible marital love and sensible friendship. Her sensibility is apparent in her approval of her sister-in-law Elizabeth Markham, married to her brother-in-law William: 'I really do love Mrs Will more than I ever expected to do, she has so much feeling, so good a heart, I am quite delighted to have this opportunity of seeing more of Her.'[35] John and Maria also subscribed to the ideal of sensible marital love in their correspondence. In one letter Maria wrote: 'The dear little tear you sent in the letter brought many into my eyes, unfortunately in my haste to open the seal I tore it in two, but not enough to prevent my seeing it, and giving it many *many* kisses.'[36] A letter from John further emphasises their sensibility as he wrote to Maria describing his longing for her during their separation, when he slept a night in their house alone: 'I need not describe to you what I felt, in Portugal Street, every thing reminded me of my loss, I kissed your side of the bed, you will find them there when you get home again, unless you should find what I wish something more, *myself*.'[37]

Other letters in the pair's correspondence show a distinctly stoic sensibility, whereby, feeling was tempered by fortitude and rationality in the manner John Dwyer described Adam Smith as encouraging in his second edition of *Theory of Moral Sentiments* published in 1790.[38] In a letter from December 1797, Maria wrote: 'do not suspect me so unworthy of you, as not constantly to endeavour to suppose myself with that firmness, which taking it in a serious light, it is our Duty to do in every situation in life',[39] and that she showed her

---

[33] NMM, MRK/107/2/13, John to Maria, 22 December 1798.

[34] John Dwyer, *Virtuous Discourse: Sensibility and Community in Late Eighteenth-Century Scotland* (Edinburgh, 1987), 3.

[35] NMM, MRK/107/3/7, Maria to John, 27 October 1797.

[36] NMM, MRK/107/3/21, Maria to John, 20 July 1798.

[37] NMM, MRK/107/2/2, John to Maria, 15 September 1797.

[38] Dwyer, *Virtuous Discourse*, 6 and 38–39.

[39] NMM, MRK/104/3/11, Maria to John, 16 December [1797].

GENDER AND PARENTHOOD: THE POWER OF BROKERS   189

feelings 'to the world as little as any one; under a smiling countenance there may be found many an aching heart'.[40] Fortitude to behave rationally but to still feel sentimentally underpinned Maria's views on male authority and female autonomy. Maria defined and discussed gender roles and norms in her letters which reveal to us her perceived position and how she styled herself. Understanding how she wanted to come across in her letters explains the lack of explicit references to her brokering patronage. In one letter, she mentioned how John's sister's fortitude at the prospect of relocating to her husband's plantation in the West Indies made Maria pity her more than if she had shown 'womanish feelings'. This prompted Maria next to say: 'a proper firmness, is as necessary for our sex, as in yours'.[41] Maria also emphasised the husband as the head of the family. In one letter, she wrote, 'how odd that I should ever have been afraid of you, god knows perhaps you might now be glad if I was so sometimes, as it might keep me in order'.[42] However, her jovial tone subverts this standard of behaviour, revealing an acknowledgement that Maria acted with a certain amount of autonomy, often potentially against John's wishes. John's pet name for Maria was, rather condescendingly, 'squib',[43] referring to her temper, but it does suggest that she had a degree of independence.

Maria's sensibility may have masked her role as broker in the epistolary record but her self-fashioning in her letters to John reveals that she did not consider herself to be in a position of autonomous strength in his absence. In fact, her letters moralise and sympathise on the dangers of female isolation. She commented on the delicacy of her position in his absence: 'I should like to have your full opinion upon this subject, for I consider a woman's situation during the absence of her husband as the most delicate possible'.[44] This is part of a stronger trend in her correspondence where she worried over doing what John would have wanted. In the same letter she wrote: 'I am satisfied that you will believe I shall try to act in *every*, the *most trifling* thing, as I think you would approve; I therefore do particularly wish to know your ideas perfectly'. She was asking whether he thought she should go to London or back to Yorkshire when she left Wales in 1798.[45] In another letter she wrote: 'it is pleasant to me that you approve my agreement with Robert, for indulgent as you ever are to me, yet I cannot help being always fearful of not doing *exactly* as you would wish, were you at my elbow to direct me'.[46] Of course, Maria was twelve years younger than Markham, so much of her searching for advice

[40] Ibid.
[41] NMM, MRK/107/3/5b, Maria to John, 14 October 1797.
[42] NMM, MRK/107/3/10, Maria to John, [unknown date].
[43] NMM, MRK/107/3/14, Maria to John, 14 February [1798].
[44] Ibid.
[45] Ibid.
[46] Emphasis in original. NMM, MRK/107/3/13, Maria to John, 11 February 1798.

190 PATRONAGE AND THE BRITISH NAVY, 1775–1815

and concern over his views in her letters reflects her comparative inexperience. However, seeking approval suggests that Maria was operating with a certain amount of autonomy in management of their affairs and by extension their patronage, rather than simply relying on her many male relations.

However, Maria's autonomy was always in relation to John and their partnership. Their familiar network saw Maria as half of a whole unit made up of John and herself. She jokingly commented in one of her letters that she was convinced 'the world in general do not know you are absent' because all of her invitations were made to him as well as her.[47] Invitations made out to both Maria and John suggests that their social circle viewed her as irrevocably tied to him and, therefore, as a point of contact with him while he served at sea. Certainly, establishing their familiar network from mentions in their letters in Chapter 2 illustrated Maria's position and the efforts of connections to be introduced to her and secure access to Markham and his naval patronage. On the other hand, their extended social circle may have ignored Markham's absence as a polite means to avoid acknowledging their necessary separation which had connotations of naval wives' infidelity.[48] Of course, it may also have just been easier, with less chance of accidental impoliteness, to invite both John and Maria, in case John returned to England unexpectedly. However, this does reflect that Maria was firmly linked to Markham in public perception, meaning that the informal face-to-face requests which would have been made to him, were he present, were instead made to Maria. The practical element of face-to-face meetings coupled with Maria's semantic emphasis on feeling and friendship means that Maria may have subconsciously obscured her role as an agent of their patronage partnership.

Maria's moralising also reveals the limitations of female patronage independence. Even in the absence of husbands, other male members of the domestic sphere acted as limits on female autonomy. This seems to have been partly enforced by what Henry French and Mark Rothery refer to as gender templates being translated into a 'normative code' which then enters 'common sense'.[49] Maria's moralisation on reputation reflects this. She mentioned reputation as the one thing 'more fatal to our sex' and wrote:

> I have heard many say "what does it signify what the world thinks, provided I do nothing that is actually wrong" in the world we must live, and the good

[47] NMM, MRK/107/3/20, Maria to John, 29 May 1798.

[48] This letter discusses Maria's fears over her reputation and these associations. NMM, MRK/107/3/19, Maria to John, 20 March 1798.

[49] Henry French and Mark Rothery, 'Hegemonic Masculinities? Assessing Change and Processes of Change in Elite Masculinity, 1700–1900', in John Arnold and Sean Brady (eds.), *What Is Masculinity? Historical Dynamics from Antiquity to the Contemporary World* (London, 2011), 159.

GENDER AND PARENTHOOD: THE POWER OF BROKERS   191

opinions of it once lost, every thing that is bad soon follows. This holds good with respect to the society young women live in more than anything, and however amiable and innocent they may be, she will be judged of by her companions.[50]

Women who subscribed to this therefore isolated themselves, seeing only approved acquaintances, which likely severely limited their patronage brokering abilities.

One letter from Maria reveals the effect of her concern for her reputation on her ability to act as a patronage broker. Maria asked for his approval of her plan to not allow male visitors to her house in London in the morning:

> When I have your sanction it will relieve all difficulties and doubt with respect to *Male* morning visitors I shall make the matter very easy, by a general order when I first get to town; and if I am quizzed, by a certain friend of yours for never being at home, I shall tell him at once that tho' I trust perfectly free from that pondary and nonsense (which in my opinion is the greatest proof of folly) I do not during your absence like the style of having *even your friends* lounging in.[51]

She was probably referring to Edward Riou who, as we saw in Chapter 2, Maria disinvited because his regular morning visits made her uncomfortable.[52] Gendered space and societal norms of politeness therefore limited when and where a man could meet and make a patronage request face-to-face with a female broker. Indeed, other letters in John and Maria's correspondence suggest that this restriction was a common one advised to the young wives of officers serving abroad. Maria wrote that Hugh Seymour had told her that he gave his wife Horatia the same advice to restrict male visitors.[53] Part of the fear was the damage that could be done to a woman's reputation by seeing men in the morning when women were more likely to be unchaperoned. Reportedly, Seymour did not warn his wife from a lack of 'confidence in her propriety of conduct' but rather to protect her reputation.[54] Certainly, in the rest of her letter Maria passed on a story of the infidelity of naval wives told to her by another woman, whom she referred to as 'Mrs L', who said there were some who presented their husbands with babies only five months after their return.[55] This reveals the moral confines of the gendered domestic space for women. In juxtaposition, Maria mentioned how she liked being visited by the

50 NMM, MRK/107/3/20, Maria to John, 29 May 1798.
51 NMM, MRK/107/3/16, Maria to John, 17 February 1798.
52 NMM, MRK/107/3/18, Maria to John, 9 April 1798.
53 NMM, MRK/107/3/19, Maria to John, 20 March 1798.
54 Ibid.
55 Ibid.

192 PATRONAGE AND THE BRITISH NAVY, 1775–1815

Wycombes and passed on John Henry Petty's (the earl of Wycombe) wishes to be remembered to Markham. The implication here is that the presence of Lady Wycombe made Maria more comfortable and therefore allowed Petty to talk with her and to fortify his connection with Markham.[56]

Maria was either uninvolved in her and Markham's patronage, or her self-fashioning as a sentimental friend meant that she under-represented her role as broker. However, some applications to Markham suggest she was involved at more than a superficial level. The request from Francis Smith, self-reportedly rector of Grendon and vicar of Eardesly in Hertfordshire, for his nephew to become a lieutenant of marines came via Maria.[57] Others mentioned Maria as a possible way to make their request. Sarah D'Oyly apologised for soliciting Markham directly on behalf of her brother's illegitimate son, Captain George Blake, saying that she would have gone through either Maria or George Talbot Rice but she did not know if they were in town.[58] D'Oyly was part of Markham's wider familiar circle. Her sister Anne had married Wellbore Ellis, the first baron Mendip and a Westminster-Christ Church connection of Markham's father's friend the first earl of Mansfield. D'Oyly's connection to Markham seems to have come particularly through her sister's friendship with his father, as her letter mentioned a previous favour granted Blake on her behalf: 'the [Archbishop] was so very kind from Friendship to Lady Mendip, to obtain, the very desirable rank of Post for Capt Blake: and I believe Sir, that we were much obliged to you likewise for that favour'.[59] She also mentioned how George Talbot Rice had applied to St Vincent on Blake's behalf.

D'Oyly's request reveals the male-to-female structures which facilitated patronage of this sort. Captain George Blake had no connection to Markham or St Vincent directly himself, so could not rely on professional credentials of the service to support his request. That meant his connection to his aunts was his route to patronage solicitation. D'Oyly was embedded in the same Westminster-Christ Church circle as the Markhams and Maria's family, including her brother. D'Oyly also married Christopher D'Oyly, a friend of her brother-in-law, in 1765. Christopher D'Oyly was MP for Wareham and then Seaford until 1784, and had supported Lord North's government along with William Markham and Maria's father.[60] Christopher D'Oyly died in 1795, leaving Sarah a widow. Her sister Anne was also a widow by the time they made their requests on behalf of George Blake, Wellbore Ellis having died in February 1802.[61] Both D'Oyly and Lady Mendip are more apparent in the

---

56 NMM, MRK/107/3/18, Maria to John, 9 April 1798.
57 NMM, MRK/104/2/104, Smith to Maria Markham, 15 November [1801].
58 NMM, MRK/104/4/11, D'Oyly to Markham, 1 August 1803.
59 Captain George Blake made post-captain 29 April 1802. TNA, ADM/9/2/262.
60 Namier and Brooke, *House of Commons 1754–1790*, ii.336–337.
61 Ibid., ii.397–400.

GENDER AND PARENTHOOD: THE POWER OF BROKERS   193

patronage exchange because as widows they assumed a greater responsibility managing patronage and brokering requests from their extended network. This also made it acceptable for D'Oyly to write to Markham directly. Their widowhood, however, did not necessarily mean they had assumed control of patronage which they had previously been disengaged from. Rather, D'Oyly mentioned seeing either Maria or her brother, which suggests that she had previously conducted her patronage face-to-face. It also reveals that visiting Maria was a secure way to solicit Markham's patronage and that it was not unusual or even gendered.

D'Oyly and Lady Mendip's role in Blake's preferment, and D'Oyly mentioning her approaching Maria with the request, reveals a female-to-female patronage network, which although it did not exclude men was also not solely reliant on them as Maria's self-fashioning would suggest. Other letters point towards a female-to-female network being used to solicit Markham while he was at the Admiralty. Martha Peckard, wife of the Reverend Peter Peckard, Dean of Magdalene College and a prominent abolitionist, solicited Markham on behalf of her friend's husband, Lieutenant Joseph Stephenson.[62] Once again, Peckard was part of Markham's wider familiar circle and she passed on news of his family staying with her on their way to Bishopthorpe. She also signed her letter familiarly 'Adieu! Adieu!'. Peckard's application was to assist Lieutenant Stephenson's original request not to be superseded. She forwarded a letter that her friend Mrs Stephenson had sent her, worrying that Lieutenant Stephenson had not been explicit about his family's distressed circumstances. The application relied on a female-female connection. The request also echoed the emphasis on friendship and charity that Maria placed in her letters. Peckard was also widowed in 1797, so she may have written to Markham directly because of the absence of her male counterpart.[63] On the other hand, her involvement in patronage may have previously gone unrecorded as it was conducted informally in face-to-face visits. The death of her husband prompted her direct application to Markham by letter, thus leaving a written record of her engagement.

D'Oyly and Peckard's letters show that Maria was involved in managing requests to Markham, especially in marshalling the informal requests of other female connections, which seems to have also been a common aspect of other women's involvement. Not all female requests came through Maria, however. Lady Elizabeth Fane brokered the appointment of her acquaintance Lieutenant Daniel Ivie.[64] Her letter passed on thanks to Markham for the

---

[62] NMM, MRK/104/4/5, Martha Peckard to Markham, 30 May 1802; John Walsh, 'Peckard, Peter', *ODNB*, vol. 43, 374–375; MRK/104/2/108, Stephenson to Markham, 23 May 1802.

[63] NMM, MRK/107/3/11, Maria to John, 16 December 1797.

[64] NMM, MRK/104/4/51, Elizabeth Fane to Markham, [unknown date].

194 PATRONAGE AND THE BRITISH NAVY, 1775–1815

appointment and apologised for not thanking him sooner, but Ivie had been ill and his agent had not informed him of his appointment. She also mentioned how Ivie's illness 'prevented his calling as usual at the Admiralty'.[65] This suggests that while Fane was soliciting Markham directly by letter, Ivie was attempting to make direct solicitation at the Admiralty in person. However, despite Ivie's possibly multiple and unsuccessful visits, he does not appear to have written to Markham to thank him himself, which suggests he was not in direct contact with him. Rather, Fane passed on their joint thanks: 'I am commission'd by Mr Ivie to say everything that ought, and much more than can be said on his behalf; he is indeed grateful beyond expression'. She may of course have written Ivie's thanks on his behalf because he was ill; however, she explicitly referred to Ivie as 'my recommendation' in her letter. She also requested Markham's continued interest in Ivie as she ended her letter: 'I trust you will never have reason to repeat your attention to my recommendation in this instance, but on the contrary will have every inducement to continue to him the honour of your patronage'. Fane's husband, John, MP for Oxfordshire, also wrote to Markham brokering requests.[66] Elizabeth Fane's brokering of Ivie's request, therefore, was not a product of her husband's absence. Rather, Elizabeth Fane's letter reflects a normal standard of female independent engagement in patronage that is not well-represented in Maria's personal letters to Markham.

Certainly, other patronage letters to Markham show how female brokers acted independently on behalf of male connections. A letter from Captain John Oakes Hardy mentioned that Lady Sophia Hesketh, a close female relation, had previously solicited St Vincent for his interest. Hardy wrote to Markham to request that he remind St Vincent that he was eager for a more active service than provided by his service on *St Albans* in home-waters. He included St Vincent's response to his relation in a postscript at the end of the letter where he wrote: 'It is but proper to communicate a letter from Lord St Vincent to a near relation, who kindly interested herself about me.'[67] He did not overtly stress his relation's gender but he was sure to make her station clear by including St Vincent's response including his address of her, 'Madam, the interest your Ladyship takes', as well as dropping her name at the very end of the letter: 'This answer must have been received by Lady Hesketh *previous* to my *application* for the command on the Coast of Guinea.'[68] Hesketh's status carried weight in her brokering of Hardy's patronage, even though she did not ask for anything particular. Hardy's

[65] Ibid.

[66] NMM, MRK/104/1/6–8, John Fane to Markham, 10 July 1803, 14 July 1803 and 27 July 1807.

[67] NMM, MRK/102/3/9, Hardy to Markham, 11 March 1802.

[68] Emphasis in original. Ibid.

GENDER AND PARENTHOOD: THE POWER OF BROKERS

inclusion of her general approach to St Vincent and his general response of support represents Hesketh's power as a broker because of her social status as well as her independence in the exchange.

Chalus has demonstrated that gender mattered less for those of higher rank in their pursuit of patronage.[69] Naomi Tadmor also noted that women were excluded from political patronage lower down the social scale while their male counterparts were active participants despite their also lacking the property which would enable them to vote.[70] Women of lower status, however, could act as independent brokers in their own extended networks. Mary Higg, who ran a lodging house in Plymouth dock, acted as broker for warrant officers and lower-status captains who otherwise faced difficulties in addressing Markham directly unless already known to him through mutual service. In 1803, Higg brokered the request of the carpenter Thomas Sampson, who was husband of the woman she employed to look after her sick mother. She wrote a letter of recommendation for Sampson which he then delivered to Markham at the Admiralty personally. The letter also reveals that Markham had obliged Higg previously by appointing Sampson to the frigate *Thames*, as she wrote: 'The Bearer is Thomas Sampson who you was so good as to appoint Carpenter of the Thames frigate, which ship is now in Dock for the purpose of being broke up.'[71] There are no more letters from Higg in the collection but some requests suggest she acted on behalf of other non-related male connections. Captain Delamore Wynter mentioned in a letter to Markham in 1806 that he was 'made known' to Markham on Markham's last visit to Plymouth and that he had 'reason to believe that several times after that period you were so good as to remember me, through the medium of my good friend Miss Higgs'.[72] Her position as an independent owner of a lodging house gave her a powerful network position because it allowed her to forge connections with many officers of different statuses.

Her connection to Markham is not entirely clear. She seems to have been fairly friendly with him, adding as a postscript to her letter about Sampson that she 'shall send some Pilchards in the course of a fortnight'.[73] Perhaps Markham stayed in her inn when he visited Plymouth. Certainly, he mentioned other women in Plymouth who could arrange lodging for himself and Maria including one 'Susannah', which suggests that officers used favoured lodging houses when in port and consequently forged connections with their owners.[74] On the other hand, it seems possible that their connection was not solely born

[69] Chalus, *Elite Women*, 146.
[70] Tadmor, *Family and Friends*, 222.
[71] NMM, MRK/104/4/44, Higg to Markham, 24 August 1803.
[72] NMM, MRK/102/6/47, Wynter to Markham, 18 March 1806.
[73] NMM, MRK/104/4/44, Higg to Markham, 24 August 1803.
[74] NMM, MRK/107/2/15, John to Maria, 1 February 1800.

196 PATRONAGE AND THE BRITISH NAVY, 1775–1815

of location and necessity. Higg's late uncle, Benjamin Kennicott, although only the son of a town clerk, attended Oxford in 1744 through the patronage of his sister's employers.[75] After taking his doctorate in divinity he seems to have become well-connected within Markham's Oxford-Christ Church network, particularly with the Dean Cyril Jackson whom he mentioned in his will alongside Higg and her mother in Plymouth dock.[76]

Higg's patronage independence came from her ability to mix with different levels of society. There are other examples of female patrons acting as the brokers in networks that extended between social levels in wider British society. Like Higg, women in other businesses, such as grocers or servant-hiring agencies, acted as a bridge between both classes and genders. Their work put them in contact with both prospective employers and employees, while their gender allowed them to forge vast networks of connections through local shops.[77] Higg's position similarly facilitated the requests of warrant officers and artificers in the dockyards. The dockyards were principally a male space and the wives of workers were even forbidden to approach the yard perimeter in some yards, to prevent theft.[78] However, the wives of artificers had connection to one another outside yard hierarchies which, in some ways, put them in a stronger position to broker patronage than their male counter-parts. Chapter 6 demonstrates that the wives of artificers in Plymouth dockyard frequently organised the entry of all classes of artificers and labourers into the yard.[79] Higg, as an unmarried woman, was also in a powerful position to broker requests from these strong female networks, as it meant that she had fewer requests to make on behalf of a marriage partnership, and could afford to trouble connections, such as Markham, more frequently on behalf of others.

Many higher-status female brokers also acted independently, but often because their male counterparts were absent through service abroad, or the death of their husbands meant they assumed greater patronage responsibility. Lady Sarah Frankland, the widow of Admiral Thomas Frankland, dictated a letter to Markham in May 1804 to request a promotion for her grandson Lieutenant George Whinyates. She was explicit that she addressed Markham

[75] Sabine Baring-Gould, *Devonshire Character and Strange Events* (London: John Lane, Bodley Head, 1908), 369–374.

[76] TNA, PROB 11/1108/111 Will of Benjamin Kennicott, D.D. Christ Church Oxford, 9 September 1783.

[77] See in particular Peter Collinge's work on Jane Williamson: Peter Collinge, 'Female Enterprise in Georgian Derbyshire, c.1780–1830' (unpublished PhD thesis, University of Keele, 2015); Peter Collinge, 'Enterprise, Activism and Charity: Mary Pickford and the Urban Elite of Derby, 1780–1812', *Midland History* 45:1 (2020), 36–54.

[78] Morriss, *Royal Dockyards*, 94.

[79] See *The Sixth Report of the Commissioners of Naval Inquiry. Appendix: Plymouth yard, Woolwich yard* (London, 1804).

GENDER AND PARENTHOOD: THE POWER OF BROKERS   197

'in the absence of' Lieutenant-Colonel William Frankland of North York militia.[80] However, unlike other female brokered requests, Frankland did not place herself directly within the exchange, nor cast favour or obligation on herself. Rather, by expressly operating as broker during her male counterpart's absence, Frankland styled herself as a conduit to his patronage rather than an active participant. In this, she aligned herself more with other women of her class and the fashion for a more informal approach to patronage. Lady Sophia Hesketh, of a similar status to Frankland, as the wife of a baronet, may have framed her letter to St Vincent in a similar way. Regardless of how she styled herself, Hardy viewed her as an active broker in his interest, which suggests that some women were inclined to under-report their participation in patronage.

Some female applicants were reluctant to appear overly active in managing the patronage of their absent husbands. Jemima Crozier requested a government position for her husband who was a captain in the marines serving in the West Indies. She wrote: 'a prospect appears of there being more Vacancies to fill up in the much wish[d] for department, he is so desirous to get I fear his being abroad will disappoint him of it'. She emphasised his distance and consequent inability to approach Markham himself in her next line: 'he knows nothing of the bustle we are in'.[81] Although she acted independently on behalf of her absent husband she also emphasised her need for him at home, similar to how Maria emphasised her need for Markham's advice when he was absent. Crozier wrote:

> I catch at every shadow of a hope that seems likely to bring him home to me and my family his eldest son is now grown a young man and is yet unprovided for, tis a great charge on me. He is a fine lad, was Crozier with me all I hope wou[d]. go on to our wish.[82]

Crozier was in part probably also referring to her husband's role in the education of her son, which was a real tension in the lives of naval officers and their families when fathers were by necessity so often absent.[83] Her reluctance to own her patronage independence, however, also supports the argument that there was a cultural expectation that women did not engage in the more formal, explicit side of patronage unless pushed to by the necessity of widowhood or their husband's great distress.[84]

On the other hand, a joint letter from Elizabeth and Thomas Bailey, written on the reverse of each other, reveals the understanding of a partnered approach

---

[80] NMM, MRK/104/4/56, Frankland to Markham, 13 May [1804].
[81] NMM, MRK/104/4/13, Crozier to Markham, 6 June 1803.
[82] Ibid.
[83] Gill, *Naval Families*, 74–85.
[84] Lincoln, *Naval Wives*, 15–16.

198   PATRONAGE AND THE BRITISH NAVY, 1775–1815

to patronage.[85] Elizabeth Bailey addressed her letter to Maria as 'Honoured madam' and wrote that she had 'taken the liberty of writing you a few lines as my husband was writing to Captain Markham ... to thank you for your goodness'. She mentioned a mutual acquaintance, Anne Ricketts, Lady Northesk, whose kindness, alongside Maria's, allowed Bailey and her husband to settle in Poole.[86] Thomas Bailey, on the other hand, wrote to Markham to supply him with his certificate from his time serving under Markham's command aboard *Centaur*, from 1797 to 1800, when he was detained aboard *Ville de Paris* and put on that ship's books. This meant he missed out on *Centaur*'s prize money and he requested Markham see that he got what was owed to him. He did not thank Markham in his letter but Elizabeth thanked both Maria and Lady Northesk. Their favour seems to have been solicited and secured by visits from Elizabeth. Although the naval patronage of ensuring the certificate was signed was pursued by the male side of the partnership, the patronage relationship that facilitated and strengthened that request was one forged by women. The fact that Elizabeth and Thomas wrote their letters on the same piece of paper also suggests that John and Maria were perceived in the same way, as a patronage partnership, with Maria dealing with the more informal connection maintenance and Markham managing the distribution of appointments.

Other female brokers acting in Britain seem to have trod a fine line between placing all the favour on their absent husbands, consequently styling themselves as conduits, and taking ownership of their role as independent brokers, to whom favour and credit were due. After all, acting as broker was more than just being a conduit for patronage between a patron and client; bestowing an appointment on a broker's client also bestowed favour on the broker and created a tie of obligation between broker and patron.[87] For some, the solution was to style the request as coming from both themselves and their husband, as a patronage partnership. Mary Dickens passed on news of her nephew being made a sub-lieutenant in the West Indies and at the same time indirectly asked for Markham's favour in ensuring her own son, Lieutenant Samuel Dickens, had his sub-lieutenant's commission approved by the board. Her brother-in-law, Colonel Richard Mark Dickens, was in India with the Thirty-Fourth Cumberland Regiment, so it seems that she adopted the mantle of broker for these various family members, maintaining their connection to

[85] NMM, MRK/104/4/6, Elizabeth and Thomas Bailey to Maria and John, 14 June 1802.

[86] Anne Ricketts was married to Admiral William Carnegie, seventh earl of Northesk, and was St Vincent's niece. Kenneth Breen, 'Carnegie, William, seventh earl of Northesk', *ODNB*, vol. 10, 196.

[87] J. Boissevain, *Friends of Friends: Networks, Manipulators and Coalitions* (Oxford, 1974), 154.

GENDER AND PARENTHOOD: THE POWER OF BROKERS   199

Markham through the passing on of thanks and news.[88] She wrote: 'Having been informed by Mr Dickens you had the goodness to assure him you would make use of your interest to have his nephew Mr George Dickens confirmed ... I have the pleasure of acquainting you he has lately been made a sub-lieut on board the Shark Sloop at Jamaica', and she went on to write: 'allow one to add that Mr Dickens unites with me in requesting your farther influence for a full Lieu^cy for which favour we shall both be most truly grateful'.[89] Even in the absence of her male counterpart, therefore, Mary Dickens made sure the favour was clearly bestowed on them both rather than just herself.

The conferring of obligation on the wives of officers is not perhaps surprising when we consider their restricted position in society. After all, the wives of officers relied on their husband's position for their own security. Lieutenant Daniel Carpenter framed his request for active duty as a favour to his wife, as it meant he was better able to support her. Carpenter wrote to Markham several times over the course of his career, his first letter dating from 1803 when he was recommended to Markham's patronage by a mutual acquaintance.[90] In his letters he often mentioned Harriet, and recommended her to Markham's friendship, and used her as a means of softening his own appeals for Markham's favour. In September 1803, he wrote: 'You will be inclined to serve her by favouring me with such a Cruise as may turn out to Advantage' and 'Mrs Carpenter you will find on enquiry, to be deserving of any Acts of friendship with which you may be pleased to favour her.'[91] In a letter from November 1804, Carpenter mentioned Markham's correspondence with Harriet after her letter in April that year about her concern with the state of *Viper*. His phrasing reveals the couple's patronage partnership, as he wrote: 'Agreeable to the advice you did me the honor to favor me with in your very friendly letter to Mrs Carpenter'.[92] Daniel and Harriet then, as a married unit, were also a patronage partnership. Harriet engaged in the informal part of the exchange even when she was not in direct correspondence with Markham. When she did contact Markham directly she could ask for advice or request changes in situation that would be more risky or difficult for Daniel to do. Daniel applied for active service, for faster, better ships, and for recommendation but relied upon Harriet to directly approach Markham on a matter which could so easily have backfired. Complaining about a ship's condition, especially a cutter such

---

[88] *A List of all the Officers of the Army and Royal Marines on Full and Half-Pay with an Index: and a Succession of Colonels* (War Office, 1805), 170; *Historical Record of the Thirty-Fourth or, The Cumberland Regiment of Foot: containing an account of the Regiment in 1702 and of its subsequent services to 1844* (London, 1844), 44.

[89] NMM, MRK/104/4/23, Dickens to Markham, 25 January 1807.

[90] NMM, MRK/103/1/19, Carpenter to Markham, 10 August 1803.

[91] NMM MRK/103/1/21, Carpenter to Markham, 23 September 1803.

[92] NMM, MRK/103/1/22, Carpenter to Markham, 27 November 1804.

200   PATRONAGE AND THE BRITISH NAVY, 1775–1815

as *Viper*, could be seen by some patrons as ungrateful, and could damage a carefully fostered patronage connection, as we saw with Thomas Searle in Chapter 4. Harriet styled her application as a request for advice rather than action. Couching her letter in her anxiety and female naivety, therefore, Harriet prevented herself and Daniel from appearing overbearing.

As we have seen, widows often acted independently for their sons or relations but their power in the exchange was often limited through the loss of their husband, and the male half of the patronage partnership shown in the Carpenters' and the Baileys' applications. A long letter to Markham from Lady Elizabeth Collier clearly demonstrates the problems naval widows faced in their attempts to secure patronage for their sons and connections. Collier wrote to Markham to ask for his interest in her son Captain Francis Collier. She opened her letter by apologising for missing Markham when she visited the Admiralty, where she could have put her request to him in person. Collier was the widow of Vice-Admiral George Collier, who had died in April 1795, meaning that she took on the principal role in brokering the patronage exchange. However, Collier's aim at the Admiralty was to persuade Markham to act as guarantor with both Thomas Grenville, the First Lord, and Admiral Alexander Cochrane, the station commander-in-chief. Her own recommendation appeared to count for very little.

She began by overtly emphasising her son's personal skill and merit: 'I most solemnly would not appeal for if my son was not pre-eminently deserving and who has I must ever think been very ungenerously and unjustly dealt with'.[93] But she bolstered her request by outlining her son's other patrons and recommendations by describing her meeting with the First Lord:

> In the interview with Grenville about a month ago I requested his writing to the Commander of the Leeward Islands Station; I left with him a slight memorandum of my son's service, I produced some letters from his immortal friend Lord Nelson; Lord St Vincent; Sir Samuel Hood and *warm memories from Sir Alexander Cochrane* (in a letter of his in my possession) the whole of which Mr Grenville admitted were the most honourable testimonials.[94]

Collier was restricted in how far she could recommend her son. Despite being very well versed in the patronage mechanisms of the navy, she needed the recommendations of other officers to support her application.[95] Her recom-

---

[93] NMM, MRK/104/4/54, Collier to Markham, 6 January 1807.

[94] Emphasis in original. Ibid.

[95] In part of her letter she wrote that her son's commission for a death vacancy was before the board for ten months where she acknowledged that 'form only was necessary and not favour'. NMM, MRK/104/4/54, Collier to Markham, 6 January 1807.

GENDER AND PARENTHOOD: THE POWER OF BROKERS 201

mendation of her son was no guarantee of his merit, or she felt it was not enough to secure the attention of those she applied to.

Women could, and did, act as brokers for their male connections, but their restricted position in society determined by their gender put physical and cultural limitations on their patronage. They were restricted in the times and places they could meet with male contacts. Their recommendations may have counted for less because they had no naval experience to act as guarantee of their judgement. Women who aligned themselves with the fashion for sensibility also self-limited their patronage when they styled themselves as friends rather than patrons. However, the restricted female gendered position meant that most female requests were brokered requests, and this meant that they were able to include more anxiety or concern for the client's distress than if the application were for themselves, where such affect could be considered ungrateful, undutiful or duplicitous. Motherly anxiety was also a central part of many female applications to Markham's favour. Bailey has noted that there was an assumption in eighteenth-century literature that women were naturally anxious over their children, and so overt displays of motherly 'feeling' were perhaps expected in female requests.[96]

Collier finished her letter by emphasising her motherhood. She wrote that she felt 'as a mother most poignantly the disappointments and neglect of one who has merited so differently and to you Admirals who can appreciate so well what is due to a gallant young officer'. She excused her solicitation of Markham with a far more emphatic display of parental anxiety than other letters in the collection: 'Forgive my having intruded this length, which my feelings have naturally betrayed me into, but not to trespass with the pain and mortification I endure beyond I fear what I have already done.'[97] Other female letters to Markham did not emphasise their motherhood to this extent, but rather couched their applications in the anxiety of the gender-neutral parent. Frances Shippardson ended her request to Markham for her son's promotion by writing: 'I trust the solicitude of a Parent will plead my excuse with you'.[98] Similarly, Rebecca Brett's letter was brief and straightforward as she wrote: 'may I now hope my Dear Sir for your influence on the present Occasion, that my son may be appointed to some ship'.[99] Of course, parenthood was a position adopted by both genders and naturally made men as well as women brokers for their children, and thus gave them the same licence to express anxiety and repeat troublesome requests.

[96] Bailey, *Parenting in England*, 38.
[97] NMM, MRK/104/4/54, Collier to Markham, 6 January 1807.
[98] NMM, MRK/104/4/33, Shippardson to Markham, 19 March [1804].
[99] NMM, MRK/104/4/2, Brett to Markham, 20 May 1802.

Parenthood

The role of father and the role of mother carried different weights in patronage requests. The importance of the father is undeniable. His own service acted as a guarantee of the son's education, behaviour and innate skill. His recommendation carried with it a reputation for good judgement in non-familial appointments. Granting the son the favour of Admiralty interest also conferred favour onto the father, fulfilling the Admiralty's obligation to the long-serving officer.[100] Mothers had comparatively little power of recommendation. However, their role as physical provider and gendered stereotypes of women as naturally, parentally anxious meant that they had in many ways more power in requests of a difficult nature or those lacking honour, such as in the removal of their male connections from dangerous stations, or in repeated solicitations in the face of refusal. The role of the parent is also marked in the way that extended relations applied on behalf of their familial connections, their requests taking on a referred parental position, rather than simply that of an interested broker.

Fathers often used their own long service as reason for their children to be employed, and to excuse directly writing to Markham. Lieutenant-Colonel Frederick Wetherall wrote to request Markham's political influence in Portsmouth to get his son placed in the Portsmouth Academy, where boys were taught sea skills and navigation before going to sea.[101] Wetherall wrote: 'I trust that the request of an old officer anxious for the prosperity of his Son will plead an apology for his troubling you.'[102] Wetherall used both his greater patronage position as a long-serving officer and his fatherly anxiety. The importance of long service was emphasised even more clearly in a letter from John Goddard, who requested that his son be placed on the candidacy list for a commission in the marines. Goddard directly employed his own long service to support his request, as well as his son's anxiety to be commissioned: 'he anxious to become a solider, emboldens me to hope on the score of my own long service in the navy, that my tender of his service may be accepted at this juncture'.[103] Goddard's position as father made him more intimately involved in the exchange than a usual broker. He actively offered up his son's service, as if it were his own. His own long service, therefore, was more than just a guarantee of good judgement, it also drew on Markham's obligation to see to the fulfilment of the request.

The need to support large families was also a constant tension in male requests. Those who did not secure post-captaincy during a period of war

---

[100] Gill, *Naval Families*, 87–97.
[101] Cavell, *Midshipmen and the Quarterdeck Boys*, 26–29.
[102] NMM, MRK/105/3/33, Wetherall to Markham, 27 May 1802.
[103] NMM, MRK/105/6/30, Goddard to Markham, 1 July 1803.

GENDER AND PARENTHOOD: THE POWER OF BROKERS   203

could be stuck in a low-paid position on half-pay during the peace.[104] Many applications came to Markham from men in their twenties and thirties who were still lieutenants. These men often had growing families to support on very little pay and their applications were fraught with the tension of needing to admit their family situation but also the knowledge that the Admiralty did not look well on self-serving applications that tried to use any reason for employment other than merit or connection. Officers in the navy relied on patronage to support their families, but they could not acknowledge the need for patronage because it suggested a lack of skill. Men were also limited in their ability to represent their situation because doing so ran counter to the eighteenth-century ideal of fathers efficiently providing for their children.[105] It is worth noting, however, that the petitions of ordinary seamen, dockyard workers and their families almost all emphasise familial distress or concerns ahead of listing service credentials and connections. Gill also demonstrates that many female petitioners were more inclined to frame their requests in terms of female dependence if their husband was killed or wounded in the service, even in cases where they had their own independent incomes.[106]

One letter from Captain Charles Herbert, whom we met at the beginning of Chapter 3, shows the connection between mentioning the need to support a large family and the Admiralty's obligation to a long-serving officer and his children. Herbert applied to Markham on behalf of the son of James Mounsher, who had served as a purser in the navy for 'near thirty years' and had 'left his large family with little (might I say nothing) but what claims they may have as children of an old and upright servant'.[107] Once again, the father's long service and connection to Herbert are what prompted his solicitation on their behalf. The importance of the role of father is clear in this letter as his service and position continued to affect the application even after his death. Perhaps even more so, as the need to support a large family no longer carried with it the connotations of self-serving requests or bad parenting and could tap directly into charitable patronage. However, the request was unsuccessful, as evidenced by Markham's clerical note at the bottom of the letter which outlined St Vincent's stop on patronage until all those named on the previous First Lord's candidate list had been seen to.[108]

The level of consideration given to an applicant having a large family is perhaps best represented in James Hardy's letter to Markham. Hardy was the brother of John Oakes Hardy who had applied to Markham's patronage several times and had encouraged James Hardy to apply for Markham's influence

---

[104] Rodger, *Command of the Ocean*, 380; Wilson, *British Naval Officers*, 108–109.
[105] Bailey, *Parenting in England*, 146–155.
[106] Gill, *Naval Families*, 199–222.
[107] NMM, MRK/102/3/29, Herbert to Markham, 29 March [1801].
[108] Ibid.

204   PATRONAGE AND THE BRITISH NAVY, 1775–1815

with St Vincent. He wrote: 'I am well aware that to say my having a Family which Employment would the better enable me to support, is not considered at the Public Board as having any additional weight.'[109] This suggests that although Markham may personally have approved of the charitable bestowal of appointments to support families, he needed more palatable reasons than the need for more pay to persuade the other Admiralty commissioners to fulfil the request. This goes some way to explaining why male applicants mentioned their large family in combination with other attributes such as long service, good character or engagement in certain actions. Hardy certainly employed this tactic, as he went on to write: 'altho my rank as Post Captain does not unfortunately add any additional Claim yet in place of there I offer what I trust, you will think gives me some Claim that of 33 years uninterrupted service and that too with a fair unsullied Character'. Hardy's request was successful, as a note from Markham at the bottom of the letter reveals.[110]

The reputation of a father also carried weight in extended familial requests, or in requests made by those members of the extended familial circle who were intrinsic in the operation of patronage.[111] Captain Edward Roe applied to Markham on behalf of his nephew who was the son of a marine. Roe's own reputation as a captain and his familial connection already acted as a guarantee of his request, so he did not necessarily need to emphasise his nephew's father. However, Roe mentioned both his nephew's father and the fact that he came from a large family: 'I beg leave to solicit your Interest to obtain a Lieutenancy for a Nephew of mine, fifteen years of age, and the son of a respectable officer in that Corps having a large family'.[112] He also stressed how the favour would be conferred on both himself and the father, similar to the way female brokers urged that the favour be bestowed on both themselves and their husbands. He wrote: 'your complying with my request I shall always consider as a distinguish'd mark of attention at the same time that it will be conferring a lasting obligation on the father'. Fatherhood carried the weight of the father's own service and respectability into patronage requests. Applicants were eager to include reference to the father, even if he himself did not make the request.

Female referred parental connections, however, in some cases omitted the role of the father. One letter from Catherine Graham emphasised her role as mother to her godson George Fortescue, when she requested Markham's involvement in moving his commission in the marines from the Portsmouth Division to Plymouth, to be closer to her. As her request was for a transfer

---

[109] NMM, MRK/102/3/18, Hardy to Markham, 6 June 1802.

[110] Ibid.; TNA, ADM 36/16766, Muster Book: HMS Leda August 1802–June 1803; Hardy entered as captain 7 September 1802.

[111] Ben-Amos, *Culture of Giving*, 47–70; Tadmor, *Family and Friends*, 113–115.

[112] NMM, MRK/102/5/47, Roe to Markham, 1 July 1803.

GENDER AND PARENTHOOD: THE POWER OF BROKERS 205

rather than promotion, the omission of Fortescue's service history and merit is not unusual. However, in the rest of her letter Graham emphasised her motherly position and parental anxiety to a much greater degree than other godparents. She wrote:

> if thro' your interest it cou'd be altered to Plymouth I shou'd feel particularly obliged and grateful to you, my God son is a fine lad, and as a perfect stranger to the World it wou'd afford me the greatest gratification to have him under my protection, that I might in some measure supply the place of the valued mother he is deprived of.

She also excused her request with anxiety as Collier did: 'My anxiety on his account I hope will plead my excuse for addressing you'.[113]

Graham's letter is not inherently gendered in her desire to have her charge under her 'protection' from the world. Bailey has clearly established that tender, protective parenthood was a mantle shouldered by both mothers and fathers.[114] Young men were also well-known for behaving rashly. Captain Charles Tyler requested Markham's assistance in having his son reinstated to his rank after he was discharged for leaving his ship without permission to go to Rome with 'a Female'.[115] Tyler emphasised the death of the boy's mother in a way that implied that it was her absence that caused the error in his son's judgement, thus diverting blame away from any assumption of his own negligence causing the disaster: 'Captain Mundy of the Hydra speaks very handsomely of Charles as an officer, but in this unfortunate case a Female seduced him to quit Malta and go to Rome, where he has squandered the greatest part of the money left by his good Mother'.[116] Again the absence of the mother may not be in itself a gendered association of women with better behaved sons, although there have been numerous links made by historians between women and gentility.[117] Bailey argues that the end of the eighteenth century saw a rise in the involvement of fathers in the raising of their children and the importance of the mother-father unit in parenting, meaning that any single parent could invoke the absence of their partner as reason for charity or distress.[118] Of course, Collier's letter reveals the problems faced by widows which widowers did not encounter.

Although both men and women acted as brokers for their children, and so were more ready to use parental anxiety as a reason for their application,

---

[113] NMM, MRK/104/4/16, Graham to Markham, 22 May [1801].
[114] Bailey, *Parenting in England*, 28–39.
[115] NMM, MRK/102/6/6, Tyler to Markham, February 1806.
[116] Ibid.
[117] See Carter, *Emergence of Polite Society.*
[118] Bailey, *Parenting in England*, 51–53.

206   PATRONAGE AND THE BRITISH NAVY, 1775–1815

women's restricted position in society and earning capability meant that many female letters invoked financial distress more often than they did moral distress. Equally, the restrictions placed on male gendered position by duty and perceived capability meant that many male applicants were not so able to admit their need for patronage outside the bounds of a desire to serve their country. Officers who lacked the support of influential connections, whose status or political followings offered more in return to an Admiralty commissioner, therefore, were more restricted in their ability to appeal to charitable patronage, which consequently limited the impact of their applications.

Gender in Solicitation Letters

Male and female requests to Markham were not, in many ways, that different from one another. Chalus found that there was little to distinguish the patronage letters of elite women in their style and content from those written by their male counterparts.[119] The same seems to have been true of naval patronage letters. Gendered restrictions had a considerable effect on the things that men and women requested, but the natural variation, dependent on the applicant's social circle, status and how they fashioned themselves, had a much greater effect on their style of application than their gender. Of course, it is impossible to view a letter in isolation from the writer's social position. Female letters, therefore, had a greater tendency towards apology and deference, while male letters stressed duty and service history. However, some female brokers couched their letters in what we could call a naval style of solicitation and many male applicants also expressed their anxiety as well as their sensibility in their heartfelt gratitude for Markham's interest in them.

The few female templates in Thomas Cooke's *Universal Letter-Writer*, first published in 1771/2, were more apologetic regardless of the status of the writer.[120] In one letter about courtship entitled 'From the young Gentleman's mother to the young Lady', the fictional mother writes: 'Dear Miss, if you find any thing in these lines improperly written, you will candidly excuse it, as it coming from the hands of a parent, in behalf of an only beloved, and dutiful son'.[121] On the other hand, a male request from 'a Gentleman of decayed Circumstances in the Country, to another lately returned from the East-Indies, recommending his Son to his Protection', is frank and brief, without apologising for any potential impropriety: 'the bearer, my eldest son, is just twenty, and is very desirous of going to the East-Indies; but my circumstances are such, that it is not in my power to give him any assistance, nor indeed do

---

[119] Chalus, *Elite Women*, 155–156.
[120] Bannet, *Empire of Letters*, 318.
[121] Cooke, *The Universal Letter-Writer*, 60.

I know in what manner to proceed in an affair of so much importance'.[122]
Of course, the fictional relationship between the correspondents is different,
the former being a new correspondent and the latter a lapsed acquaintance.
However, the stylistic differences reflect this trend in appropriate male and
female letter-form.

A typical male patronage request to Markham at the Admiralty tended to
be direct and not overly apologetic or sentimental. Captain Henry Lidgbird
Ball's application to Markham is a good example of typical male style:

> My Dear Admiral Markham
>
> I hope you will pardon the liberty of addressing you in behalf of a Mr
> William Millett sub Lieut of His Maj[s] Brig Jackall as I understand that rank
> is to cease and they are to be promoted in due time. May I beg the favour
> of his being appointed to this ship as he is a most deserving good Man as
> we have a vacancy for a Lieut. I am My Dear Admiral your much Obliged
> and Most Sincerely
>
> H L Ball[123]

On the other hand, female requests to Markham tended to be longer, more
apologetic, and emphasised distress or their need for his attention more
forcefully. A letter from Alicia Hillier to Markham is representative of this
typical form of female application:

> Sir,
>
> I know not in what way to apologize to you for this liberty, but your candor
> and generosity will I trust forgive me, if my request be deem'd an improper
> one but as you once did me the honour to say you wou'd wish to render
> Mr Hillier any service in your power I am Sir embolden by that to entreat
> your interest in procuring for Mr H any situation or those in any of the
> Dock Yards or Ports, a Guardship or in any of the Public Offices a Place
> to employ his time as he has so long been used to an active life he knows
> not what to do with himself and as you Sir must be acquainted both with
> his ability and Character I trust you will not think him an improper Object
> to bestow your favours on *for believe me Sir you will not bestow them on
> any more grateful* Mr H knows not of my writing this as he has said he
> shou'd consider it improper to make a second request to you after your
> recent goodness to his Brother nor I know not of any excuse to plead but
> that of interceding for a Husband, and to you Sir from the knowledge I have
> of your familys good nature and disposition I flatter myself if my request

[122] Ibid., 123.
[123] NMM, MRK/102/1/12, Ball to Markham, 19 November 1806.

208   PATRONAGE AND THE BRITISH NAVY, 1775–1815

you cannot accede to you will forgive me, I wou'd not have then troubled you but as I know M^r H has made every application in his power without effect therefore I must again Sir ask your Pardon and shall always have great pleasure in thinking myself Sir

Your most grateful and much
Obliged
Humble serv^t
A Hillier[124]

Ball's letter is efficient, unapologetic and confident whereas Hillier's is careful and conciliatory. However, the two requests are not directly comparable. Ball's letter was a straightforward request to have a meritorious lieutenant appointed to a vacancy on his ship. Ball made no mention of his connection to Millett, and he may not have had any patronage connection to him other than wanting to secure effective officers for his crew. If he was connected to Millett he had no need to cloud his request with any connotations of self-service through obliging family, friends or political connections rather than selecting for merit alone. Of course, this book has shown that these considerations were a fundamental part of naval patronage, but Ball was also entitled by his rank as a captain to approach the Admiralty for the transferral of officers for the best running of his ship, regardless of connection. Hillier, on the other hand, was not entitled to Markham's attention through her service. Her husband's previous solicitations had already failed, and so her requests could be deemed more troublesome, especially as his failure to secure the step he wanted was most likely the result of the severe lack of vacancies in 1802 and not because Markham actively refused to assist him. Both Ball and Hillier acted as brokers, but Hillier was intimately connected to the success of her husband's application, whereas Ball could always solicit for a different lieutenant. Therefore, Hillier's request was a last attempt at success and her language, drawing on sympathy and charity, naturally reflects her greater need.

Certainly, Hillier's request was not that different from male requests also in difficult circumstances. Captain John Allen applied to Markham in 1807 for his assistance in getting him actively employed after several years on half-pay. Like Hillier, he opened his letter with an apology: 'It is with a considerable degree of Diffidence and reluctance I take the liberty of addressing you being perfectly unknown.'[125] He also appealed to Markham's public character as Hillier had done: 'as an officer High in Rank as you Sir are, and one of the Lord Commissioners of the Admiralty. With this view of your Public situation, it is, that I wish to appeal to you, Sir, and that in so doing, you will not think me presuming too much.' Like some of the female requests mentioned in the

[124] NMM, MRK/104/4/4, Hillier to Markham, 23 May 1802.
[125] NMM, MRK/102/1/5, Allen to Markham, 4 March 1807.

GENDER AND PARENTHOOD: THE POWER OF BROKERS 209

previous section, he also expressed his anxiety: 'It has ever been my most anxious wish to be actively Employ'd in the service.' In the rest of his letter he repeatedly emphasised his father's long service, and, consequently, what he felt the Admiralty owed him. He wrote: 'from my late fathers rank, I was naturally induced to suppose I might have opportunity's of being as they were of service to my country but unfortunately (for what reason I know not) I have been since a Post Captain unemployed'. His style is very similar to the style of Collier's letter beseeching Markham's interest in her son, mentioned in the previous section. She also emphasised his father's long service and his own merit.[126] Rather than a female style, therefore, these letters represent a style of petition characterised by the difficult circumstances of the writer rather than their gender.

Female writers were in a different position from their male counterparts in the navy. Not being in command of a ship, they were never in a position, as Ball was, to make a standard request free of connotations of serving their family or themselves. In some respects, a more direct comparison would be with requests from men outside the navy. However, many of the non-naval male requests Markham received are indistinguishable in tone and style from those of men serving in the navy; although there are certain stylistic traits which suggest a letter was written by a civilian rather than an officer, beyond of course obvious references to their occupation or, in the case of officers, their ship.

Non-naval male writers tended to direct their applications to Markham if they were already acquainted with him, so their letters were often more familiar and less formal. William Baker wrote to Markham when he missed seeing him at the Admiralty, to solicit him on behalf of his son. He wrote: 'My dear sir! I was unwilling to stop you in your way through Mr Parker's Room, this morning when I perceived you was in a hurry to proceed to Lord St Vincents apartments. I should otherwise have troubled you on *Two* matters of business.'[127] This style is very similar to that of captains who were also acquainted with Markham. Commander Edward Crofton wrote to request Markham's influence in his application to Grenville for a different sloop. He wrote: 'Should I be so fortunate through your interference to obtain the object of my desires, it will if possible strengthen the attachment I have to that goodness, which you have always shown to [me].'[128]

Non-naval male requests did not tend to apologise as much as female requests to Markham, or in cases where they did, they did so by saying they

[126] NMM, MRK/104/4/54, Collier to Markham, 6 January 1807.

[127] NMM, MRK/104/5/20, Baker to Markham, 25 June 1803.

[128] NMM, MRK/102/1/164, Crofton to Markham, 12 November [1806]; Crofton was transferred to *Wanderer* 23 December 1806, TNA, ADM 36/1800 Muster Book: HMS *Wanderer* January 1807–August 1807.

would not waste his time apologising for taking the liberty to address him. John Wharton, MP for Beverley in Yorkshire, mentioned in Chapter 4, wrote to Markham: 'from the uniform kindness I have experienced from you I do not think it necessary to trespass on your time by making apologies'.[129] This had the dual benefits of, on the one hand, not offending Markham by assuming he was inconvenienced by their letter and, on the other, acknowledging that his kindness to them meant they were importuning him. Those male requests that did apologise did so briefly. John Goddard, in requesting Markham's influence to have his son placed on the list of future promotions in the marines, apologised very briefly by writing only: 'I take the liberty to trespass on your goodness to request your kind aid in the furthering my views'.

Compare this to a female request of a similar level of acquaintance from Elizabeth Robinson where she opened her letter with: 'I humbly flatter myself your goodness, will excuse my presumpssion in addressing a Gentleman, of your abbillity, Sir your public character induces me humbly to hope, you will condescend to befriend a Widow and 2 infant Orfans'.[130] Robinson's request has more in common with poor relief letters than the patronage requests of commissioned officers. Thomas Sokoll has argued that deferential tone and a 'modest emphasis' on distress were rhetoric features of pauper letters, although the examples he analyses in his study often go above and beyond a modest expression of their miserable circumstances.[131] Robinson's request, therefore, is styled as personal but deferential relief, rather than invoking the clarity of purpose, brevity and formality of officers' letters. Of course, Robinson's situation was different from Goddard's in that she was trying to get her sons into the Naval Asylum at Greenwich rather than trying to place her son in a school. Robinson's use of a style more similar in tone to poor relief letters was a result of her social position rather than her gender.

The other female letters which apologise to Markham do so because they made repeated troublesome requests. Even in those cases which were not a product of repeated failure or extreme distress, such as Anne Hillier or Harriet Carpenter's requests, female applicants excused their letters with their female or motherly anxiety. Take for example how Lady Anne Bickerton opened her request for Markham to tell her how long her husband Admiral Richard Bickerton would be absent:

> The very great anxiety of mind, and heavy affliction I am suffering, in consequence of the painful state of suspense I still continue to experience on the subject of my Beloved Husbands return, has induced me to be troublesome to you, and I trust you will oblige me by answering the enquiry I have taken the liberty of making.[132]

---

[129] NMM, MRK/104/3/46, Wharton to Markham, 18 January 1807.
[130] NMM, MRK/104/4/19, Robinson to Markham, 11 April 1806.
[131] Sokoll, 'Writing for Relief', 100.
[132] NMM, MRK/104/4/36, Bickerton to Markham, 5 July 1802.

GENDER AND PARENTHOOD: THE POWER OF BROKERS 211

The request for information was not in itself a nuisance but it was often denied, which perhaps is why Bickerton prefaced her request with such anxiety. Equally, female brokers excused their requests with their parental anxiety as Frances Shippardson did in her letter: 'I hope you will excuse the liberty I take in addressing you on a subject that is of so much importance to my son'.[133] Of course, as we saw in the previous section, both mothers and fathers excused their applications with their parental anxiety, and it was an extremely typical, non-gendered style of request.

The expression of anxiety was also not restricted to apologetic female letters. Indeed, male anxiety extended to include shipboard discipline, lack of promotion and obliging connection. Captain George Jones expressed his 'anxiety' in reference to his need to oblige a 'respectable Gentleman'. He wrote: 'I trust a great anxiety to serve a very respectable gentleman will with you prove a sufficient appology for my being thus troublesome'.[134] The letter implied that Markham had a reputation for appreciating the difficulties of patronage solicitation and maintenance of ties, and thus Jones saw his patronage anxiety as reasonable grounds for a favourable application. Similarly, other captains expressed their anxiety in seeing to the needs of their youngsters and followings. Captain Richard Williams requested the discharge of his protégé because he had no ship to 'apprentice' him in and wrote that, in favouring him, Markham would 'relieve me of the anxious care which it causes in my mind'.[135] Captain William Johnstone Hope also used his anxiety when asking for Markham to supply him with the names of those men staying employed after the signing of the Treaty of Amiens in 1802 and the inevitable reductions in employment at the onset of peace, so that he could see his own followers well-placed. He wrote:

> Would you also do me the favour at your leisure to let me know the names of a few of the young men likely to keep employed in the Peace, as I have several very fine young men whom I am anxious to look out for berths for in time, that they may not be adrift upon their Friends hands.[136]

Male and female letter style was determined more by their circumstances than their gender. There are stylistic traits in Hillier's letter, however, which mark it out as a particularly female request. She mentioned her writing without her husband's knowledge, which is not a trope which appears in any of the male letters in the collection. After all, this style of letter was often written in cases where the male half of the patronage partnership could not honourably make the request or his gendered position prevented his admitting to his distressed circumstances. Harriet Carpenter could colour her letter to Markham

---

133 NMM, MRK/104/4/33, Shippardson to Markham, 19 March [1807].
134 NMM, MRK/102/3/77, Jones to Markham, 16 July 1803.
135 NMM, MRK/102/6/34, Williams to Markham, 5 June 1806.
136 NMM, MRK/102/3/60, Hope to Markham, 21 December 1801.

212 PATRONAGE AND THE BRITISH NAVY, 1775–1815

with her wifely anxiety and naivety. In turn, this allowed her to frame her letters to Markham as requests for advice rather than action, meaning that she maintained his interest but also protected herself and Daniel from damaging their connection to Markham by appearing overbearing.[137]

Certainly, other female brokers used this gambit in approaching Markham, some going as far as to plead their male counterpart's ignorance of their application, thus absolving any male blame accrued from the misfire of a request. Elizabeth Dashwood pleaded her husband's ignorance of her application because he had already applied to other members of the board. She wrote: 'Will you then my dear Sir aid and assist me. I say me, for in truth Capt D is ignorant of my, perhaps, intruding letter, for which I shall ever consider myself under many obligations.'[138] Although it was commonplace for clients and brokers to solicit more than one patron, Dashwood's apologetic tone suggests impropriety in her approaching Markham. There are four letters from Dashwood in the Markham collection, all between May and July 1803, as she was soliciting for Admiralty favour to get her husband a ship. In this context, she appears to be the main broker for the Dashwoods, and it does seem that her position as female broker meant that her repeated solicitations were, perhaps, excused. Certainly, she only mentioned Captain Dashwood as joining her in her thanks once she had secured Markham's interest, as she wrote in June 1803: 'Although I may appear troublesome yet I cannot avoid expressing my thanks for your kind apearances of serving me and mine. I have communicated to Capt D the contents of your highly pleasing letter and he joins me in my sentiments of esteem and gratitude.'[139] Interestingly, in her following letters Dashwood stressed that the obligation was bestowed upon her alone, as the interest of the Admiralty was not providing her husband with an active situation with the speed she would like and her application perhaps became once again 'troublesome'. She wrote on 11 June: 'permit me my dear sir to look for your support on this occasion, and be assured I shall consider myself infinitely obliged to you'.[140]

Male requests may have used anxiety, if it did not suggest their own inadequacy, and female brokers were perhaps better able to make difficult applications. However, not all female letters in the Markham collection relied on female stereotypes of distress and anxiety to excuse impertinent applications. Rather some were very brief, much closer to male naval requests, suggesting an awareness of a naval style of application subscribed to by both men and women. Rebecca Brett was very brief in her request to have her son appointed to a frigate. She wrote: 'I humbly request your Interest

---

[137] NMM, MRK/104/4/14, Carpenter to Markham, 26 April 1804.
[138] NMM, MRK/104/4/38, Dashwood to Markham, 30 May 1803.
[139] NMM, MRK/104/4/9, Dashwood to Markham, 4 June 1803.
[140] NMM, MRK/104/4/39, Dashwood to Markham, 11 June 1803.

GENDER AND PARENTHOOD: THE POWER OF BROKERS 213

in a more particular manner as having been acquainted with his Father, and to whom I did some little time ago state my claim for his children'.[141] She emphasised Markham's connection to her late husband, Captain Peircy Brett, and reminded him of her previous request. She did not, however, emphasise her motherhood or anxiety. In fact, she in some ways distanced herself as she wrote 'his' children rather than 'my'. However, in her next sentence she implied the favour was bestowed upon her, rather than her children: 'may I now hope my Dear Sir for your influence on the present Occasion, that my son may be appointed to some ship, I dare not presume to point out any, but if it could be to a Frigate I should be the more Obliged'.[142]

Other letters were as brief as Brett's. Ann Wallis wrote only two sentences in her request: the first, 'I venture to solicit your protection of Andrew Cumings whose services are represented in the enclosed copy of a memorial, the original will follow in a post or two addressed to the First Lord'; and the second, 'My wishes to recommend to your protection an old servant of his King and Country who has a wife and numerous family dependant on him for support; will I trust plead my excuse for this intrusion on your valuable time, and requesting you will offer my best compliments to the honourable Mrs Markham, and good wishes to the little ones.'[143] She emphasised duty as first and foremost among her reasons for applying to Markham but also followed that with a brief acknowledgement of Cumings's family circumstances.

One letter from Margaret Stuart was similarly concise despite her reportedly close connection to Markham which would have allowed for a greater transfer of news or gossip. She wrote: 'I am persuaded our very old acquaintance will justify me in your opinion for the liberty I take in including a letter to Lord St Vincent and further requesting you to add your interest towards procuring my son active employment.'[144] She then included another captain's recommendation of her son and that he wanted to serve his country in active employment rather than in the perhaps more comfortable position in the sea fencibles: 'I can with confidence refer you to Capt Pierrepont for his good conduct in his present employment wᶜʰ however lucrative does not satisfy a disposition for actual service and a wish to signalize himself at this moment of danger.'[145]

Mary Webster also wrote a brief and succinct letter requesting Markham's interest in her son who had been a prisoner of war for several years and, having passed as lieutenant, awaited a recommendation from Admiral Dacres to see him promoted on *Hercule*. She mentioned his father's service in lieu of his own, writing: 'I have presumed to trouble you (in consequence of my

[141] NMM, MRK/104/4/2, Brett to Markham, 20 May 1802.
[142] NMM, MRK/104/4/1, Brett to Markham, 20 May 1802.
[143] NMM, MRK/104/4/10, Wallis to Markham, 12 June 1803.
[144] NMM, MRK/104/4/15, Stuart to Markham, 29 April 1804.
[145] Ibid.

214   PATRONAGE AND THE BRITISH NAVY, 1775–1815

late husband, having sail'd with you as Carpenter of the Hannibal)'.[146] She did couch the favour in terms of friendship, 'in the hopes of obtaining that friendship Sir from you, has been the occasion of my taking this liberty', but crucially used it in terms of formal friendship rather than the affective, feeling friendship exhibited by other female applicants to Markham. In many respects, Webster's letter echoes the restrained requests of commissioned officers' wives, such as Brett or Wallis. As her husband had been a warrant officer, she may have self-consciously employed this style because she was writing on behalf of her son's rise in status to lieutenant. Certainly, the wives of other warrant officers, such as Elizabeth Bailey and Elizabeth Robinson, wrote in a way much more typical of letter manuals of the period.[147] This suggests that this brief style of female application was related particularly to the wives of commissioned officers, from naval families, meaning that gender was less important in the patronage exchange than social circle, family and social position.

Gendered tropes, therefore, affected the style of an applicant's request to some extent, but ultimately, requests were varied and employed multiple epistolary fashions to achieve different ends. Male requests show greater variation because female gendered position meant many of their patronage requests happened face-to-face and so do not leave such a trace in the written record. Anxiety was a trope that both genders used in their applications but female letters tended to be more apologetic and male letters more direct. However, this was as much associated with cultural pressures and self-fashioning, as well as restricted position and the role of women in male-female patronage partnerships, as it was with a particular male or female style. Women were more apologetic in applications because they tended to apply face-to-face, or via female networks, and, therefore, had more need to excuse writing directly to Markham.

On the other hand, Markham was expected to at least consider requests from serving officers for the good of the service and in honour of their sacrifices for their country.[148] Female requests may have been more apologetic because they shouldered the more difficult requests in their patronage partnership, being less likely to offend Markham by excusing their requests with their female naivety and inexperience. However, women were not limited to writing only in this way. The letters of Brett, Wallis and Stuart show that proactive female brokers embedded in naval circles could be as brief and direct as their male counterparts in simple requests. There was no such thing, therefore, as a male and a female patronage letter, but rather only letters which were affected by gendered position.

---

[146] NMM, MRK/104/4/17, Webster to Markham, 23 March 1806.

[147] Bannet, *Empire of Letters*, 64–71.

[148] Gill, *Naval Families*, 138.

Conclusion

In looking at patronage through the lens of the navy, it is important to consider the role played by gender. The lack of a consistent difference in male and female written applications shows how susceptible patronage requests were to individual style and personality. It also suggests that there was a naval style of application which men and women drew upon when approaching Markham at the Admiralty. Equally, the fashion for sensibility translated differently in male and female gendered position. Male naval patronage was particularly susceptible to stoic sensibility which meant that men couched their requests in terms of their passionate duty for the service, but under-represented their need for assistance in case it appeared insincere or self-serving. Women at the higher levels of society downplayed their active involvement as brokers. Rather, their involvement became about their affective friendships with those they recommended or how they acted out of duty to their husbands, sons, or brothers, styling themselves as conduits for male patronage.[149] However, female brokers were not nearly as powerless in patronage as their self-styling and lack of governmental position would suggest.

Men and women acted in patronage partnerships. Women maintained informal social connections that underpinned solicitation, and could solicit more effectively than male counterparts for potentially risky requests or when they were closer to the patron in status or connection. In some cases, subscribing to a naval style of request seemed to be more important than the applicant's gender, the act of broker being all that distinguishes their letters in the collection. There certainly was, however, a gendered aspect to some of these requests, with female brokers self-consciously or maybe unconsciously employing female stereotypes to excuse or support requests where their own power to return the favour in the exchange was restricted. This certainly was the case for experienced brokers such as Collier, who plainly had a detailed knowledge of the inner workings of Admiralty patronage, but still had to rely on her female anxiety to excuse her repeated solicitations of multiple patrons. It does seem that the greater the risk of a request, the more women employed female stereotypes. And as was the case with Harriet and Daniel Carpenter, there was a strength in solicitation that could be gained by women shouldering the burden of riskier or potentially damaging requests, as they could frame them indirectly. Women existed in both naval and civilian contexts through their connection to their fathers, husbands and sons, and their effective involvement in Admiralty patronage solicitation made female brokers vital to naval careers.

[149] Ibid., 16–17.

6

Fees and Resistance: Lower-Level Patronage

I am sure, the man had need to be fortified doubly and trebly, for his Honor's sake, against the natural Impressions of Friendship, even if he had no servants by whom he himself profited from the extra-work done in the yards.

Ambrose Serle to Charles Middleton, 16 January 1790[1]

Writing to his friend Charles Middleton, Comptroller of the Navy, Ambrose Serle suggested that one of the greatest contributors to dockyard inefficiency was that the senior yard officers were overly inclined to promote their friends. His solution was to allow master shipwrights and the principal officers and clerks of the yards larger perquisites to fortify them against the 'natural impressions of friendship'.[2] His proposal encapsulates the difference in eighteenth-century perception of the patronage of the elite and that of the labouring classes; a sea officer's gentlemanly honour guaranteed the virtue of his appointments, whereas a shipwright's allegiance had to be bought.[3]

This book has demonstrated that individuals conducted their patronage in a wide variety of ways. Connection and merit were both required in the bestowal of naval appointments and applicants trod a fine line between the two in soliciting Admiralty patrons such as Markham.[4] When we expand our discussion to include the careers of non-officers, however, patronage is often transformed into a discussion of community power or lack of autonomy.[5] After all, the Navy Board had official control of appointments in the dockyards and many seamen were gathered onto ships from local ports and some via the press-gang.[6] The lower orders of society appear in the record of elite patronage only in extreme circumstances, such as when they asked to be

---

[1] NMM, MID/1/168.

[2] Ibid.

[3] Morriss, 'Government and Community'; Lunn and Day (eds.), *Labour Relations*, 29.

[4] See Rodger, *Wooden World*; or Gill, *Naval Families.*

[5] See Gill, *Naval Families*, 195–197.

[6] Morriss, *Royal Dockyards*, 167; Dancy, *Myth of the Press Gang*, 45–49.

FEES AND RESISTANCE: LOWER-LEVEL PATRONAGE   217

released from impressment or to secure superannuation. To gain these favours they petitioned their social superiors rather than writing the sort of direct solicitation letter we see made to Markham from the elite and middling sorts.

Historians have often used petitions and poor relief letters as a window into the predicaments and feelings of those lower down the social scale. Thomas Sokoll illustrated the styles and language of letters seeking poor relief which bear a striking resemblance to the language of solicitation letters addressed to Markham at the Admiralty.[7] Ellen Gill has also used the petitions of artificers in the Royal Dockyards to examine their conception of family and duty.[8] The mechanism of petitions allowed those socially distant from a patron to solicit their support without prior acquaintance. The gulf in their social proximity, such a great determining factor in the construction of networks and, therefore, the operation of patronage, has prompted historians such as Gill to conceive of applications by petition as separate from naval patronage.[9]

Patronage relied on acquaintance or brokered acquaintance with the patron, something that was difficult to achieve for many lower down the social scale. However, some applicants from the middle and upper sorts wrote directly to Markham without prior acquaintance, and the language they used to draw on his charity and duty bears a striking resemblance to the language of petitions. The greatest difference between non-gentleman ranks of the navy and commissioned officers and wardroom warrant officers, such as surgeons, chaplains and pursers, was that the gentleman ranks moved in similar social circles to Markham.[10] Sea officers had claim to gentility because of their commission and Evan Wilson argued this distinction was deliberately cultivated on board ship through dining practices and even teaching young boys who would become officers to dance.[11] Surgeons, chaplains and pursers claimed gentility through their education and connections.[12] Officers' gentility cast their requests in an honourable light as well as granting them access to Markham through his familiar network.[13] Officers may have written letters using the language of petition but they did not have to resort to the formal layout that Gill demonstrated dockyard artificers used to gain Admiralty attention.[14]

Harold Perkin argued that social position in the eighteenth century was too individually incremental to be understood within hegemonic divisions of

---

[7] Sokoll, 'Writing for Relief', 92–111.
[8] Gill, *Naval Families*, 199.
[9] Ibid., 103–139.
[10] See Wilson, *British Naval Officers*, 105–116.
[11] Ibid., 192.
[12] Ibid., 193.
[13] Ibid., 196–197.
[14] Gill, *Naval Families*, 199–222.

working, middle and upper class.[15] David Cannadine further emphasised that social position in the eighteenth century is best understood on an individual basis.[16] In terms of patronage, social level determined an individual's social circle and consequently who an individual could politely approach for assistance. Chapters 2 and 3 demonstrated the influence of Markham's familiar network on his own patronage and the effect that social level had on the way his correspondents solicited his attention or how he responded to them. Class, translated into patronage terms, refers to an artificer's or seaman's access to these circles or their exclusion because of their social origins and physical labour.

A lack of personal access to Admiralty and Navy Board patrons, however, did not mean that seamen and artificers had no patronage autonomy. Patronage was a system of recommendation, wherein an individual's network determined their access to appointments, career progression and social support. As such, it operated at all levels of society and was not restricted to the social elite. Far from not being involved in patronage, Serle felt that artificers in the dockyard were more inclined to promote from their network of friends within the yard rather than select for skill. This was somewhat hypocritical of Serle, especially as he had just been made Navy Board secretary solely because of his friendship with Charles Middleton.[17] However, his suspicion illustrates that artificers had extensive networks within the yard and their local parishes which limited Navy Board control. As we have seen among the elite and middling sorts who directly approached Markham, recommendations for appointments took varied routes through an individual's network and did not necessarily rely on directly soliciting a superior within the occupational hierarchy.

This chapter considers how patronage networks operated within the Royal Dockyards as a case study into patronage among the lower levels of society. The dockyards provide a stable base from which to reconstruct the networks for sections of society where less epistolary evidence survives. Admiralty description books record the hierarchal connections within the yard in apprenticeships and work-gangs. Parish records, particularly marriage registers and vestry minutes, provide tantalising glimpses of how artificers integrated with their local communities and their potential networks of acquaintance. Connections in the local church and community also acted to bypass the hierarchical structures which, as Roger Knight has argued, limited the influence of

---

[15] Harold Perkin, *The Origins of Modern English Society, 1780–1880* (London, 1969), 26.

[16] David Cannadine, *Class in Britain* (London, 1998), 27.

[17] Gareth Atkins, 'Wilberforce and His Milieux: The Worlds of Anglican Evangelicalism, c.1780–1830' (unpublished PhD thesis, University of Cambridge, 2009), 174.

FEES AND RESISTANCE: LOWER-LEVEL PATRONAGE 219

ordinary artificers within the yard.[18] Artificers may not have been frequently in direct correspondence with men like Markham at the Admiralty but they had access to patronage networks of their own.

Control of Appointments

Control in the dockyard technically rested with the principal officers: the commissioner, the master attendant, and the master shipwright.[19] The social composition of the yard determined which officer had the most control over appointments. The networks of shipwrights and artificers within the yard were defined by friendships made outside, particularly dependent on local religious denominations and communities. In Portsmouth, the master attendant controlled most yard appointments because he was deeply involved in the non-conformist church that the majority of dockyard workers attended.[20] In Plymouth, the master shipwright seems to have been in control, with men from different sections of the yard paying him for their appointments.[21] Within the hierarchy, the clerks were also important brokers. Often connected to other inferior members of the yard through family and friendships, the clerks acted as points of connection with senior officers. Most premiums for entry to Plymouth yard came to the master shipwright via the clerk or the clerk's wife.[22] In Woolwich, the assistants and quartermen held significant patronage control.

The assistants were senior dockyard officers in charge of specific areas of the yard and workforce, and they answered directly to the master shipwright. The second assistant to the master shipwright at Woolwich was also the master caulker and oversaw the men who caulked the ships by filling the space between planking in the hulk with oakum. Some assistants were young officers who had been apprenticed to other senior officers. Knight named these dockyard officers the 'elite' of the dockyard.[23] They were on a career trajectory

---

[18] R. J. B. Knight, 'Sandwich, Middleton and Dockyard Appointments', *Mariner's Mirror* 57:2 (1971), 179.

[19] See Appendix IV for detail on yard hierarchy.

[20] John Field, 'The Diary of a Portsmouth Dockyard Worker', *Portsmouth Archives Review* 3 (1978), 39–64.

[21] 'Item No.126: List of Persons employed in His Majesty's yards at Plymouth, who have paid Considerations for their several Appointments, with the Sums received for the same, and to whom paid; taken from the Depositions of the Parties, before Commissioner Fanshawe', *The Sixth Report of the Commissioners of Naval Inquiry. Appendix: Plymouth yard, Woolwich yard* (London, 1804), 419–421. Hereafter cited as the *Sixth Report.*

[22] This will be explored in detail in the second section.

[23] Knight, 'Sandwich, Middleton and Dockyard Appointments', 179.

220   PATRONAGE AND THE BRITISH NAVY, 1775–1815

which would take them eventually to the rank of master shipwright. These young officers tended to move readily between yards, filling assistant positions as vacancies arose.[24] Some assistants rose more slowly from being ordinary shipwrights and quartermen, the inferior officers who led the work-gangs. These men tended to be less mobile or had advanced up the ranks in smaller, overseas yards where there was more chance of promotion.

Beneath assistants the foremen were another layer of command. Depending on the yard and demand for labour, there could be up to three foreman positions: foreman of the yard, foreman afloat, who oversaw work being done on recently launched ships, and foreman of new works, who oversaw contracts undertaken in merchant yards. Foreman of new works was not a permanent position and was often awarded to a quarterman of good character or one of the assistants to the master shipwright.[25] The other two foreman positions were a step on the ladder for quartermen aiming for promotion to assistant.

The day-to-day labour of dockyards was organised by shipwrights, skilled artisans who formed the backbone of parish communities local to the yard. In 1801, there were 3,793 shipwrights out of a total of 10,436 artificers and labourers in the six major yards, the smaller depots around the coast and in overseas stations.[26] The other artificers were not as numerous as the shipwrights – the caulkers, riggers, house carpenters, sawyers, joiners, sailmakers and smiths.[27] However, in the local community these men were often on a similar social level to shipwrights and officers. For example, Daniel Eldridge, master sailmaker at Woolwich, was deeply involved in the vestry meetings alongside the master shipwright until 1783.[28] By the end of the eighteenth century these artificers were not allowed apprentices by the Navy Board, which reduced their access to one mode of influence in the yard.[29] There were also labourers in the yard who were responsible for the hauling of material, among other tasks, and specialised labourers named scavelmen, who erected scaffolding around ships and dug trenches where needed.[30] In certain yards, community and friendship connections gave labourers patronage power, such as Reuben Brooks discussed in the third section.

St Vincent's moves towards centralisation which restricted the autonomy of commanders-in-chief in the Mediterranean, as we saw in Chapter 1, also heavily affected the dockyards. The reforms were aimed at improving yard

---

[24] Ibid., 180–181.

[25] Morriss, *Royal Dockyards*, 139.

[26] NMM, ADM/B/214, Admiralty In-Letters, An Account Answering the Number of Artificers borne in His Majesty's several Dock Yards, Navy office, 14 April 1804.

[27] Appendix IV.

[28] LMA, P97/MRY/050, St Mary Magdalene, Woolwich: Vestry Minutes.

[29] Morriss, *Royal Dockyards*, 105.

[30] Ibid., 246.

FEES AND RESISTANCE: LOWER-LEVEL PATRONAGE   221

efficiency and focused particularly on the patronage structures of the yard and artificers' network power. Samuel Bentham, brother to Jeremy Bentham, suggested a complete restructuring of the apprenticeship system. His concern, and that of St Vincent, was that an apprentice's wages went to his master, who was then supposed to give a portion back to the boy's parents for his upkeep.[31] In practice, the wages seem to have incentivised otherwise busy men to focus on training their apprentices.[32] However, Bentham was suspicious that many masters took the wages without properly training the boys. He suggested removing the indentures – which were often organised privately between the shipwright and the apprentice's family – from the masters and binding them instead to a principal officer in the yard. The shipwright would then be named 'instructor' to the apprentice, and the apprentice's pay divided between the instructor and the parents.

There were several problems with this plan. First, Bentham and St Vincent misunderstood the nature of apprenticeships within the yard networks. It quickly became clear that most masters gave a large proportion of the apprentice's wage to his family. In centralising apprentice control, Bentham also reduced their pay, which meant that families of apprentices received less than under the traditional system.[33] Apprentices were also only given to 'deserving men' in the yard, who were then 'shoaled', in other words, organised into gangs of workmen of tiered ability.[34] Unfortunately, this resulted in the creation of gangs where half the workers were untrained boys, who could not do the work required, meaning their instructors had to work harder to make their wage from task-work.[35]

This, albeit misguided, attempt to ensure the quality of shipwright education was motivated in part by fundamental distrust of the presence of fees in these kinds of agreements. But it was also perhaps partly rooted in underlying suspicion and misunderstanding of the familial structures of apprenticeship that already existed in the yards. Roger Morriss, in his extensive study of the Royal Dockyards, noted that not only was most dockyard patronage based on familial connections, its influence was also an essential factor in the workforce's resistance to modernisation, calling it a 'traditional system more productive of useful connections and profit than of educated shipwrights'.[36]

Administratively, however, the process was not as simple as a shipwright deciding to train his own son. Even before Bentham's reforms of 1802, the

---

[31] Ibid., 110–111.

[32] Knight, 'Sandwich, Middleton and Dockyard Appointments', 180.

[33] Morriss, *Royal Dockyards*, 111.

[34] Ibid., 29 and 111.

[35] Task-work was the system where men were paid by the jobs they completed. Ibid., 112.

[36] Morriss, 'Government and Community', 28; Morriss, *Royal Dockyards*, 113.

222   PATRONAGE AND THE BRITISH NAVY, 1775–1815

Navy Board technically controlled who was eligible to take on apprentices. The description books for Chatham and Sheerness yards show that out of a total of 718 shipwrights, 178 were allowed apprentices, and only fifteen of those were allowed more than two.[37] Petitions from shipwrights to the Navy Board asking to be allowed apprentices reveal one level of how permission for apprenticeships was obtained, but description books suggest that eligibility was decided at a bureaucratic level within the yard itself, most likely based on connections of friendship and professional obligation. Ilana Krausman Ben-Amos argued that most apprentices in wider eighteenth-century society were indentured to friends of the family and indentures were organised through family connections. This was especially true of urban apprenticeships but rural apprenticeships also saw adolescents sent away from home to extended familial connections.[38] Keith Snell, on the other hand, emphasised the importance of the parish poor relief system in placing apprentices with masters, especially in the south-east of England, suggesting that family had a much less significant role in the careers of some in the lower levels of society than it did for many of the middling and elite who wrote to Markham at the Admiralty.[39] Realistically, it is difficult to discern what instigated the connection between masters and apprentices in the dockyards, whether it was prior acquaintance, familial obligation, or professional necessity.

Familial Connections

We rarely have records for the dockyards that reveal the direct action of recommendation in the way that is available to us for the predominantly middling and elite levels of society that solicited Markham at the Admiralty. However, an unusual description book for the small naval dockyard at Deptford gives us a glimpse into these patterns of behaviour. Seeming to cover entries from 1746 to 1796, the book records typical information about shipwrights' time of entry, age, married status, apprenticeship yard and other service or physical details that could identify them. From 1770, it also recorded notes on who recommended them for entry to the yard.[40]

---

[37] TNA, ADM 106/2975, Chatham Description Book 1779. Total No. Shipwrights: 546; Shipwrights allowed one apprentice: 81; Shipwrights allowed two apprentices or above (master shipwright, assistants, foremen): 9; Apprentices granted by Navy Board warrant: 16; ADM 106/2982, Sheerness Description Book 1779. Total No. Shipwrights: 172; Shipwrights allowed one apprentice: 43; Shipwrights allowed two apprentices (master shipwright, assistants, foreman): 6; Apprentices granted by Navy Board warrant: 23.

[38] I. K. Ben-Amos, *Adolescence and Youth in Early Modern England* (London, 1994), 77–95.

[39] Keith Snell, *Annals of the Labouring Poor: Social Change and Agrarian England, 1660–1900* (Cambridge, 1985), 232–236.

[40] TNA, ADM 106/2993 Deptford: artificers and labourers 1780–1796.

FEES AND RESISTANCE: LOWER-LEVEL PATRONAGE

Between 1770 and 1789, over a quarter of all recommendations recorded were from family members. But this dwindled to only slightly more than a tenth for the final six years of recommendations recorded in the book between 1790 and 1796. This was perhaps in part because of waves of reform to the dockyard system, including apprenticeships, following the widespread strike action and subsequent dismissals of 1775.[41] Certainly, the book records almost three times as many recommendations for the period 1770–1779 as for the following ten years 1780–1789.

All but one of the family recommendations between 1770 and 1789 were for the entry of apprentices. In 1770 to 1779, at least ten of these were made by the apprentice's father who was already serving in the yard. Within this number only two were also apprenticed directly to their fathers who recommended them: John Penny, whose father of the same name was a quarterman, and James Talbutt, whose father, also of the same name, was foreman to the master mastmaker. Even in this period of what seems to be comparatively greater influence of family on the arrangement of apprenticeships, there were limits on how many apprentices an artificer could take on, and when. Within the network of the yard, it could also be advantageous to have sons apprenticed to others in possibly more beneficial positions. For instance, Talbutt's brother Robert also entered the yard as an apprentice two years later on his father's recommendation, but rather than being apprenticed to his father, he was instead attached to Thomas Jones, 'acting quarterman to Mr Williams', presumably Sir John Williams, the Naval Surveyor.

The period 1770–1779 also shows many familial recommendations from outside the yard, which could be quite diverse. John Pike was entered as the apprentice of pro-quarterman Charles Searnell, after being recommended by his father who was listed simply as a 'gardener'. Francis Webster was recommended for entry as an apprentice by his 'mother a widow in Church Street', the main street in Deptford. The charitable inclusion of the sons of widows from the local community was an important part of yard culture, although after 1779 the charity seems to have been limited primarily to their entry at an earlier age as oakham boys rather than shipwright apprentices.[42] Giving a valuable apprenticeship position to the son of a widow may not have been entirely altruistic though. Webster was apprenticed to quarterman James Hughes, who had recommended his own son to be entered as an apprentice to the yard only a few months earlier in July, but slightly more advantageously as servant to the foreman of the yard, William Lancaster. Perhaps Hughes took on Webster as a charitable favour in return for his own son's good placement in the yard.

In the period 1790–1796, there were fewer overall recommendations from family members, but in contrast to 1770–1779, most were from fathers or

---

[41] R. J. B. Knight, 'From Impressment to Task Work: Strikes and Disruption in the Royal Dockyards 1688–1788', in Lunn and Day (eds.), *Labour Relations*, 1–14.

[42] See the recommendations of oakham boys: TNA, ADM 106/2993 ff.46–47.

224 PATRONAGE AND THE BRITISH NAVY, 1775–1815

brothers serving in the yard rather than relations outside, and only four were for apprentices. The only apprentice to be recommended by and apprenticed to his father was James Penney, who entered in September 1792 on the recommendation of his father, shipwright John Penney, who may well have been connected to the large influential 'Penny' family in the yard mentioned above. Most of the recommendations of apprentices recorded in this period were made either by Martin Ware, the master shipwright, or John Harris, the boatswain of the yard. However, entering the yard from the recommendation of one of these principal officers did not necessarily guarantee a more advantageous position for the apprentice. Certainly Harris recommended apprentices who would be attached to the master boatbuilder or the foreman of the yard, but he also recommended others who were apprenticed to quartermen or ordinary shipwrights. The apprentices recommended by their family members were placed just as well. David Green, noted as being recommended as 'nephew of Patrick Howitt, shipwright', was apprenticed to the master shipwright. Nor were those that recommended them necessarily from well-established shipwright families in the yard. George Wilson, for instance, was apprenticed to the foreman of the yard in 1791 through the recommendation of his father, David Wilson, who had entered in September 1770 after moving from his apprenticeship yard in Sunderland.[43]

These recommendations show that by the 1790s the family connections that had the most influence were ones already *within* the yard. This was also true of appointments beyond apprenticeships. Several of the non-apprenticeship familial recommendations in the period 1790–1796 were on behalf of shipwrights entered on 11 May 1790, when a warrant from the Navy Board directed the yard to increase its complement from 391 to 420. Several of these shipwrights had already served in the yard, such as Adam Goodman, who was recommended to be entered again by his brother, presumably James Goodman, who was also a shipwright in the yard. John Berry was also re-entered at the age of 28 on recommendation from his father, of the same name, a well-established quarterman. This is not to say that the extended family of yard artificers did not have any influence. Mrs Limberry, the widow of the recently deceased boatswain of the yard, recommended the shipwright John Williams for entry in 1791, on behalf of 'her son's maid Jane'. Other external brokers may have also had familial connections within the yard that are not so obvious from the description book alone. This was certainly the case when we look at the apprenticeships of Woolwich dockyard in the following period.

The Woolwich description book of 1802 records the names, ages and dates of entry of the apprentices of the yard and to whom they were apprenticed. It is a useful foundation from which to consider the use of familial ties in

---

[43] TNA, ADM 106/2978 Deptford: artificers and labourers, riggers 1779.

FEES AND RESISTANCE: LOWER-LEVEL PATRONAGE   225

dockyard patronage, particularly in securing entry to a yard or organising apprenticeships to senior officers which could lead to later promotions.[44] Of the fifty-six apprentices listed in the 1802 Woolwich description book, thirty-three were born in the parish of St Mary Magdalene, Woolwich. Fourteen of these were the sons of other men in the yard or had extended family serving in the yard. Only four were apprenticed directly to their fathers: John Andrew Hall was apprenticed to his father Isaac Hall; George Coake had his eldest son George Coake as his servant; William Mallack had his son John Mallack apprenticed to him; and Robert Knowles was servant to his father John Knowles who was assistant to the master shipwright and had transferred from Sheerness in 1796.[45]

Like Deptford, many of the apprentices in Woolwich in 1802 were not apprenticed to their fathers in the yard. James Nicholson had Thomas Lloyd apprenticed to him, and his son, George Nicholson, was apprenticed to John Hillman, the overseeing quarterman.[46] George Nicholson began his apprenticeship and entered into the yard before Lloyd, so his appointment to Hillman was probably because of his senior rank. As an overseeing quarterman, Hillman could provide better future connections for young Nicholson, as well as officer training beneficial for later promotion. In another instance, William Fuller junior was apprenticed to Thomas Wallbridge, and his father, William Fuller senior, had an apprentice named William Round. William Round entered the yard in 1798, whereas William Fuller junior entered two years later in April 1800, perhaps explaining why he was apprenticed to Wallbridge rather than his own father. There is no ostensible connection between Round and Fuller to explain why Fuller would take on an apprentice which would prevent him from taking on his own son. The apprenticeship may have been organised by the Navy Board rather than between Fuller and his connections although there is no suggesting of an order in the description book. Alternatively, it is possible that Fuller had already made an agreement to have his son apprenticed

---

[44] All following examples of apprenticeships mentioned are drawn from this document, unless otherwise stated. TNA, ADM 106/2895, Woolwich Description Book 1802.

[45] LMA, P97/MRY/009, St Mary Magdalene, Woolwich, Composite Register, baptisms, burials, Jan 1779–Dec 1799, John Andrew Hall son of Isaac and Sarah Hall born 27 August 1783; George Coake son of George and Mary Coake born 7 October 1785; John Mallack son of William and Elizabeth Mallack, born 8 June 1784; LMA, P75/PAU/001, St Paul, Deptford, Composite Register, baptisms Jun 1730–Jun 1788, burials Jun 1730–Jun 1788, marriages Jun 1730–Mar 1754, Robert Knowles son of John and Mary Knowles baptised 6 November 1786.

[46] LMA, P97/MRY/009, St Mary Magdalene, Composite Register, Thomas Lloyd son of John and Amy Lloyd born 11 December 1784; George Nicholson son of James and Elizabeth Nicholson 3 December 1782.

226 PATRONAGE AND THE BRITISH NAVY, 1775–1815

to Wallbridge. As the section on James Jagoe's network will show, Wallbridge came from a well-connected shipwright family. In this case, apprenticing a son outside of the family could be motivated by securing connection within a profitable network and not just by the opportunity to train under a master of senior rank.

There were, however, apprenticeships in Woolwich that were undoubtedly organised through family connections, just not in so clear a way as father and son. The quarterman Job Davis had his nephew Jabez Edwards as his apprentice, a fact only made obvious from his will which named Jabez Edwards as his executor along with his other nephew Edward Edwards junior.[47] Both were the sons of his sister Ann and her husband Edward Edwards senior, a prominent member of the local community in his role as church clerk.[48] Similarly, John Swanson, another quarterman, had his grandson John Coombs as his apprentice. John Coombs was the son of Richard Coombs and Elizabeth Swanson, John Swanson's daughter.[49] Elsewhere in the yard, John Coombs's cousin, William Coombe, was apprenticed to Robert Smith.[50] William Coombe was the son of William Coombe and Susannah Swanson, another of John Swanson's daughters. Interestingly, Susannah and William Coombe had another son named Robert Smith Coombe in 1793, four years before their eldest son William Coombe entered the yard as Robert Smith's servant.[51] This suggests that William Coombe secured his position as Smith's apprentice through the connection of his widowed mother.[52] The late William Coombe senior was described as a waterman in John Swanson's will of 1808 so it is quite likely that his son's entry into the yard was also through the influence of his grandfather John Swanson.[53]

A look at the mobility of shipwrights between yards in the description books from 1779 also shows the importance of family. The majority served in the yard in which they were first apprenticed and many appear to have been apprenticed in the yard closest to the parish where they were born.[54] The

[47] TNA, PROB/11/1784/51, Will of Job Davis, Gentleman of Woolwich, Kent, 9 April 1831.

[48] LMA, P97/MRY/050, St Mary Magdalene, Woolwich: Vestry Minutes.

[49] LMA, P97/MRY/009, St Mary Magdalene, Woolwich, Composite Register Jan 1779–Dec 1799.

[50] It seems to have been coincidence that the sisters married men with similar surnames rather than clerical error.

[51] LMA, P97/MRY/009, St Mary Magdalene, Woolwich, Composite Register Jan 1779–Dec 1799.

[52] Ibid., Robert Smith Coombe born 1793.

[53] TNA, PROB/1483/88, Will of John Swanson, late Quarterman in His Majesty's Dock Yard of Woolwich, Kent, 16 July 1808.

[54] See Table 6.1. The data for whether the yard was their home yard or not is not as comprehensive as their apprenticeship yard as not all description books recorded the

FEES AND RESISTANCE: LOWER-LEVEL PATRONAGE   227

shipwright Jacob Thorpe's petition illustrates the importance of family in a home parish. Thorpe had entered Woolwich from Portsmouth by Navy Board orders to meet labour demand. He requested that the Navy Board officially enter him at Woolwich because he had served his apprenticeship there and his family still lived in the parish.[55] Similarly, Richard Randall applied in 1765 to be entered at Deptford after serving twenty years in Woolwich, so he could 'be with two of his children who live with his father-in-law there'.[56] John Woodger also asked to be removed from Woolwich to be with his family in Chatham.[57] Both of these shipwrights had served around twenty years in Woolwich yard before asking to be removed to their original yards. In her larger survey of artificer petitions Gill found that family was the primary reason given for assistance, over both skill and length of service.[58] Some petitions also reveal the difficulties shipwrights faced in being removed to a yard where they did not have such extensive familial networks. One petition from shipwrights and 'other artificers' who had been recently entered at Woolwich yard asked for the Navy Board to allow them to borrow wages while they waited for their quarterly pay. The petition states that as 'some of them are strangers in the place and others have no friends', the dealers would not advance them any money.[59] In a system where the Navy Board moved men frequently to meet demand, it is surprising that removal from home yards caused such a problem. The refusal to extend credit to these shipwrights suggests that most mobility between the yards was organised within an artificer's friendship or professional network, which the Woolwich apprenticeships suggest included many familial ties.

Fees and Non-Familial Networks

Even a glance at the Deptford recommendations shows the influence that non-familial connections had on yard employment. Some of these connections were plainly rooted in local networks, especially for a yard like Deptford which was surrounded by merchant yards. For example, Mary Slade, wife of the naval surveyor of the yard Thomas Slade, recommended the shipwright John Keare for entry in 1773, who had served his apprenticeship in 'Messrs

---

home parish. TNA, ADM 106/2975: Chatham 1779; ADM 106/2979: Plymouth 1779; ADM 106/2980: Portsmouth 1779; ADM 106/2982: Sheerness 1779; ADM 106/2984: Woolwich 1779; ADM 106/2986: Deptford 1784.

[55] TNA, ADM 106/1205/224, Petition of Jacob Thorpe, 4 March 1771.

[56] TNA, ADM 106/1142/156, Petition of Richard Randall, 20 July 1765.

[57] TNA, ADM 106/1174/168, Petition of John Woodger, 12 January 1767.

[58] Gill, *Naval Families*, 199–216.

[59] TNA, ADM 106/1185/60, Petition of shipwrights and other artificers, Woolwich, 28 September 1770.

228   PATRONAGE AND THE BRITISH NAVY, 1775–1815

Wells' yard in Rotherhithe. Others seem to have followed the movement of artificers between yards, as seems to have been the case for shipwright William Parker, who was recommended by William Halley for entry in July 1779, perhaps because they had both served their apprenticeships in Hull.[60] Similarly, Robert Scott was recommended for entry in 1790 by John Garrett who had served with him in Halifax yard, and even originally entered Deptford in 1778 at the same time as Scott, but had remained in the yard when Scott instead requested to be discharged in 1782.[61]

However, the nature of the connection, and therefore of the recommendation itself, is not so obvious for some. George Peacock, for example, was recommended to be entered to the yard in 1783 by shipwright George Bridges, although Bridges had served his apprenticeship in Deptford, while Peacock had served in Leith.[62] The quarterman Prince Frederick, similarly, recommended a shipwright named William Tiddy to be entered in 1780, despite Tiddy having served his apprenticeship in Norfolk, whereas Frederick, the adopted son of a Deptford shipwright, Robert Robinson, had served his own in the yard in 1747.[63] Even with the records of these recommendations having taken place it is difficult to discern the nature of their relationships and the reason for the recommendation, in the way we can for Markham's connections for whom letters of requests or recommendations survive.

An investigation undertaken by the commissioners of the naval inquiry set up by St Vincent in 1801 to investigate abuses in the dockyards reveals an extra layer of how these non-familial connections functioned in recommendations for entry to the yards. Item number 126 in the appendix of the *Sixth Report of the Commissioners of Naval Inquiry*, published in 1804, is a table of all the gratuities, meaning gifts of money, paid for entry and promotion in Plymouth yard at the end of the eighteenth century.[64] The subsequent items include interviews with the recipients and payees of gratuities, which provide more detail as those interviewed tried to defend themselves. Like the Deptford recommendations, it gives a glimpse into who was involved in brokering appointments to the yard.[65]

---

[60] TNA, ADM 106/2978 Deptford: artificers and labourers, riggers 1779.

[61] TNA, ADM 106/ 2978; ADM 106/2991.

[62] TNA, ADM 106/2991.

[63] TNA, ADM 106/2991; ADM 106/1048/159 Margaret Robinson, wife of Shipwright Robert Robinson of Deptford Yard. Her husband is at present incapacitated and on his behalf asks that a young man, Prince Frederick, whom they have brought up since a child, may be entered as his servant in place of his former servant whose time has expired. 1747 Nov 4.

[64] 'Item No.126: List of Persons employed in His Majesty's yards at Plymouth, who have paid Considerations for their several Appointments, with the Sums received for the same, and to whom paid; taken from the Depositions of the Parties, before Commissioner Fanshawe', *Sixth Report.*

[65] 'Item 127–133', *Sixth Report*, 422–429.

FEES AND RESISTANCE: LOWER-LEVEL PATRONAGE   229

Most of the money seems to have been paid on the understanding that it was to be passed on to Thomas Pollard, the master shipwright between 1784 and 1793. Those investigated may have been trying to avoid accusations of corruption themselves by blaming Pollard, who had died by the time of the investigation in 1803. Certainly, Robert Duins, the first clerk to the master shipwright, staunchly maintained that the money he received directly from the seven men listed had been 'for the use of Mr Pollard'. When he was initially questioned whether he knew Pollard had been in the habit of taking money for entry to the yard, Duins answered: 'Yes, I do believe he was, but not through me.'[66] To take Duins at his word that all the gratuities made their way to Pollard does not undermine the value of the network that the investigation uncovered. The friendships and connections used to get the money to Pollard are also likely to have been the connections used to exert influence over appointments, as well as forming the chain that facilitated recommendation.

Figure 6.1.1 illustrates the payment of gratuities. Each connection where money was paid includes the amount in pounds, shilling and pence along the connecting line. Each broker recorded as having paid at least one payment to Pollard is also represented connected by a line. Those who by nature of their role as messenger or clerk were connected to the master shipwright but were not recorded as having directly passed money to him are represented with a dotted line. Those brokers listed in the inquiry who were not ostensibly connected to Pollard have been grouped into scavelmen, labourers and women, represented in the box 'Others Accepting Fees' and in further detail in Figure 6.1.5. The brokers who accepted payment from multiple applicants, such as Robert Duins and Mrs Rippon, are represented with the number of applicants they took payment from collected within a circle. The details of these connections can be seen expanded in Figures 6.1.2–6.1.4.

The inquiry reveals several important elements about the construction of networks of recommendation and influence at Plymouth. First, the first clerk to the master shipwright was a position of significant influence within the yard. Duins received payment for appointments directly from seven men. Indirectly, he had influence on the entry of at least three more men, and both his wife and daughter also brokered appointments, as can be seen in Figure 6.1.2. The inquiry shows that a broker's influence was not determined by his or her position within the yard hierarchy. As we can see in Figure 6.1.3, Luke Hammett, an ordinary joiner in the yard, received gratuities from twelve applicants, ranging from £3 3s to £14 14s.[67] Some of the payments to Hammett were listed as 'for Mr Pollard'. However, not all the payments were listed

[66] 'Item No. 130: The Examination of Mr Robert Duins', *Sixth Report*, 424.

[67] James Ladd, scavelman and also Ezekiel Hendey, labourer; John May, sawyer, *Sixth Report*, 420.

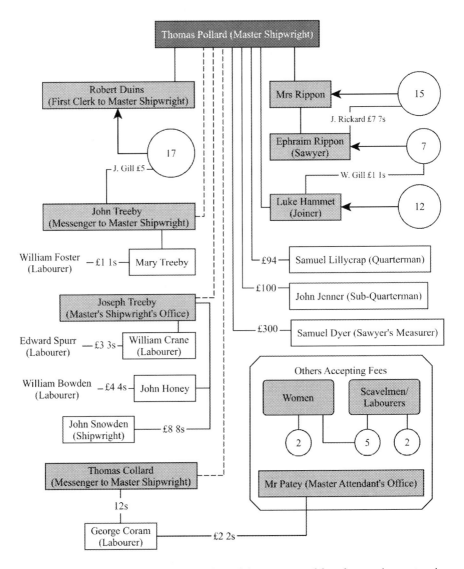

Figure 6.1.1 Plymouth gratuities: overview of the payment of fees for appointment and promotion in Plymouth yard. Source: *The Sixth Report of the Commissioners of Naval Inquiry. Appendix 126. Plymouth yard, Woolwich yard* (London, 1804), 419–421.

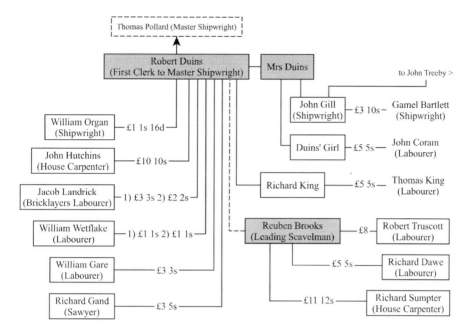

Figure 6.1.2 Plymouth gratuities detail, Robert Duins.

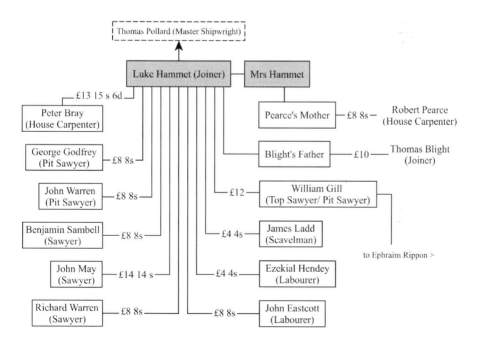

Figure 6.1.3 Plymouth gratuities detail, Luke Hammet.

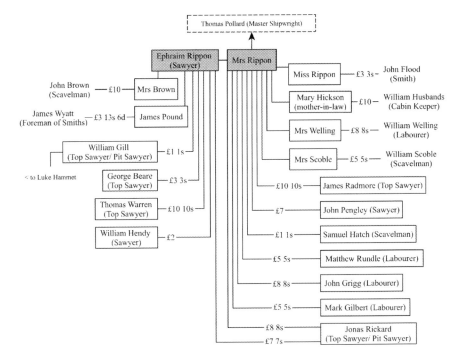

Figure 6.1.4 Plymouth gratuities detail, Mrs Rippon.

as such, which suggests that Hammett had influence in the yard besides his connection to the master shipwright.[68]

Women also acted as key brokers in the network, a point which is easy to overlook if we focus solely on the apprenticeship records considered in the first section. Duins stated that Pollard employed 'principally women' in the collection of payments when he was pressed about 'what persons' did he remember that 'Mr Pollard employed, in receiving money from artificers and labourers for their entry in this dockyard?'[69] Duins again avoided implicating himself or men still working in the yard by saying that women had been the main brokers. If true, it suggests that Pollard was tapping into a female patronage network already operating in and around the yard. Certainly, several women received the payment of gratuities for themselves and Pollard. The shipwright Gamel Bartlett paid £3 10s to Mrs Duins via his friend John Gill.[70]

---

[68] See John Eastcott, labourer, *Sixth Report*, 421.

[69] *Sixth Report*, 424.

[70] Gamel Bartlett was recorded with the abbreviated name Gam^l and so could either have been Gamel, Gammel or Gamaliel.

FEES AND RESISTANCE: LOWER-LEVEL PATRONAGE   233

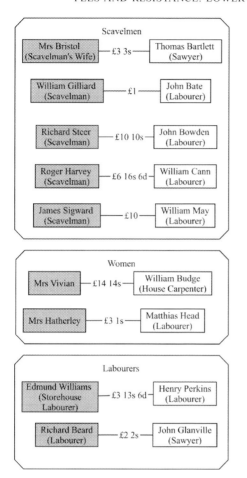

Figure 6.1.5 Plymouth gratuities, others accepting fees

John Gill did not pay his own gratuity to Mrs Duins, but rather paid a higher gratuity to John Treeby, a labourer employed as the messenger to the master shipwright. It is possible that Gill entered before Bartlett, and by the time of Bartlett's entry had formed a connection to Mrs Duins, thus bringing down the cost of the fee by missing out John Treeby as a connection. The payment of a lesser fee was not because of Mrs Duins's gender. Her daughter received a gratuity of £5 5s from John Coram for entry as a labourer.

Female-to-female connections also facilitated the entry of a number of artificers and illustrate the extent of the influential network which operated outside the yard. As we can see in Figure 6.1.4, William Welling entered the yard as a labourer when his wife paid Mrs Rippon, the wife of the sawyer Ephraim Rippon, £8 8s. Other payees reported that Mrs Rippon passed the fees directly to Pollard. Whether this was a direct transaction or it went through

234 PATRONAGE AND THE BRITISH NAVY, 1775–1815

other connections, perhaps through Mrs Duins, is unclear. Robert Pearce also gained entry as a house carpenter after his mother paid a fee of £8 8s to Mrs Hammett, the wife of Luke Hammett, the joiner mentioned previously (see Figure 6.1.3). In this instance, it is possible that there was a level of pre-existing acquaintance between Mrs Hammett and Mrs Pearce as the inquiry also noted that the gratuity was paid 'some Months after Entry', which suggests Hammett was confident in the future payment of the fee. Morriss argued that the payment of fees in the dockyards circumvented patronage as a system of friendship and trust.[71] However, Mrs Pearce's payment suggests that the fees operated alongside friendship recommendations. Other female recipients were also listed in the inquiry and are represented in Figure 6.1.5. A wife's familial and political connections could also be drawn upon for patronage. William Scoble's wife who paid Mrs Rippon after his entry into the yard was also noted as having given 'her brother-in-law' a fee of £4 4s 'for his Influence with Sir John Call, by whose Recommendation Deponent was entered in the Yard'.[72] Scoble was only a scavelman but his wife's connections are a good illustration of the extent of lower-level patronage networks as well as the fluidity of eighteenth-century social level.

Of these women, Mrs Rippon appears to have taken the most gratuities. Three of these gratuities were paid by female connections on the applicant's behalf.[73] The notes for John Grigg and Mark Gilbert's payments suggest that Mrs Rippon managed to secure fees by saying they were for the master shipwright, which in turn suggests that female brokers were not necessarily perceived as having power over appointments.[74] Grigg's note reads 'as he believes, for Mr Pollard' and Gilbert's 'who said it was for Thomas Pollard'. Neither shipwright seems to have trusted that Rippon actually passed the fees on to Pollard; however, both artificers gained entry to the yard so either Rippon was connected to Pollard or she was well-connected in other ways in the yard to secure their appointments. Rippon was the wife of an ordinary sawyer and her position as a broker for so many connections neatly reveals how patronage networks extended beyond the yard hierarchy.

Male connections outside the yard were also important in the Plymouth network. John Jenner, who in 1803 was the foreman of the masthouse, where the masts for ships were shaped, was listed as having paid Pollard £100 for his promotion. However, Jenner stated that he believed that his 'friend Mr

[71] Morriss, 'Government and Community', 22.

[72] *Sixth Report*, 420.

[73] Mrs Welling, wife of William Welling, paid £8 8s for his entry as a labourer; Mary Hickson, mother-in-law to William Husbands, paid £10 for his entry as a cabin keeper; Mrs Scoble, wife of William Scoble, paid £3 5s for his entry as a scavelman. *Sixth Report*, 420.

[74] John Grigg paid £5 5s; Mark Gilbert paid £8 8s. *Sixth Report*, 421.

FEES AND RESISTANCE: LOWER-LEVEL PATRONAGE   235

John Henderson' had paid the sum of £100 to Pollard for his appointment to sub-quarterman, a position below quarterman. Jenner stressed that when Henderson had paid the gratuity he 'had given up all kinds of business', although he had at one time been employed in the yard and after that had been an agent for the delivery of stores.[75] However, Henderson had continued actively to operate as a broker with connections in the yard, which suggests that personal networks and connections were more important in yard patronage than the influence afforded by position in the yard hierarchy.

Friendship was intimately associated with the payment of fees. The shipwright John Snowden paid £8 8s to John Treeby for his entry to the yard. The inquiry also notes, however, that Snowden heard Treeby say that more shipwrights would be entered the next day if applicants made 'Mr Duins their friend by a few pounds'.[76] Some of the payments also seem to have been made without the appointee's knowledge, but through a sense of obligation to their familial connections. Jenner, the foreman of the masthouse, mentioned previously, stated that Henderson was no relation but he believed that he had made the payment because 'he esteemed me particularly on my Uncle's Account'. John Jenner's uncle was the late John Jenner, master shipwright at Woolwich, who had also served several years as an officer at Plymouth, where he presumably forged his connection with Henderson.

Certainly, an interview with Richard Steer suggests that charity was a significant part of the payment of fees. Steer was a scavelman who 'had been a long while in the Yard'. He 'applied to the Builder', most likely referring to the master boatbuilder who was a senior officer beneath the master shipwright, for the entry of John Bowden who had promised to pay him £10 10s 'for the Good' of Steer's family. Reportedly the builder told him 'that when a vacancy happened he [Bowden] should be entered';[77] and 'upon some vacancies occurring, I again applied to the Builder and he [Bowden] was entered'. The gratuity Steer mentioned was paid after Bowden entered the yard and he stressed once again it was for 'the Good of my Family'.[78] He also stressed that he had not been the means for entering any other men to the yard either with or without gratuity, perhaps to further emphasise that he took the fee because he had to, rather than making a habit of what the Navy Board considered corruption.

The interviews with those who received fewer gratuities reveal the importance of friendship between connections and how the payment of gratuities was facilitated by a pre-existing patronage network. Reuben Brooks, who was a leading scavelman, said that the fees taken from Richard Sumpter,

[75] *Sixth Report*, 425.
[76] Ibid., 419.
[77] Ibid., 422.
[78] Ibid., 422.

236 PATRONAGE AND THE BRITISH NAVY, 1775–1815

Richard Dawe and Robert Truscott were for his own use and that he managed to get their entrance to the yard because of his friendship with Duins. He said: 'he being a Friend to me he got it done; but he did not know that any Money was to be paid for it'. Contrary to Duins's testimony, which painted the taking of payment as motivated by hierarchical corruption instigated by Pollard, Brooks's statement shows that it was the personal connections between the yard artificers and officers that facilitated entry and appointments.

Furthermore, Brooks's testimony suggests that the financial side of these appointments was a bonus to the recipient rather than their prime motivation. When questioned whether he had been offered or received money to 'get persons advanced' within the yard, he answered: 'I have not received any, but it has been offered to me both by shipwrights and caulkers, to get them advanced'. He also stated that a 'great number' of applications had been made to him and money offered, adding 'I dare say Hundreds'.[79] With so many soliciting him, Brooks most probably made decisions about who to recommend based on their strong personal connection to him or the financial incentive they offered him. However, he also emphasised in his testimony that: 'the sums offered were so great that I would not have any thing to do with it', which suggests that the money was not his central object in accepting fees.

Despite this, the sums paid to him for his recommendation to Duins were relatively high. Richard Sumpter paid him £12 12s to be entered as a house carpenter. A house carpenter's basic pay was 1s 10d a day but they earned overtime and had an allowance of four pence a day in 'chips', which meant they were allowed to take four pence's worth of waste wood or materials from the yard, or as much as they could rest on one shoulder.[80] Even so, Sumpter's fee was just over two-thirds of his basic income for a year. A scavelman, however, earned even less with a basic rate of only 1s 6d.[81] Clerks received a salary and had more financial stability. However, they anticipated the payment of fees and gratuities for entry into the yard as part of their income. The first clerk to the master shipwright at Chatham yard up until 1801 received a salary of £40, roughly twice as much as a house carpenter's annual basic pay. In 1784, the first clerk to the master shipwright at Chatham also received £51 in fees and gratuities.[82] Brooks may not have taken higher fees because he felt it put him at risk of accusations of corruption. His testimony suggests, however, that it was most likely a combination of both the financial incentive and a close personal connection which secured entry to the yard, as appears to have been the case with apprenticeships.

Plymouth yard was the only yard in which the naval inquiry investigated the payment of gratuities in such detail. The commissioners were more concerned

79 Ibid., 423.
80 Morriss, *Royal Dockyards*, 101.
81 Ibid., 101.
82 Ibid., 133.

FEES AND RESISTANCE: LOWER-LEVEL PATRONAGE 237

with abuse at the higher levels of the yard although the same system of fees operated in other yards.[83] The Plymouth gratuities reveal the network of non-familial connections inside and outside the yard's hierarchy used for entry and promotion. The list and interviews suggest that an artificer's best route to appointment was through friendship with clerks in the master shipwright's office, such as Duins, but also to have a female connection brokering on his behalf outside the yard. Brooks was in a position to be solicited by these 'hundreds' of applicants because of his friendship with Duins. Without this report into gratuities, their connection and the role of women would be difficult to discern from the yard description books and Navy Board letters. Brooks's dismissal of the financial aspect of the gratuities also suggests that connection mattered in dockyard patronage more than money. Serle's claim that shipwrights could be bought, therefore, was no more true for shipwrights than it was for sea officers.

Woolwich Timber Master James Jagoe's Network

The network and career of James Jagoe, the timber master at Woolwich yard between 1801 and 1803, is a useful case study of the mechanisms of patronage in the dockyard and the integration of dockyard networks within the local community. Jagoe was fairly representative of the middling level of shipwrights; advantageously apprenticed in the yard where he was born, moving only between two yards in his career, rising steadily but not with the speed Knight argues distinguished the yard 'elite'.[84] He was active in Woolwich dockyard's parish church, St Mary Magdalene, even holding the position of churchwarden between 1793 and 1798.[85] The marriage records of his daughter also reveal familial ties within the yard itself, through her marriage in 1795 to the shipwright Joseph Brain, who also appeared often in the vestry minutes of St Mary Magdalene.[86]

Jagoe served his apprenticeship in Plymouth yard to John Jenner, the assistant to the master shipwright at the time. He then entered Plymouth yard as an ordinary shipwright on 10 February 1758.[87] In 1778, he was serving as a pro-quarterman, an acting position beneath quarterman, under the charge of Anthony Manley, who was overseer of the work-gang.[88] In December that year, Manley recommended Jagoe for full quarterman and he appears as such in the 1779 Plymouth description book, where he was also listed as being a

---

[83] Ibid., 127.

[84] Knight, 'Sandwich, Middleton and Dockyard Appointments', 176.

[85] LMA, P97/MRY/050, St Mary Magdalene, Woolwich: Vestry Minutes.

[86] LMA, P97/MRY/024, St Mary Magdalene, Register of Marriages, Joseph Brain married Unity Rich Jagoe, 1 October 1795.

[87] TNA, ADM 106/2979, Plymouth 1779.

[88] TNA, ADM 106/1244/369, Navy Board In-Letters: 4 December 1778.

238 PATRONAGE AND THE BRITISH NAVY, 1775–1815

'sober man' and a 'Good workman'.[89] Jagoe entered Woolwich in January 1782 as a quarterman, aged 40, married with four children, having served eighteen years and one month at Plymouth yard. By 10 August he was promoted to second foreman of the yard, under the authority of Stephen Jones, the first foreman, who also came from Plymouth.[90] Jagoe's next promotion traceable in the record was his appointment to assistant to the master shipwright in 1801.[91] In 1803 he returned to Plymouth by a Navy Board warrant dated 30 March, and was then appointed assistant to the master shipwright at Plymouth yard, a rank he retained until November 1810 when he was superannuated.[92]

Jagoe's moves coincided with the movement of his patrons Jenner and Manley. Jenner's final position before his death was as master shipwright at Woolwich between April 1779 and December 1782, so Jagoe probably entered Woolwich yard in January 1782 through Jenner's influence. Certainly, Jagoe appears to have had a close connection to Jenner, beyond the professional tie of master and apprentice, as he acted as witness to Jenner's will, drawn up in 1782.[93] In addition, Manley entered Woolwich in December 1779 as master boatbuilder and was quickly moved to master mastmaker in January 1780.[94] Both positions were ones of authority but were inferior to being assistant to the master shipwright. In 1781 Manley returned to Plymouth as master boatbuilder, a position which he held until the end of 1786. In March 1787 Manley was re-entered to Woolwich and this time was promoted to second assistant to the master shipwright.[95] When Jagoe first entered Woolwich he had access to hierarchical ties. However, Manley left in 1781 and Jenner died in 1782 so their influence on his behalf was likely limited when Jagoe first arrived. Jagoe had to use other connections in and around the yard to secure patronage.

Jagoe's position as timber master allows us to partially recreate his network as it might have stood between 1801 and 1803, providing us with a window into the sorts of connections and routes to patronage support he developed in the previous twenty years of his time at Woolwich.[96] The timber master was responsible for the inspection of purchased timber, its qualification as inferior or superior quality, and its subsequent allocation from the timber yard to ships being built.[97] In the Woolwich description book created in approxi-

---

89 TNA, ADM 106/2979, Plymouth 1779.

90 TNA, ADM 106/2984, Woolwich 1779. Entered 13 July 1779.

91 TNA, ADM 6/27/273, Warrant dated 25 July 1801.

92 TNA, ADM 6/28/124, Warrant dated 30 March 1803; ADM 6/31, Warrant dated 6 November 1810.

93 TNA, PROB 11/1099/245, Will of John Jenner, master shipwright, 1783.

94 TNA, ADM 6/22/71, Warrant dated 13 December 1779.

95 TNA, ADM 6/23/386, Warrant dated 3 March 1787.

96 TNA, ADM 106/2985, Woolwich 1802; Morriss, *Royal Dockyards*, 88.

97 *Cobbett's Parliamentary Debates*, 7 (London, 1812), 179–180.

FEES AND RESISTANCE: LOWER-LEVEL PATRONAGE   239

mately 1802, a number of shipwrights were noted as being employed by the timber master. Two apprentices in particular were recorded as being servants explicitly to 'James Jagoe Timber Master'.[98] It is difficult to determine exactly when the data was added to the Woolwich description book. The notes which mark out men as employed by the timber master appear to have been made at the same time as the rest of the information, which suggests that the notes refer to Jagoe. It is likely that Jagoe was inspecting timbers in the capacity of assistant to the master shipwright before he was officially warranted as timber master. In this case, it is possible that the men he selected were also already working under his direct authority.

Figure 6.2 illustrates Jagoe's network centred on his employment of men in the timber yard, in combination with surrounding connections drawn together from the parish records for St Mary Magdalene and the Woolwich description books of 1802 and 1779. The men Jagoe employed in the timber yard give an insight into his friendship network and professional allegiances. As a position of high responsibility and escape from task-work Jagoe chose men closely connected to him or who had credentials from other respected members of the yard and local community.

This illustration gives an impression of three factors in Jagoe's network: the role of the vestry of St Mary Magdalene, the employment of shipwrights well-integrated in the yard through family connections, and the importance of apprentices. Those shipwrights and senior yard officers who appeared frequently in the vestry minutes alongside Jagoe between 1782 and 1802 are illustrated here marked as black circles, family connections are depicted by the dashed line, and apprenticeships by an arrow with a line that is either solid or broken depending on whether the apprenticeship was active or was from the period before 1801–1803. All of those who were listed in the 1802 description book as working under the timber master are included here. However, for simplicity's sake, not all of the shipwrights who appeared in the vestry minutes alongside Jagoe as active members of the church and vestry as signees, commissioners or serving in positions like churchwarden or sidesman, are depicted. These included prominent members of the yard who had also come from Plymouth such as John Jenner, Anthony Manley and Stephen Jones, mentioned above, as well as Robert Shipster, William Sture and Robert Rundle. Other shipwrights whom we encountered in the previous section on apprenticeships, such as John Swanson and William Coombe, also appeared in the minutes. This suggests the overlap between shipwrights' involvement in the local community and their ability to take on the privilege of apprentices.

Taking on apprentices was one way a new quarterman to a yard could secure his position, as well as strengthen his financial security by receiving

---

[98] TNA, ADM 106/2985, Woolwich 1802.

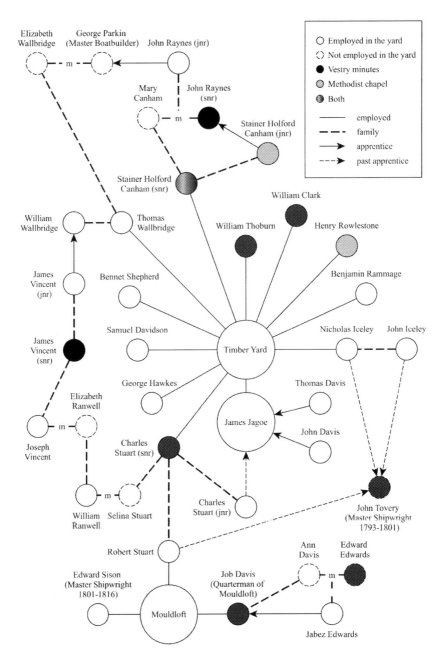

Figure 6.2 James Jagoe's network. The timber yard 1801–1803. Source: LMA, P97/MRY/008-009, P97/MRY/050, P97/MRY/024, St Mary Magdalene Woolwich; TNA, ADM 106/2984 Woolwich 1799, ADM 106/2985, ADM 106/2979, IR 1/31-36, PROB 11/1099/245, PROB 11/1381/24, PROB 11/1400/29, PROB 11/1483/88, PROB 11/1532/63, PROB 11/1549/528, PROB 11/1784/51, PROB 11/1858/188, PROB 11/2123/368, RG 4/1770.

FEES AND RESISTANCE: LOWER-LEVEL PATRONAGE   241

their wages.[99] During his time at Woolwich, Jagoe trained six apprentices, three of which are shown in Figure 6.2 because of their connection to his time as timber master. Two of these were Thomas and John Davis, who were apprenticed to him in April 1800 and 1801 respectively, and were the apprentices noted in the description books as being servants to 'James Jagoe Timber Master'. It is unclear exactly to whom these two were connected. However, it is striking that there were other Davis's in the yard who were also very prominently connected in the vestry.

Figure 6.2 illustrates one of these possible relations: Job Davis. Davis, whom we have encountered already in this chapter taking on his nephew Jabez as his apprentice, was deeply involved in the church. He was a frequent signee of the minutes, acted as overseer of the poor on several occasions as well as holding other vestry offices.[100] As already mentioned, his sister Ann was also married to Edward Edwards, the vestry clerk.[101] Alongside his influence in the vestry, Davis also had influence in the dockyard. He was the quarterman of the mouldloft, an important position for an ordinary shipwright to rise to. The mouldloft was where the designs of ships were drawn out on the floor for the measuring and warping of timber, and was under the direct command of the master shipwright.[102] The apprentices destined to rise to senior positions were often employed in the mouldloft. The quarterman in charge would have supervised the manual labour, directed by the master shipwright, and it would have given him many patronage opportunities. Job Davis had his nephew apprenticed in the mouldloft.[103] Davis's position of relative privilege in the yard and his dedication to the vestry suggest that Thomas and John Davis may well have been extended relations, which in turn would suggest importance of vestry friendships in the appointment of apprentices.

Certainly, the pattern of Jagoe's apprentices suggests that they were an important part of his integration into the yard and local community, either as a way to strengthen new connections or as a result of these connections. His first two apprentices in 1782, Henry Brock and Robert Mather Watson, do not appear to have been connected to any artificers in the yard.[104] However, Watson continued to be closely associated with Jagoe after his apprenticeship and

[99] Morriss, *Royal Dockyards*, 122.

[100] LMA, P97/MRY/050, St Mary Magdalene, Woolwich: Vestry Minutes.

[101] LMA, P97/MRY/009, Composite Register: baptisms, births and burials, 29 October 1787.

[102] Morriss, *Royal Dockyards*, 112.

[103] TNA, ADM 106/2985, Woolwich 1802.

[104] The apprenticeships are traceable through the stamp duty Jagoe paid on the indenture premium they offered to enter his service. TNA, IR1/31, Board of Stamps: Apprenticeship Books. Robert Mather Watson: October 1782 f.109; Henry Brock: 15 March 1782 f.110.

242 PATRONAGE AND THE BRITISH NAVY, 1775–1815

even appears to have followed Jagoe to Plymouth, where he was promoted to foreman afloat.[105] Watson also became highly involved in the vestry, probably through his connection to Jagoe.[106]

Once Jagoe's involvement in the vestry increased, in 1785, as indicated by his first appearance as a signee of the minutes in September that year, he began taking on the sons of more prominent shipwright families as his apprentices.[107] Of the six apprentices Jagoe took on during his time at Woolwich, we can say with some confidence that two came from prominent shipwright families that were also connected to the vestry: William Eldridge in 1786 and Charles Stuart in 1787, who also appears in Figure 6.2.[108] Stuart's father and Eldridge's grandfather were both frequent signees of the vestry minutes alongside Jagoe. His greater involvement in the church may have led to a friendship connection or alliance which then prompted him to take the boys as apprentices. Both Eldridge and Stuart paid apprentice premiums of £24, which appears to have been the standard fee for shipwrights' apprentices in Woolwich in those years.[109] Ten pounds of Eldridge's premium was paid on his behalf by Mrs Wiseman's Charity, which paid for the upkeep, education and apprenticeship premiums (of up to £10) of six orphans of Woolwich shipwrights.[110] The payment of the standard premium and consequent stamp tax suggests that Eldridge's family supplied the extra £14, and Jagoe did not take on Eldridge out of charity. In Jagoe's case, his taking on Stuart and Eldridge may also have increased his influence in the yard. Both boys had well-connected families.

Eldridge was well-connected through his grandfather, Daniel Eldridge, who until his retirement in 1784 was the master joiner of the yard, in charge of the joiners and carpenters responsible for fitting out newly crafted vessels, as well as furnishing them. It was a senior position for an artificer. Eldridge's aunt was

---

[105] TNA, ADM 6/28, Commission and Warrant Book, 8 December 1803.

[106] LMA, P97/MRY/050, St Mary Magdalene, Woolwich: Vestry Minutes.

[107] Ibid., f.67.

[108] TNA, IR1/33, Board of Stamps: Apprenticeship Books, William Eldridge: 12 June 1786 ff.30–31; Charles Stuart: 11 May 1787 ff.112–113. With indentures of seven years it is likely that these apprenticeships overlapped with those of Watson and Brock. It is unclear how Jagoe managed to act as master to all four apprentices at the same time. It is possible that Brock may have died, because he does not appear in ADM 106/2985, Woolwich 1779. But that would still mean that Watson's final years overlapped with both Eldridge and Stuart. In this case, Jagoe was flouting Navy Board code. Morriss, 'Government and Community', 22; H. Richardson, 'Wages of Shipwrights in HM Dockyards, 1496–1788', *Mariner's Mirror* 33 (1947), 265–274.

[109] Shipwrights Robert John Nelson and Job Davis were also paid as much by their apprentices. TNA, IR1/33, Board of Stamps: Apprenticeship Books, William Hills: 11 May 1787 f.113; William Morris: 4 January 1788 f.172.

[110] LMA, P97/MRY/076, Accounts of Mrs Wiseman's Charity.

FEES AND RESISTANCE: LOWER-LEVEL PATRONAGE 243

also married to Benjamin Pidcock, who was clerk to the master attendant.[111] The Plymouth gratuities showed that connection to a senior clerk could give individuals and families significant influence within the yard. Both Pidcock and Daniel Eldridge were also involved in the vestry. Pidcock appears only once in 1787, but Daniel Eldridge was a frequent signee between 1772 and 1782 at which point he seems to have retired from some of his extra responsibilities in the years leading up to his death in 1786.[112] He appeared alongside other dockyard men such as Robert Rundle, Robert Shipster and older shipwrights such as Joseph Canham, who was the father of Stainer and Mary Canham depicted in Figure 6.2 to whom we shall return shortly.[113] The Eldridges' earlier involvement in the vestry perhaps prompted Jagoe to take on William Eldridge from Mrs Wiseman's Charity. The charity aligned itself with the Anglican church, and the master in charge of the education of the six boys had to be a member of the church.[114] So Jagoe's involvement in the vestry in positions of responsibility, like governor of the workhouse, is probably what allowed him to take on Eldridge as his apprentice, and to therefore form a bond with the influential Eldridge family.

William Eldridge's aunt and uncle also appear to have been connected to Sarah Tippett, wife of Edward Tippett who was second assistant to the master shipwright. Sarah Tippett witnessed the marriage of Anne Eldridge and Benjamin Pidcock in 1780.[115] There may have been a level of familiar connection between Anne and Sarah, which suggests Pidcock was in a position of considerable influence within the yard. In 1786, when William Eldridge was entered as Jagoe's apprentice, Tippett was the second assistant at Plymouth, so he most likely did not exert any direct influence on the apprenticeship. It is also likely that Sarah Tippett went with him to Plymouth, so was no longer acting as a broker in the parish. Tippett's position in Plymouth also did not overlap with Jagoe's, Tippett entering in 1785 and Jagoe having moved to Woolwich in 1781. Anthony Manley, however, was still serving in Plymouth, and potentially was in communication with Jagoe. Not only, therefore, was Eldridge's family entrenched in positions of influence and authority within the yard itself, but his family were also potentially in brokered connection with Jagoe. By accepting an apprentice as well-connected as Eldridge, Jagoe

[111] LMA, P97/MRY/024, Register of Marriages: St Mary Magdalene, Woolwich, 29 November 1780.

[112] TNA, PROB 11/1141/304, Will of Daniel Eldridge, Gentleman of Woolwich, 29 April 1786.

[113] LMA, P97/MRY/050, St Mary Magdalene, Woolwich: Vestry Minutes.

[114] LMA, P97/MRY/076, Accounts of Mrs Wiseman's Charity.

[115] LMA, P97/MRY/024, Register of marriages: St Mary Magdalene, Woolwich, 29 November 1780.

244   PATRONAGE AND THE BRITISH NAVY, 1775–1815

strengthened his position in the yard by becoming integrated within Pidcock's network, as well as potentially favouring his own patronage connections.

Certainly, his taking on Charles Stuart, potentially twisting the Navy Board's rules, was most likely motivated by the strength of the Stuarts' connections as shipwrights and artificers within the yard. Charles Stuart was the son of an ordinary shipwright also named Charles Stuart, represented in Figure 6.2. The wills of both Stuart senior and his shipwright brother William Stuart show strong connections with the Ranwells, another shipwright family. Stuart senior jointly owned the commonhold on a windmill in Plumstead, near Woolwich, with William Ranwell.[116] The proximity of the two families is perhaps best represented by the marriage of Selina Stuart, Stuart senior's daughter, to William Ranwell's son.[117] William Ranwell also witnessed William Stuart's will.[118] The families were also connected to the Wallbridges who, Figure 6.2 shows, were also well-connected within the yard. Elizabeth Ranwell, Selina Stuart's sister-in-law, was married to Joseph Vincent who was mentioned in William Ranwell's will of 1814 as a shipwright of Woolwich, although he is not listed in the 1802 Woolwich description book.[119] Joseph Vincent was potentially the brother of James Vincent who was the father of James Vincent junior, who in turn was apprenticed to William Wallbridge.[120] Wallbridge's niece was married to George Parkin, the master boatbuilder.[121] As shown in Figure 6.2, Jagoe employed both Stuart senior and Thomas Wallbridge, William Wallbridge's brother, in the timber yard in 1802, which reflects his connection to them as well as their position within the yard community. His selection, or perhaps his acceptance, of Charles Stuart junior as his apprentice in 1787, therefore, could reflect his integration within the Woolwich professional and community networks.

It is likely that Jagoe selected men to assist him in the inspection of timber based on the value of their connection, network potential and trustworthiness. Between 1801 and 1804 the supply of timber to the royal yards became a particular focus in St Vincent's reforms. His accusations of corruption broke down the government's relationship with the timber contractors, as well as his instigation of a system within the yards called 'conversion', where timber

---

[116] TNA, PROB 11/1532/63, Will of Charles Stuart, Shipwright of Woolwich, 3 April 1812.

[117] Ibid.

[118] TNA, PROB 11/1858/188, Will of William Stuart, Shipwright of Woolwich, 5 February 1836.

[119] TNA, PROB 11/1549/528, Will of William Ranwell, Shipwright of Woolwich, 29 November 1813.

[120] TNA, ADM 106/2985, Woolwich 1802.

[121] TNA, PROB 11/1381/24, Will of Thomas Wallbridge, Shipwright of Woolwich, 6 September 1802.

FEES AND RESISTANCE: LOWER-LEVEL PATRONAGE 245

masters had to examine every piece of timber and 'determine a specific purpose' to decide on the value at the point of purchase.[122] Among other problems, it was argued in parliament in 1806 that this system put the merchant contractors to considerable cost for no guaranteed return and put timber masters under pressure to buy only superior quality timber or risk their reputation. There was a suspicion that the system also incentivised timber masters to mark timber at a lower quality to bring the price down or to provide surplus timber which they could then profit from selling on themselves.[123] This quote from John Jeffery reflects on how timber masters were viewed after the supply of timber had been disrupted during St Vincent's administration:

> I conceive, sir, that these regulations, when exercised with candour and justice, according to their true spirit, are beneficial; but when exercised by persons who do not strictly consult the mutual interest of the individual and the public, and who are in a measure awed by the responsibility of their situation, they become detrimental.[124]

Jeffery opposed St Vincent and the implication in his speech was that shipwrights were naturally untrustworthy.

Several of the men employed by Jagoe do appear to have been well-connected in the yard, to one another or to Jagoe himself. Charles Stuart senior was employed in the yard probably because of his connection to Jagoe through their involvement in the vestry and Jagoe's taking on of Charles Stuart junior as his apprentice. Equally, Thomas Wallbridge was connected to the Stuarts through extended relations, illustrated by his brother's taking on James Vincent as his apprentice. Besides Stuart, three other members of the timber yard illustrated in Figure 6.2 also appear in the vestry minutes: William Thoburn, William Clark and Stainer Canham.[125] William Thoburn entered the yard in 1800 and appears to have had no familial links in the yard or the parish at that time although he served his apprenticeship at Woolwich. He became involved in the vestry and at a public meeting in 1802 stood for election to a committee charged with investigating parish complaints, alongside James Jagoe, Charles Stuart and Robert Watson, Jagoe's old apprentice.[126] As it is unclear in the Woolwich description book when the men of the timber yard were selected, it is possible that Thoburn was selected because of his involvement in the vestry with Jagoe. Of the dockyard men who stood for election, only Charles Stuart garnered enough votes to make the committee

---

[122] *Cobbett's Parliamentary Debates*, 7, 177–180; Morriss, *Royal Dockyards*, 88–89.
[123] *Cobbett's Parliamentary Debates*, 7, 178; Morriss, *Royal Dockyards*, 88.
[124] *Cobbett's Parliamentary Debates*, 7, 178.
[125] Ibid.
[126] LMA, P97/MRY/050, St Mary Magdalene, Woolwich: Vestry Minutes.

246 PATRONAGE AND THE BRITISH NAVY, 1775–1815

of twelve, which illustrates his standing in the community and highlights the importance of his friendship with Jagoe, despite being technically outranked by him. William Clark also appeared in the vestry minutes for the first time in 1802, so perhaps it was his employment by Jagoe as timber master that instigated his involvement in the parish community rather than the other way around.[127] Clark is recorded in the 1802 book as having entered Woolwich yard in 1793 and having served his apprenticeship in Whitby, so he did not have the same childhood connections within the yard as some of his peers. However, interestingly, he does seem to have been Jagoe's neighbour and is recorded in the parish overseer's accounts as living next door to him in Unity Place, alongside other shipwrights involved in the vestry such as John Beck, Thomas Guyer and William Hellard.[128]

Stainer Canham is also an interesting inclusion in the timber yard. He also came from a well-established dockyard family; several of the men were also employed in the yard and some of the women were also married to other shipwrights. Stainer Canham's sister, Mary Canham, was married to the shipwright John Raynes.[129] Raynes was the churchwarden between 1801 and 1802 and had long served in the vestry alongside Jagoe, so it is possible Raynes's friendship with Jagoe played into his brother-in-law's employment in the timber yard.[130] Stainer Canham also appears as a signee in the vestry minutes but, interestingly, he was also a member of the non-conformist church, Queen Street Chapel. He registered four of his children with the church in December 1798, including his son Stainer Holford Canham who was apprenticed to his uncle, John Raynes.[131] Appearing in the vestry minutes even after registering at the Baptist church was also not unusual for shipwrights at Woolwich. Three other shipwrights who registered their children at the chapel also appear in the vestry minutes: George Coake, James Fincham

[127] LMA, P97/MRY/050, St Mary Magdalene, Woolwich: Vestry Minutes. Public meeting 23 February 1802.

[128] LMA, P97/MRY/075, St Mary Magdalene, Woolwich: Overseer's accounts June 1800–October 1805.

[129] LMA, P97/MRY/024, St Mary Magdalene, Register of Marriages, May 1763– Aug 1796, John Rayns married Mary Canham, 31 January 1784; Mary Canham's uncle, Henry Canham, included Raynes in his will of 1803 as his 'good friend': TNA, PROB 11/1400/29, Will of Henry Canham, Shipwright of Woolwich, Kent, 12 November 1803; George Canham, Henry Canham's son and Mary and Stainer Canham's cousin, was also a shipwright in the yard: LMA, P97/MRY/008, Composite Register: baptisms, marriages and burials, 16 November 1768.

[130] LMA, P97/MRY/050, St Mary Magdalene, Woolwich: Vestry Minutes.

[131] TNA, RG 4/1770, KENT: Woolwich, Queen Street Chapel (Baptist): births. Stainer Holford Canham son of Stainer and Rebecca Canham, born 2 February 1787, registered 15 December 1798.

FEES AND RESISTANCE: LOWER-LEVEL PATRONAGE 247

and Richard Dunmall, which at the very least suggests the intersection of friendship networks.[132]

Unlike the Stuarts, Canham's association with Jagoe is most firmly traceable to his employment in the timber yard and his signing of the vestry in 1802. His father, Joseph Canham, had been involved in the vestry, but only up until 1781, before Jagoe came to Woolwich. However, Canham had a large, extended family, as well as connection to both the Baptist and Anglican church, which gave him community power. Employing an older, well-connected shipwright like Canham in the timber yard, therefore, may have been strategic. Certainly, only one other shipwright in the timber yard was a member of the chapel, Henry Rowlestone.[133] Rowlestone's connection to Jagoe is not at all apparent. Perhaps he employed him on his merit alone, but Stainer Canham's wide spread of connections in the yard, as well as his involvement in both churches, strongly suggests that there was a friendship connection between Rowlestone and Canham, and Canham used his influence to have them both employed in the respected role in the timber yard.

Jagoe also seems to have selected men who may not have been personally connected to him but were meritorious and well-connected. Nicholas Iceley came from another large Woolwich family and was apprenticed to the late master shipwright John Tovery in 1795, as was his brother John Iceley in 1797.[134] To have two boys apprenticed to a master shipwright, the Iceleys must have had access to considerable capital and connection, an especially impressive feat when only one family member seems to have served above the rank of ordinary shipwright, 66-year-old Nicholas Iceley who served as a 'leading man' among the sailmakers.[135] Roger Knight argued that the large apprenticeship premiums which master shipwrights demanded effectively outpriced most ordinary shipwrights.[136] James Jagoe does not seem to have been especially favoured by their powerful connection John Tovery, despite also being involved in the vestry. After all, his promotion to assistant came

[132] TNA, RG 4/1770, Queen Street Chapel (Baptist): births. George Coake, son of George and Mary Coake of St Mary's, Woolwich, born 7 October 1785, registered 4 November 1798; John Fincham, son of James and Mary Fincham St Mary's Woolwich, no birth date, registered 2 November 1798; Mary Ann Dunmall, daughter of Richard and Martha Dunmall, born 23 November 1791, registered 3 January 1800; LMA, P97/MRY/050, St Mary Magdalene, Woolwich: Vestry Minutes.

[133] TNA, RG/1770, Queen Street Chapel (Baptist): births. Sarah Rowlestone, daughter of Henry and Sarah Rowlestone, born 22 August 1788, registered 28 November 1798.

[134] TNA, IR1/36, Board of Stamps: Apprenticeship Books, 1794–1799, John Tovery for Nicholas Iceley, 3 January 1795; TNA, ADM 106/2985, Woolwich 1802.

[135] TNA, ADM 106/2985, Woolwich 1802.

[136] Knight, 'Sandwich, Middleton and Dockyard Appointments', 179.

248   PATRONAGE AND THE BRITISH NAVY, 1775–1815

with Edward Sison's appointment to master shipwright after Tovery's death. It is possible, therefore, that Jagoe was not well-connected to the Iceleys. Furthermore, Edward Sison does not seem to have particularly favoured the Iceley boys. Neither of the Iceley boys were employed in the mouldloft under Edward Sison. Rather, he appears to have put Nicholas Iceley in the timber yard, to perhaps free up space in the mouldloft for his own apprentices. The timber yard was less prestigious than the mouldloft, but was a position that was still beneficial enough that the large Iceley family would not be dissatisfied.

Alternatively, Nicholas Iceley's employment by Jagoe might have been prompted instead by the skills he undoubtedly learnt while apprentice to the master shipwright. Certainly, it is difficult to establish the reason for some of the younger men's selection, which suggests that there were other factors involved than their connection. Four of the eleven men employed by Jagoe in the timber yard were below the age of 30: William Thoburn, Nicholas Iceley, George Hawkes and Benjamin Rammage. It is difficult to trace any level of connection within the yard or community for Benjamin Rammage who entered in 1797 having served his apprenticeship in Chatham, or for George Hawkes, despite being recorded in the 1802 book as having entered in 1798 soon after he had finished his apprenticeship at Woolwich. Rammage, at least, was also noted in the 1802 book as being of 'good' character, which suggests that trust-worthiness and merit may have been ultimately what prompted his inclusion, perhaps strengthened by a recommendation from a connection in Chatham where he had recently been apprenticed. Hawkes, however, is somewhat of a mystery. We could assume that he had some connections within the yard from having served his apprenticeship there, although what these were are not at all clear. It is also difficult to discern what prompted Jagoe's employment of the last two men: Samuel Davidson and Bennet Shepherd. However, both shipwrights were in their forties and had served at Woolwich for the whole of their careers, recorded in the 1802 book as entering respectively in August 1775 and 1782. It is quite possible, therefore, that Jagoe simply selected the older men, or was told to employ them, because of their long standing in the yard.

Jagoe's network reveals the multiple factors involved in employment within the dockyard. Lower-level patronage was marked by the importance of community integration, which meant that men of different social statuses could be profitably connected. The female involvement is perhaps less apparent in Jagoe's network than was visible in the investigation into Plymouth gratuities. However, the unknown connections between men who otherwise appear to be carefully managing patronage connections suggest that more connections were managed by women than is represented in Figure 6.2. The involvement of dockyard men in the parish church of St Mary Magdalene was a significant part of their patronage network. Not only would the men potentially spend more time outside the yard together

FEES AND RESISTANCE: LOWER-LEVEL PATRONAGE 249

in vestry meetings and in overseeing the poor but also their involvement in the church acted as a guarantee of their behaviour. It is not so unusual therefore for many of the men in the timber yard to have been involved in the church, given the responsibility of the position.

Jagoe's career could have faced a problem when he lost his patron John Jenner in 1782. However, perhaps it was never his goal to stay so well-connected. After all, a master shipwright had many apprentices seeking his patronage throughout his career and it was unrealistic that he would be able to look to all of them all of the time. Instead Jagoe's involvement in the parish church gave him access to the friendship circles of the dockyard, which did not necessarily follow the vertical hierarchy of the navy. Those families with influence were also not necessarily those with the highest social position or financial security. Jagoe's apprentice William Eldridge was an orphan of a shipwright, which is why part of his apprentice premium was paid for by Mrs Wiseman's Charity. His grandfather was also dead by 1787. His aunt however was well-placed, and this meant that Eldridge gave Jagoe access to these networks as well. The exact nature of relationships laid out in a network sketch like Figure 6.2, gathered from disparate, dry and sometimes contradicting evidence, will always be difficult to judge. However, the coincidental connections in the vestry, intermarriages, and the continued association of apprentices and their masters all suggest that friendships inside and outside the yard were the cornerstone of dockyard careers, patronage and community.

Artificer Mobility and Wide-Ranging Networks

Familial and familiar connections in the yard and in the local parish were the foundation of patronage in the dockyards. The networks, although fluctuating through the natural variations in friendships and enmities, appear to have been largely static and tied to the yard where the artificers served their apprenticeship for most of their time. The experiences of shipwrights, therefore, do not seem directly comparable to the experiences of other non-gentlemen of the navy such as seamen and inferior warrant officers, carpenters, gunners and mates. The lives of seamen were characterised by their mobility, which often prevented their building stable families on shore, let alone nurturing entrenched networks of support in port-towns or elsewhere.[137] Shipwrights, on the other hand, lived with their families, could engage in local communities and the clear majority served their entire careers in one yard (Table 6.1).

---

[137] Lincoln, *Naval Wives*, 136–137; although Elin Jones also stressed that some naval wives went to sea with their sailor husbands: Jones, 'Masculinity, Materiality and Space', 123 and 146.

Some shipwrights, however, did not serve their whole time in the yard they apprenticed in or the parish in which they were born. Senior dockyard officers often moved between yards to fill vacancies and to gain promotion.[138] Artificer mobility, reflected in their apprenticeship records, gave them the labour confidence to resist the pressures for reform from the Navy Board.[139] Inferior officers such as quartermen also moved to find promotion or to follow their patrons. Jagoe followed his patrons to Woolwich in 1782 and did not return to Plymouth until 1803 after he had established himself and been promoted. Shipwrights also moved between British and overseas yards, often only serving part of their time in stations such as Jamaica or Halifax before returning to Britain.[140] These movements, although organised through Navy Board orders or through petitioning the Admiralty, provided connections between the artificers of different naval yards which could be drawn upon for patronage support. Certainly, Philip MacDougall, in his discussion of late eighteenth-century strike action in the dockyards, stressed that the links between trades within the yards extended to other yards and allowed artificers to contact one another to orchestrate labour force resistance.[141] The mobility of warrant officers and seamen was also largely organised through the Navy Board or Admiralty. Seamen may not have had control over where their ship was to be stationed but nor did many sea officers. Jeremiah Dancy also demonstrated that seamen for ships in home-waters were largely employed through volunteering rather than through impressment.[142] Seamen had volition in their service and that service provided them with connections around the globe.

As we have seen, Markham's mobility in service provided him with a wide-ranging network of multiple weaker ties which fundamentally defined and facilitated his patronage. He did not choose which station he served in but followed Admiralty orders. Yet, his service in the West Indies and the Mediterranean provided him with new network connections who solicited him for patronage when he joined the Admiralty. Involuntary mobility, therefore, did not preclude the creation of networks, but in some cases facilitated wider-ranging networks than would be possible in a less mobile service. The official movement of artificers and seamen may have also assisted their creation of networks which they drew upon for patronage support. Illiteracy and financial restrictions limited the modes of connection maintenance that the lower orders

[138] Knight, 'Sandwich, Middleton and Dockyard Appointments', 180–181.

[139] Morriss, 'Government and Community', 26.

[140] Gwyn, *Ashore and Afloat*, 78.

[141] Philip MacDougall, 'The Changing Nature of the Dockyard Dispute 1790–1840', in Lunn and Day (eds.), *Labour Relations*, 41.

[142] Dancy, *Myth of the Press Gang*, 72.

FEES AND RESISTANCE: LOWER-LEVEL PATRONAGE   251

could use. However, many shipwrights could write or had access to someone in their strong local networks who could.[143] Similarly, at sea, the close-knit communities on ship and in port-towns meant that illiterate seamen also had the means to send letters.[144]

This final section illustrates the degree of artificer mobility between naval yards, from other maritime centres such as Liverpool or Bristol, as well as from smaller river yards, such as Chester, to reveal the extent of potential networks of correspondence and patronage support. Seamen were also drawn to enter the service from port and river towns.[145] Also many shipwrights, sailmakers and riggers served time at sea, so there is considerable overlap in the backgrounds of both artificers and seamen and their potential networks. Both voluntary and official artificer mobility, therefore, provides us with a comparison for the patronage of non-gentlemen ranks in the navy, which are much harder to reconstruct.

This section uses the description books for each of the six major yards, beginning in 1779, to map shipwright movement between yards as well as the geographical dispersal of apprenticeship yards.[146] The books have been amalgamated from smaller records, organising artificers alphabetically (other than the Deptford book) and by trade, with inserts of physical descriptions and work character. Their creation seems to have been instigated by a need to keep track of artificers discharged after the general dockyard strike of 1775, and subsequent local strikes throughout the American Revolutionary War.[147] Crucially, they record where each artificer apprenticed and whether they served in other yards or at sea. The Plymouth description book also records the place or parish where the artificer came from. This allows us to build a picture of artificer backgrounds and their potential connections.[148]

---

[143] A good example of the rate of shipwright literacy is in the signing of records for the payment of superannuation pay, as well as the witnessing of shipwright wills.

[144] Lincoln, *Naval Wives*, 137.

[145] See Dancy's discussion of the background of sailors: Dancy, *Myth of the Press Gang*, 49–51.

[146] TNA, ADM 106/2975, Chatham 1779; ADM 106/2979, Plymouth 1779; ADM 106/2980, Portsmouth 1779; ADM 106/2982, Sheerness 1779; ADM 106/2984, Woolwich 1779; ADM 106/2986, Deptford 1784.

[147] R. J. B. Knight, 'From Impressment to Task Work: Strikes and Disruption in the Royal Dockyards 1688–1788', in Lunn and Day (eds.), *Labour Relations*, 9–10.

[148] The books cover the years up to 1783 or 1791 so the data in this section is not representative of the total number of shipwrights borne in a yard in 1779 but rather of the trend in backgrounds of shipwrights.

252 PATRONAGE AND THE BRITISH NAVY, 1775–1815

Table 6.1   Movement of shipwrights from the yard of their apprenticeship.

Yard	Shipwrights apprenticed in current yard	Shipwrights apprenticed in other naval yards	Shipwrights apprenticed in other naval yards and current yard	Total apprenticed in other naval yards	Shipwrights apprenticed in merchant yards
Portsmouth	582	41	8	49	149
Plymouth	584	44	22	66	285
Chatham	457	26	25	51	40
Sheerness	111	28	13	41	16
Woolwich	178	69	16	85	49
Deptford	191	39	16	55	58
TOTAL	2,103	247	100	347	597

Total apprenticed in other yards: 944

Sources: TNA, ADM 106/2975, Chatham 1779; ADM 106/2979, Plymouth 1779; ADM 106/2980, Portsmouth 1779; ADM 106/2982, Sheerness 1779; ADM 106/2984, Woolwich 1779; ADM 106/2986, Deptford 1784.

As we have seen, apprenticeships are a strong indicator of an individual's network.[149] In Woolwich, many of the apprentices were indentured to their fathers or uncles. Jagoe did not apprentice his own son in the yard, but he instead took on the sons of influential members of the vestry, consolidating his position.[150] Where a shipwright was apprenticed, therefore, reflects his familiar patronage network. Certainly, Table 6.1 shows that 69 per cent of shipwrights remained in the yard they apprenticed in, which suggests that their network was also restricted to the yard and surrounding parish. The Plymouth 1779 description book records artificer parishes as well as their apprentice yard and it shows that most shipwrights in both naval and merchant yards apprenticed in the yard closest to the parish they were born in.[151]

However, Table 6.1 also shows that 11.4 per cent of shipwrights served their apprenticeship in other Royal Naval yards before entering their current yard. Jagoe's network revealed the importance of an apprentice's connection

[149] Catherine Beck, 'Uncovering the Unrecorded: The Patronage of Artificers in the Royal Dockyards 1778–1802', *Transactions of the Naval Dockyard Society* 13 (August 2020), 17–28.

[150] Jagoe's son appears to have been a musician and played the organ in the parish church.

[151] TNA, ADM 106/2979, Plymouth 1779.

FEES AND RESISTANCE: LOWER-LEVEL PATRONAGE 253

to his master for a successful career. Jagoe followed his own master, John Jenner, to Woolwich. Equally, Jagoe's apprentice Watson followed Jagoe to a promotion in Plymouth in 1804. Moving to a yard other than their apprentice yard suggests that shipwrights followed their patrons or were connected in another way to their new yard. Of course, many of the moves may have been organised by the Navy Board to meet wartime demand for shipwrights in certain yards.[152] A shipwright who moved from his apprentice yard also brought with him connections to his extended family, master and colleagues who remained behind. The moves, therefore, created extended networks between the yards which could facilitate the movement of other shipwrights.

Also, not all the shipwrights recorded in Table 6.1 necessarily served their apprenticeship in the same yard as their parish. Only the Plymouth description book records shipwrights' parish of origin, so the data is limited; however, there are individual examples which show that shipwrights born in the parish of one naval yard served their apprenticeship in another. If apprenticeships relied on the familiar connection of the apprentice's family to the shipwright who was to act as master, then these cases of a move from home parish to apprentice yard suggest familiar networks between shipwrights in the Royal Naval yards. John Gill apprenticed in Woolwich but was born in Plymouth dock.[153] Gill was one of the shipwrights mentioned in the naval inquiry into the fees paid for entry into Plymouth yard, represented in Figure 6.1 in the second section of this chapter. When Gill returned to Plymouth yard, he paid £5 to John Treeby, the messenger to the master shipwright, to be entered as a shipwright.[154] Other shipwrights paid much larger gratuities of up to £100 for their entry to the yard, so the £5 fee may reflect Gill's return to his parish network and consequent support. His move to Woolwich for his apprenticeship also supports the trend in Jagoe's network for strong connections between Woolwich and Plymouth shipwrights. The Plymouth description book also includes other examples of shipwrights who moved to Plymouth for their apprenticeship from other yards. John Simson was born in Portsmouth but apprenticed in Plymouth yard.[155] An undated description list of work-gangs in Deptford, c.1807, also records James Trinnaman, who was born in Plymouth dock but served his apprenticeship in Deptford.[156]

---

[152] Gill, *Naval Families*, 207.

[153] TNA, ADM 106/2979, Plymouth 1779.

[154] *Sixth Report*, 419.

[155] TNA, ADM 106/2979, Plymouth 1779.

[156] This document is catalogued as a pay list for Portsmouth. However, many of the shipwrights listed apprenticed in Deptford yard. The only date in the entire document is for a promotion of a quarterman in 1807. This suggests that the list recorded shipwrights employed at Deptford yard in c.1807. On the other hand, the list may record work-gangs of shipwrights who had been transferred to Portsmouth, from

254 PATRONAGE AND THE BRITISH NAVY, 1775–1815

The move from parish of origin to apprentice yard also occurred in the merchant yards. Some were moves to the nearest local yard. William Johnson was listed as being born in Edinburgh and apprenticed in Leith.[157] Some followed trade and sea routes to their closest, largest port. Brothers David and William Hughes were born in Holyhead, Anglesey, but served their apprenticeships in Liverpool and Chester before joining Deptford yard. Robert Mercer also seems to have followed trade routes, as he was born in Hull but served his apprenticeship on the river Thames.

Some moved a more considerable distance. Robert Brown was born in Lancaster but apprenticed in Milbrook, a merchant yard opposite Plymouth, before joining the naval yard.[158] One other shipwright in Plymouth was born and served part of his apprenticeship in Lancaster and was possibly Robert Brown's brother. William Brown entered Plymouth yard in September 1755 and Robert entered in November.[159] Robert Brown potentially forged connections with Plymouth yard when he moved to Milbrook from Lancaster in c.1748, which his brother William may have used to arrange his own entry to the yard before Robert in September. Certainly, there seem to have been strong connections between the naval yards and their surrounding merchant yards. Many of the shipwrights in the 1779 description books who apprenticed in merchant yards came from yards nearby, suggesting that extended networks seen in the rest of this chapter included the surrounding merchant yards. However, the Navy Board also gave incentives to merchant shipwrights to join naval yards at the commencement of a war which naturally drew on the closest yards.[160]

Most shipwrights who served their apprenticeship outside the naval yards did so in yards focused mainly in Cornwall, the south coast, South Wales and the Bristol Channel, the Medway and the Thames. Almost all, except for a few bizarre exceptions, served in coastal communities or in river towns.[161]

Deptford, to meet demand, consequently meaning that many of the shipwrights in the list will have apprenticed at Deptford. Because of this uncertainty this list has been used sparingly in this analysis and does not appear in any of the tables of shipwright numbers or maps of distribution of apprentice yards. However, the individual examples reflect the movement history of shipwrights, regardless of whether they served in Deptford or Portsmouth at the time the list was created. The list is referred to as the Deptford pay list for c.1807 in the body of this chapter, but will be referenced as the Portsmouth pay list to avoid confusion. TNA, ADM 30/62, Pay List for shipwrights (Portsmouth) 1800.

[157] TNA, ADM 106/2979, Plymouth 1779.

[158] TNA, ADM 106/2979, Plymouth 1779.

[159] Ibid., f.10.

[160] Morriss, 'Government and Community', 22.

[161] One shipwright in Portsmouth yard was recorded as having apprenticed in Tyndrum, in the Scottish Highlands, and another in Plymouth as having apprenticed in Buxton in Derbyshire.

FEES AND RESISTANCE: LOWER-LEVEL PATRONAGE

However, the wide dispersal of apprentice yards suggests that not all moves from merchant yards to naval yards were motivated by Navy Board orders. Shipwrights voluntarily moved to the larger naval yards for the benefits of guaranteed service, medical care and potential access to superannuation pay.[162] As we have seen in Jagoe's career and in the Plymouth gratuities, entry to the yards relied on friendship networks. The brothers Robert and William Brown from Lancaster and David and William Hughes from Anglesey moving to the same naval yards together suggests that moves to naval yards were not all coincidence or arbitrary official decisions but were motivated by familiar connection. In this case, the geographical span of the yards where shipwrights served their apprenticeships shows the extent of the potential familiar networks that facilitated appointments in the six major yards.

Movement to yards was also not solely motivated by geographical proximity. Several shipwrights came from Scottish ports. William Buchan entered Plymouth yard in March 1749 having apprenticed on the river Forth in Stirling. Similarly, Thomas Adams entered Plymouth in January 1778 from his apprenticeship in Borrowstouness near Falkirk in the Firth of Forth. One Scottish shipwright who entered Plymouth yard also apprenticed on the Isle of May at the mouth of the Firth of Forth.[163] There was a naval base at Leith, where three shipwrights in Plymouth, Portsmouth and Sheerness served their apprenticeships.[164] Equally, the port-towns of Dundee and Aberdeen provided shipwrights to the major yards. Hector Lyall entered Portsmouth yard in April 1780 having just served his apprenticeship in Dundee.[165] Jonathan McCure entered Deptford yard in June 1755 aged around 32 and so had probably served part of his time in Aberdeen where he was apprenticed.[166]

Several shipwrights also came from port-towns in Wales. Jonathan Evans entered Deptford yard in February 1771 having served his apprenticeship in Aberystwyth.[167] Fifteen shipwrights who entered Plymouth yard had served their apprenticeships in Swansea and six in Milford Haven, before the new yard at Milford was built between 1801 and 1809.[168] Coming from outside the yard's parish also did not prevent these shipwrights from integrating in the yard community or gathering influence. Evan Davis entered Plymouth yard in October 1755 having apprenticed in Tenby, but rose to quarterman and was allowed one apprentice.[169]

---

[162] Morriss, 'Government and Community', 22–23.
[163] TNA, ADM 106/2979, Plymouth 1779.
[164] Ibid.; ADM 106/2980, Portsmouth 1779; ADM 106/2982, Sheerness 1779.
[165] TNA, ADM 106/2980, Portsmouth 1779.
[166] TNA, ADM 106/2986, Deptford 1784.
[167] Ibid.
[168] TNA, ADM 106/2979, Plymouth 1779.
[169] Ibid.

256   PATRONAGE AND THE BRITISH NAVY, 1775–1815

Shipwrights also joined the naval yards having apprenticed in other large ports, particularly Dublin, Bristol, Hull, Liverpool and the ports on the Tyne: Newcastle, Gateshead, and North and South Shields. Deptford and Plymouth had the most shipwrights from large trade ports, probably because they were surrounded by other merchant yards to which merchant shipwrights may have moved before entering the naval yard. For example, a shipwright apprenticed in the north-west could travel on board a merchant vessel to these ports and then gain entry to the naval yard once they had established connections in the community. By 1813, the Navy Board actually posted adverts in large ports such as Liverpool and Hull, to draw merchant shipwrights to the naval yards. During the labour crisis caused by St Vincent's attempts at reform and the reductions he made in the yards, shipwrights were given passes from Liverpool to the southern naval yards in the tenders transporting impressed seamen.[170] Those apprenticed in naval depots and docks associated with the navy, such as Deal, Falmouth, Harwich and Yarmouth, could similarly seek passage on naval vessels to travel to the larger yards. In this case, the movement of shipwrights to the naval yards may have been initially one of convenience; the incentives of pay and security drew them to join the navy, and they went to whichever yard they could get to by naval or merchant ship.

Certainly, some shipwrights served time at sea in between their move from their apprentice yard to the naval yard, because the dates of their sea service are listed in the description book. William Buchan, who had apprenticed in Stirling, served seven years at sea before his entry to Plymouth yard.[171] Hector Lyall also served one month at sea, which suggests he joined the navy at Dundee, travelled to the south coast and then joined Portsmouth yard in 1780.[172] Interestingly this was also the case for labourers and other artificers who came from Scotland or Ireland. James Hall, a riggers labourer from Aberdeen, entered Plymouth yard in June 1778 after serving five years at sea. James German, a sawyer from Limerick, entered Plymouth in November 1767 after serving seven years at sea.[173] Serving at sea may have given shipwrights and artificers from merchant yards the experience to be taken on in a naval yard. Their mobility through their sea service may have also given them connections in the major naval ports which they later drew upon for entry.

Many shipwrights who served in overseas yards also served some time at sea, which suggests that they either joined the navy as carpenters and then decided to join a yard, or they used their sea service to journey to Britain. Daniel Harriott entered Plymouth in July 1782 having apprenticed in Bermuda but serving six years at sea. Similarly, Benjamin Philips entered Plymouth

[170] Morriss, *Royal Dockyards*, 107.
[171] TNA, ADM 106/2979, Plymouth 1779.
[172] TNA, ADM 106/2980, Portsmouth 1779.
[173] TNA, ADM 106/2979, Plymouth 1779.

FEES AND RESISTANCE: LOWER-LEVEL PATRONAGE 257

in November 1781 from Philadelphia having served four years at sea.[174] Harriott and Philips both served during the American Revolutionary War so they probably joined the navy initially, when demand for their services on board ships was high, and later decided to join the dockyards, perhaps once their ships had been paid off.

Certainly, the description books show that not all of the shipwrights who apprenticed in overseas yards served at sea. Shipwrights came from having apprenticed in naval yards in Port Royal and Kingston, Jamaica, Halifax, Nova Scotia and Gibraltar.[175] Naval ships frequently sailed between these ports, meaning that shipwrights could send letters and gifts or, like Daniel Harriott, could return to Britain. Many shipwrights in these communities also often left family connections back in Britain and maintained connection to home ports. Mary West in Woolwich petitioned the Admiralty to have the wages of Solomon West, a shipwright in Jamaica, paid to her on his authority.[176] She also requested that shipwright Thomas Travers's wages be paid to her from Jamaica.[177] Solomon West may have been Mary West's husband or, perhaps, her brother. Thomas Travers may have also been related through marriage or was perhaps a familiar or business connection. West's petition reveals the extent of connection to Britain from foreign yards, which may have even provided the facility for the movement to British yards of shipwrights who apprenticed abroad. Shipwrights also came from other foreign ports. Two shipwrights came from Boston, Massachusetts to Plymouth. The first was George Fisher who entered in January 1756, and the second was Thomas Blyth who entered in 1770.[178] Another, James Marven, entered Portsmouth in February 1782 from Providence in Rhode Island.[179]

Movement from foreign yards was also not restricted to shipwrights. Some artificers also apprenticed in overseas yards. William Willoughby, a smith, entered Deptford in July 1785 from Boston. Jeremiah Hancock, a rigger, entered Plymouth yard in September 1770 from New York.[180] The riggers were the most mobile of the artificers, many of them also serving many years at sea. Both John Burley and Peter Lawson were riggers at Plymouth who were recorded as having been born in Stockholm. They both had also served over twenty years at sea and so are perhaps the most directly comparable to

---

[174] Ibid.

[175] TNA, ADM 106/2986, Deptford 1784; ADM 106/2982, Sheerness 1779.

[176] TNA, ADM 106/1262/340, Petition of Mary West of Woolwich to the Admiralty, 10 April 1780.

[177] TNA, ADM 106/1262/338, Petition of Mary West of Woolwich to the Admiralty, 4 April 1780.

[178] TNA, ADM 106/2979, Plymouth 1779.

[179] TNA, ADM 106/2980, Portsmouth 1779.

[180] TNA, ADM 106/2979, Plymouth 1779.

the sort of patronage networks seamen had after a long career in the navy. A study of the parish connections of riggers may provide interesting comparisons with the sea service, and is a strong topic for future research.

These moves, however, may have been influenced by the need for shipwrights during mobilisation and not the result of shipwrights drawing on their extended networks. Rather, shipwrights in busy trade ports answered the Navy Board's call for artificers to meet the demand for the building and repair of ships. Presumably, those with enough capital could also 'make friends' with key brokers in the yards like Robert Duins, the clerk to the master shipwright at Plymouth, to allow their entry on their arrival. However, if shipwrights entered voluntarily, or even if they entered by Navy Board order, once they were in the yard they forged connections to their colleagues and became integrated in local communities, just as Jagoe had done at Woolwich. Having apprenticed in a merchant yard outside the local community was not a bar on promotion or being allowed apprentices within the yard, so we can assume there was little prejudice towards coming from a naval or merchant establishment. Many of the shipwrights were also married with children, some in a time-frame which suggests they married locally. Jonathan Garrett, aged 27, who entered Deptford in July 1778 after serving his apprenticeship in Halifax, Nova Scotia, was married and had one child.[181] Others, however, may have brought their families with them. Thomas Blyth, who entered from Boston, was married with seven children, an impressive feat if he had married a local woman, having only entered in 1770.[182] Of course, this does not account for second marriages, step-children, twins or if the children were born close together, which was not unusual. Some shipwrights may also have served in a local merchant yard before entering the naval yard and so could still have married locally even if the number of children they had from their date of entry seems unreasonably high. Either way, the second section of this chapter showed the importance of women in the Plymouth patronage system, so having a local wife, or indeed any female relation living with them, would assist their entry to the yard.

The Woolwich description book for 1802 and the pay list for Deptford c.1807 also show that the trend for shipwrights who had apprenticed in naval yards was not restricted to the 1770s and the American Revolutionary War. Even after the peacetime reductions of 1802, Woolwich had more shipwrights who had apprenticed in merchant yards than those who had apprenticed in the other six main naval yards.[183] Out of the 251 shipwrights listed in the Deptford list, 63.3 per cent were from merchant yards or smaller naval bases, the largest of any of the lists included in this study.[184] The list may have been created

[181] TNA, ADM 106/2986, Deptford 1784.
[182] TNA, ADM 106/2979, Plymouth 1779.
[183] TNA, ADM 106/2895. Woolwich 1802.
[184] TNA, ADM30/62, Pay List for shipwrights (Portsmouth) 1800.

FEES AND RESISTANCE: LOWER-LEVEL PATRONAGE 259

to record work-gangs which contained shipwrights from other yards rather than those who apprenticed in Deptford or naval yards. However, the number listed is in line with the peacetime reductions of 1802 and the subsequent increase again in 1803 at the recommencement of the war, so it is probably representative of the makeup of Deptford yard.[185] In this case, corroborated by the statistics from Woolwich yard, shipwrights clearly continued to enter the naval yards after serving their apprenticeship in merchant yards in both war and peace, and not just as a result of incentives during mobilisation.

In 1779 and 1802, therefore, there were established communities in the naval yards of shipwrights who had come from across Britain and abroad. These shipwrights may have influenced the entry of shipwrights coming from their home-towns or apprentice yards. Some of the wills of the Woolwich shipwrights show a network of family ties beyond Woolwich itself. Thomas Guyer had a niece who married a glazier in Windsor.[186] Benjamin Pidcock had numerous relations and inherited a freehold in Derbyshire.[187] Also his daughter-in-law, Katharine Mary Constable, was from St Kitts in the West Indies.[188] In this way, far from being isolated or completely dependent on local communities, the demography of the dockyards reveals that the lower orders of society had wide-ranging networks. These connections could be drawn upon for patronage in the same way as Markham's weaker ties drew on their connection to him at the Admiralty.

The movement of shipwrights between yards and to service at sea after their apprenticeships also provides ground for comparison with warrant officers and seamen. 11.8 per cent of shipwrights at Portsmouth had served at sea. Other artificers such as sailmakers and riggers also usually served a part of their career at sea. Navy Board In-Letters reveal that at least some appointments of shipwrights to ships were made by the recommendation of the ship's captain. Captain Samuel Barrington applied to have Charles Beeler, of Woolwich yard, entered as the carpenter's mate of *Venus* in 1770.[189] Similarly, shipwright William Knight was recommended by the master shipwright at Woolwich to Captain John Raynor to act as carpenter's mate on board the sloop *Swift*.[190]

[185] Morriss, *Royal Dockyards*, 106.

[186] TNA, PROB 11/2123/368, Will of Thomas Guyer, Shipwright of Woolwich, 1850.

[187] TNA PROB 11/1279/79, Will of Benjamin Pidcock, Gentleman of Woolwich, Kent, 1796.

[188] TNA, HO 107/1588, 1851 Census Woolwich Dockyard Parish: Woolwich (1,6), Katharine Mary Pidcock wife to Benjamin Pidcock born 1787.

[189] TNA, ADM 106/1185/270, Navy Board In-Letters, Captain Barrington, 10 October 1770.

[190] TNA, ADM 106/1180/64, Navy Board In-Letters, petition of William Knight, 20 June 1769.

260 PATRONAGE AND THE BRITISH NAVY, 1775–1815

A key difference between dockyard patronage and that available to seamen was the direct involvement of women. The wives of dockyard artificers appear in the record as points of connection between intermarrying families, like the Raynes and the Canhams, or Jagoe's daughter and Joseph Brain in Woolwich yard. The report on gratuities in Plymouth yard also showed that women acted as vital brokers and patronage facilitators within dockyard and community networks. As with the male vestry connections in James Jagoe's network, female connections transcended status and hierarchy in the yard, connecting labourers to the clerk to the master shipwright. These connections were most likely maintained by face-to-face meetings and mutual support in childcare and sharing of resources, one of the cornerstones of lower-level social networks.[191]

The Portsmouth cabin-keeper, William Webber, recorded the sorts of social activity where dockyard artificers and their female relations maintained female-to-female and community connections. He recorded that a female-only cricket match was played at Milton on Monday 14 March 1813.[192] He also mentioned going to 'Richard's house' for tea and supper as well as he and his wife Sally looking after the house of someone named 'Bill' after his wedding.[193] A study of female networks in the naval port-towns may reveal the same mechanisms in place for seamen. Certainly, Mary Higg, mentioned in Chapter 5, acted as a link to the Admiralty for seamen and warrant officers. Higg's position was maintained through her ownership of a boarding house in Plymouth dock, but she was not directly tied to any male relations at sea, which highlights how women could participate within these networks without male relations of their own and would not otherwise appear in Admiralty or Navy Board records.[194] Higg's independence, and Mrs Duins and Mrs Rippon in Plymouth acting as vital, status-crossing brokers, suggests that female connections of seamen were also the main patronage facilitators on shore.

Involvement in the local religious community also in many ways differentiates dockyard patronage from lower-level sea-going patronage. The vestry at Woolwich offered men who came from outside the yard a chance to establish themselves and their wives and children within the local parish community in positions which would also act as guarantees of their character and behaviour. The vestry, in some ways, acted as an environmental broker, recommending men like Jagoe to his superior officers for promotion and to be allowed more apprentices, because he proved himself reliable in his work in the community and his connection to other parish officers.

---

[191] Ben-Amos, *Culture of Giving*, 45–46.

[192] Field, 'Diary of a Portsmouth Dockyard Worker', 51.

[193] Ibid., 57 and 63.

[194] See insurance records for property on George Street: LMA, MS 11936/359/555858, Records of Sun Fire Office 28 March 1789.

FEES AND RESISTANCE: LOWER-LEVEL PATRONAGE   261

Religious community also affected connection and patronage in Portsmouth yard. John Field, the transcriber of the diary of William Webber, stressed that there was a strong tradition of non-conformist churches in the dockyard towns which transcended hierarchical connection. In the non-conformist church in Portsmouth, ordinary shipwrights were active members alongside the master attendant, who was an officer of a similar status to the master shipwright who was in charge of all the ships coming in and out of the yard.[195] Studies have been done into the connections between a patron's religion and his role in office. Gareth Atkins has looked into the evangelism of Charles Middleton and whether he promoted his religious friends above all others. However, Atkins demonstrated that this was not the case with Middleton's distribution of patronage, nor did Markham's religiosity and ties to the Anglican church through his father overtly influence his distribution of patronage.[196]

There are similarities but not direct comparisons to be drawn in relation to the operation of lower-level patronage in the dockyard and at sea. At an essential level, the demography and culture on board ship, as well as isolation from local communities and female brokers, changed lower-level patronage at sea. Woolwich yard had a full complement of 900 artificers, labourers and wardens.[197] Within that the yard had 286 shipwrights, 233 other artificers and 234 labourers and scavelmen. A 74-gun third rate like *Centaur* was designed for a full complement of 640 men. When Markham sailed in 1800 he mustered 540 men: 491 in the ship's company, 32 volunteer boys, 93 marines, and one 'widow's man' where the wages of one man were given to the superannuation of a seaman or his widow.[198] Unlike the dockyards, there were more labourers than artificers in a ship's company in the sense that the ordinary seamen and able-seamen far outnumbered carpenters and riggers. The demands of the ship also enforced a very rigid hierarchy that artificers moving between yard and sea famously baulked at. Roger Morriss highlights a case in 1782 where a shipwright was beaten on board *Diomede* while it was in dock at Plymouth, which he then complained of to the Admiralty.[199]

The cross-status connections apparent in the largely skilled and, therefore, valuable workforce of the dockyards, and the involvement in a stable community such as the local parish church, gave dockyard artificers considerably more patronage power than seamen. However, seamen had wide-ranging connections similar to the connections of shipwrights explored here. Their wives and families often lived in port-towns alongside dockyard workers, and artificers

---

[195] Field, 'Diary of a Portsmouth Dockyard Worker', 48.

[196] Gareth Atkins, 'Religion, Politics and Patronage in the Late Hanoverian Navy c.1780–c.1820', *Historical Research* 88:240 (2015), 272–290.

[197] TNA, ADM 106/2895, Woolwich 1802.

[198] TNA, ADM36/14166, HMS *Centaur* 18 February–November 1800.

[199] Morriss, 'Government and Community', 28.

served both in port and at sea. Therefore, the two groups were not necessarily distinct from one another. The mobility of shipwrights provides us with a comparison for the sea service. Shipwrights coming from merchant yards managed to enter the strong friendship networks in the naval yards which controlled entry and promotion, despite the distance of their apprentice yards and the associated connections. Either they did it through Navy Board orders, or there were familiar connections between naval and merchant yards which are invisible to us today. There may, therefore, have also been similar networks between the non-gentleman ranks of the sea service.

Conclusion

Patronage was rooted firmly in local and religious communities for the lower levels in the Royal Dockyards. Their involvement in the church meant that hierarchical barriers in the yard could be surpassed. Elite officers in the yard tapped into these networks in order to choose who to promote to inferior officer positions. The position of men like Jagoe spanned the elite and the non-elite of the yard. He rose to an elite position, but he did so slowly, and assisted by both his patrons above him in the hierarchy and his association with other dockyard men within the church. Undoubtedly, his reputation as a 'good workman' was also vital in his ability to rise. As with service at sea, patronage relied on both merit and connection. Those workmen who had bad character were the ones who moved most frequently between yards, highlighting the importance of local parish communities. Even those who served in overseas yards, where chances of promotion were higher, often returned to the yard of the parish in which they born or the one in which they were apprenticed.

Some yards often exchanged workers, such as Sheerness and Chatham or Woolwich and Plymouth. This can be partly explained by their proximity to one another and demand for labour depending on the course of the war. Sheerness and Chatham often exchanged men because they needed to grow and decrease rapidly depending on what ships were being refitted and where the major action of the war was happening, in the Channel or in the Mediterranean.[200] The connection between Woolwich and Plymouth is a little more obscure. Of all the yards, Plymouth received the most men who had trained in merchant yards. But the men who appear at Woolwich were all apprenticed in the royal yard at Plymouth. This suggests that the motivating factor was a network that extended between Woolwich and Plymouth, perhaps forged principally through the movement of elite officers such as Jenner or Manley, but then reinforced by the movement of inferior officers who became entrenched in the local communities, like James Jagoe, William Sture and Robert Rundle. For

[200] Morriss, *Royal Dockyards*, 98.

these men, involvement in the vestry was of even more importance perhaps than in the local parish. It gave them connections within the new yard, their wives and children connections in the local community, and above all else acted as a guarantee of good character.

As much as with elite social circles, patronage formed a part of lower-level social machinery, which is at its most obvious in dockyard communities. The cross-status integration of shipwrights in the church and through marriages gave them community power which most importantly acted as guarantee of their character and trustworthiness for the more mobile officers coming into the yard, outside that community. Just as Markham relied on the trusted recommendations of officers he had served with to appoint lieutenants, principal officers of the dockyard relied on the recommendations of the men deeply involved in the local community and, therefore, who had the most to lose from a bad recommendation. It was the same system which facilitated career promotion and informal support.

CONCLUSION

> I have no connection with him, but should be happy if it were in my power in the smallest degree to promote the welfare of a Man who is I understand as remarkable for the performance of domestic duties as for the high spirit and intrepidity of an English seaman.
>
> Matthew Montagu to Earl Spencer, 27 November 1798[1]

Edward Riou was invalided from the West Indies with a severe attack of yellow fever in 1794, and was out of active service for four years. In 1795, he secured command of a royal yacht, *Princess Augusta*, so did not languish on half-pay as so many other officers did, and once his health had improved by 1798, he personally applied to Lord Spencer in visits and by letter for a more active situation.[2] When his efforts were rebuffed by the Admiralty, he sought Montagu's assistance despite being personally unknown to him. Spencer told Montagu in a prompt reply to his letter in November that he chose not to appoint Riou to a command because he was concerned Riou's health would not bear winter service:

> I shall be very happy to employ Capt Riou when I have a ship at my disposal which will be properly calculated for him and I hope that his health will be such as to enable him to undertake the charge. My doubts upon which point have been a great measure the cause of his not having been more actively employed some time since.[3]

Riou had a long, distinguished career. As a midshipman, he served with Captain Charles Clerke on *Discovery*, part of James Cook's third voyage to the Pacific in 1776. He also captured the imagination of the eighteenth-century public and secured his promotion to post-captain when he saved almost his entire crew, and the convicts he was transporting, from *Guardian*

---

[1]   NMM, RUSI/NM/235/ER/4/3.

[2]   See NMM, RUSI/NM/235/ER/4/3, Riou to Spencer, 16 March 1798, 8 August 1798 and 11 November 1798.

[3]   NMM, RUSI/NM/235/ER/4/3, Spencer to Montagu, 27 November 1798.

CONCLUSION

when it struck an iceberg *en route* to Australia in 1789.[4] He embodied the naval ideals of fortitude, duty to the service and strict moral character. He also had a reputation for modesty and steadiness, central to the values which marked naval patronage. Thomas Byam Martin described him as: 'Free from the arrogance and foolishness of the enthusiast, he entertained a deep sense of every Christian obligation; it was this that gave him a serenity of mind which no peril, however sudden and appalling, could disturb; it was his sheet anchor.'[5] Even so, Riou remained out of active service for another seven months before finally securing the frigate *Amazon* in June 1799.

Riou's career provides a counterpoint to Markham's. Riou entered the navy in 1774 and served with Markham as a midshipman aboard *Romney* in 1775.[6] As Chapter 2 demonstrated, Markham had multiple, powerful connections who ensured that, by the end of the American Revolutionary War, he passed as lieutenant and made post-captain. Markham was by no means a bad sailor, but neither was his career exceptional. Rather, his time in the navy was characterised by the influence of his connections and his ability to foster the goodwill of his superiors. Riou, on the other hand, was not as well-connected, although he did have acquaintances who acted on his behalf. Indeed, in a letter to Spencer in 1798, Riou mentioned that Charles Greville had recommended him to the command of *Princess Augusta* in 1795, which prevented him recovering from his illness on half-pay.[7] He also made lieutenant before the end of the war in 1780.[8] His career was marked by his securing appointments which allowed him to distinguish himself, like serving on Cook's voyages. He was far from being unsuccessful, but rather his success was more intimately associated with his service than Markham's had been.

Yet, Markham's career progressed more quickly. When he was invalided from the West Indies, a year after Riou, he was only out of active service for two years, and that seemed to be largely voluntary. He recovered from his illness, married his wife Maria, and when he was well again, he secured command of *Centaur* in 1797.[9] Of course, we speculated in Chapter 1 about how ill Markham was when he left *Hannibal* in 1795, so perhaps the speed of his regaining a command reflects his better health rather than his stronger patronage. Markham also owed much of his later success to having befriended St Vincent, who approved of Markham's steady temperament and liked his willingness to bend to his somewhat draconian personality and style of

[4]   M. D. Nash, 'Riou, Edward', *ODNB*, vol. 46, 998–999.
[5]   Richard Vessey-Hamilton (ed.), *Letters and Papers of Admiral of the Fleet Sir Thomas Byam Martin, 1773–1854* (NRS, 1902), i.44.
[6]   Markham, *A Naval Career*, 27.
[7]   NMM, RUSI/NM/235/ER/4/3, Riou to Spencer, 11 November 1798.
[8]   Nash, 'Riou, Edward'.
[9]   Markham, *A Naval Career*, 120–134.

command.[10] The contrast in Riou and Markham's careers, however, highlights the impact of connections, both inside and outside of the navy, on naval promotion. Contrary to the ideals represented in solicitation letters, which emphasised meritorious service coupled with an expectation for modesty in not over-emphasising skill or need, even a model officer like Riou needed connection to succeed.

The role of connection in naval history has not been ignored. It is a histo-riographical commonplace to present merit and connection operating alongside one another in naval advancement. N. A. M. Rodger argued that patronage was the 'spring which drove the machine of naval promotion' entirely because it relied on well-connected officers promoting talented subordinates.[11] Recent works by S. A. Cavell, Evan Wilson and Ellen Gill all stress that an officer needed a combination of talent and friends to further his career.[12] Some studies, such as Michael Lewis's early survey, have focused a little too much on the abuses of the system and in making judgements of whether an officer's skill, or meritorious service, really deserved the promotions he received.[13] This book has not followed this line. It has not built a database of applicants' patronage success to judge whether it was deserved or not. The success of applications is extremely difficult to gauge on an individual basis, let alone for all the correspondents within the collection. Secondly, patronage corruption, although the rallying cry of many reformers in the French Revolutionary and Napoleonic wars, obscures the reality that patronage was unavoidable.[14] In essence, patronage did not disappear with the advent of examinations and the rise of the working class. The term merely became subsumed within broader conceptions of reputation, friendship and trust.[15]

Whether an officer, artificer, seaman, or their relations recognised their role in patronage, they were part of the system which formed the structure of eighteenth-century society. When a government official made an appointment based on an applicant's merit, he bestowed a patronage favour. When an individual

[10] Rodger, *Command of the Ocean*, 476–477 and 479; Davey, *In Nelson's Wake*, 35 and 139.

[11] Rodger, *Wooden World*, 301.

[12] Wilson, *British Naval Officers*, 127–129; Cavell, *Midshipmen and the Quarterdeck Boys*, 101–103 and 200; Gill, *Naval Families*, 137.

[13] Lewis, *A Social History of the Navy*, 226–227.

[14] Bourne, *Patronage and Society*, 16–21; Philip Harling, *The Waning of 'Old Corruption': The Politics of Economical Reform in Britain 1779–1846* (Oxford, 1996), 1–2 and 15–17; Joanna Innes, '"Reform" in English Public Life: The Fortunes of a Word', in A. Burns and J. Innes (eds.), *Rethinking the Age of Reform: Britain 1780–1850* (Cambridge, 2003), 87–89.

[15] Sunderland, *Social Capital*, 1–14; Basil Greenhill and Ann Giffard, *Steam, Politics and Patronage: The Transformation of the Royal Navy 1815–1854* (London, 1994); Bourne, *Patronage and Society*, 187–191.

CONCLUSION 267

passed on the recommendation of a close friend, they acted as broker. When the wife of a naval captain asked for advice from an Admiralty commissioner on how to solve her husband's poor situation, she made a patronage request. Patronage was much more than direct applications for assistance or bestowals of favour, it was the maintenance of intricate networks of support which were susceptible to both offence and fashion.

In the navy, the style of patronage varied greatly depending on the location of an officer's network or the station in which they served. Disease and types of service affected the number and profitability of vacancies available. Access to gift-goods and local connections also made some stations more desirable than others. This meant that certain stations were extremely competitive, causing recommendations and the quality of an officer's connections to be vital in the distribution of limited appointments. The distance of a station from the Admiralty, and the consequent difficulties in the communication of orders, also determined who an officer had to approach to secure an appointment. In stations like the East Indies where the commander-in-chief had considerable control, he took advantage to promote his own following. The Admiralty dominated appointments in home-waters and increasingly annexed the distribution of appointments in the Mediterranean to satisfy demand from influential applicants in Britain who had the power to topple the ministry. However, the Admiralty was also open to requests from commissioned and warrant officers across the navy, and previous acquaintance was not as essential as in stations controlled by the networks of the senior admirals. It was not a question of the morality of Admiralty control or captain autonomy, but rather, how the geography of the navy determined access to brokers and patrons.

Patronage, after all, was personal. It was a system of trust, whereby a patron trusted that the request made to them was for the good of their service, their ministry, their local parish or their family. As with all hiring practices, the manager took it on trust that the applicant was telling the truth about their professional ability or moral character.[16] Personal acquaintance acted as a guarantee of that trust, especially if strengthened by affective friendship. Gentility carried connotations of honour and duty, which meant that an individual's social rank could also act as a guarantee, where strong personal affection with the patron was lacking.[17] This is why members of the nobility wielded such considerable brokering power. It is also why members of the lower orders of society, such as the skilled craftsmen of the dockyards, did not wield the same recommendation power as the Navy Board or Admiralty.[18]

---

[16] Sunderland, *Social Capital*, 207; for sociological discussion of reputation and trust see Lin, *Social Capital*, 147–149.

[17] Wilson, *British Naval Officers*, 196–200.

[18] Knight, 'Sandwich, Middleton and Dockyard Appointments', 179.

268   PATRONAGE AND THE BRITISH NAVY, 1775–1815

However, other values of competence, religious responsibility and the payment of gratuities acted as guarantees within their own networks.

An individual's network, therefore, was moulded by their need for patronage, as well as shaping their ability to access and distribute it. Intimate connections drawn from family and affective friendships provided a stable core of support. Markham's early network was centred on his family in Yorkshire and their London houses in Bloomsbury Square and South Audley Street. His father's connections formed his social circle, supported his initial entry into the navy and secured his speedy promotions. Later in his career, his social circle was centred on his wife, Maria, who acted as a connection to him for their friends when he served at sea. The weaker ties in Markham's network, however, facilitated his distribution of patronage to a greater degree.

Even a fraction of those mentioned in John and Maria's correspondence as visiting them, or writing to them, reveal the proliferation of weaker ties in Markham's immediate social circle. As social equals, these connections could use their position in the shared social circle to approach Maria and to make requests face-to-face. The benefit of an informal face-to-face meeting was that the request could be couched even more firmly in terms of affective friendship than in a letter, where the artifice was more apparent. The very act of a visit in some ways presented the connection as closer than it may have been.[19] Also, depending on the applicant's social status, or their level of interconnection with other prominent members of a social circle, Maria would not have been able to politely refuse their requests.[20] The patronage partnerships between men and women in marriage, in some ways, mediated this. A wife could approach a patron in difficult situations where requests for removal from dangerous or unprofitable service compromised a man's honour. Equally, a wife could draw on tropes of her naivety to excuse refusals to requests from influential, but troublesome, members of her social circle. Brokers made it easier for more connections to solicit a patron, but they also protected the patron from the displeasure of a client in refusing their request. Even so, Markham was wary of allowing Maria to over-extend her social circle and bring him into connection with people who he felt would be more difficult to refuse because of their social status.

Markham's wide network of correspondence from his naval connections also reveals the variety of men in the navy who would have considered Markham their 'friend' at the Admiralty. Some strengthened their connection through their integration with his familiar network, particularly through

---

[19] Whyman, *Sociability and Power*, 94–95; Ingrid H. Tague, *Women of Quality: Accepting and Contesting Ideals of Femininity in England, 1690–1760* (Woodbridge, 2002), 197 and 221; Chalus, *Elite Women*, 83–87.

[20] Whyman, *Sociability and Power*, 95–96; Granovetter, 'Strength of Weak Ties', 1361–1362.

CONCLUSION   269

the association of their wives with Maria. This was primarily motivated by intimate and affectionate friendships, but it was also driven by a practical need for mutual support between naval wives in their separation from their husbands. Naval wives supported one another by sharing news they received from husbands serving abroad to alleviate the worries of their friends who had heard nothing because of the difficulties of communication.[21] Being able to ask for patronage, couched in terms of affectionate assistance, rather than troublesome demands, meant there was less strain on requests from these connections. Patronage access was not the motivating factor in their formation, but it was an essential by-product.

Some of Markham's naval connections maintained their relationship with him through the giving of gifts such as wine or by offering reciprocal favours in the form of vacancies he could fill on their ships. Others had connection through their shared service or mutual rank. The senior admirals in command of squadrons and fleets had ample cause to write to Markham about official administration. But this also acted to strengthen their connection to him so that they were also able to ask for patronage favours. The patronage requests made from his naval connections varied greatly in style. Many requests for appointments or promotion were subsumed within wider correspondence about naval organisation. These letters were couched in terms of duty and expedience. A sense of duty legitimised the entitlement of officers who believed they deserved to be considered first, because of their position on the seniority list. Markham's response to applicants who voiced their displeasure, however, reveals that Admiralty patronage relied just as much on carefully maintained personal connections as any other form of eighteenth-century patronage.

The veneer of duty meant that, so long as applicants trod the line between modesty and demanding assistance, they could forge a personal connection through their need for patronage alone. Gill's close reading of familial correspondence reveals this tension in young officers and she argued that they 'drew a fine line between acceptable and unacceptable intervention in their naval careers'.[22] Duty and merit were intimately tied, and most officers saw patronage as a means for their skills to be recognised and advanced.[23] The entitlement found in political requests was not entirely absent, but rather was grounded in a belief that, as a hard-serving, patriotic officer, they deserved to be employed.

Of course, most officers were not in a position to demand attention or even to imply that their service required their employment. A great many

---

[21] Lincoln, *Naval Wives*, 65–66; Gill, *Naval Families*, 67–74.

[22] Gill, *Naval Families*, 105.

[23] Wilson, *British Naval Officers*, 127–129; Rodger, 'Honour and Duty at Sea, 1660–1815', 425–447.

270   PATRONAGE AND THE BRITISH NAVY, 1775–1815

officers remained lieutenants for their entire careers.[24] They consequently phrased their applications to Markham carefully. Brevity was key, but their sense of duty, willingness to serve and fortitude to bear their situation if they must, characterised their letters. Their restricted position meant that the reciprocity implicit in other requests became lost within tropes of charity. In these instances, female brokers could further emphasise distress where male writers were bound by their stoicism and duty not to express it.[25]

The variety of female styles of application serves to highlight that there was a naval style of solicitation letter distinct from civilian trends. Naval style was brief, direct and emphasised long service and fortitude, which translated as a flexibility in where they were willing to serve. Writers, of course, embellished where needed, or included other tropes of male and female anxiety and affective friendship. Most of all, this naval style was vague about the 'obligation' created by the exchange, which obscured the reciprocity at the heart of naval patronage. This opened naval patronage beyond the personal, allowing for applicants to approach Admiralty commissioners even without previous acquaintance or introduction.

The same patronage structures existed for those lower down the social scale. The exchange of money and fees for apprenticeships and entry to the dockyards was part of wider gift-giving practices, which included the giving of wine as seen in Markham's network, used to strengthen bonds.[26] Gentility did not act as a guarantee in recommendations, but rather moral character and involvement in religious communities. The importance of female networks is stark in the artificer patronage of Plymouth in Chapter 5, as is the potential extent of shipwright connections between the naval and merchant yards throughout Britain and across the Atlantic. The social circumstances of Jagoe at Woolwich were undoubtedly different from those of Markham, as an admiral and a gentleman, but they both relied on the trust relationships of their colleagues, friends and families to secure their positions and to assist those around them.

This book has gone further than previous studies of patronage. It has empirically established the active involvement of non-elite men and women in patronage as patrons and brokers, rather than simply supplicants or the objects of charity. Its analysis of the implicit forms of participation alongside the more obvious role played by men like Markham has uncovered the operation of patronage beneath layers of familial, bureaucratic and cultural pressure. This redefines how scholars of eighteenth-century Britain, the navy and other

---

[24] Rodger, 'Commissioned Officers' Careers', 101–102 and 119; Wilson, *British Naval Officers*, 38–41.

[25] Lincoln, *Naval Wives*, 66–67.

[26] Ben-Amos, *Culture of Giving*, 105 and 173.

CONCLUSION 271

institutions conceive of friendship and patronage, and the role that patronage played in eighteenth-century society.

This much wider definition of patronage includes the connection maintenance and trust relationships of elite and middling women as well as non-elite artisans. Many studies consider many aspects that were essential to patronage, such as the careful consolidation of relationships through visitations or church meetings, only within their discussions of separate spheres, sociability or community.[27] The difficulties arise when these terms are used in opposition to patronage. It has been demonstrated here that patronage was a pervasive mechanism which operated within social structures with a considerable amount of individual variation. In establishing this, it dismantles the restrictive model which draws a distinction between patronage and friendship or community support, by which patronage is used to refer exclusively to the connection maintenance and exploitation of connections by aristocrats and politicians, while friendship and community support is generally used to frame the participation of women and the lower orders. The connotation that elite patronage was self-serving but the support based in friendships and communities was inherently altruistic diminishes the impact, variation and pragmatism of particularly female and lower-level networks. Equally, this book has established that close, affectionate relationships and patronage were not mutually exclusive, as some studies present them.[28] Rather, the likelihood of face-to-face meetings coupled with ideals of sensible friendship made the patronage conducted within these relationships less explicit. Even so, the distinction between the role of affectionate friendships and the pragmatic obligations of more typical patronage relationships can elucidate the variety of factors involved in an officer's success.

The association of patronage exclusively with the elite creates a tendency for scholars to frame essential structural aspects such as the networks of officers' wives in terms of sensible or affectionate friendship and to reduce the patronage solicitations of the family and friends of sailors to community support. Conflating patronage with elite influence obscures the limitations imposed on the patronage of women and the lower orders by their socio-economic circumstances. Social status and gender certainly affected patronage control. William Murray, first earl of Mansfield, as a titled gentleman with ties to government had greater economic impact through his patronage than Mary Higg had, as a female owner of a dockside lodging house in Plymouth, but that does not mean that the ties of obligation she managed and the appointments she arranged were not a part of patronage. Nor does it mean that all of Mansfield's patronage was governed entirely by expedience rather than his sense of duty

---

[27] See Gill, *Naval Families*, 197–199; Garrioch, *Neighbourhood and Community*; Whyman, *Sociability and Power.*

[28] Gill, *Naval Families*, 103–120, 139–144, 171, 195–197, 199.

272 PATRONAGE AND THE BRITISH NAVY, 1775–1815

or his affection for the individual he promoted. In dismantling the division between elite patronage and community support, this book provides a more rigorous model of patronage as it operated throughout all levels of society.

Widening the definition of patronage and considering it as a mechanism of trust within a variety of networks uncovers the web of obligations, trust and reputation which underpinned social systems, ranging from election campaigns to the honour-bound but essentially practical distribution of appointments in the navy. These structures of trust and recommendation operated throughout the early modern period and well into the twentieth century. Necessity drove patronage but the way individuals distributed their favour and framed their engagement was deeply affected by social and cultural pressures and expectations.

With that in mind, let us return to Pellew's quote about the 'wheel' of patronage.[29] His letter to Markham has appeared several times in the preceding chapters and several naval historians have used it to demonstrate the inherent reciprocity of naval patronage.[30] However, this book has demonstrated that, although hugely varied, a significant proportion of all eighteenth-century patronage occurred in non-explicit forms beneath a veneer of fashionable sensibility, friendship, duty and honour. Pellew's letter, therefore, is clearly overly explicit about the nature of his patronage expectations. Far from being representative of naval values in patronage, his over-explanation reveals his own frustration with some Admiralty commissioners' tendency to neglect the reciprocity and expectations of favour he felt were at the core of patronage. His unambiguous reference to the 'wheel' of patronage is a pointed comment on Markham's own devotion to sensible stoicism in his response to requests, meaning that he emphasised duty, honour and friendship before the form of reciprocal favour which encouraged entitled demands for attention. This may have angered Pellew but it gave Markham vital flexibility and protection in how he responded to the huge number of requests he received. By failing to explicitly acknowledge his patronage, he ensured his freedom from satisfying the requests of applicants who had strengthened their connection to him through previous favours or by familiar maintenance such as gift-giving and network integration. Yet, the ill-defined edges of this ideal are revealed by the degree of Markham's offence when George Cuthbert betrayed him in the 1818 Portsmouth election.[31] Markham felt that the favours he bestowed on those who applied to him were reciprocal, but only when it suited him.

Markham's attitude and Pellew's letter in many ways epitomise the conflicting, ill-defined and yet overwhelmingly pervasive nature of patronage

[29] NMM, MRK/101/13/100, Pellew to Markham, 15 August 1806.

[30] Rodger, *Command of the Ocean*, 513; Taylor, *Commander*, 201; Gill, *Naval Families*, 105; Wilson, *British Naval Officers*, 116.

[31] NMM, MRK/106/2/19, Draft of a letter, Markham to Cuthbert, 30 July 1818.

CONCLUSION   273

which shaped eighteenth-century society. The practical necessity of securing
social position, promotion or employment operated beneath layers of fashion,
cultural expectation and socio-economic restrictions. Exchanges occurred
between varying degrees of friendship and connection and acted as guarantees
of a person's competence, or, at the very least, that they could provide access
to the assistance of their connections. These networks operated at all levels
of society, both laterally within social status groups and vertically within
occupational and social hierarchies. There was a huge amount of individual
variation in how patrons, brokers and clients sought after and distributed
patronage and in how they framed their participation. But patronage was
essentially a mechanism of trust founded on an individual's ability, character
and connections.

The intrinsic quality of patronage within society highlights the importance
of connection and the devastation of exclusion. Which brings us back to where
we began, with Russel White's entreaty for Markham's support. Having 'no
other frind' who could offer assistance was a very real danger for individuals
at the edges of eighteenth-century society.[32] The drive to consolidate and
expand networks defined manners and fashions across all social levels as well
as shaped communities. Naval historians have variously called patronage the
'spring' which drove the machinery of promotion or the 'oil' that greased it.[33]
In wider society, it has been called the glue which bound society together.[34]
But rather than a small part that worked within eighteenth-century social
machinery, we could more appropriately call patronage the machine itself.

[32] NMM, MRK/104/3/49, White to Markham, 30 June 1802.

[33] Rodger, *Wooden World*, 301; Cavell, *Midshipmen and the Quarterdeck Boys*,
10–11

[34] Cavell, *Midshipmen and the Quarterdeck Boys*, 10–11; Peck, *Court Patronage*,
4.

APPENDIX I:
JOHN MARKHAM'S CAREER

Date		Ship	Rating	Location
Entered 11 March	1775	*Romney* (50)	Midshipman	
	1776	*Perseus* (20)		North America
March	1777	*Pearl* (32)		West Indies/ North America
May		*Perseus* (20)		
	1778	Ship-wrecked in a prize Returned to Britain		
11 March	1779	*Phoenix* (36)		Britain
21 July		*Roebuck* (44)	Acting-lieutenant	North America
15 May	1780		3rd Lieutenant	
June			1st Lieutenant	
14 April	1781	*Confederacy*	(Prize)	
		Royal Oak (74)	Lieutenant	Newfoundland/
22 August		*London* (90)	Lieutenant	North America
October			1st Lieutenant	
13 January	1782	*Hinchinbrooke* (28)	Acting-commander	Jamaica
13 March		Fireship *Volcano*	Acting-commander	
16 May		*Zebra* (16)	Commander	
28 May		Court martial	*Dismissed from the service*	

APPENDIX I 275

4 December		*Restored to the service*	Britain
9 December		*Carysfort* (28)	Acting-captain
3 January	1783		Post-captain
19 June		*Sphinx* (20)	
November			Mediterranean
	1784		
May	1785		
16 October	1786	Paid off	Britain
		Half-pay	
24 June	1793	*Blonde* (38)	Channel
6 January	1794	*Blonde* (38)	West Indies
			Barbados
February			Martinique
April			Channel
18 August		*Hannibal* (74)	
April	1795		West Indies
27 June			Sant Domingue
September		On shore, hospital	Port Royal, Jamaica
November		Invalided from *Hannibal*, yellow fever	
		Half-pay	
29 March	1797	*Centaur* (74)	
September			Nore
21 November			Ireland
25 May	1798		Cadiz
7 November			Minorca
February	1799		Mediterranean
May			Majorca
6 August			Channel

February	1800			*Blockade of Brest*
18 February	1801	ADMIRALTY *under St Vincent*	Commissioner	Britain
12 November	1802		MP Portsmouth	
23 April	1804		Rear-Admiral of the Blue	
15 May	1804	LEFT ADMIRALTY		
26 January	1806	ADMIRALTY *under Howick*	Commissioner	
13 September		ADMIRALTY *under Grenville*		
24 March	1807	LEFT ADMIRALTY		
	1809		Vice-Admiral	
	1818	Lost his seat at Portsmouth to Admiral George Cockburn		
	1819		Admiral	
	1820	Re-gained his seat	MP Portsmouth	

Sources: MRK/100/1/14-18 and 39, service certificates and commissions 1775–1804; MRK/107/1/3, 6–7, 12, 15–16, 18 and 20, letters to his father 1777–1784; MRK/100/1/1–2, 5 and 21–24, orders 1779–1794; MRK/100/8/1–2, court martial order and minutes, 28 May 1782; MRK/100/2/33, 35 and 126, orders 1783–1785; Clements Markham, *A Naval Career during the Old War: Being a Narrative of the Life of Admiral John Markham, M.P. for Portsmouth for Twenty-Three Years (Lord of the Admiralty, 1801–4 and 1806–7)* (London, 1883), 26–30, 44–56, 65–82, 102–119, 134–153, 169–205, 220–242; R.G. Thorne (ed.), *The History of Parliament: The House of Commons 1790–1820* (Woodbridge, 1986), iv.546–548.

APPENDIX II: CONNECTIONS

Markham's Family

Maria Rice
(b.1773–d.1810)

Married John Markham 1796
Visited Bishopthorpe 1797
Visited Dynevor castle November
1797– February 1798
Portugal Street, London March–June 1798
Visited Kenwood House, London June 1798
Visited Bishopthorpe July–October 1798
Visited Becca Hall, Aberford
November 1798
Visited Dynevor castle December
1798–February 1799
Portugal Street, London March 1799
Visited Bishopthorpe June 1799
Took lodgings at Plymouth dock
August 1799–March 1800
Livermead Cottage, Torquay
February 1800–January 1801
Admiralty Apartments 1801–1802
Ades, Sussex April 1802–1810
Died in childbirth at Ades 1810

Four children:
John Markham 1801
William Rice Markham 1803
Frederick Markham 1805
Maria Francis Markham 1806

Family:
Parents
George Rice (b.1724–
d.1779) *m*.1756
Cecil de Cardonnel,
second baroness Dynevor
(b.1735–d.1793) (see below)

Siblings
Henrietta Rice (b.1758) *m*.1788
Magens Dorien Magens
(b.1761), a London banker and
East India Company director
(*MP for Carmarthen 1796;
Ludgershall 1804–1812*)

George Talbot Rice (b.1765–
d.1852) *m*. Frances Townsend,
dau. Thomas Townsend, first
viscount Sydney (see below)

Reverend Edward Rice
(b.1776–d.1862) *m*.1800
Charlotte Lascelles, illegitimate
dau. General Francis Lascelles
Westminster school c.1788
Christ Church, Oxford
1794–1802

Parents

William Markham   *m.*1759   **Sarah Goddard**
(b.1719–d.1807)   (b.1738–d.1814)
Westminster school 1733;   *dau.* John Goddard,
king's scholar 1734   merchant in
Christ Church, Oxford 1738–1752   Rotterdam
Headmaster Westminster school 1753–1764
Dean of Rochester 1765–1767
Dean of Christ Church, Oxford 1767–1777
Bishop of Chester 1771–1776
Preceptor to the Prince of Wales 1771–1776
Archbishop of York 1776–1807

Siblings

William Markham   *m.*1795   **Elizabeth Bowles,**
(b.1760–d.1815)   *dau.* Oldfield Bowles of
Westminster school 1767;   North Ashton, Oxford.
king's scholar 1773   Her uncle was Reverend
Private secretary to Warren Hastings,   Abraham Elton, fifth
Governor-General of India [1777]   baronet Elton
Writer East India Company (Bengal) 1777
Assistant to Resident of Benares 1778
Resident of Benares 1781–1783
Returned to England 1784
Took up residence at Becca Hall,
Aberford, Yorkshire 1784

George Markham   *m.*1788   **Elizabeth Sutton**
(b.1763–d.1822)   divorced   (b.1772–d.1856)
Westminster school 1771;   1803   *dau.* Sir Richard Sutton,
king's scholar 1776   first baronet Sutton,
Christ Church, Oxford 1780–1803   of Norwood House,
Prebendary of Southwell 1787–1802   Nottinghamshire
Canon of York 1787   (*Westminster school*
Chancellor of York 1787–1802   *1744–1749; Trinity*
Rector of Beeford, Yorkshire 1788–1791   *College Cambridge*
Rector of Stokesley, Yorkshire 1791   *1749; Under-secretary*
Archdeacon, Cleveland 1797   *of state 1766–1772; Lord*
Dean of York 1802   *of Treasury 1780–1782)*

APPENDIX II 279

Henrietta Markham
(b.1764–d.1844)

*m.*1784

Ewan Law
(b.1747–d.1829)
son Reverend Edmund
Law, Bishop of
Carlisle, brother of
Edward Law, first earl
of Ellenborough
East India Company
1763–1777
MP for Westbury
1790–1795
MP for Newtown 1802
Commissioner of Naval
Inquiry 1802–1805

Elizabeth Markham
(b.1765–d.1820)

*m.*1796

William Barnett
(d.1832)
Westminster school 1777

David Markham
(b.1766–d.1795)
Westminster school 1774;
king's scholar 1780
Christ Church, Oxford 1784–1785
Lieutenant of 7th Regiment 1785
1st Lieutenant of 76th Regiment 1788
Captain 1789
Major c.1791
Commanded 20th Regiment
in West Indies 1791
Lieutenant-colonel 1794
Killed at Sant Domingue 1795

Robert Markham
(b.1768–d.1837)
Westminster school 1776;
king's scholar 1782
Christ Church, Oxford 1786–1794
Rector of Barton-in-Fabis,
Nottinghamshire 1794–1796
Prebendary of York 1792–1833
Archdeacon of West Riding and
Chancellor of Richmond, Yorkshire 1794
Rector, Bolton Percy, Yorkshire 1796
Vicar of Bishopthorpe 1797
Prebendary of Carlisle 1801
Archdeacon of York 1802

*m.*1797

Frances Clifton *dau.*
Sir Gervase Clifton,
sixth baronet of Clifton,
Nottinghamshire

Osborne Markham
(b.1769–d.1827)
Westminster 1778; *king's scholar* 1783
Christ Church, Oxford 1787–1794
Lincoln's Inn 1790; *called to the bar* 1794
Chancellor of diocese of York 1795–1818
Commissioner of Navy Board 1803–1805
MP for Calne 1806–1807

*m.*1806
*m.*1821

Lady Mary Thynne
(d.1814) *dau.* Thomas
Thynne, first
marquess of Bath
Martha Jervis *dau.*
Captain William Henry
Jervis, nephew of John
Jervis, earl of St Vincent

Alicia Markham
(b.1771–d.1840)

*m.*1794

**Reverend Henry
Forster Mills**
(b.1769–d.1827)
Westminster school
1776; *king's scholar* 1782
Christ Church,
Oxford 1786–1793
Prebendary of
York 1795–1797
Rector of
Barton-in-Fabis,
Nottinghamshire 1796
Preceptor of York
1797–1802

Georgina Markham
(b.1772–d.1793)

Frederica Markham
(b.1774– d.1860)

*m.*1797

**David William
Murray**, third
earl of Mansfield.
(b.1777–d.1840),
son David Murray,
seventh viscount
Stormont and second
earl of Mansfield
Westminster school
1786; *king's scholar* 1790
Christ Church,
Oxford 1794
Became third earl
of Mansfield 1796
Lieutenant 7th
Regiment of foot 1798
Captain 44th Regiment
of foot 1802
Lord Lieutenant of
Clackmannanshire
1803–1840

APPENDIX II   281

Anne Markham
(b.1778– d.1808)

Cecilia Markham   *m*.1808   Reverend Robert
(b.1783–d.1865)   Philip Goodenough
                                                       (d.1826), *son*
                                                       Samuel Goodenough
                                                       (b.1743–d.1827)
                                                       Westminster school
                                                       1784; *king's scholar* 1788
                                                       Christ Church, Oxford
                                                       1792; BA 1796; MA 1799

Westminster-Christ Church Circle

(Arranged by date of entry to Westminster school or Christ Church, Oxford)

William Murray, first earl of   *m*.1738   **Lady Elizabeth Finch**
Mansfield (b.1705–d.1793)   (d.1784), *dau*. Daniel Finch,
Son David Murray, fifth   seventh earl of Winchilsea and
viscount Stormont (d.1731)   second earl of Nottingham
Westminster school 1718
Christ Church, Oxford 1723–1730
Lincoln's Inn 1724; *called*
to the bar 1730
Solicitor-General 1742–1754
MP for Boroughbridge 1742–1756
Attorney-General 1754–1756
Created baron of Mansfield 1756
Lord Chief Justice 1756–1788
Created earl of Mansfield
(Nottinghamshire) 1776
Created earl of Mansfield
(Middlesex) 1792

APPENDIX II

Granville Leveson-Gower, first
marquess of Stafford and second
earl Gower (b.1721–d.1803)
Westminster school 1731;
king's scholar 1736
Christ Church, Oxford 1740
MP for Bishop's Castle 1744–1747
Courtesy title of Viscount
Trentham 1746–1754
MP for Westminster 1747–1754
Became second earl Gower 1754
MP for Lichfield 1754
Commissioner of the
Admiralty 1749–1751
Privy Councillor 1755
Lord lieutenant of
Staffordshire 1755–1800
Lord privy seal 1755–1757
Master of the horse 1757–1760
Mater of the wardrobe 1760–1763
Lord chamberlain 1763–1765
Lord president of the council
1767–1779, 1783–1784
Lord privy seal 1784–1794
Created first marquess
of Stafford 1786

*m.*1744 **Elizabeth Fazarkerly**
*m.*1748 (d.1746)
*m.*1768 **Lady Louisa Egerton**
(d.1761), *dau.* Scroop
Egerton, first duke of
Bridgewater, and niece of
fourth duke of Bedford
Four children including:
Louisa Leveson-Gower

Lady Susanna Stewart,
marchioness of Stafford
(b.1742–d.1805), *dau.*
Alexander Stewart, sixth
earl of Galloway and Lady
Catherine Cochrane, *dau.*
of John Cochrane, fourth
earl of Dundonald
Woman of the bedchamber to
Princess Augusta 1761

George Rice (b.1724–d.1779)
Son Edward Rice and Lucy
Morley Trevor (cousin once
removed of Thomas Pelham
Holles, duke of Newcastle)
Christ Church, Oxford 1742
MP for Carmarthenshire 1754–1779
Lord Lieutenant of
Carmarthenshire 1755–1779
Commissioner of the Board
of Trade 1761–1770
Privy Councillor 1770
Treasurer of the chamber 1770–1779

*m.*1756 **Cecil de Cardonnel**,
second baroness Dynevor
(b.1735–d.1793), *dau.*
William Talbot, first earl
Talbot and first baron
Dynevor (1710–1782)
Became second baroness
Dynevor 1782
Four children including:
George Talbot Rice
Maria Rice

John Skynner (b.1724–d.1805)
Westminster school 1735;
king's scholar 1738
Christ Church, Oxford 1742–1751
Lincoln's Inn 1739; *called
to the bar* 1748
*Attorney-general to duchy
of Lancaster* 1770–1777
King's counsel 1770
Recorder for Woodstock 1771–1780
Second justice of Chester 1772–1777
MP for New Woodstock 1771–1777
Recorder for Oxford 1776–1797
Knighted 1777
*Chief Baron of the
Exchequer* 1777–1787
Privy Councillor 1787

*m.*1778 **Martha Burn** (d.1797)

David Murray, seventh viscount
Stormont and second earl of
Mansfield (b.1727–d.1796)
Son David Murray, sixth
viscount Stormont (d.1748),
nephew of William Murray,
first earl of Mansfield
Westminster school 1739;
king's scholar 1740
Christ Church, Oxford 1744–1748
Became Viscount Stormont 1748
*Envoy-extraordinary to
Saxony-Poland* 1755
Ambassador to Vienna 1763–1772
Ambassador to Paris 1772–1778
*Lord Justice General for
Scotland* 1778–1794
*Secretary of state for the northern
department* 1779–1782
President of the council
1783, 1794–1796
Became earl of Mansfield 1793

*m.*1759   **Henrietta Frederica de**
*m.*1776   **Berargaard** (b.1736–
d.1766), *dau.* Graf Heinrich
von Bünau, a Saxon
minister and diplomat

Louisa Cathcart, countess
of Mansfield (b.1758–d.1843),
dau. Charles Cathcart,
ninth lord Cathcart

APPENDIX II

Samuel Goodenough (b.1743–d.1827) *m.*1770
Westminster school c.1755;
king's scholar 1756
Christ Church, Oxford 1760–1772
Undermaster of Westminster
school 1766–1770
Established private school in
Ealing, Middlesex 1772
Vicar of Cropredy, Oxfordshire 1797
Canon of Windsor 1798–1802
Dean of Rochester 1802–1808
Bishop of Carlisle 1808

Elizabeth Ford, *dau.* Dr
James Ford, physician
to Queen Charlotte
Three children including:
Robert Philip Goodenough

Cyril Jackson (b.1746–d.1819)
Westminster school c.1756;
king's scholar 1760
Christ Church, Oxford 1764–1781
Sub-preceptor of Prince of Wales
with William Markham 1771–1776
Preacher of Lincoln's Inn 1779–1783
Canon of Christ Church 1779
Rector of Kirkby in Cleveland 1781
Dean of Christ Church 1783–1809
Prebendary at Southwell 1786

Archibald MacDonald, first baronet   *m.*1777
Macdonald (b.1747–d.1826)
Westminster school [unknown
entry date]; *king's scholar 1760*
Christ Church, Oxford 1764–1772
Lincoln's Inn 1765; called
to the bar 1770
MP for Hindon 1777–1780
King's Counsel 1778
Second justice of South
Wales circuit 1780–1788
MP for Newcastle-
under-Lyme 1780–1793
Solicitor-general 1784–1788
Attorney-general 1788–1793
Privy Councillor 1793
Chief Baron of the
Exchequer 1793–1813
Created first baronet Macdonald 1813

Lady Louisa Leveson-Gower
(d.1827), *dau.* Granville
Leveson-Gower and Lady
Louisa Egerton (see above)

APPENDIX II   285

George Talbot Rice, third baron   *m*.1794   **Frances Townsend**,
Dynevor (b.1765–d.1852)   *dau*. Thomas Townsend
Westminster school 1773;   first viscount Sydney
in school lists 1781
Christ Church, Oxford 1783–1786
Mayor of Carmarthen 1790
MP for Carmarthenshire 1790–1793
Became third baron Dynevor 1793
and took name de Cardonnel
Lord Lieutenant
Carmarthenshire 1804–1852
Resumed name Rice 1817

Sources: G. F Russell Barker and Alan H Stenning (eds.), *The Record of Old Westminsters: A Biographical List of all those who are known to have been educated at Westminster School from the earliest times to 1927*, 2 vols. (London, 1928), i.57, 382, 389, 506 and ii.604, 620–623, 647, 675–678, 782, 852; Clements Markham, *A Naval Career during the Old War: Being a Narrative of the Life of Admiral John Markham, M.P. for Portsmouth for Twenty-Three Years (Lord of the Admiralty, 1801–4 and 1806–7)* (London, 1883); David Frederick Markham, *A History of the Markham Family* (London, 1854), 54–84; Nigel Aston, 'Markham, William', *ODNB*, vol. 36, 697–700; William C. Lowe, 'Gower, Granville Leveson-, first marquess of Stafford', *ODNB*, vol. 23, 116–117; James Oldham, 'Murray, William, first earl of Mansfield', *ODNB*, vol. 39, 992–1000; James Price, 'Goodenough, Samuel', *ODNB*, vol. 22, 772–774; H. M. Scott, 'Murray, David, seventh Viscount Stormont and second earl of Mansfield', *ODNB*, vol. 39, 884–887; Peter Thomas, 'Rice, George', *ODNB*, vol. 46, 649; David Lemmings, 'Skynner, Sir John', *ODNB*, vol. 50, 890–891; W. R. Ward, 'Jackson, Cyril', *ODNB*, vol. 29, 470–473; R. K. Webb, 'Elton, Sir Charles Abraham, sixth baronet', *ODNB*, vol. 18, 342; R. G. Thorne (ed.), *The History of Parliament: The House of Commons 1790–1820* (Cambridge, 1986), iv.486, 548.

APPENDIX III:
PORTSMOUTH CORPORATION

The corporation was elected by a vote of the existing corporation members and, therefore, was structured around the network of friendship and familial obligations which also facilitated patronage. The table shows who sat in the corporation meetings according to John Carter's notes on the corporation between 1795 to 1818. The mayor was elected each year and prominent members in the corporation took it in turns. Those who were not elected mayor that year were often elected as one of the three magistrates instead. The most prominent members of the corporation appeared most often as mayor or magistrates.

Year	Mayor	Magistrates	Aldermen elected	Aldermen deceased
1795	John Godwin	Thomas White of Milton Sir John Carter William Carter		
1796	Sir John Carter	Thomas White Thomas White of Milton William Carter		
1797	Stephen Gaselee	John Godwin Thomas White William Goldson	Stephen Gaselee William Goldson Rev. George Cuthbert	Thomas White of Milton
1798	Rev. George Cuthbert	Sir John Carter Thomas White John Godwin		William Carter
1799	William Goldson	Sir John Carter John Godwin Stephen Gaselee		

APPENDIX III

1800	Sir John Carter	Thomas White Stephen Gaselee William Goldson		Henry Bonham
1801	John Godwin	Stephen Gaselee William Goldson Rev. George Cuthbert	Thomas Bonham John Adam Carter	Rev. William White
1802	Stephen Gaselee	Sir John Carter William Goldson Rev. George Cuthbert		
1803	Rev. George Cuthbert	John Godwin Sir John Carter William Goldson		
1804	Sir John Carter	John Godwin Stephen Gaselee William Goldson		
1805	William Goldson	John Godwin Stephen Gaselee Rev. George Cuthbert		
1806	John Adam Carter	Stephen Gaselee Rev. George Cuthbert Sir John Carter		Thomas White
1807	John Godwin	Sir John Carter Rev. George Cuthbert William Goldson		
1808	Rev. George Cuthbert	William Goldson John Adam Carter Samuel Spicer	Arthur Atherley Samuel Spicer Joseph Smith	Sir John Carter
1809	Samuel Spicer	John Godwin William Goldson Joseph Smith		John Adam Carter
1810	Joseph Smith	John Godwin William Goldson Rev. George Cuthbert	Edward Carter	Stephen Gaselee
1811	Edward Carter	William Goldson Rev. George Cuthbert Samuel Spicer		

APPENDIX III

1812	James Carter	John Godwin William Goldson Joseph Smith	James Carter Henry White	
1813	Henry White	John Godwin William Goldson Edward Carter		William White
1814	William Goldson	Samuel Spicer Edward Carter James Carter	John (Bonham) Carter	
1815	Samuel Spicer	Edward Carter James Carter Sir Henry White		
1816	Edward Carter	William Goldson James Carter Sir Henry White	George Atherley	
1817	James Carter	Samuel Spicer Sir Henry White George Atherley		John Godwin William Goldson
1818	Daniel Howard		George Grey Daniel Howard	

Source: HRO, Bonham Carter Papers, 94M72/F31/2, Election Notebook [1818].

APPENDIX IV:
I: HIERARCHY AND OCCUPATIONS IN THE ROYAL DOCKYARDS

Role	Description
Commissioner	Often a retired admiral or captain, appointed by either Admiralty or Navy Board. Had technical control of all appointments in the yard but usually conceded to master attendant and master shipwright.

Principal Officers

Role	Description
Master Shipwright	Responsible for all the shipwrights, caulkers and labourers working in the yard itself on both new builds and repairs. Also, responsible for carpenters, smiths and sawyers at work in the yard. Oversaw the master caulker, master sailmaker, master smith, master ropemaker as well as the assistants to the master shipwright.
Master Attendant	Responsible for piloting ships in the harbour and shipwrights, artificers and labourers at work on ships afloat: those that had just been launched but not fully-fitted, those out of dry-dock, or those laid up in ordinary. These artificers were most commonly riggers, sailmakers and house carpenters.

Principal Clerks

Role	Description
Clerk of the Cheque	Saw to the pay and largely controlled the appointments of the clerks in the offices of the yard.
Clerk of the Survey	Reviewed materials coming into the yard from contractors and saw to the provision of the different sections of the yard.

290 APPENDIX IV

Naval Storekeeper	Saw to victualling of the yard and cabin-keepers who were the storekeepers for individual sections of the yard. In smaller overseas yards the clerk of the cheque, clerk of the survey and the naval storekeeper were often one role and the term was largely interchangeable.
Clerk of the Ropeyard	In charge of the provision of stores and the mustering of the ropemakers in those yards with a rope yard: Plymouth, Portsmouth, Woolwich and Chatham.

Senior Officers and Clerks

Assistant(s) to the Master Shipwright	In charge of specific areas of the yard and workforce, and they answered directly to the master shipwright. They were the most senior officers in the yards below master shipwright. Some yards had up to three assistants. Each assistant was allowed three apprentices.
Master Caulker	In charge of the caulkers of the yard. In the six main yards the second assistant to the master shipwright also held this role.
Master Boatbuilder	Sometimes interchangeable with the master shipwright, depending on the size of the yard. In larger yards appears to have been on a level with assistants and directly answered to the master shipwright.
Timber Master	Responsible for the inspection of purchased timber, its qualification as inferior or superior quality and its subsequent allocation from the timber yard to ships being built. The position was only introduced in 1801 and the title was often given to an assistant who had already been doing the surveying of timber.
Boatswain of the Yard	Immediately subordinate to master attendant and oversaw ships ordinary in the yard.
Other Masters	Each group of artificers had a master in the large yards: master mastmaker, master measurer, master rigger, master sailmaker, master house carpenter, master joiner, master smith, master bricklayer, master painter (see below for artificer descriptions).

APPENDIX IV

291

Senior Foremen

Foreman of the Yard	In charge of all of the artificers and labourers in the yard. Answered to the master shipwright and assistants. Smaller yards and bases often only had a foreman of the yard and no other senior foremen.
Foreman Afloat	Oversaw work being done on recently launched ships.
Foreman of New Works	Oversaw contracts undertaken in merchant yards. It was not a permanent position and was often awarded to a quarterman of good character or one of the assistants to the master shipwright.

Foremen and Inferior Officers

Foreman of the Masthouse	In charge of the men shaping masts.
Foreman of Caulkers	Directly subordinate to master caulker.
Foreman of Shipwrights	Answered to foreman of the yard. The quartermen in charge of individual work-gangs were immediate subordinates. The number of foremen depended on the size of the yard.
Quarterman of the Masthouse	In charge of individual work-gangs in the shaping of masts.
Quarterman of the Mouldloft or Mouldhouse	The mouldloft was where the designs of ships were drawn out on the floor for the measuring and warping of timber and was under the direct command of the master shipwright. The quarterman supervised the manual labour directed by the master shipwright.
Quarterman of Shipwrights	The senior shipwrights in charge of work-gangs of roughly fifteen men.
Cabin-Keeper	Storekeeper for individual sections of the yard, housed in smaller 'cabins' on site. Responsible particularly for provisions of expensive materials such as copper and to keep a watchful eye out for fraudulent behaviour.

Artificers and Labourers

Shipwright	Undertook much of the skilled work building and repairing ships in the yard.
Caulker	Skilled workmen who filled the gaps in between the boards of the ship's hull with oakum made from old rope, to make it watertight.

292 APPENDIX IV

Riggers	Responsible for the fixing of rigging in ships about to launch and often served part of their career at sea.
Sailmakers	Crafting, affixing and repairing sails.
House Carpenter	Distinct from shipwrights because they specialised in the construction of the wooden housing of the ship.
Ship's Carpenter	Many of the skilled workmen in the yard served at sea as ship's carpenters, particularly shipwrights and house carpenters but sometimes also caulkers.
Sawyers	Responsible for the cutting and shaping of wood needed for ship construction.
Joiners	Responsible for wooden fixtures of ships.
Smiths	Responsible for metal fixtures of ships as well as anchors.
Labourers	Responsible for the hauling of material etc.
Scavelmen	Specialised labourers who dug trenches and erected scaffolding to facilitate the construction of ships.
Wardens and Porters	Oversaw the yard, especially at night. Positions often held by old or infirm yard workers.

Sources: ADM 106/2975, Navy Board: Dockyard Description Books, Chatham: artificers (alphabetical), 1779; ADM 106/2979, Navy Board: Dockyard Description Books, Plymouth 1779; ADM 106/2980, Portsmouth: 1779. ADM 106/2982, Sheerness: 1779; ADM 106/2984, Woolwich: 1779; ADM 106/2985, Woolwich: 1802. ADM 106/2986, Deptford: 1784; *Cobbett's Parliamentary Debates*, 7, 178; Roger Morriss, *The Royal Dockyards during the Revolutionary and Napoleonic Wars* (Leicester, 1993), 88, 112–139, 167–170; Julian Gwyn, *Ashore and Afloat: The British Navy and the Halifax Naval Yard before 1820* (Ottawa, 2004), 73–74; N. A. M. Rodger, *The Command of the Ocean: A Naval History of Britain, 1649–1815* (London, 2004).

BIBLIOGRAPHY

Manuscript and Archival Sources

National Maritime Museum (NMM), Greenwich

ACG/P/17, Martindale Powell to his mother, 12 June 1805.

ADM/B/214, Admiralty In-Letters, An Account Answering the Number of Artificers borne in His Majesty's several Dock Yards, Navy office, 14 April 1804.

CRK/3/83– 84, Collier to Nelson, 28 December 1800 and 21 March 1803.

DUC/8, Letters of Admiral John Thomas Duckworth, commander-in-chief Jamaica 1802.

FOW/2/1, Letters to Midshipman/Lieutenant George Fowke from Major Thomas Thorpe Fowke 1783–1791.

MID/1/68, Loose In-Letters to Charles Middleton, first Baron Barham, 1805.

PER/1/23 and 32, Letters of George Perceval to his mother 1807–1808.

PER/1/40, Letters of George Perceval to his father 1811.

RUSI/NM/235/ER/4/3, Papers of Captain Edward Riou: Letters from Lord Spencer.

RUSI/NM/235/ER/4/4, Papers of Captain Edward Riou: The Shakespeare Club (i.e. The Navy Society).

The Markham Collection

MRK/100/2/221–223, Letters from John Hunter, Lisbon, 1798.

MRK/101/1, Letters from St Vincent, 1800–1807.

MRK/101/3, Letters from Admiral Lord Keith, 1801–1807.

MRK/101/4, Letters from Admiral George Murray, 1801–1807.

MRK/101/6 Letters from Admiral Stanhope, Sir Richard Strachan and Rear-Admiral John Sutton, 1801–1807.

MRK/101/7/, Letters from Sir Isaac Coffin, Sir Charles Cotton, Sir Thomas Pasley, 1801–1807.

MRK/101/13, Letters from Flag Officers 1801–1807

MRK/102/1, Letters from Captains A–C.

MRK/102/2, Letters from Captains D–G.

MRK/102/3, Letters from Captains H–K.

MRK/102/4, Letters from Captains L–O.

MRK/102/5, Letters from Captains P–S.

MRK/102/6, Letters from Captains T–Y.

MRK/103/1, Letters from Lieutenants A–J.

MRK/103/2, Letters from Lieutenants K–W.

MRK/104/1, Letters from Public and Warrant Officers A–J.

294   BIBLIOGRAPHY

MRK/104/2, Letters from Public and Warrant Officers K–S.
MRK/104/3, Letters from Public and Warrant Officers T–Z.
MRK/104/4, Letters from Women (Chronological).
MRK/104/5, Letters from the Public (Various).
MRK/105/3, General Correspondence 1800–1810.
MRK/105/6, Letters from and about Royal Marines 1800–1810.
MRK/106/1–49, Letters from Sir John Carter and the Carter family 1802–1806.
MRK/106/2/1–20, Letters from Reverend George Cuthbert 1803–1818.
MRK/106/3, Letters from Portsmouth Corporation and constituents 1801–1820.
MRK/106/4/1–6, Letters from the Portsmouth Corporation 1803–1807.
MRK/107/1–38, Letters from his father William Markham, 1774–1784.
MRK/107/2/1–83, Letters to his wife Maria Markham, 1796–1809.
MRK/107/3/1–39, Letters from his wife Maria Markham, 1797–1798.
MRK/107/4/1–32, Letters from his family, 1776–1822.
MRK/108/2/1–18, Letters from Lord Mark Kerr, 1799–c.1802.
MRK/108/4/1–67, Letters from his friends, c.1787–c.1807.

The British Library, Manuscript Collection, London (BL)

Add MS 31167, Papers of Lord St Vincent, letter-book of secret official letters, 23 November 1795–27 March 1807.
Add MS 31168, Papers of Lord St Vincent, letter-book to commissioned officers, 17 February 1801–22 January 1823.
Add MS 31170, Papers of Lord St Vincent, letter-book to promiscuous, 17 February 1801–16 February 1807.
Add MS 31173, Papers of Lord St Vincent, letters to the First Lords and secretary of the Admiralty, 5 May 1800–1 April 1807.
Add MS 86495, Keith Papers, Letters from George Keith Elphinstone to Mary Elphinstone, 1797–1799.
Add MS 86496, Keith Papers, Letters from George Keith Elphinstone to Mary Elphinstone, 1799–1800.

Cadbury Research Library and Special Collections, University of Birmingham (CRL)

JER/407, Jerningham Letters, Lady Frances Jerningham to Lady Charlotte Bedingfeld, 4 June 1806.
JER/810, Jerningham Letters, Lady Frances Jerningham to Lady Charlotte Bedingfeld, 29 October 1814.
JER/813, Jerningham Letters, Lady Frances Jerningham to Lady Charlotte Bedingfeld, 31 October 1814.
JER/816, Jerningham Letters, Lady Frances Jerningham to Lady Charlotte Bedingfeld, 10 November 1814.
JER/870, Jerningham Letters, John Cary to Lady Charlotte Bedingfeld, 2 June 1815.

BIBLIOGRAPHY   295

Huntingdon Library (HL), California

ST102, Stowe Papers, Thomas Grenville: Promotion Books.

Hampshire Record Office (HRO), Winchester

94M72/F31/2, Bonham Carter Papers, John Bonham Carter Election Notebook [1818].
94M72/F36, Bonham Carter Papers. 'Notes on Electors' in John Bonham Carter's Notebook.
94M72/F49–52, Bonham Carter Papers. Diaries of Joanna (Smith) Bonham Carter.
94M72/Z3, Bonham Carter Papers. Borough Election Manual and County Election Manuals 1818–1835.

London Metropolitan Archives (LMA)

MS 11936/359/555858, Records of Sun Fire Office, 28 March 1789.
P75/PAU/001, St Paul, Deptford: Composite Register, Baptisms, Marriages, Burials 1730–1788.
P97/MRY/008–009, St Mary Magdalene, Woolwich: Composite Register, Baptisms, Marriages, Burials, 1768–1799.
P97/MRY/024, St Mary Magdalene, Woolwich: Register of Marriages, 1763–1796.
P97/MRY/050, St Mary Magdalene, Woolwich: Vestry Minutes.
P97/MRY/075, St Mary Magdalene, Woolwich: Overseer's accounts June 1800–October 1805.
P97/MRY/076, Accounts of Mrs Wiseman's Charity.

National Library of Scotland (NLS), Edinburgh

ACC9572, Scrap Books of Admiral Mark Kerr.

Scone Palace Archives and Collections (Scone), Perth

NRAS776/Box15, Letters to David Murray, Viscount Stormont, 1779–1781.
NRAS776/Box110/Bundle1, Letters from David Murray, Viscount Stormont, to William Markham, Archbishop of York. 1757–1793.
NRAS776/Bundle1235, Letters from Colonel Charles Cathcart to David Murray, Viscount Stormont, 1783–1788.
NRAS776/Bundle1384, Miscellaneous Correspondence of David Murray, Viscount Stormont, 1779–1781.
NRAS776/Bundle579, Personal Correspondence of David William Murray, third earl of Stormont, 1796–1797.
NRAS776/Box95/Folder2, Miscellaneous Personal Correspondence.

The National Archives (TNA), Kew

ADM 6/22, Admiralty: Commission and Warrant Book, 1779–1782.
ADM 6/28, Admiralty: Commission and Warrant Book, 1801–1804.
ADM 6/31, Admiralty: Commission and Warrant Book, 1810–1813.

296 BIBLIOGRAPHY

ADM 9/2–3, Admiralty: Survey Returns of Officers' Services. Captains' Services.

ADM 9/6–8, Admiralty: Survey Returns of Officers' Services. Lieutenants' Services.

ADM 30/62, Navy Board: Pay List for Shipwrights (Portsmouth) 1800.

ADM 36/10595, Admiralty: Royal Navy Ships' Musters (Series I): HMS *Sphinx*, 28 June–3 October 1783.

ADM 36/11389–11390, Admiralty: Royal Navy Ships' Musters (Series I): HMS *Blonde*, 1 July 1793–November 1796.

ADM 36/13666–13667, Admiralty: Royal Navy Ships' Musters (Series I): HMS *Hannibal*, 1 August 1794–February 1796.

ADM 36/14162–14168, Admiralty: Royal Navy Ships' Musters (Series I): HMS *Centaur*, April 1797–30 April 1802.

ADM 36/15344, Admiralty: Royal Navy Ships' Musters (Series I): HMS *Dragon*, August 1801–June 1802.

ADM 36/16530, Admiralty: Royal Navy Ships' Musters (Series I): HMS *St George*, December 1804–June 1805.

ADM 106/1142/156, Navy Board In-Letters: Petition of Richard Randall, 20 July 1765.

ADM 106/1174/168, Navy Board In-Letters: Petition of John Woodger, 12 January 1767.

ADM 106/1180/64, Navy Board In-Letters: Petition of William Knight, 20 June 1769.

ADM 106/1185/60, Navy Board In-Letters: Petition of shipwrights and other artificers, Woolwich, 28 September 1770.

ADM 106/1185/270, Navy Board In-Letters: Captain Barrington, 10 October 1770.

ADM 106/1205/223, Navy Board In-Letters: Petition of Jacob Thorp, 4 March 1771.

ADM 106/1244/369, Navy Board In-Letters: Plymouth Yard, 4 December 1778.

ADM 106/1262/338, Petition of Mary West of Woolwich to the Admiralty, 4 April 1780.

ADM 106/1262/340, Navy Board In-Letters: Petition of Mary West of Woolwich to the Admiralty, 10 April 1780.

ADM 106/2975, Navy Board: Dockyard Description Books, Chatham: artificers (alphabetical), 1779.

ADM 106/2979, Navy Board: Dockyard Description Books, Plymouth: artificers (alphabetical), 1779.

ADM 106/2980, Navy Board: Dockyard Description Books, Portsmouth: artificers (alphabetical), 1779.

ADM 106/2982, Navy Board: Dockyard Description Books, Sheerness: artificers (alphabetical), 177.

ADM 106/2984, Navy Board: Dockyard Description Books, Woolwich: artificers, 1779.

ADM 106/2985, Navy Board: Dockyard Description Books, Woolwich: artificers and labourers, 1802.

ADM 106/2986, Navy Board: Dockyard Description Books, Deptford: shipwrights (alphabetical), 1784.

ADM 196/68/349, Officers' Service Records (Series III): George Stuart.

BIBLIOGRAPHY 297

ADM 196/4/141, Officers' Service Records (Series III): David Edwards.
HO 107/1588, 1851 Census Woolwich Dockyard Parish: Woolwich (1,6), Katharine Mary.
IR 1/31–33, Board of Stamps: Apprenticeship Books, 1784–1788.
IR 1/36, Board of Stamps: Apprenticeship Books, 1794–1799.
PROB 11/1099/245, Wills and Probate: Will of John Jenner, master shipwright, 1783.
PROB 11/1108/111, Wills and Probate: Will of Benjamin Kennicott, D.D. Christ Church Oxford, 9 September 1783.
PROB 11/1141/304, Wills and Probate: Will of Daniel Eldridge, Gentleman of Woolwich, 29 April 1786.
PROB 11/1381/24, Wills and Probate: Will of Thomas Wallbridge, Shipwright of Woolwich, 6 September 1802.
PROB 11/1400/29, Wills and Probate: Will of Henry Canham, Shipwright of Woolwich, Kent, 12 November 1803.
PROB 11/1483/88, Wills and Probate: Will of John Swanson, late Quarterman in His Majesty's Dock Yard of Woolwich, Kent, 16 July 1808.
PROB 11/1493/281, Wills and Probate: Will of Meabron otherwise Meaban Holmes, formerly First Lieutenant belonging to His Majesty's Ship Amelia but late First Lieutenant belonging to His Majesty's Ship Uranie, 28 February 1809.
PROB 11/1532/63, Wills and Probate: Will of Charles Stuart, Shipwright of Woolwich, 3 April 1812.
PROB 11/1549/528, Wills and Probate: Will of William Ranwell, Shipwright of Woolwich, 29 November 1813.
PROB 11/1771/432, Wills and Probate: Will of Thomas John Williamson, Purser in the Royal Navy of Hampton Court, 3 May 1830.
PROB 11/1784/51, Wills and Probate: Will of Job Davis, Gentleman of Woolwich, Kent, 9 April 1831.
PROB 11/1858/188, Wills and Probate: Will of William Stuart, Shipwright of Woolwich, 5 February 1836.
PROB 11/2123/368, Wills and Probate: Will of Thomas Guyer, Shipwright of Woolwich, 1850.
RG 4/1770, KENT: Woolwich, Queen Street Chapel (Baptist): Births. 1781–1836.

University of Aberdeen Special Collections (UoA)

MS3540, George Keith 10th Earl Marischall: letters, 1768–1778.

University of Nottingham Manuscripts and Special Collections (UoN)

Pw F 3.007, Papers of William Henry C. Cavendish-Bentinck, 3rd Duke of Portland (1738–1809), Portland (Welbeck) Collection. Letter from George Collier to Duke of Portland, 24 October 1794.

298 BIBLIOGRAPHY

Printed Primary Material

Anon., *Historical Record of the Thirty-Fourth or, The Cumberland Regiment of Foot: containing an account of the Regiment in 1702 and of its subsequent services to 1844* (London, 1844).

The Naval Chronicle for 1812: Containing a general and biographical history of the Royal Navy of the United Kingdom; with a variety of original papers on nautical subjects, 27, January–June (London, 1812), 273.

Austen, Jane, *Pride and Prejudice* (first printed 1813; London, reprint 2003).

—— *Mansfield Park* (first published 1814; Oxford, reissue 1990).

Brydges, Egerton, *Collin's Peerage of England: Genealogical, Biographical, and Historical*, 5 vols. (London, 1812).

Burke, John, *A General and Heraldic Dictionary of the Peerage and Baronetage of the British Empire*, 5th edn (London, 1837).

—— *A Genealogical and Heraldic History of the Commoners of Great Britain and Ireland*, 4 vols. (London, 1838).

Cooke, Thomas, *The Universal Letter-Writer; or, New Art of Polite Correspondence* (Gainsborough, 1801).

Edgeworth, Maria, *Patronage* (first printed 1814; reprint London, 2011).

Field, John, 'The Diary of a Portsmouth Dockyard Worker', *Portsmouth Archives Review* 3 (1978), 39–64.

Girdlestone, Thomas, *Essays on the Hepatitis and Spasmodic Affections in India; founded on observations made while on service with His Majesty's troops in different parts of that country* (London, 1787).

Hoffman, Frederick, *A Sailor for King George: The Journals of Captain Frederik Hoffman R.N. 1793–1814* (London, 1901; reprint 1999).

Nugent, Maria, *Lady Nugent's Journal of Her Residence in Jamaica from 1801 to 1805* (Kingston, 1966).

Slight, Henry and Julian, *Chronicles of Portsmouth* (London, 1828).

Government and Parliamentary Papers

The Sixth Report of the Commissioners of Naval Inquiry. Appendix: Plymouth Yard, Woolwich Yard (London, 1804).

A List of all the Officers of the Army and Royal Marines on Full and Half-Pay with an Index: and a Succession of Colonels (War Office, 1805).

Cobbett's Parliamentary Debates, 7 (London, 1812).

Published Letter Collections

Aspinall, Arthur (ed.), *The Later Correspondence of George III*, 2 vols. (Cambridge, 1967).

Brenton, Edward Pelham (ed.), *Life and Correspondence of John, Earl St Vincent*, 2 vols. (London, 1838).

Castle, Edgerton (ed.), *The Jerningham Letters (1780–1843): Being Excerpts from the Correspondence and Diaries of the Honourable Lady Jerningham and her Daughter Lady Bedingfeld*, 2 vols. (London, 1896).

BIBLIOGRAPHY 299

Navy Records Society

Bonner-Smith, David (ed.), *Letters of Admiral of the Fleet the Earl of St Vincent while First Lord of the Admiralty 1801–1804*, 2 vols. (Navy Records Society, 1927).

Hughes, Edward (ed.), *The Private Correspondence of Admiral Lord Collingwood*, 2 vols. (Navy Records Society, 1957).

Markham, Clements (ed.), *Selections from the Correspondence of Admiral John Markham during the Years 1801–4 and 1806–7* (Navy Records Society, 1904).

Vessey-Hamilton, Richard (ed.), *Letters and Papers of Admiral of the Fleet Sir Thomas Byam Martin, 1773–1854* (Navy Records Society, 1902).

Newspapers

'Portsmouth Saturday June 20 1818', *Hampshire Telegraph and Sussex Chronicle (Portsmouth, England)*, 976 (June, 1818).

Secondary Sources

Arnold, D., *Warm Climates and Western Medicine* (Amsterdam, 1996).

Atkins, G., 'Religion, Politics and Patronage in the Late Hanoverian Navy c.1780–c.1820', *Journal of Historical Research* 88:240 (May, 2015), 272–290.

Bailey, J. (Bergiato), *Parenting in England 1760–1830: Emotion, Identity and Generation* (Oxford, 2012).

Bannet, E. T., *Empire of Letters: Letter Manuals and Transatlantic Correspondence, 1688–1820* (Cambridge, 2005).

Beck, C., 'Uncovering the Unrecorded: The Patronage of Artificers in the Royal Dockyards 1778–1802', *Transactions of the Naval Dockyard Society* 13 (August, 2020), 17–28.

—— 'Patronage and Insanity: Tolerance, Reputation and Mental Disorder in the British Navy 1740–1820', *Historical Research* 94:263 (February, 2021), 73–95.

Ben-Amos, I. K., *Adolescence and Youth in Early Modern England* (London, 1994).

—— *The Culture of Giving: Informal Support and Gift-Exchange in Early Modern England* (Cambridge, 2008).

Berg, T., *The Lives and Letters of an Eighteenth-Century Circle of Acquaintance* (Aldershot, 2006).

Bodemann, Y. M., 'Relations of Production and Class Rule: The Hidden Basis of Patron-Clientage', in B. Wellman and S. D. Berkowitz, *Social Structures: A Network Approach* (Cambridge, 1988).

Boissevain, J., *Friends of Friends: Networks, Manipulators and Coalitions* (Oxford, 1974).

Bourne, J. M., *Patronage and Society in Nineteenth Century England* (London, 1986).

Brant, C., *Eighteenth-Century Letters and British Culture* (London, 2006).

Burkolter, V., *The Patronage System: Some Theoretical Remarks* (Basel, 1976).

300   BIBLIOGRAPHY

Burns, A., 'English "Church Reform" Revisited, 1780–1840', in A. Burns and J. Innes (eds.), *Rethinking the Age of Reform: Britain 1780–1850* (Cambridge, 2003).

Burns, A. and Innes, J. (eds.), *Rethinking the Age of Reform: Britain 1780–1850* (Cambridge, 2003).

Cannadine, D., *Class in Britain* (London, 1998).

Carter, P., *Men and the Emergence of Polite Society, Britain 1660–1800* (London, 2001).

Cavell, S. A., *Midshipmen and the Quarterdeck Boys in the British Navy 1771–1831* (Woodbridge, 2012).

Chalus, E., *Elite Women in English Political Life c.1754–1790* (Oxford, 2005).

Charters, E., *Disease, War and the Imperial State: The Welfare of the British Armed Forces during the Seven Years' War* (London, 2014).

Coats, A., 'Bermuda Naval Base: Management, Artisans and Enslaved Workers in the 1790s: The 1950s Bermudian Apprentices' Heritage', *Mariner's Mirror* 95:2 (March, 2013), 149–178.

Colley, L., 'Whose Nation? Class and National Consciousness in Britain, 1750–1830', *Past and Present* 113 (1986), 97–117.

Collinge, P., 'Enterprise, Activism and Charity: Mary Pickford and the Urban Elite of Derby, 1780–1812', *Midland History* 45:1 (2020), 36–54.

Dancy, J., *The Myth of the Press Gang: Volunteers, Impressment and the Naval Manpower Problem in the Late Eighteenth Century* (Woodbridge, 2015).

Davey, J., *In Nelson's Wake: The Navy and the Napoleonic Wars* (London, 2015).

Deitz, B., 'Mobile Objects: The Space of Shells in Eighteenth-Century France', *British Journal for the History of Science* 39:3 (September, 2006).

Dwyer, J., *Virtuous Discourse: Sensibility and Community in Late Eighteenth-Century Scotland* (Edinburgh, 1987).

Earle, R. (ed.), *Epistolary Selves: Letters and Letters-Writers 1600–1945* (Ashgate, 1999).

Eisenstadt, S. N. and Roniger, L., 'Patron-Client Relations as a Model of Structuring Social Exchange', *Comparative Studies in Society and History* 22:1 (1980), 42–77.

——— *Patrons, Clients and Friends: Interpersonal Relations and the Structure of Trust in Society* (Cambridge, 1984).

Ellis, M., *The Politics of Sensibility: Race, Gender and Commerce in the Sentimental Novel* (Cambridge, 1996).

Fedorak, C., *Henry Addington, Prime Minister, 1801–1804: Peace, War, and Parliamentary Politics* (Akron, 2002).

Fisher, D., *The History of Parliament: The House of Commons 1820–1832*, 6 vols. (Cambridge, 2009).

Foy, C., 'The Royal Navy's Employment of Black Mariners and Maritime Workers 1754–1783', *International Journal of Maritime History* 28:1 (2016), 25.

French, H. and Rothery, M., 'Hegemonic Masculinities? Assessing Change and Processes of Change in Elite Masculinity, 1700–1900', in J. Arnold and S. Brady (eds.), *What Is Masculinity? Historical Dynamics from Antiquity to the Contemporary World* (London, 2011).

BIBLIOGRAPHY

Garrioch, D., *Neighbourhood and Community in Paris, 1740–1790* (Cambridge, 1986).

Gellner, E. and Waterbury, J. (eds.), *Patrons and Clients in Mediterranean Societies* (London, 1977).

Gill, E., *Naval Families, War and Duty in Britain 1740–1820* (Woodbridge, 2016).

Granovetter, M., 'The Strength of Weak Ties', *American Journal of Sociology* 78:6 (May, 1973), 1360–1380.

Greenhill, B. and Giffard, A., *Steam, Politics and Patronage: The Transformation of the Royal Navy 1815–1854* (London, 1994).

Gwyn, J., *Frigates and Foremasts: The North American Squadron in Nova Scotia Waters 1745–1815* (Vancouver, 2003).

—— *Ashore and Afloat: The British Navy and the Halifax Naval Yard before 1820* (Ottawa, 2004).

Haggerty, S., *The British-Atlantic Trading Community 1760–1810: Men, Women, and the Distribution of Goods* (Leiden, 2006).

Haggerty, S. and Haggerty, J., 'Visual Analytics of an Eighteenth-Century Business Network', *Enterprise and Society* 11:1 (March, 2010), 1–25.

Harling, P., *The Waning of 'Old Corruption': The Politics of Economical Reform in Britain 1779–1846* (Oxford, 1996).

Innes, J., '"Reform" in English Public Life: The Fortunes of a Word', in A. Burns and J. Innes (eds.), *Rethinking the Age of Reform: Britain 1780–1850* (Cambridge, 2003), 71–97.

Jenks, T., *Naval Engagements: Patriotism, Cultural Politics, and the Royal Navy 1793–1815* (Oxford, 2006).

Jones, V., *Women in the Eighteenth Century: Constructions of Femininity* (London, 1990).

Kadushin, C., *Understanding Social Networks: Theories, Concepts and Findings* (Oxford, 2012).

Kettering, S., *Patrons, Brokers, and Clients in Seventeenth-Century France* (Oxford, 1986).

Knight, R. J. B., 'Sandwich, Middleton and Dockyard Appointments', *Mariner's Mirror* 57:2 (1971), 175–192.

—— 'From Impressment to Task Work: Strikes and Disruption in the Royal Dockyards 1688–1788', in K. Lunn and A. Day (eds), *History of Work and Labour Relations* (London, 1999), 1–20.

—— *Britain Against Napoleon: The Organization of Victory, 1793–1815* (London, 2013).

Ledbury, M., 'Patronage', in *The Oxford Handbook of the Ancien Régime* (Oxford, 2012).

Lewis, M., *A Social History of the Navy 1793–1815* (London, 1960).

Lin, N., *Social Capital: A Theory of Social Structures and Action* (Cambridge, 2001).

Lincoln, M., *Representing the Royal Navy: British Sea Power, 1750–1815* (Aldershot, 2002).

—— *Naval Wives and Mistresses 1750–1815* (London, 2007).

Lunn, K. and Day, A. (eds.), *History of Work and Labour Relations in the Royal Dockyards* (London, 1999).

BIBLIOGRAPHY

MacDougall, P., 'The Changing Nature of the Dockyard Dispute 1790–1840', in K. Lunn and A. Day (eds), *History of Work and Labour Relations in the Royal Dockyards* (London, 1999), 41–65.

Markham, C., *A Naval Career during the Old War: Being a narrative of the life of Admiral John Markham, M.P. for Portsmouth for Twenty-Three years (Lord of the Admiralty, 1801–4 and 1806–7)* (London, 1883).

—— (ed.), *Selections from the Correspondence of Admiral John Markham during the Years 1801–4 and 1806–7* (Navy Records Society, 1904).

Martin, J. L., *Social Structures* (Princeton, 2009).

Matthews, H. C. G. and Harrison, B. (eds.), *The Oxford Dictionary of National Biography* (Oxford, 2004).

McCranie, K., *Admiral Lord Keith and the Naval War against Napoleon* (Gainesville, 2006).

McGilvary, G. K., *East India Patronage and the British State: The Scottish Elite and Politics in the Eighteenth Century* (London, 2008).

Morriss, R., *The Royal Dockyards during the Revolutionary and Napoleonic Wars* (Leicester, 1993).

—— 'Government and Community: The Changing Context of Labour Relations, 1770–1830', in K. Lunn and A. Day (eds.), *History of Work and Labour Relations in the Royal Dockyards* (London, 1999).

—— *Naval Power and British Culture, 1760–1850: Public Trust and Government Ideology* (Aldershot, 2004).

—— *The Foundations of British Maritime Ascendancy: Resources, Logistics and the State, 1755–1815* (Cambridge, 2011).

Morrow, J., *British Flag Officers in the French War, 1793–1815: Admiral's Lives* (London, 2018).

Namier, L., *The Structure of Politics: At the Accession of George III*, 2nd edn (London, 1957; reprint London, 1961).

Namier, L. and Brooke, J. (eds.), *The History of the House of Commons 1754–1790*, 3 vols. (Woodbridge, 1964).

O'Neill, L., *The Opened Letter: Networking in the Early Modern British World* (Philadelphia, 2014).

Payne, R., *Ecclesiastical Patronage in England, 1770–1801: A Study of Four Family and Political Networks* (Lampeter, 2010).

Pearsall, S., *Atlantic Families: Lives and Letters in the Later Eighteenth Century* (Oxford, 2008).

Peck, L. L., *Court Patronage and Corruption in Early Stuart England* (Boston, 1990).

Perkin, H., *The Origins of Modern English Society, 1780–1880* (London, 1969).

Porter, R., *English Society in the Eighteenth Century* (London, 1982; reprint 1990).

Reiter, J., *The Late Lord: The Life of John Pitt 2nd Earl of Chatham* (Barnsley, 2017).

Richardson, H., 'Wages of Shipwrights in HM Dockyards, 1496–1788', *Mariner's Mirror* 33 (1947), 265–274.

Rodger, N. A. M., *The Wooden World: An Anatomy of the Georgian Navy* (Glasgow, 1986).

BIBLIOGRAPHY

—— *The Insatiable Earl: The Life of John Montagu, Fourth Earl of Sandwich 1718–1792* (London, 1993).

—— 'Commissioned Officers' Careers in the Royal Navy, 1690–1815', *Journal for Maritime Research* 3:1 (2001), 85–129.

—— 'Honour and Duty at Sea, 1660–1815', *Historical Research* 75:190 (November, 2002), 425–447.

—— *The Command of the Ocean: A Naval History of Britain, 1649–1815* (London, 2004).

Schmidt, S. W., Guasti, L., Landé, C. H. and Scott J. C. (eds.), *Friends, Followers, and Factions: A Reader in Political Clientelism* (London, 1977).

Scott, J., *When the Waves Ruled Britannia: Geography and Political Identities, 1500–1800* (Cambridge, 2011).

Scott, J. C., 'Patron-Client Politics and Political Change in South-East Asia', *American Political Science Review* 66:1 (1972), 91–113.

Silverman, S. F., 'Patronage and Community-Nation Relationships in Central Italy', in S. W. Schmidt, L. Guasti, C. H. Landé and J. C. Scott (eds.), *Friends, Followers, and Factions: A Reader in Political Clientelism* (London, 1977).

Snell, K., *Annals of the Labouring Poor: Social Change and Agrarian England, 1660–1900* (Cambridge, 1985).

Sokoll, T., 'Writing for Relief: Rhetoric in English Pauper Letters 1800–1834', in A. Gestrich, S. King and L. Raphael (eds.), *Being Poor in Modern Europe: Historical Perspectives 1800–1940* (Oxford, 2006).

Steele, I., *The English Atlantic 1675–1740: An Exploration of Communication and Community* (Oxford, 1986).

Stone, L., *The Family, Sex and Marriage in England 1500–1800* (London, 1977).

Sunderland, D., *Social Capital, Trust and the Industrial Revolution 1780–1880* (London, 2007).

Sunter, R., *Patronage and Politics in Scotland* (Edinburgh, 1986).

Tadmor, N., *Family and Friends in Eighteenth-Century England: Household, Kinship, and Patronage* (Cambridge, 2001).

Tague, I. H., *Women of Quality: Accepting and Contesting Ideals of Femininity in England, 1690–1760* (Woodbridge, 2002).

Taylor, S., *Commander: The Life and Exploits of Britain's Greatest Frigate Captain* (London, 2012).

Thorne, R. G., *The History of Parliament: The House of Commons 1790–1820*, 5 vols. (Woodbridge, 1986).

Ward, P., *British Naval Power in the East 1794–1805: The Command of Admiral Peter Rainier* (Woodbridge, 2013).

Wareham, T., *Frigate Commander* (Barnsley, 2004).

Weingrod, A., 'Patrons, Patronage and Political Parties', in S. W. Schmidt, L. Guasti, C. H. Landé and J. C. Scott (eds.), *Friends, Followers, and Factions: A Reader in Political Clientelism* (London, 1977).

Wellman, B. and Berkowitz, S. D., *Social Structures: A Network Approach* (Cambridge, 1988).

Whyman, S., *Sociability and Power in Late Stuart England* (Oxford, 1999).

Williams, S., 'The Royal Navy and Caribbean Colonial Society during the Eighteenth Century', in J. McAleer and C. Petley (eds.), *The Royal Navy and the British Atlantic World, c.1750–1820* (London, 2016).

304   BIBLIOGRAPHY

Wilson, E., *A Social History of British Naval Officers 1775–1815* (Woodbridge, 2017).

Wolf, E., 'Kinship, Friendship, and Patron-Client Relations in Complex Societies', in M. Banton (ed.), *The Social Anthropology of Complex Societies* (London, 1966).

Unpublished Works

Atkins, G., 'Wilberforce and His Milieux: The Worlds of Anglican Evangelicalism, c.1780–1830' (unpublished PhD thesis, University of Cambridge, 2009).

Bracknall, M., 'Lord Spencer, Patronage and Commissioned Officers' Careers, 1794–1801' (unpublished PhD thesis, University of Exeter, 2008).

Collinge, P., 'Female Enterprise in Georgian Derbyshire, c.1780–1830' (unpublished PhD thesis, University of Keele, 2015).

Convertito, C., 'The Health of British Seamen in the West Indies, 1770–1806' (unpublished PhD thesis, University of Exeter, 2011).

Jones, E. F., 'Masculinity, Materiality and Space on Board the Royal Naval Ship, 1756–1815' (unpublished PhD thesis, Queen Mary University London, 2016).

Williams, S., 'The Royal Navy in the Caribbean 1756–1815' (unpublished PhD thesis, University of Southampton, 2015).

Wilson, E., 'The Sea Officers: Gentility and Professionalism in the Royal Navy 1775–1815' (unpublished PhD thesis, University of Oxford, 2014).

INDEX

acting appointments 23, 32, 34, 36
  commissions 28, 31, 33, 121
    captain 34
    lieutenant 34, 82, 111, 121, 123, 126
    Markham's 12, 113
  quarterman 223
Admiralty 7, 8, 10–15, 19–20
  board 1–2, 7, 13, 29, 51, 88–9, 103–4,
    108, 129–30, 133, 141, 146–7, 157,
    164, 198, 212
  first lord(s) 31, 155, 160, 178, 213
    Barham, Lord 141 *see also*
        Middleton, Charles
        (Comptroller of the Navy)
    connection to 64, 95
    delegating patronage 21–2
    displeasure of 89
    Grenville, Thomas 13, 78, 83,
      148–9, 161, 200
    Howick, Lord (Charles Grey) 35,
      165
    Markham's influence with 14, 83
    Melville, Viscount (Henry
      Dundas) 35, 128, 149
    politics 146–61
    pressure on 31, 92, 146, 160
    Sandwich, Earl of (John
      Montagu) 9–10, 146
    St Vincent, Earl 1, 10, 12, 30,
      92, 147, 149 *see also* Jervis,
      Admiral John
  patronage 21, 100, 146–161
    control of appointments 28–30,
      108
    list of candidates 20, 22, 29–30,
      140, 151, 153, 203
  structure 21–4
advancement
  hopes for 139, 143
  patronage, a tool of 86
  role of merit and connection 266

use of friendship 183, 188
agent
  connection maintenance 41
  passing information 121, 194
  recommendation by 104
applicant
  captain 114, 120, 129
  civilian 15, 20
  lieutenant 45, 56, 115, 120, 128,
    139–41, 209
  midshipman 30, 116–17
  naval women 95
  warrant officer 1–2, 82, 84–5, 106–7,
    112–13, 119, 128–9, 135–6
applications
  need for flexibility 20, 48–9, 108–11,
    138
  need to be undemanding 108, 160
  reason for support *see also* obligation
    long service 102, 120, 148, 164–5,
      202–4, 209, 213–14
    need to support family 107, 123,
      128, 135, 169, 202–4, 213
    shared service 98–9, 110, 113–16
  success 90, 92, 105–6, 109, 114–15,
    121, 127, 204
    partial 111–12
  unsuccessful 102–3, 111–12, 115–16,
    120, 135, 140, 147, 151–2, 167,
    203
appointments
  acting 23, 28, 31–2, 34, 36, 121
  artificers 232–4, 236, 237 *see also*
    dockyard
  control of 21–4, 28–30, 108, 219–22
  opportunity 44, 104
  routine requests 94, 96, 100–3

Bengal 13, 68
Bertie, Captain Albermarle 131–4, 142

Bishopthorpe, Yorkshire   58, 61–3, 66–7,
      71, 74, 185, 187, 193
broker
      captain   103–4, 108–11, 207–8, 211
      civilian   18, 20, 63, 67, 92, 110, 129,
            209
            family friend   63, 67
      commander   102–3, 112
      dockyard
            family   223–7, 239, 241
            network connections   259
            payment of fees   227–36
            women   223–4, 227, 232–4, 257
      female   185–201, 204–8, 210–15,
            223–4, 232–4, 260–1, 270 *see
            also* Markham, Maria
            family friend   50, 192–3
            friend   42
            limits on   190–1, 200–1, 205–6
            lower level   195–6, 197–8, 210,
                  223–4, 226, 232–4, 257,
                  260–1
            naval women   20, 73, 91, 93, 95,
                  123–4, 181, 198–200, 210–14,
                  223–4, 226, 257
            widow   192–3, 196–7, 200–1, 205,
                  210, 223–4, 226
      Markham's family   68–9
      parental   20, 67, 96, 116, 120–1, 125,
            140, 152, 154, 163–5, 170, 172,
            198–206, 223–6
      political   98, 152–3, 155, 158–9, 165,
            194
      warrant officer
            boatswain   136, 142
            carpenter   82, 113–14
            purser   203
Brooks, Reuben (leading
      scavelman)   220, 235–7
Buller, Captain Edward   94, 104, 127–9
Buller, Getrude (wife of)   127–9

Carpenter, Harriet   123–4, 181, 199–200,
      211–12
Carpenter, Lieutenant Daniel   43, 122–4,
      142, 181, 183, 199 *see also* court
      martial & followers
Carter, Sir John   150, 161–3, 167–70 *see
      also* Portsmouth Corporation
Channel (Home waters)   12, 18, 28–9, 43,
      47, 73–4, 76, 80–1, 147, 183, 185–6,
      262

charity
      claim to patronage   7, 51
      dockyard appointments   223
      familial support   54
      female brokers' appeals to   193, 205,
            208, 270
      less demanding requests   183
      Markham's sense of   94, 120–2, 135
      Mrs Wisemans Charity   242–3, 249
      payment of fees   235
child of the service   102, 113, 120, 124 *see
      also* broker, parental
Christ Church, Oxford   11, 55, 57–63,
      67–8, 98fn15, 187, 192, 196,
      Appendix 2
church
      Queen Street Chapel (non–conformist
            church), Woolwich   246–7
      St Mary Magdalene (Anglican
            Church), Woolwich   242–3,
            245–7, 260
client   22, 25, 31, 146, 148, 149, 179, 198,
      201 *see also* recipient
      broker and patron   198, 212, 268, 273,
            181
      patron–client   4, 6, 11, 162
commanders–in–chief   10, 12, 21–5, 29,
      32–6, 39, 48, 90, 144, 220
      Cochrane, Alexander   200
      Collingwood, Cuthbert   10, 30–1
      Duckworth, John Thomas   33–6, 42
      East–Indies   34, 267
      Keith, Admiral   30–2, 153 *see also*
            Elphinstone, Admiral George
            Keith
      Nelson, Horatio   142
      Pellew, Edward   14, 35, 140
      Rodney, George   65
      West Indies   36, 38
community
      church   23–4, 218, 242–3, 245–7,
            260–1
      dockyard   24, 244, 246, 248, 249,
            255–6
            coming from outside   36–8, 237–8,
                  255–6
            Deptford   222–4, 227–8
            Halifax   36–8
            Plymouth   39
            Portsmouth   260
            Woolwich   224–7, 238–9, 241–4,
                  246–9

INDEX

local   23, 38, 220, 223, 226, 237, 239, 241, 263
    mercantile   37
    political   54
power   36–7, 39, 216, 220, 247, 263
support   38, 182
vs patronage   16, 182, 216, 220, 271–2
connection
    benefits of   105
    female–to–female   191–3, 195, 198, 224, 233
    influential   29, 37, 58, 92–3, 105 *see also* influence
    lapsed acquaintance   42–3, 75, 114–15, 206–7
    local   24, 36–9, 42, 47, 67, 139, 159, 160, 187, 196, 218, 223, 226–8, 239, 241, 249, 254, 260
    maintenance   25, 27, 29, 40–2 *see also* gift giving & letters
    personal   4–6, 50, 101, 103, 106–7, 146, 161, 163, 173, 236, 267
    political   9, 32, 91–2, 98, 101, 110, 125, 128, 144–80
    troublesome   32, 162
correspondence   28, 53, 77, 182, 219, 269 *see also* letters
    distance   25–7
    frequency   52, 56, 78, 82–6, 92–3, 118
corruption   4, 9, 16, 145–7, 149, 170, 235–6, 266
    accusations of   10, 155, 229, 236, 244
court martial   33–4, 46, 125, 126–32
    assistance   12–14, 65, 125, 127–8
    Best, Samuel (surgeon)   130–1
    Carpenter, Lieutenant Daniel   123–5
    Markham   12, 65
    Morgan, James (boatswain)   128
    Nops, Lieutenant John George   126–7
    vacancies   33–4
Croft, William   30, 35, 67, 82, 108, 117, 187 *see also* followers
Cuthbert, Reverend George   163, 167, 170–1 , 175–9 *see also* Portsmouth Corporation

damage *see also* reputation
    entitlement and expectation   107, 131–4, 168–70
    failure to fulfil request   133, 174
    insanity   130–1

reputation   20, 76, 89, 103 119, 125–7, 152
dockyards
    brokers
        family   223–7, 239, 241
        network connections   259
        women   223–4, 227, 232–4, 257
    Chatham   222, 227, 236, 248, 252, 262
    church networks   239–49, 260–1 *see also* St Mary Magdalene
    commissioner   23, 24, 32
    community   24, 36–9, 244–9, 255–6
    control of appointments   23–4, 219–22
    Deptford   222–5, 227–8, 252–5, 257–9
    enslaved labourers   38–9
    geography   24
    Halifax   23, 32, 33, 36–8, 228, 258
    payment of fees   228–37
    Plymouth   195–6, 219, 228–39, 242–3, 251–8, 260, 262
    Portsmouth   161, 252, 256–7, 259–61
    reforms   16, 152, 161
    shipwright apprentices   222–7, 241–2
    strike   250–1
    Woolwich   55, 219–20, 224–7, 237–49, 252–3, 257–62
D'Oyly, Sarah   157, 192–3
Duckworth, Admiral John Thomas   33, 35–6, 41, 81–2 *see also* commanders–in–chief
Duins, Mrs   232–4, 260
Duins, Robert (first clerk to master shipwright)   229, 235–7, 258
duty
    blurred edges of patronage   14
    deflecting risk   142
    familial   54, 96, 184, 217
    female   183, 188, 213, 215
    gentility and honour   267
    language of patronage   7–8 , 270
    language of petitions   217
    Markham's sense of   51, 94, 137
        to constituents   133, 135
        to followers   113
        to long service   120
        to strangers   119, 121–2
    moulding relationships   138
    politics   144, 163, 175–9
    regulating reciprocity   180
    restrictions on male applicants   206

308 INDEX

to the service   133, 141, 162, 166, 173, 215, 265

East Indies   3, 24–5, 34–5, 38, 139–40, 149, 161, 206, 267
ill–health   19–20, 46, 119
Elphinstone, Admiral George Keith
broker   46
commander–in–chief   30–2, 153
gift–giving   41
Naval Society   80–1
reciprocity with Markham   82, 121, 136
Scottish network   56, 64
Elton, Henry   67, 83, 117, 187 *see also* followers
expectation
as hindrance   131–3, 160
differences between naval and political   162
disguising   138, 142
face–to–face meetings   15
familial support   96
female behaviour   197, 266
letters of introduction   36
misjudging   88, 138
patronage exchange   7, 94, 272
personal connection   103, 107
old shipmates   114
reciprocity   7, 106, 134, 141
sharing news   75

first lord *see under* Admiralty
followers   35, 68, 81, 98–9, 101, 111–12, 132, 211 *see also* protégés
Bennet, Commander John Astley   103, 112
Carpenter, Lieutenant Daniel   43, 122–4, 142, 181, 183, 199
Croft, William   30, 35, 67, 82, 108, 117, 187
Elias, Joseph (midshipman)   116–17
Elton, Henry   67, 82, 117, 187
Grossett, Walter   42, 72, 84, 108
Hoffman, Frederick   46–7, 81, 114
Kelly, Jonathan   67, 187
Kittoe, Robinson (purser)   83–4
Littlehales, Captain Bendall Robert   83, 108
MacDonald, Fred   62, 187
Pearkes, Lieutenant John   139, 140, 141

Richbell, Lieutenant Thomas   72, 73, 83, 168
Robinson, Thomas (boatswain)   136–7, 142
Wooldridge, Lieutenant William   139, 140, 141
friendship   1, 18, 27, 56, 57, 103, 235, 258
cynical use of   183
difficult to categorise   52
disappointment   140
gift–giving   41
intimacy   54–6, 83, 86, 112
language of patronage   1, 19, 56–8, 124, 148, 156, 192, 199
lapsed   114
networks   24, 73, 192, 222, 227, 239, 247–9, 255
non–elite   220, 222, 227, 234, 246–7, 255, 262
obligation   6, 7, 117, 170
politics   148
sensible ideals of   2–3, 57
shared service connection   1, 18
style of patronage
female   51, 188, 190, 193, 214 *see also* broker, female
politics   156
service and duty   179–80
suspicion of   103, 216

gentlemanly masculinity   41, 217
gift–giving   40–2, 85–6
Goldson, William   163, 167–9, 175 *see also* Portsmouth Corporation
government
Addington ministry   30, 149–50, 154, 158, 161
'All the Talents' ministry   13
connections   58, 65, 123, 160
influence
assumed   88, 151
pressure of   92–3, 146, 166
local   36–7, 56
support for   151, 153, 155, 160, 172, 174, 175
vs corporation   177
vs party   159
Grossett, Walter   42, 72, 84, 108 *see also* followers

Hammett, Luke (ordinary joiner)   229, 232, 234

INDEX

Hardy, Captain John Oakes 8, 23, 115, 194–5, 203
Herbert, Captain Charles 88–90, 94–5, 101–2, 108, 141, 203
Hesketh, Lady Sophia 194, 197–8
Higg, Mary 15, 92, 195–6, 260, 271
Hillier, Alicia 207–8, 211
Hoffman, Frederick 46–7, 81, 114 *see also* followers
honour *see also* duty
 claim to patronage 51, 55
 deflecting criticism 166, 176–7
 fashion for 8, 14
 Markham's sense of 162
 patronage of health 46

illegitimate child 13, 37, 68, 94, 133, 157–8, 192
ill–health
 damage to career 115–16, 119
 hot climates 19–20, 45–6
 insanity 130–1
influence
 connection 29, 37, 58, 92–3, 105
 government 88, 92–3, 146, 166
 Markham with first lord 14, 83
injury *see under* ill–health
interest
 beyond patronage exchange 11
 damage to 89
 implicit 64, 94, 105, 121–2, 136, 148, 157
 language of patronage 36, 89, 113–14, 128, 166, 168, 177
 politics 152, 160
  Admiralty 145–6
  in East Indies 149
  party 146
  Portsmouth Corporation 163, 166, 168, 171–3, 177
  St Vincent 149–50
 weight of connections 90, 138
intimacy 57–8, 60, 64, 114, 117, 185 *see also* friendship
Ireland 12, 24, 27, 43, 57, 75, 141, 151, 183, 186, 256

Jagoe, James (Timber Master)
 apprentices 241–4
 female relatives 237, 260
 integration in Woolwich yard 237–9, 258

mapping network 55
mobility with patron 252–3
timber yard network 237–50
vestry 242–3, 245–7, 260 *see also* St Mary Magdalene
well–connected shipwrights 226
Jamaica 12, 18, 24–5, 33, 36, 38, 41–2, 44–5, 48, 69–70, 199, 250, 257
Jervis, Admiral John (Earl St Vincent)
 accusations of corruption 168–9
 as first lord 1, 10, 12, 30–1, 89, 92, 147, 149
 Channel Fleet 28–9
 dockyards 220–1, 228, 244–5, 256
 management of appointments 21
 offence 89
 political patronage 148–61
  influence with Portsmouth Corporation 161
  obliging political enemies 156
  refusal because of politics 154–5
 preference of flexibility 20
 suspicion of patronage 22, 29
  against sons of nobility & MPs 92, 95, 98, 102
 The Naval Society 80–1

Kantzow, Lucy de 42, 84
Keith, Admiral Lord *see under* Elphinstone, Admiral George Keith
Kerr, Captain Lord Mark 55, 95, 108, 112

letters *see also* correspondence
 connection maintenance 25, 27, 29
 frequency 52, 56, 78, 82–6, 92–3, 118
 of introduction 27, 34–6, 106–7
 speed 27–8

Markham
 career 11–13
 family 57–77, 159, 172, 176
  Markham, Frederica 60, 62–3, 66, 72
  Markham, Maria 7, 12, 27–8, 39, 47, 60–2, 66–7, 70–7, 81–4, 86, 111, 183–193, 195, 198, 265, 268–9
  Markham, Robert (Archdeacon of York) 68–9, 170, 172–3
  Markham, William (Archbishop of York) 11, 15, 47, 50, 57–8, 60–4, 71, 176, 192

310 INDEX

school friend   72
ships
   Blonde   46, 81–2, 113–14, 139
   Centaur   35, 42, 47, 62, 67–8, 70,
      72–4, 81–4, 108, 113, 116–18,
      132, 136, 139, 168, 185, 198,
      261
   Hannibal   46–7, 70, 82, 113–14,
      139, 214
   Perseus   1–2, 75, 84, 116
   Roebuck   12, 64, 68, 113
   Romney   56, 63–4, 75, 112, 265
   Sphinx   12, 42, 64, 82
   Zebra   65
masculinity   40, 183-4
   gentility   41, 217
   gift-giving   40
   merit   185
Mediterranean   10, 12, 18, 24–5, 27–32,
   40–8, 68, 75, 81, 112, 140, 183, 186,
   250, 262, 267
   health   31
members of parliament   69, 98, 125, 129,
   144, 145, 147, 150–61, 163, 171, 176,
   210
   Markham as MP   161–80
   naval MPs   144–5
merit
   Admiralty priority   32, 147–8, 203,
      208
   and political obligation   158, 168–70
   deflecting criticism   156–7, 164–5
   dockyards   247–8
   emphasis of   103, 119, 138, 200
   masculinity   185
   meritocracy   9, 105
   of parent   209
   recommendations based on   105
messmates   1, 54, 75, 84, 99, 115–16
Middleton, Charles (Comptroller of the
   Navy)   33, 141, 216, 218, 261 *see
   also* Admiralty, first lord(s)
Murray, David (Viscount Stormont,
   second Earl of Mansfield)   27, 58,
   60–5, 71
Murray, David William (third Earl of
   Mansfield)   60, 72, 170

Naval Society (Naval Club of 1765)   56,
   80–1
naval women
   brokers   20, 73, 91, 93, 95, 123–4, 181,

      198–200, 210–14, 223–4, 226,
      257
   wives   73–6, 123–4, 181, 199, 200,
      211–12
Navy Board   34, 37, 218, 220, 224–5,
   227, 235, 238, 250, 254–6
   control of appointments   21, 23–4,
      216, 222, 253
Nepean, Evan (admiralty secretary)   29,
   33, 132

obligation
   and flexibility   108–18
   brokers   106–7, 202
   distrust   142
   family   54, 96, 217
   follower   105
   friendship   6, 7, 117, 170
   political   151, 153, 160, 162, 165–6,
      170, 176, 177
   shared service   112–16, 139
   stretched   120

patronage
   as social mechanism   4, 16, 271–3
   between administration and personal
      favour   29, 90, 96, 100, 127,
      133, 134
   language of
      anxiety   119, 121, 199–200, 202,
         205, 209, 210–14
      duty   7–8, 270
      friendship   1, 19, 56–8, 124, 148,
         156, 192, 199
      interest   36, 89, 113–14, 128, 166,
         168, 177
      merit   103, 119, 138, 200
   limits on   109, 120, 131, 142, 147–8,
      160, 165, 208
   female brokers   190–1, 200–1,
      205–6
Pellew, Admiral Edward   7, 14, 35, 39,
   106, 139–40, 149, 154, 181, 272
Perkins, Captain John   7, 18–19, 38, 41,
   45, 47–8, 57, 69–70, 108
petitions   2, 16, 164, 182, 203, 209, 217,
   222, 227, 250, 257
Portsmouth Corporation   98, 150, 161–78
protégé   32, 67–8, 82, 187, 211 *see also*
   followers

INDEX

311

Queen Street Chapel (non–conformist church), Woolwich 246–7

recipients
- captain 42, 158, 195–6, 203–4
- commander 209
- house carpenter 234–5
- labourer 233–4, 236
- lieutenant 20, 32, 98, 100, 102, 110–11, 147, 155–6, 158, 192–4, 198
- marine 150, 154, 204–5
- midshipman 159–60 *see also* followers
- scavelman 234
- shipwright 223–8, 232–3, 235
- warrant officers 113
  - boatswain 95, 113, 119
  - carpenter 112–13, 195, 259
  - gunner 103
  - purser 102, 106, 203
reciprocity 4–7, 81–2, 126, 131–5, 143, 150, 164, 170
- gift–giving 85–6
- honour & duty 180
- limits on 120, 130–1, 134–5, 137, 270
- quid pro quo 148, 164, 170, 179, 181
- stretched 90, 94, 106, 134, 138, 141, 143, 180
- the 'wheel' 7–8, 106, 131, 133, 181, 272
reputation
- appointments by 100–1
- damage 20, 76, 89, 103, 119, 125–7, 152
Rice, George Talbot (MP for Carmarthenshire) 61, 70, 187, 192
Rice, Maria *see under* Markham, Maria
Richbell, Lieutenant Thomas 72–3, 83, 168 *see also* followers
Riou, Captain Edward 55–6, 72, 80, 83–4, 112, 191, 264–6
Rippon, Mrs 229, 233–4, 260
risk 78, 103, 106, 122, 126–7, 162–3
Robinson, Elizabeth (widow) 210
Robinson, Thomas (boatswain) 136–7, 142 *see also* followers
Rodney, Admiral George 18, 27, 45, 65

Saunders, James (Purser) 41, 84–5
Scotland 24, 31, 41, 56, 66, 72, 255–6
- politics 31, 64, 158

sea fencibles 114–15, 139, 168
Searle, Captain Thomas Searle 166, 168–70, 180
sensibility 183, 192, 215, 272
- self–fashioning 188–90, 201, 206
ships
- *Albatross* 159
- *Alexander* (Lazaretto) 166
- *Andromeda* 124
- *Argo* 41
- *Aurora* 102
- *Barfleur* 82
- *Beaulieu* 83, 128
- *Bittern* 85
- *Blanche* 45
- *Blonde see under* Markham, ships
- *Brune* 8
- *Camel* 35
- *Camilla* 113
- *Centaur see under* Markham, ships
- *Champion* 123
- *Cheerful* 43–4, 122–3
- *Convert* 122
- *Culloden* 35, 129
- *Cyane* 42
- *Defender* 126
- *Determinee* 126
- *Diamond* 114
- *Diomede* 261
- *Dragon* 84, 121, 156
- *Dreadnaught* 113, 126
- *Duchess of Cumberland* 128
- *Elk* 139
- *Endeavour* 45
- *Eugenie* 117
- *Expedition* 123
- *Foudroyant* 121
- *Gelykheid* 106
- *Goliath* 104
- *Grasshopper* 169
- *Hannibal see under* Markham, ships
- *Harrier* 139
- *Hazard* 129–30
- *Hercule* 44, 123, 213
- *Hibernia* 147
- *Isis* 128
- *Lark* 125
- *Malta* 132
- *Martin* 68
- *Mermaid* 139
- *Monarch* 82
- *Neptune* 126

312 INDEX

Penelope 111
Perseus 168, 169 *see also under*
Markham, ships
Phaeton 109
Piercer 128
Prince of Wales 160
Princess Augusta 127
Psyche 140
Punch 45
Pylades 102
Roebuck 75 *see also under* Markham,
ships
Romney see under Markham, ships
Royal George 135
Salvador del Mundo 135–6
Santa Dorotea 119
Speculator 123
Sphinx see under Markham, ships
St Albans 194
St George 84
Sulphur 103
Surinam 56
Swift 259
Tartar 18, 41, 47, 69
Temeraire 126
Turbulent 127
Union 113
Venus 259
Ville de Paris 198
Viper 43, 122, 124, 181, 199, 200
Zebra see under Markham, ships
shipwright *see also* dockyards
apprentices 222–7, 241–2
mobility 249–62
Sick and Hurt Board 21 *see also*
Transport Board
*Sixth Report of the Commissioners of
Naval Inquiry* 228–37
social capital
as patronage 4, 6
reputation and trust 266–7
Somerville, Captain Phillip 121–2, 126,
134, 138
St Mary Magdalene (Anglican Church),
Woolwich 242–3, 245–7, 260
St Vincent, Earl *see under* Jervis, Admiral
John
Stopford, Captain Robert 95, 100–2

strangers 8, 103–4, 107, 118–24, 133 168,
205, 227

Transport Board 130–1 *see also* Sick and
Hurt Board
Troubridge, Admiral Thomas (at
admiralty) 21, 35, 100, 118, 129,
144, 149–50, 160–1
trust 9, 10, 105, 134–8, 175, 177
lack of 135–7

vacancies
accusations of corruption 169
Admiralty control 29–34, 45
availability 19–20, 38–40, 43, 45,
48–9
limited 8–11, 208
mobility 220, 250
offered as reciprocity 85–6, 109, 150
'on the spot' 39
promise of 235
refusal 110, 135
routine requests 93, 100–1
routine vs personal brokerage 103,
110, 147, 207–8

Wales 47, 188–9, 254–5
politics 60, 187
Walker, John (purser) 106–7, 122, 133,
138
Wallbridge, Thomas (shipwright) 225–6,
244–5
warrant officers 14, 46, 95–6, 100–1, 102,
113, 195–6, 214, 217, 249–50, 259
boatswain 95, 113, 119, 136–42
carpenter 1–2, 18, 82, 84–5, 112–14,
135–6, 195, 259
gunner 103
purser 102, 106–7, 203
West Indies 12, 18–20, 27, 33–9, 42,
44–8, 69, 81, 110, 139, 189, 197–8,
250, 259, 264–5
ill–health 19–20, 45–7, 264
Leeward Islands 24, 33, 42, 44–5,
65, 200
Westminster School 11, 55, 57–8, 61, 63,
66–8, 72, 192
White, Russel (carpenter) 1, 6, 16, 84,
108, 112–13, 135–6, 273

Printed in the United States
by Baker & Taylor Publisher Services